ATHENAEUS
VII

ATHENAEUS

THE DEIPNOSOPHISTS

WITH AN ENGLISH TRANSLATION BY
CHARLES BURTON GULICK, Ph.D.

ELIOT PROFESSOR OF GREEK LITERATURE EMERITUS
HARVARD UNIVERSITY

IN SEVEN VOLUMES

VII

CAMBRIDGE, MASSACHUSETTS
HARVARD UNIVERSITY PRESS
LONDON
WILLIAM HEINEMANN LTD
MCMLXXI

American
ISBN 0-674-99380-2

British
ISBN 0 434 99345 x

First printed 1941
Reprinted 1957, 1961, 1971

Printed in Great Britain

TO

THE MEMORY

OF

MY DAUGHTER

ANNE

CONTENTS OF VOLUME VII

PREFATORY NOTE

With this volume the work begun twenty-five years ago, but often interrupted, now reaches its conclusion. Undertaken at the suggestion of the late John Williams White, it was at first planned to base the Greek text on Kaibel's edition. It soon became evident, however, that in spite of Kaibel's indispensable contributions to the study of Athenaeus, a new examination of Marcianus A and the Paris excerpts was necessary. Various circumstances conspired to prevent a complete collation of the first ten books, but the text of the last five has been revised with the help of my own photographs, the monograph by Clara Aldick, and especially the admirable edition of the Epitome (Paris and Florence Excerpts) by Dr. Simon Peter Peppink. The untimely death of this brilliant Netherlands scholar has brought grievous loss to the cause of classical philology in general and to the study of Athenaeus in particular.

Naturally the attentive reader will discover inconsistencies caused by the protracted publication of the several volumes. These I regret, but I apologize for them only to those who have never committed any. Even to-day, after a century and a quarter of research and discovery, Schweighäuser's despairing exclamation may be repeated : " Quot

PREFATORY NOTE

difficultates in molestissimo huius operis edendi labore ! "

In the Indexes, prepared with the devoted aid of my wife, effort has been made to show as completely as possible the vast scope and encyclopaedic nature of Athenaeus's work. Additional notes, as well as some corrections which demanded immediate record, have been added in the Indexes.

Many of my colleagues at Harvard have given generously of their time and knowledge in helping to elucidate parts of the text. Meriting special mention are George Henry Chase, Hudson Professor of Archaeology, Carl Newell Jackson, now Eliot Professor of Greek Literature, Henry Bryant Bigelow, Professor of Zoology, and the late Benjamin Lincoln Robinson, Curator of the Gray Herbarium. The Reverend A. Lumb, of the Merchant Taylors' School, kindly permitted me to consult and make use of valuable emendations not already published. I must also acknowledge my debt to critics of previous volumes, on both sides of the ocean.

With all its difficulties, *The Deipnosophists* remains, as the Abbé de Marolles described it in 1680, " un ouvrage délicieux."

C. B. G.

HARVARD UNIVERSITY
November 1939

ABBREVIATIONS

Allinson = *Menander*, in Loeb Classical Library.
Aristoph. = Aristophanes.
Aristot. = Aristotle.
Athen. = Athenaeus.
Brandt = *Parodorum Epicorum Graecorum Reliquiae*, ed. P. Brandt, 1888.
Diehl = *Anthologia Lyrica*, ed. E. Diehl, 1922–1924.
Diels = *Poetarum Philosophorum Fragmenta*, ed. Hermann Diels, 1901.
Diels³ = *Vorsokratiker*, 3rd edition.
Edmonds = *Elegy and Iambus*, in Loeb Classical Library.
= *Lyra Graeca*, in Loeb Classical Library.
F.H.G. = *Fragmenta Historicorum Graecorum*, ed. C. Müller.
Frag. ep. = *Epicorum Graecorum Fragmenta*, ed. G. Kinkel.
G. and H. = Grenfell and Hunt, *Hellenica Oxyrhynchia*.
H.S.C.P. = *Harvard Studies in Classical Philology*.
Hort = *Theophrastus*, in Loeb Classical Library.
I.G. = *Inscriptiones Graecae*.
J. = Jacoby, *Fragmente der griechischen Historiker*.
Kaibel = *Comicorum Graecorum Fragmenta*, ed. G. Kaibel (for Epicharmus, Sophron, Sopater).
Kock = *Comicorum Atticorum Fragmenta*, ed. Th. Kock.
Olivieri = *Frammenti della commedia greca*, Naples, 1930.
*P.L.G.*⁴ = Bergk, *Poetae Lyrici Graeci*, 4th edition.
*P.L.G.*⁵ = 5th edition of the preceding work, Vol. i. (Pindar), by Schroeder, 1900, reprinted with a new appendix (*P.L.G.*⁶), 1923. Vols. ii. and iii. reprinted with indices bv Rubenbauer, 1914.
Powell = *Collectanea Alexandrina*, ed. J. U. Powell, Oxford, 1925.

ABBREVIATIONS

P.-W.   = Pauly-Wissowa, *Real-Encyclopädie*.
S.V.F.   = *Stoicorum Veterum Fragmenta*, ed. H. von Arnim, 1903.
Script. Al. M. = *Scriptores Historiarum Alexandri Magni*.
T.G.F.   = *Tragicorum Graecorum Fragmenta*, ed. A. Nauck, 2nd edition.

The references are to pages, unless otherwise indicated.

In the case of an ancient author whose work is known only through quotations, a proper name following a reference indicates the modern editor or compiler of the quoted fragments. Thus, " Frag. 200 Rose " means the edition of Aristotle's *Fragmenta* by Valentin Rose ; " Frag. 72 Gaede," Gaede's edition of the *Fragmenta* of Demetrius of Scepsis, etc.

PERSONS OF THE DIALOGUE

AEMILIANUS MAURUS, grammarian.

ALCEIDES OF ALEXANDRIA, musician.

AMOEBEUS, harp-player and singer.

ARRIAN, grammarian.

ATHENAEUS OF NAUCRATIS, the author.

CYNULCUS, nickname of a Cynic philosopher, Theodorus.

DAPHNUS OF EPHESUS, physician.

DEMOCRITUS OF NICOMEDIA, philosopher.

DIONYSOCLES, physician.

GALEN OF PERGAMUM, physician.

LARENSIS (P. Livius Larensis), Roman official, *pontifex minor, procurator patrimonii*.

LEONIDAS OF ELIS, grammarian.

MAGNUS, probably a Roman.

MASURIUS, jurist, poet, musician.

MYRTILUS OF THESSALY, grammarian.

PALAMEDES THE ELEATIC, lexicographer.

PHILADELPHUS PTOLEMAEENSIS, philosopher.

PLUTARCH OF ALEXANDRIA, grammarian.

PONTIANUS OF NICOMEDIA, philosopher.

RUFINUS OF NICAEA, physician.

TIMOCRATES, to whom Athenaeus relates the story of the banquet.

ULPIAN OF TYRE, Roman jurist and official.

VARUS, grammarian.

ZOÏLUS, grammarian.

ATHENAEUS

ΑΘΗΝΑΙΟΥ ΝΑΥΚΡΑΤΙΤΟΥ ΔΕΙΠΝΟΣΟΦΙΣΤΩΝ

ΙΔ

ΒΟΤΡΥΣ δὲ ὅτι μὲν κοινὸν δῆλον. σταφυλῆς δὲ
μέμνηται, καίτοι δοκοῦντος τοῦ ὀνόματος Ἀσια-
γενοῦς εἶναι, Κράτης ἐν δευτέρῳ Ἀττικῆς Διαλέκτου, ἐν τοῖς Ὑμνοις τοῖς ἀρχαίοις φάσκων ἀντὶ
τοῦ βότρυος τὴν σταφυλὴν κεῖσθαι διὰ τούτων·

αὐτῆσι σταφυλῇσι μελαίνῃσιν κομόωντες.

ὅτι δὲ καὶ παρ᾽ Ὁμήρῳ ἐστὶν παντὶ δῆλον.
Πλάτων δὲ ἐν ὀγδόῳ Νόμων καὶ βότρυς καὶ στα-
c φυλὰς ὀνομάζει διὰ τούτων· " ὃς ἂν ἀγροίκου
ὀπώρας γεύσηται, βοτρύων εἴτε καὶ σύκων, πρὶν
ἐλθεῖν τὴν ὥραν τὴν τοῦ τρυγᾶν ἀρκτούρῳ σύν-
δρομον, εἴτ᾽ ἐν τοῖς αὐτοῦ χωρίοις εἴτε καὶ ἐν
ἄλλων, ἱερὰς μὲν ν[1] ὀφειλέτω τῷ Διονύσῳ δραχμάς,
ἐὰν ἐκ τῶν αὐτοῦ δρέπῃ, ἐὰν δ᾽ ἐκ τῶν[2] γειτόνων,
μνᾶν, ἐὰν δ᾽ ἐξ ἄλλων, δύο μέρη τῆς μνᾶς. ὃς δ᾽
ἂν τὴν γενναίαν νῦν λεγομένην σταφυλὴν ἢ[3] τὰ
γενναῖα σῦκα ἐπονομαζόμενα ὀπωρίζειν βούληται,
ἐὰν μὲν ἐκ τῶν οἰκείων λαμβάνῃ, ὅπως ἂν ἐθέλῃ
d καὶ ὁπόταν βούληται καρπούσθω, ἐὰν δ᾽ ἐξ ἄλλων

---

[1] ν' added from Plato.
[2] δ' ἐκ τῶν Plato: δὲ καὶ τῶν A.
[3] ἢ added from Plato.

2

THE DEIPNOSOPHISTS OF ATHENAEUS OF NAUCRATIS

BOOK XIV (*continued*)

Grapes. That these are universal is well known. Although the form staphylê, bunch of grapes, seems to be of Asiatic origin, Crates quotes it in the second book of his *Attic Dialect*,[a] saying it occurs instead of botrys in the ancient Hymns, as follows : " Coiffed with the very clusters of black grapes." But every one knows the word staphylê is to be found in Homer.[b] Plato in the eighth book of *Laws* has both words, botrys and staphylê, in this passage[c] : "Whoever tastes common fruit, such as grapes (botryes) and figs, before the coming of harvest-time, coinciding with the rising of Arcturus,[d] whether on his own farms or on those of another, let him pay fifty drachmas sacred to Dionysus, if he gather them from his own land ; if from his neighbours', a mina, and if from any others', two-thirds of a mina. And whoever desires to gather what are now called the ' choice ' grapes or the ' choice ' figs, so-named, if he take them from his own lands let him harvest them how he will and whenever he desires,

---

[a] Wachsmuth 65. See Allen, Sikes, and Halliday, *Hom. Hymns*[2] 97.

[b] *e.g.* describing the shield of Achilles, *Il.* xviii. 561

ἐν δ' ἐτίθει σταφυλῇσι μέγα βρίθουσαν ἀλωὴν
καλὴν χρυσείην· μέλανες δ' ἀνὰ βότρυες ἦσαν.

βότρυες occurs only here in Homer, σταφυλή five times elsewhere.   [c] 844 D.

[d] The heliacal rising, middle of September.

3

μὴ πείσας, ἑπομένως[1] τῷ νόμῳ τῷ μὴ κινεῖν ὅ τι
μὴ κατέθετο, ἐκείνως αἰεὶ ζημιούσθω." ταῦτα μὲν
ὁ θεῖος Πλάτων. ἐγὼ δὲ πάλιν ζητῶ τίς ἡ γενναία
σταφυλὴ καὶ τίνα τὰ γενναῖα σῦκα. ὥρα οὖν ὑμῖν
ζητεῖν, ἕως ἐγὼ περὶ τῶν ἑξῆς παρακειμένων
διεξέλθω." καὶ ὁ Μασσούριος ἔφη·

μηδ᾽ ἀναβάλλεσθαι ἔς τ᾽ αὔριον ἔς τε ἔνηφι.[2]

γενναῖα λέγει τὰ εὐγενῆ ὁ φιλόσοφος, ὡς καὶ
Ἀρχίλοχος·

πάρελθε, γενναῖος γὰρ εἶς.

ἢ τὰ ἐπιγεγεννημένα[3] οἷον τὰ ἐπεμβεβλημένα.[4] ὁ
γὰρ Ἀριστοτέλης καὶ ἐπεμβολάδας[4] ἀπίους ὀνομάζει τὰς ἐγκεκεντρισμένας. Δημοσθένης ἐν τῷ
ὑπὲρ Κτησιφῶντος· "σῦκα καὶ βότρυς καὶ ἐλαίας
συλλέγων." Ξενοφῶν ἐν Οἰκονομικῷ· "ὑπὸ τοῦ
ἡλίου γλυκαίνεσθαι τὰς σταφυλάς." οἴδασιν δὲ οἱ
πρὸ ἡμῶν καὶ τοὺς ἐν οἴνῳ συντιθεμένους βότρυς.
Εὔβουλος γοῦν ἐν Κατακολλωμένῳ φησίν·

ἀλλὰ παραλαβὼν ἀκράτῳ κροῦε καὶ δίδου πυκνὰς
καὶ βότρυς τρώγειν ἀνάγκαζ᾽ αὐτὸν ἐξ οἴνου
συχνούς.

[1] ἑπόμενοσ A.
[2] Mazon: ἔστ᾽ ἔνηφι A, ἔστ᾽ ἔννηφι Kaibel.
[3] CE: ἐπιγεγενημένα A.
[4] ACE: ἐμβεβλημένα and ἐμβολάδας Harpocration.

---

[a] Jowett cites *Laws* 913 β τὸ μὴ κινεῖν τὰ ἀκίνητα; so Herod.
vi. 134.
[b] The speaker is Ulpian.
[c] Hes. *Opp.* 410.
[d] "Choice" is Jowett's rendering of γενναῖα, which Plato,

but if he take them from others' lands without their
consent, let him, in that event, always be fined according to the law which ordains that one must not meddle
with [a] what he has not stored up himself." Thus the
divine Plato. But I [b] again ask, What is meant by the
" choice " grapes and what are the " choice " figs? It
is high time, therefore, that you seek the answer
while I discourse on the viands served in order. And
Masurius said, quoting [c]: "And put nought off till the
morrow nor the day after to-morrow." By "choice"
the philosopher means "high-bred," [d] as also Archilochus [e]: " Pass, for you are a high-bred man"; or, in
the case of figs, those which have been born or produced upon, that is, grown by grafting (epemballo).
Aristotle, indeed, calls [f] pears which have been
grafted epembolades. [g] Demosthenes in the speech in
defence of Ctesiphon [h]: " Picking up figs and grapes
(botrys) and olives." Xenophon in Oeconomicus [i]:
" For the grapes (staphylai) to be sweetened by the
sun." The men who came before us know about the
practice of putting grapes down in wine. Eubulus,
for example, says in Glued Together [j] : " Come, take
him along and knock [k] him out with unmixed wine ;
give him drink on drink, and make him eat a lot of

Rep. 372 B, uses of barley-cakes, μάζας γενναίας, "generous,"
and ironically of tyranny, ἡ γενναία δὴ τυραννίς, Rep. 544 c ;
εὐγενής means virtually the same, "well-born," "noble,"
in Modern Greek "nice."

 [e] P.L.G.⁴ ii. 415, Diehl i. 240.
 [f] Frag. 274 Rose.
 [g] Rather, embolades. See critical note 4.
 [h] De Cor. 262, of the wandering barnstormer Aeschines.
 [i] xix. 19 ὅταν δὲ καιρὸς ᾖ ὑπὸ τοῦ ἡλίου ἤδη γλυκαίνεσθαι.
 [j] Kock ii. 181.
 [k] κρούω "knock" seems to be a slang term for getting a
man drunk, like σείω "shake," Athen. 168 c (vol. ii. p. 262).

ὁ δὲ τὸν Χείρωνα πεποιηκὼς τὸν εἰς Φερεκράτην
f ἀναφερόμενόν φησιν·

ἀμυγδάλας καὶ μῆλα καὶ μιμαίκυλα
καὶ μύρτα καὶ σέλινα κἀξ οἴνου βότρυς
καὶ μυελόν.

ὅτι δ' ἐν ταῖς Ἀθήναις διηνεκεῖς ἦσαν αἱ ὀπῶραι
πᾶσαι, μαρτυρεῖ Ἀριστοφάνης ἐν Ὥραις. τί οὖν
παράδοξον ἱστορεῖν δοκεῖ Ἀέθλιος ὁ Σάμιος ἐν
πέμπτῳ Σαμίων Ὥρων λέγων; "σῦκον καὶ
σταφυλὴ καὶ ὁμομηλὶς καὶ μῆλα καὶ ῥόδα δὶς τοῦ
674 ἐνιαυτοῦ ἐγίνετο[1]." Λυγκεὺς δ' ἐν τῇ πρὸς
Διαγόραν Ἐπιστολῇ ἐπαινῶν τὸν κατὰ τὴν Ἀτ-
τικὴν γινόμενον Νικοστράτειον[2] βότρυν καὶ ἀντι-
τιθεὶς αὐτῷ τοὺς Ῥοδιακούς φησιν· "τῷ δ' ἐκεῖ
καλουμένῳ βότρυι Νικοστρατείῳ[2] τὸν Ἱππώνειον[3]
ἀντεκτρέφουσι βότρυν, ὃς ἀπὸ Ἑκατομβαιῶνος
μηνὸς ὥσπερ ἀγαθὸς οἰκέτης διαμένει τὴν αὐτὴν
ἔχων εὔνοιαν."

Ἐπεὶ δὲ πολλάκις ὑμῖν εἴρηται περί τε κρεῶν
καὶ ὀρνίθων καὶ περιστεριδίων,[4] ἔρχομαι κἀγὼ
λέξων ὅσα ἐκ πολυαναγνωσίας εὑρεῖν ἠδυνήθην
b παρὰ τὰ προειρημένα. ΠΕΡΙΣΤΕΡΙΟΝ οὕτως ἔστιν
εὑρεῖν εἰρημένον παρὰ Μενάνδρῳ ἐν Παλλακῇ·

μικρὸν ἐπιμείνας[5] προστρέχει,
"ἠγόρακά σοι περιστέρια ταδὶ[6]" λέγων.

---

[1] Kaibel: ἐγένετο ACE.
[2] CE: νικοστράτιον, νικοστρατίωι A.
[3] ἱππώνιον CE: ἱππώνιον A.
[4] καὶ περιστεριδίων deleted by Kaibel.
[5] Clericus: ἐπέμεινασ A.

6

grapes in wine." The author of *Cheiron*, generally
attributed to Pherecrates, says [a] : " Almonds, apples,
arbutus-berries, myrtle-berries, celery, grapes in
wine, and marrow." That all the fruits were to be
found in Athens throughout the year is attested by
Aristophanes in *The Seasons*.[b] What is there to
wonder at, then, in what Aëthlius of Samos records
in the fifth book of his *Chronicles of Samos* ? He
says [c] : " The fig, the grape, the medlar, apples, and
roses grew twice a year." Lynceus in his *Letter to
Diagoras*, praising the Nicostrateian grape which
grows in Attica, and contrasting with it the Rhodian
kinds, says : " In competition with the Nicostrateian grape, as it is called over in Athens, they grow
the Hipponeian grape, which, beginning with the
month of Hecatombaion,[d] abides throughout the year
with the same loyalty that a faithful servant exhibits."

Since you have often discussed the subject of meats
and fowls, including pigeons,[e] I too am going to tell
what I have been able to discover in the course of
wide reading, over and beyond what has already been
said. The diminutive word for pigeon (peristerion)
is to be found in this form used by Menander in *The
Concubine*[f] : " After waiting a little he runs up to
her and says, ' I have bought you these pigeons in

[a] Kock i. 191. For μιμαίκυλα see 50 e-f (vol. i. p. 220).
[b] Kock i. 536, Athen. 372 b (vol. iv. p. 186). Xen. *Vectig.*
i. 3 καὶ μὴν ὅσαπερ οἱ θεοὶ ἐν ταῖς ὥραις ἀγαθὰ παρέχουσι, καὶ
ταῦτα πάντα ἐνταῦθα πρωαίτατα μὲν ἄρχεται, ὀψιαίτατα δὲ
λήγει (cited by Kock).
[c] *F.H.G.* iv. 287.
[d] Late June or early July.
[e] 373 a-406 c (vol. iv. pp. 188-338).
[f] Kock iii. 109, Allinson 420.

---

[g] ταδὶ added by Cobet.

ὁμοίως Νικόστρατος "Αβρᾳ·

τοῦτ' ἀξιῶ·

τοὐρνιθάριον,[1] τὸ περιστέριον, τὸ γάστριον.

'Αναξανδρίδης ἐν 'Αντέρωτι[2]·

περιστέρια γὰρ εἰσάγων[3] καὶ στρουθία.

Φρύνιχος Τραγῳδοῖς·

περιστέριον δ' αὐτῷ τι λαβὲ τριωβόλου.

ΦΑΣΙΑΝΙΚΟΣ. Πτολεμαῖος ὁ βασιλεὺς ἐν τῷ
c δωδεκάτῳ τῶν Ὑπομνημάτων περὶ τῶν ἐν 'Αλεξ-
ανδρείᾳ βασιλείων λέγων καὶ περὶ τῶν ἐν αὐτοῖς
ζῴων τρεφομένων φησίν· " τά τε τῶν φασιανῶν,
οὓς τετάρους ὀνομάζουσιν· οὓς οὐ μόνον ἐκ Μηδίας
μετεπέμπετο,[4] ἀλλὰ καὶ νομάδας ὄρνιθας ὑποβαλὼν
ἐποίησε πλῆθος, ὥστε καὶ σιτεῖσθαι· τὸ γὰρ βρῶμα
πολυτελὲς ἀποφαίνουσιν." αὕτη ἡ[5] τοῦ λαμπρο-
τάτου βασιλέως φωνή, ὃς οὐδὲ φασιανικοῦ ὄρνιθός
ποτε γεύσασθαι ὡμολόγησεν, ἀλλ' ὥσπερ τι κει-
μήλιον ἀνακείμενον εἶχε τούσδε τοὺς ὄρνιθας. εἰ
δὲ ἑωράκει ὡς ἡμῶν ἑκάστῳ εἷς ἐστι παρακείμενος
χωρὶς τῶν ἤδη κατανηλωμένων, προσαναπεπληρώ-
d κει ἂν ταῖς πολυθρυλήτοις ἱστορίαις τῶν Ὑπομνημάτων τούτων τῶν εἰκοσιτεσσάρων καὶ ἄλλην μίαν.
'Αριστοτέλης δὲ ἢ Θεόφραστος ἐν τοῖς Ὑπομνή-

---

[1] Dindorf: εἶτ' ὀρνιθάριον A (εἶτ' Kock).
[2] Kaibel: ἀντερῶντι A.
[3] παρεισάγων Hirschig.
[4] Casaubon: μετεπόμποντο A.
[5] ἡ added by Kaibel.

---

[a] Kock ii. 220. The title "Αβρα means " favourite slave-
girl " (" mi-servante, mi-demoiselle," Navarre). A mistress
is here prescribing the proper use of words to her maid.

8

the market.' " Likewise Nicostratus in *The Pet* [a] :
" This is what I want : a little squab, a little pigeon,
a little bacon." Anaxandrides in *Anteros* [b] : " Bringing in, indeed, pigeons and sparrows." Phrynichus
in *Tragedians* [c] : " Buy from him a pigeon for threepence."

Pheasants. King Ptolemy, in the twelfth book of
his *Commentaries*, speaking of the royal palace at
Alexandria and the animals kept in it, says [d] : " Also
the kind of pheasants which they call tetaroi [e] ; not
only did he procure these from Media, but by mating
Numidian birds [f] he produced quantities of them for
food ; for it is asserted that they make a very rich
delicacy." Here you have the word of that most
illustrious king, who has admitted that he never even
so much as tasted a pheasant, but kept the very birds
we have here as a treasure carefully stored. But if
he had seen that each one of us to-day has a whole
pheasant served to us besides the food already con-
sumed, he would have filled up another book to add to
the famous stories in his *Commentaries*, now consisting
of twenty-four books.

Aristotle [g] or Theophrastus in his *Commentaries*

[b] Kock ii. 138, with the title Ἀντερῶν, " rival in love."
For Ἀντέρως see *I.G.* xiv. 1098 ; for Ἀντερῶσα 487 b (vol.
v. p. 166).

[c] Kock i. 383.

[d] *F.H.G.* iii. 188, J. 2 B 983, BD 659. Ptolemy Physcon,
also called Euergetes II, is the writer ; his subject is possibly
Philadelphus.

[e] Other forms are tetrax, tatyras. On the pheasant *cf.*
386 d, 398 b (vol. iv. pp. 246, 302).

[f] Guinea-fowls.

[g] Frag. 632 Rose. The quotation, out of place here, seems
to refer to the splendid plumage of the males.

μασι '' τῶν φασιανῶν, φησίν, οὐ κατὰ λόγον ἡ
ὑπεροχὴ τῶν ἀρρένων, ἀλλὰ πολλῷ μείζων.''

Εἰ δ᾽ ὁ προειρημένος βασιλεὺς καὶ τὸ τῶν
ΤΑΩΝΩΝ πλῆθος ἑωράκει τῶν κατὰ τὴν Ῥώμην,
καταπεφεύγει ἂν ἐπὶ τὴν ἱερὰν σύγκλητον, ὡς ὑπὸ
τοῦ ἀδελφοῦ πάλιν τῆς βασιλείας ἐξεληλαμένος.
e τοσοῦτον γάρ ἐστι τούτων τῶν ὀρνίθων τὸ πλῆθος
ἐν τῇ Ῥώμῃ ὡς δοκεῖν προμεμαντευμένον τὸν
κωμῳδιοποιὸν Ἀντιφάνην ἐν Στρατιώτῃ ἢ Τύχωνι
εἰρηκέναι τάδε·

πρὸς τῶν ταῶν[1] μὲν ὡς ἅπαξ τις ζεῦγος ἤγαγεν μόνον,
σπάνιον ὂν τὸ χρῆμα, πλείους εἰσὶ νῦν τῶν
   ὀρτύγων.
χρηστὸν ἄνθρωπον δ᾽ ἐάν τις ἕνα μόνον ζητῶν
   ἴδῃ,[2]
ὄψετ᾽ ἐκ τούτου πονηροὺς πέντε παῖδας γε-
   γονότας.

f Ἄλεξις δ᾽ ἐν Λαμπάδι·

                                              καταφαγεῖν
αὐτὸς τοσοῦτ᾽[3] ἀργύριον. οὐδ᾽ εἰ γάλα λαγοῦ
εἶχον,[4] μὰ τὴν Γῆν, καὶ ταῶς[5] κατήσθιον.

ὅτι δὲ καὶ τιθασοὺς[6] εἶχον αὐτοὺς ἐν ταῖς οἰκίαις
Στράττις παρίστησιν ἐν Παυσανίᾳ διὰ τούτων·

πολλῶν φλυάρων καὶ ταῶν[7] ἀντάξια,
οὓς βόσκεθ᾽ ὑμεῖς ἕνεκα τῶν ὠκυπτέρων.

Ἀναξανδρίδης ἐν Μελιλώτῳ·

---

[1] 397 a: τὸν ταῶν ACE.
[2] CE: δὲ ἄν τις . . . εἴδῃ A.

says : " The superiority of the cock-pheasants over
the hens is out of all proportion to what it is in other
birds, and is far greater."

Peacocks. Again, if the aforementioned king had
seen the number of peacocks we have in Rome, he
would have fled for refuge hither to the holy Senate,
as if driven out of his kingdom once again by his
brother.[a] For the number of these birds is so great in
Rome that it would seem as if the comic poet Antiphanes had divined it when he said in *The Soldier*, or
Tychon [b] : " When anyone imported just a pair of
peacocks, it was a rare thing ; but to-day they are
more numerous than quails. So if anyone looks round
and sees just one good man, presently he will see five
bad sons sprung from him." Again, Alexis in *The
Torch* [c] : " To eat up all by myself so much money !
Why, not even if I had had hare's milk, by Earth, or
had feasted on peacocks ! " That they kept them
tame in their houses is attested by Strattis in these
lines from *Pausanias* [d] : " Worth about as much as
all the poppycock and peacocks which you keep for
the sake of their wing-feathers." Anaxandrides in

---

[a] Ptolemy Philometor, who had insisted on a division of
territory and had obtained from the Roman Senate all but
Cyrene and Libya. In 163 B.C. he went to Rome to obtain
the grant of Cyprus. Polyb. xxxi. 18, xxxiii. 5.

[b] Kock ii. 99, Athen. 397 a (vol. iv. p. 296), *cf.* 397 c. For
their rarity in the fifth century *cf.* Aristoph. *Av.* 102 Τηρεὺς
γὰρ εἶ σύ; πότερον ὄρνις ἢ ταῶς;

[c] Kock ii. 340.

[d] Kock i. 718.

---

³ CE : τουσουτ' A.

⁴ Schweighäuser : γάλα εἶχον λαγοῦ ACE.

⁵ ταῶσ ACE.   ⁶ τιθάσουσ A.

⁷ ταῶν A ; see 397 e.

655 οὐ¹ μανικόν ἐστ'² ἐν οἰκίᾳ³ τρέφειν ταῶς,⁴
ἐξὸν τοσουτουὶ δύ'⁵ ἀγάλματ' ἀγοράσαι;

'Αναξίλας⁶ 'Ορνιθοκόμοις·

καὶ πρὸς ἐπὶ τούτοις τιθασὸς οἰμώζων ταῶς.⁷

Μηνόδοτος δ' ὁ Σάμιος ἐν τῷ περὶ τῶν κατὰ τὸ
ἱερὸν τῆς Σαμίας "Ηρας φησίν· " οἱ ταοὶ ἱεροί εἰσι
τῆς "Ηρας. καὶ μήποτε πρώτιστοι καὶ ἐγένοντο
καὶ ἐτράφησαν ἐν Σάμῳ καὶ ἐντεῦθεν εἰς τοὺς ἔξω
τόπους διεδόθησαν, ὡς καὶ οἱ ἀλεκτρυόνες ἐν τῇ
Περσίδι καὶ αἱ καλούμεναι μελεαγρίδες ἐν τῇ
b Αἰτωλίᾳ." διὸ καὶ 'Αντιφάνης ἐν τοῖς 'Ομοπα-
τρίοις φησίν·

ἐν 'Ηλίου μέν⁸ φασι γίνεσθαι πόλει
φοίνικας, ἐν 'Αθήναις δὲ γλαύκας. ἡ Κύπρος
ἔχει πελείας διαφόρους,⁹ ἡ δ' ἐν Σάμῳ
"Ηρα τὸ¹⁰ χρυσοῦν, φασίν, ὀρνίθων γένος,
τοὺς καλλιμόρφους καὶ περιβλέπτους ταῶς.¹¹

διόπερ καὶ ἐπὶ τοῦ νομίσματος τῶν Σαμίων ταῶς¹²
ἐστιν.

'Επεὶ δὲ καὶ τῶν μελεαγρίδων Μηνόδοτος
ἐμνήσθη, λέξομέν τι καὶ ἡμεῖς περὶ αὐτῶν. Κλύτος
ὁ Μιλήσιος, 'Αριστοτέλους δὲ μαθητής, ἐν τῷ α'
c περὶ Μιλήτου γράφει περὶ αὐτῶν οὕτως· " περὶ δὲ
τὸ ἱερὸν τῆς Παρθένου ἐν Λέρῳ¹³ εἰσὶν οἱ καλού-

---

¹ Hermann: οὐχὶ ACE.
² ἐστιν ACE.   ³ CE: οἰκίδαι A.
⁴ ταῶσ ACE.
⁵ Coraes: τοιούτουσῖδυο A, τουτοισὶ δύ' CE.
⁶ ἀναξίλαοσ A.   ⁷ ταῶσ A.
⁸ A: ἐν ἁλίαις μέν E, ἐν ἁλίειν C.

12

Melilot [a] : " Isn't it crazy to keep peacocks in the
house when for all that money you can buy two
statues ! " Anaxilas in *Poultry-Keepers* [b] : " And
what is more, on top of this, a tame peacock, dam-
mit ! " Menodotus of Samos in his work *On Objects
at the Temple of the Samian Hera* says [c] : " The peacocks are sacred to Hera. And it may be that they
were first produced and bred in Samos, and from
there were distributed among the regions beyond,
like the fowls of Persia and the meleagrides (guinea-
hens), as they are called, of Aetolia." Hence also
Antiphanes says in *Own-Brothers* [d] : " In Heliopolis,
they say, lives the phoenix, in Athens, owls, and
Cyprus has doves unlike all others, while the Hera of
Samos, they say, has that golden species of birds, the
beautiful spectacular peacocks." That is why a peacock stands on the coins of Samos. [e]

Since Menodotus mentioned guinea-hens, we also
will say something about them. Clytus of Miletus, a
disciple of Aristotle, writes about them in the first
book of his work *On Miletus* as follows [f] : " All about
the temple of the Maiden [g] in Leros are the birds called

[a] Kock ii. 145.   [b] *ibid.* 272.

[c] *F.H.G.* iii. 105, Varro, *De Re Rust.* iii. 6. 2.

[d] Kock ii. 83. On the phoenix Hdt. ii. 73 says : ἐγὼ μέν
μιν οὐκ εἶδον εἰ μὴ ὅσον γραφῇ· καὶ γὰρ δὴ καὶ σπάνιος ἐπιφοιτᾷ
σφι δι' ἐτέων, ὡς Ἡλιοπολῖται λέγουσι, πεντακοσίων.

[e] Apparently not before 200 B.C., but frequently thereafter. Head, *Greek Coins of Brit. Mus.* xv. Plate xxxvi.

[f] *F.H.G.* ii. 333. *Cf.* Pliny, *N.H.* x. 26. 74 Africae hoc
est gallinarum genus, gibberum, variis sparsum plumis.

[g] Artemis, Ael. *N.A.* iv. 42.

[9] B, Eustath. 1035. 48: διφόρουσ ACE.
[10] CE: ἤρατο A.   [11] ταῶσ ACE.
[12] ταῶσ A, ταώς C.
[13] Dalechamps: ἐν αερω A.

μένοι ὄρνιθες μελεαγρίδες. ὁ δὲ τόπος ἐστὶν
ἑλώδης ἐν ᾧ τρέφονται. ἐστὶ δὲ ἄστοργον πρὸς τὰ
ἔκγονα τὸ ὄρνεον καὶ ὀλιγωρεῖ τῶν νεωτέρων,[1]
ὥστε ἀνάγκη τοῖς ἱερεῦσιν ἐπιμελεῖσθαι αὐτῶν.
ἔχει δὲ τὸ μὲν μέγεθος· ὄρνιθος γενναίου, τὴν δὲ
κεφαλὴν μικρὰν πρὸς τὸ σῶμα καὶ ταύτην ψιλήν,
ἐπ᾽ αὐτῆς δὲ λόφον σάρκινον, σκληρόν, στρογγύλον,
ἐξέχοντα τῆς κεφαλῆς ὥσπερ πάτταλον, καὶ τὸ
d χρῶμα ξυλοειδῆ,[2] πρὸς δὲ ταῖς γνάθοις ἀπὸ τοῦ
στόματος[3] ἀρξαμένην ἀντὶ πώγωνος μακρὰν σάρκα
καὶ ἐρυθροτέραν[4] τῶν ὀρνίθων. τὴν δὲ τοῖς ὄρνισιν
ἐπὶ τῷ ῥύγχει γινομένην, ἣν ἔνιοι πώγωνα καλοῦσιν,
οὐκ ἔχει· διὸ καὶ ταύτῃ κολοβόν ἐστιν. ῥύγχος δὲ
ὀξύτερον καὶ μεῖζον ἢ ὄρνις ἔχει. τράχηλος μέλας,
παχύτερος καὶ βραχύτερος τῶν ὀρνίθων. τὸ δὲ
σῶμα ἅπαν ποικίλον, μέλανος ὄντος τοῦ χρώματος
ὅλου, πτίλοις[5] λευκοῖς καὶ πυκνοῖς διειλημμένου[6]
e οὐ[7] μείζοσιν φακῶν. οὗτοι δ᾽ εἰσὶν ἐν ῥόμβοις οἱ
κυκλίσκοι ἧσσον[8] μέλασι[9] τοῦ ὅλου χρώματος· διὸ
καὶ ποικιλίαν τινὰ οἱ ῥόμβοι παρέχονται, τοῦ μὲν
μέλανος ἔχοντες[10] λευκότερον τὸ χρῶμα, τοῦ δὲ
λευκοῦ πολὺ μελάντερον. τὰ[11] δὲ κατὰ τὰς πτέρυγας
αὐταῖς πεποίκιλται λευκῷ πριονώδεσιν σχήμασιν[12]
παρ᾽ ἄλληλα[13] κειμένοις. σκέλη δὲ ἄκεντρα ὅμοια
τοῖς ὀρνιθίοις.[14] παραπλήσιαι δ᾽ εἰσὶν αἱ θήλειαι
τοῖς ἄρρεσιν· διὸ καὶ δυσδιάκριτόν ἐστι τὸ τῶν

---

[1] νεοττῶν Herwerden.

[2] Schweighäuser: ξυλοειδέα AE, ξυλοει C.

[3] CE: σώματος A.   [4] CE: ἐρυθρωτέραν A.

14

meleagrides. The place in which they are kept is marshy. The bird is lacking in affection for its young and neglects the young chicks, so that the priests are compelled to care for them. It has the size of a high-bred cock, but a head small in proportion to its body, and bare besides, and with a fleshy comb which is hard and round, projecting from the head like a peg, and of woody colour; attached to the cheeks, beginning at the beak, is a long piece of flesh, like a beard, redder than the wattles of cocks; but that which in some birds grows on the beak, called by some the beard, it does not have; hence it is stunted at this point. It has a sharper and larger beak than the cock. Its neck is black, thicker and shorter than that of cocks. Its entire body, of a colour which in general is black, is speckled thickly with white feathers at regular distances apart, no bigger than lentils. These tiny rings are set in lozenge-shapes which are less black than the colour of the body in general; hence the lozenges present a speckled appearance, with a colour whiter than the dark part, yet a good deal darker than the white. At the wings the birds are speckled white in serrated patterns lying parallel. Their legs are without spurs, like those of chickens. The females resemble the males; hence it is hard to

[5] σπίλοις " flecks " Gesner.

[6] CE: διειλημμένων A, διειλημμένον Musurus.

[7] οὐ added by Schweighäuser.

[8] ἧσσον added by Wilamowitz; ἧττον? Cf. πάτταλον above.

[9] A: μελαντέροις CE.

[10] Wilamowitz: ἔχοντοσ AC.   [11] CE: τὸ A.

[12] Schweighäuser: σχήμασιν πυρώδεσιν AC.

[13] παρ᾿ ἄλληλα Kaibel: πρὸς ἄλληλα CE, καὶ παράλληλα A.

[14] A: ὀρνιθείοις C, ὀρνιθείοις E.

μελεαγρίδων γένος.'' τοσαῦτα καὶ ὁ περιπατη-
τικὸς φιλόσοφος περὶ τῶν μελεαγρίδων ἱστόρησεν.

f ΟΠΤΩΝ ΔΕΛΦΑΚΩΝ δὲ μνημονεύει Ἐπικράτης ἐν
Ἐμπόρῳ·

ἐπὶ τοῖς δ' ἐγὼ
μάγειρος. οὔτε Σικελία καυχήσεται
τρέφειν τοιοῦτον ἄρταμον κατ' ἰχθύων,
οὐκ Ἦλις, ἔνθα[1] δελφάκων ἐγὼ κρέα
κάλλιστ' ὄπωπα πυρὸς ἀκμαῖς ἠνθισμένα.

Ἄλεξις δ' ἐν Πονήρᾳ·

τριωβόλου κρεῖσκον ἀστεῖον πάνυ
ὕειον ὀπτὸν κἄτι[2] θερμόν, εὔχυλον,
656   τέρεν,[3] ὅταν ᾖ προσφέρων.[4]

'' Ἀθηναῖοι δ', ὥς φησι Φιλόχορος, ταῖς Ὥραις
θύοντες οὐκ ὀπτῶσιν, ἀλλ' ἕψουσι τὰ κρέα, παρ-
αιτούμενοι τὰς θεὰς ἀπείργειν τὰ περισκελῆ καύ-
ματα καὶ τοὺς αὐχμούς, μετὰ δὲ τῆς συμμέτρου
θερμασίας καὶ ὑδάτων ὡραίων ἐκτελεῖν τὰ φυόμενα.
τὴν μὲν γὰρ ὄπτησιν ἐλάττους παρέχεσθαι ὠφε-
λείας, τὴν δὲ ἕψησιν οὐ μόνον τὴν ὠμότητα περιαιρεῖν, ἀλλὰ καὶ τὰ σκληρὰ μαλάττειν δύνασθαι καὶ
τὰ λοιπὰ πεπαίνειν. ἔτι δ'[5] εὐμενέστερον καὶ
ἀκινδυνότερον πεπαίνει τὴν τροφήν. διόπερ ἐφθὸν
b ἐποπτᾶν οὔ φασι δεῖν οὐδ' ἐφέψειν. τὸ μὲν γὰρ
ἀνάλυσιν ἔχειν δοκεῖ τοῦ βελτίονος, ὥς φησιν
Ἀριστοτέλης· τὰ δὲ ὀπτὰ τῶν ἐφθῶν ὠμότερα καὶ
ξηρότερα.'' τὰ δὲ ὀπτὰ[6] κρέα καλεῖται φλογίδες.

---

[1] οὐ | κηλισενθα A.   [2] Kaibel (?): καὶ A.
[3] εὔχυλον, τέρεν Porson: εὐχυλότερον A.
[4] ὅταν ᾖ τι, πρόσφερ' (?) Porson.

distinguish the sex of guinea-fowls." All this our Peripatetic philosopher has recorded about guinea-fowls.

Roast Pig. Epicrates mentions this in *The Merchant*[a] : " After them I succeeded as chef. Sicily shall not boast that it rears such a cook when it comes to fish, not Elis either, where I have looked upon the fairest meat of porkers browned by the points of fire."[b] Alexis in *Love-lorn Lass*[c] : " Very nice is a little piece of pork worth threepence when one comes bringing it roasted and hot withal, juicy, tender." " The Athenians, however," according to Philochorus,[d] " do not roast the meat when they sacrifice to the Seasons, but boil it, entreating the goddesses to defend them from excessive heat and drought and to bring to ripeness growing things by moderate warmth and seasonable rains. For, he declares, roasting affords less benefit, whereas boiling not only takes away the rawness, but can soften tough parts and ripen the rest. Further, it ripens food more gently and at less risk. Hence they say that what has been boiled should not be roasted or boiled further. For this, it is admitted, means the dissolution of the better part of the meat, as Aristotle asserts.[e] And roasted meats are more raw and dry than boiled meats." Roasted meats are

---

[a] Kock ii. 284.
[b] Eur. *Phoen.* 1255 ἐμπύρους ἀκμάς.
[c] Kock ii. 367. The text is uncertain.
[d] *F.H.G.* i. 413.
[e] *Cf.* Aristot. *Meteor.* 380 b 21 ξηρότερα τὰ ἐφθὰ τῶν ὀπτῶν· οὐ γὰρ ἀνασπᾷ εἰς ἑαυτὰ τὸ ὑγρὸν τὰ ἑψόμενα· κρατεῖ γὰρ ἡ ἔξωθεν θερμότης τῆς ἐντός. But Philochorus (or Athenaeus) has misunderstood Aristotle.

---

[5] CE: ὅτι δ' A. [6] Musurus: ὄντα A.

Στράττις γοῦν ἐν Καλλιππίδῃ ἐπὶ τοῦ Ἡρακλέους
φησίν·

αὐτίκα δ' ἥρπασε τεμάχη
θερμάς τε κάπρου φλογίδας ἔβρυχέ τε πάνθ' ἅμα.

καὶ Ἄρχιππος ἐν Ἡρακλεῖ Γαμοῦντι·

ταδὶ δ' ἅμα[1] χοίρων ἀκροκώλια μικρῶν
ταύρου τ' αὐξίκερω[2] φλογίδες
αἱ δολιχαί τε κάπρου φλογίδες.[3]

c   Περὶ δὲ ΠΕΡΔΙΚΩΝ τί δεῖ καὶ λέγειν ἐμέ, πλεό-
νων εἰρημένων ὑφ' ὑμῶν; ἀλλ' οὐ παραλείψω τὸ
ἱστορηθὲν ὑπὸ Ἡγησάνδρου ἐν τοῖς Ὑπομνήμασιν.
φησὶν γὰρ ὅτι Σάμιοι πλεύσαντες εἰς Σύβαριν
καὶ κατασχόντες τὴν Σιρῖτιν χώραν περδίκων
ἀναπτάντων καὶ ποιησάντων ψόφον ἐκπλαγέντες
ἔφυγον καὶ ἐμβάντες εἰς τὰς ναῦς ἀπέπλευσαν.

Περὶ δὲ ΛΑΓΩΝ Χαμαιλέων φησὶν ἐν τῷ περὶ
Σιμωνίδου ὡς δειπνῶν παρὰ τῷ Ἱέρωνι ὁ Σιμω-
d νίδης, οὐ παρατεθέντος αὐτῷ ἐπὶ τὴν τράπεζαν
καθάπερ καὶ τοῖς ἄλλοις λαγωοῦ, ἀλλ' ὕστερον
μεταδιδόντος τοῦ Ἱέρωνος, ἀπεσχεδίασεν·

οὐδὲ γὰρ οὐδ'[4] εὐρύς περ ἐὼν ἐξίκετο δεῦρο.

ὄντως δ' ἦν ὡς ἀληθῶς κίμβιξ ὁ Σιμωνίδης καὶ
αἰσχροκερδής, ὡς Χαμαιλέων φησίν. ἐν Συρακού-

---

[1] Meineke: τα | διδαλλα A.
[2] Dindorf: ταξικερω A.   [3] σχελίδες Meineke.
[4] οὐδ' added by Musurus, cf. Eustath. 1821. 37 and
Aldick 26.

---

[a] " Touched by the flames," since meat was generally
roasted or broiled over an open fire.

18

called phlogides.[a] Strattis, for example, says of
Heracles in *Callippides* [b] : " Immediately he snatched
up whole slices, and hot steaks of roasted wild boar,
and gobbled them all at once." Also Archippus in
Heracles takes a Wife [c] : " Here you have together
trotters from little pigs, roast steaks from a tall-
horned bull, and the long roast steaks[d] of wild boar."

Partridges. On this subject why need I speak when
so much has already been said by you ? [e] And yet I
am not going to omit the story told by Hegesander
in his *Commentaries.*[f] He says, namely, that the
Samians after sailing to Sybaris and landing in the
territory of Siris were so frightened by partridges
suddenly flying up and making a loud noise that they
fled, going on board their ships and sailing away.

Hares. On this subject Chamaeleon says[g] in his
book *On Simonides* that the poet was once dining at
the court of Hieron, and when the roast hare was not
served to him as it had been to the other guests,
though he was afterwards given a share of it by
Hieron, he promptly parodied[h] : " Wide, indeed,
though it is, it has not reached to me." As a matter
of fact Simonides was a skinflint and greedy for gain,
Chamaeleon declares. In Syracuse, for example,

---

[b] Kock i. 715, cf. Aristoph. *Ran.* 549-578.

[c] Kock i. 680.

[d] Or, reading σχελίδες, "ribs."

[e] 388 e-390 d (vol. iv. pp. 256-264).

[f] *F.H.G.* iv. 421.

[g] Frag. 14 Koepke, p. 23. On Simonides and his re-
partees cf. 352 c (vol. iv. p. 94), 456 c (vol. iv. p. 568).

[h] *Il.* xiv. 33

οὐδὲ γὰρ οὐδ' εὐρύς περ ἐὼν ἐδυνήσατο πάσας
αἰγιαλὸς νῆας χαδέειν, στείνοντο δὲ λαοί.

P.L.G.[4] iii. 506, Diehl ii. 86, Edmonds ii. 346.

σαις γοῦν τοῦ Ἱέρωνος ἀποστέλλοντος αὐτῷ τὰ καθ᾽
ἡμέραν λαμπρῶς πωλῶν τὰ πλείω ὁ Σιμωνίδης τῶν
παρ᾽ ἐκείνου πεμπομένων ἑαυτῷ μικρὸν μέρος
e ἀπετίθετο. ἐρομένου δέ τινος τὴν αἰτίαν· " ὅπως,
εἶπεν, ἥ τε Ἱέρωνος μεγαλοπρέπεια καταφανὴς ᾖ
καὶ ἡ ἐμὴ κοσμιότης."

ΟΥΘΑΤΟΣ δὲ Τηλεκλείδης ἐν Στερροῖς[1] οὕτως
μνημονεύει·

ὡς οὖσα θῆλυς εἰκότως οὖθαρ φέρω.

ὑπογάστριον δ᾽ αὐτὸ ὠνόμασεν Ἀντίδοτος ἐν
Μεμψιμοίρῳ.

ΣΙΤΕΥΤΩΝ[2] δὲ ὀρνίθων μὲν μνημονεύει Μάτρων
ἐν ταῖς Παρῳδίαις οὕτως·

ὡς ἔφαθ᾽· οἱ δ᾽ ἐγέλασσαν,[3] ἐπήνεικάν τ᾽ ἐπὶ[4]
τούτῳ
σιτευτὰς ὄρνιθας ἐπ᾽ ἀργυρέοισι πίναξιν,
f ἄτριχας, οἰέτεας, λαγάνοις[5] κατὰ νῶτον ἐΐσας.

δελφάκων δὲ[6] σιτευτῶν ὁ φλυακογράφος Σώπατρος
ἐν Βακχίδος Γάμῳ οὕτως·

εἴ που κλίβανος ἦν, πολὺ δέλφαξ σιτευτὸς
ἔγρυξεν.[7]

δελφάκια δὲ Αἰσχίνης εἴρηκεν ἐν Ἀλκιβιάδῃ
οὕτως· " ὥσπερ αἱ καπηλίδες τὰ δελφάκια
τρέφουσιν." Ἀντισθένης[8] δ᾽ ἐν Φυσιογνωμονικῷ·
" καὶ γὰρ ἐκεῖναι τὰ δελφάκια πρὸς βίαν χορτά-

---

[1] 399 c: ἐν ἑτέροις A.
[2] Schweighäuser, cf. 384 a: σιτιστῶν ACE, Brandt.
[3] ἐγέλασαν A.
[4] επηνεινκαντεπι A, ἐπήνεγκάν τ᾽ ἐπὶ Musurus.

Hieron would send him generous supplies for his daily
needs, but Simonides would sell the greater part of
what the king sent him, keeping only a small portion
for himself. When somebody asked him the reason
he replied, " I want to show at once Hieron's munifi-
cence and my own abstemiousness."

The Udder. Telecleides mentions it thus in *Hard-
boiled* [a] : " Being a female, I naturally wear an
udder." But Antidotus in *The Faultfinder* calls the
udder a belly-piece.[b]

Fatted fowls are mentioned by Matron in his
Parodies thus [c] : " Thus spake he ; and they laughed,
and thereupon brought in fatted fowls on silver
platters, featherless, of like age, matched across their
backs as level as pancakes." And fatted pigs are
mentioned thus by the writer of farces, Sopater, in
The Marriage of Bacchis [d] : " Wherever there was an
oven, loudly a fatted pig squealed." The form
delphakia (pigs) is used by Aeschines in the dialogue
Alcibiades thus [e] : " As huckster-women feed their
little pigs." Antisthenes in *Expert in Physiognomy* [f] :
" For those women must feed their little pigs[g] whether

---

[a] Kock i. 217, Athen. 399 c (vol. iv. p. 306).

[b] Kock ii. 410 ; Athen. *loc. cit.* says ὑπογάστριον is properly
used of fish.

[c] Brandt 92 ; *cf. Il.* ii. 763-765 ἵπποι . . . τὰς Εὔμηλος
ἔλαυνε ποδώκεας ὄρνιθας ὥς, ὄτριχας (of like coat), οἰέτεας,
σταφύλῃ (mason's level) ἐπὶ νῶτον ἐΐσας.

[d] Kaibel 193.

[e] Dittmar 267, Hermann 21.

[f] F. Dümmler, *Akademika* 209.

[g] Here used *sens. obsc., cf.* 581 a (vol. vi. p. 135). For
πρὸς βίαν χορτάζειν *cf.* Alcaeus 39 πρὸς βίαν πώνην (drink).

---

[5] λαγανοῖσ A.   [6] Schweighäuser: τε A.
        [7] Schweighäuser: ἔτρυξεν ACE.
         [8] Dindorf: ἀντιφάνησ A.

21

ζουσιν." καὶ ἐν Προτρεπτικῷ δέ· " ἀντὶ δελφα-
κίων τρέφεσθαι." δέλφακα δὲ ἀρσενικῶς εἴρηκεν
657 Πλάτων ἐν Ποιητῇ·

δέλφακα δ' ὡραιότατον.[1]

Σοφοκλῆς Ὕβρει·

ἐσθίειν ἐθέλων[2] τὸν δέλφακα.

Κρατῖνος Ὀδυσσεῦσιν·

δέλφακας μεγάλους.

θηλυκῶς δὲ Νικοχάρης ἔφη·

κύουσαν δέλφακα.

καὶ Εὔπολις Χρυσῷ Γένει·

οὔκ, ἀλλ' ἔθυον[3] δέλφακ' ἔνδον[4] θῆστία·
καὶ μάλα καλήν.

καὶ Πλάτων Ἰοῖ·

πρόσφερε δεῦρο δὴ τὴν κεφαλὴν τῆς δέλφακος.

Θεόπομπος Πηνελόπῃ·

καὶ τὴν ἱερὰν σφάττουσιν ἡμῶν[6] δελφάκα.

b ΧΗΝΩΝ δὲ σιτευτῶν καὶ μόσχων Θεόπομπος ἐν ιγ΄
Φιλιππικῶν καὶ ια΄ Ἑλληνικῶν, ἐν οἷς ἐμφανίζει τὸ
περὶ τὴν γαστέρα τῶν Λακώνων ἐγκρατὲς γράφων
οὕτως· " καὶ οἱ Θάσιοι ἔπεμψαν Ἀγησιλάῳ
προσιόντι πρόβατα παντοδαπὰ καὶ βοῦς εὖ τεθραμ-

[1] δ' ὡραιότατον Casaubon: δὲ ραιοτατον A, δὲ πιότατον (?)
Kaibel.
[2] θέλων (?) Dindorf.
[3] Meineke: ου | καλλευθιον A.
[4] Kock: δελφακαωδον A.

22

they will or no." Also in his *Hortatory Discourse*[a] : "To be fed like little pigs." The form delphax is used as a masculine by Plato in *The Poet*[b] : "A very nice pig." Sophocles in *Insolence*[c] : "Willing to eat the pig." Cratinus in *The Odysseis*[d] : "Large pigs." But Nicochares used delphax as a feminine[e] : "A pregnant pig (sow)." So, too, Eupolis in *The Golden Age*[f] : "No, but they were sacrificing indoors a sow, and a mighty fine one, to Hestia." And Plato in *Io*[g] : "Bring here, then, the head of the sow." Theopompus in *Penelope*[h] : "They are slaughtering our sacred sow."

Fatted geese and calves are mentioned by Theopompus in the thirteenth book of his *History of Philip* and the eleventh book of his *History of Greece*[i] ; in these passages he illustrates the abstemiousness of the Lacedaemonians in relation to the belly-appetites, writing as follows: "The Thasians,[j] too, sent to Agesilaus when he went to their aid all kinds of small

[a] Cf. Koepke, *Chamaeleon* 36.
[b] Kock i. 631, cf. Athen. 375 b (vol. iv. p. 198).
[c] A satyric drama ; *T.G.F.*[2] 277.
[d] Kock i. 59.
[e] *Ibid.* 774.
[f] *Ibid.* 335, cf. Athen. 375 b (vol. iv. p. 198).
[g] Kock i. 615. The verses violate metre; πρόσφερε σὺ δεῦρο τὴν Kock, πρόσφερε δὲ δεῦρο τὴν Capps.
[h] Kock i. 746, perhaps said of the suitors.
[i] *F.H.G.* i. 297, 281, J. 2 B 539, cf. J. 2 B 560, G. and H. 104, 22 (a), Athen. 384 a (vol. iv. p. 234), 616 d (vol. vi. p. 321), Nepos, *Ages.* 8, Plut. *Ages.* 36.
[j] Rather, Tachôs of Egypt. See critical note 7.

---

[5] Meineke: θηστια A.
[6] Jacobs: ἡμῶν σφάττουσιν A.
[7] ACE (θάσιοι om. οἱ C): Ὀασῖται or Θηβαῖοι (?) Gulick, ὁ Ταχὼς ἔπεμψεν Wichers.

μένους, πρὸς τούτοις δὲ καὶ πέμματα καὶ τραγημάτων εἶδος παντοδαπῶν.[1] ὁ δ' Ἀγησίλαος τὰ
μὲν πρόβατα καὶ τὰς[2] βοῦς ἔλαβεν, τὰ δὲ πέμματα
καὶ τὰ τραγήματα πρῶτον μὲν οὐδ' ἔγνω· κατ-
c εκεκάλυπτο γάρ. ὡς δὲ κατεῖδεν, ἀποφέρειν αὐτοὺς
ἐκέλευσεν, εἰπὼν οὐ νόμιμον εἶναι Λακεδαιμονίοις
χρῆσθαι τοιούτοις[3] τοῖς ἐδέσμασι. λιπαρούντων δὲ
τῶν Θασίων[4] ' δότε, φησί, φέροντες ἐκείνοις,'
δείξας αὐτοῖς[5] τοὺς εἵλωτας, εἰπὼν ὅτι τούτους δέοι
διαφθείρεσθαι[6] τρώγοντας αὐτὰ πολὺ μᾶλλον ἢ
αὐτὸν καὶ τοὺς παρόντας Λακεδαιμονίων." ὅτι δὲ
τοῖς εἵλωσιν ὑβριστικῶς πάνυ ἐχρῶντο Λακεδαιμόνιοι καὶ Μύρων ὁ Πριηνεὺς ἱστορεῖ ἐν δευτέρῳ
d Μεσσηνιακῶν γράφων οὕτως· " τοῖς δ' εἵλωσι πᾶν
ὑβριστικὸν ἔργον ἐπιτάττουσι πρὸς πᾶσαν ἄγον
ἀτιμίαν. κυνῆν τε γὰρ ἕκαστον φορεῖν ἐπάναγκες
ὥρισαν καὶ διφθέραν περιβεβλῆσθαι πληγάς τε
τεταγμένας λαμβάνειν κατ' ἐνιαυτὸν ἀδικήματος
χωρίς, ἵνα μήποτε δουλεύειν ἀπομάθωσιν. πρὸς δὲ
τούτοις εἴ τινες ὑπερακμάζοιεν τὴν οἰκετικὴν
ἐπιφάνειαν, ἐπέθηκαν ζημίαν θάνατον καὶ τοῖς
κεκτημένοις ἐπιτίμιον, εἰ μὴ ἐπικόπτοιεν τοὺς
ἀδρουμένους.[7] καὶ παραδόντες αὐτοῖς τὴν χώραν
ἔταξαν μοῖραν ἣν αὐτοῖς ἀνοίσουσιν αἰεί."—χηνί-
e ζειν[8] δὲ εἴρηται ἐπὶ τῶν αὐλούντων. Δίφιλος
Συνωρίδι·

¹ A : τραγήματα παντοδαπὰ CE., τ. πλῆθος παντοδαπῶν (?)
Kaibel.
² τοὺς B, Casaubon.
³ CE : τόσούτοισ with erasure A.
⁴ Ὀασιτῶν or Θηβαίων (?) Gulick, Αἰγυπτίων Wichers.
⁵ αὐτοῖσ A : om. CE.
' Casaubon : δὲ οἶδα φθείρεσθαι ACE.

cattle and steers well fattened, and besides these cakes and every possible variety of sweetmeats. Agesilaus accepted the sheep and the large cattle, but as for the cakes and the sweetmeats, at first he did not know what they were, since they were kept covered. But when he saw them, he commanded that they be taken away, saying that it was not lawful for Spartans to use such viands. And when the Thasians [a] insisted he replied, pointing out the Helots to them, ' Take and give them to those fellows yonder,' explaining that it was much better for them to be corrupted by eating the stuff than that he and the Spartans with him should be." Now, that the Spartans treated the Helots with great insolence is recorded by Myron of Priênê in the second book of his *Messenian History*, writing as follows [b] : " Upon the Helots they enjoin any insulting practice which can lead to complete dishonour. For they have ordained that each of them shall of necessity wear a dogskin cap and be wrapped in a leather jerkin, and every year they shall receive a stated number of blows even when they are blameless, so that they may never forget that they are slaves. In addition to this, if any of them presented an appearance of vigour exceeding that of a slave, they laid upon them the death penalty, and upon their owners punishment for failure to prevent their growing fat. And after handing over to them land to work they required a certain share of the crops which the Helots were always to render to them."—" To cackle goose-fashion " is said of flute-players. Di-

[a] Egyptians? See critical note 4.
[b] *F.H.G.* iv. 461, J. 2 B 510.

---

[7] Casaubon: ἀνδρουμένουσ ACE.
[8] A: χρονίζειν C, χηνιάζειν (?) Schweighäuser.

ἐχηνίασας[1]· ποιοῦσι τοῦτο πάντες οἱ
παρὰ Τιμοθέῳ.[2]

Ἐπεὶ δὲ καὶ πετασῶνος μέρος ἑκάστῳ κεῖται,
ἣν ΠΕΡΝΑΝ καλοῦσι, φέρε τι εἴπωμεν καὶ περὶ
αὐτῆς,[3] εἴ τις τοῦ ὀνόματος μνημονεύει. κάλλισται
μὲν γὰρ αἱ Γαλλικαί,[4] οὐκ ἀπολείπονται δὲ αὐτῶν
οὔτε αἱ[5] ἀπὸ Κιβύρας τῆς Ἀσιατικῆς οὔτε αἱ
f Λύκιαι. μνημονεύει δ' αὐτῶν Στράβων ἐν τρίτῃ
Γεωγραφουμένων, ἀνὴρ οὐ πάνυ νεώτερος· λέγει
γὰρ αὑτὸν ἐν τῇ ἑβδόμῃ τῆς αὐτῆς πραγματείας
ἐγνωκέναι Ποσειδώνιον τὸν ἀπὸ τῆς στοᾶς φιλό-
σοφον, οὗ πολλάκις ἐμεμνήμεθα συγγενομένου
Σκιπίωνι τῷ τὴν Καρχηδόνα ἑλόντι. γράφει δ'
οὖν ὁ Στράβων οὕτως· " ἐν Σπανίᾳ πρὸς τῇ Ἀκυ-
τανίᾳ πόλις Πομπέλων,[6] ὡς ἂν εἴποι τις Πομπηιό-
658 πολις, ἐν ᾗ πέρναι διάφοροι συντίθενται ταῖς
Κανταβρικαῖς[7] ἐνάμιλλοι."

ΑΛΙΠΑΣΤΩΝ δὲ κρεῶν μνημονεύει ὁ τῆς κωμῳδίας ποιητὴς Ἀριστομένης ἐν Διονύσῳ·

[1] A: ἐχήνισας H. Stephanus.
[2] Τιμοθέου (?) Kock.
[3] A: ταύτης Kaibel.
[4] Kaibel: γαλαῖ καὶ A.
[5] αἱ added by Musurus.
[6] Casaubon: πόλεῖσπομπάδων A.
[7] Cf. Strabo 162: κουρικαῖο A.

---

[a] Kock ii. 567. On the title see vol. iii. p. 113 note c.
[b] Borrowed from Latin; πετασών occurs only here. The
usual term was κωλῆ, e.g. Aristoph. Plut. 1128, Athen. 368 d-f
(vol. iv. p. 168, cf. vol. i. p. 30).

philus in *Synoris* [a] : " You've cackled like a goose ; that's what all the fellows in Timotheus's house do."

Ham. Since everyone has a portion of ham set before him, called perna,[b] let us say something about it, if anyone happens to mention the word. The best, to be sure, are the Gallic,[c] and yet neither those from the Asiatic [d] Cibyra nor the Lycian hams fall far behind. Strabo mentions them in the third book of his *Geography* ; he is not a very recent authority, for in the seventh book of the same treatise he says [e] that he [f] was acquainted with Poseidonius, the Stoic philosopher, whom we have often mentioned as having associated with Scipio,[g] the conqueror of Carthage. Be that as it may, Strabo writes as follows [h] : " In Spain, near Aquitania, is the city of Pompelôn, that is to say, Pompeiopolis, in which excellent hams are put up, rivalling those of the Cantabrians."

Salted Meats. These are mentioned by Aristomenes, the writer of comedy, in *Dionysus* [i] : " These

---

[c] *Cf.* Polyb. ii. 15. 3, Varro, *R.R.* ii. 4. 11. See critical note 4, and Birt, *Kritik u. Hermeneutik* (1913), 18.

[d] *i.e.* Phrygian.

[e] Frag. 58 b Meineke, Jones (L.C.L.) iii. 383 note 6.

[f] Who ? Athenaeus understands this of Strabo himself ; but he was very young when Poseidonius died in the consulship of Marcellus. αὐτόν, by all the laws of Greek syntax, should refer to another person than the subject of λέγει, hence we should probably understand Pompey as subject of ἐγνωκέναι, *cf.* Strabo 161 end. Strabo 753 says : Ποσειδώνιος ὁ Στωϊκός, ἀνὴρ τῶν καθ' ἡμᾶς φιλοσόφων πολυμαθέστατος ; here καθ' ἡμᾶς may be used loosely, referring not only to time, but to equal origin (Asia Minor) and to the same Stoic school of thought. *Cf.* Act. Apost. xvii. 28 ὡς καί τινες τῶν καθ' ὑμᾶς ποιητῶν εἰρήκασιν.

[g] See vol. v. p. 493 note *c*, where, as here, Poseidonius wrongly stands in place of his master Panaetius.

[h] iii. 162 ; the quotation is inexact.   [i] Kock i. 692.

ἀλίπαστα ταῦτα παρατίθημί σοι κρέα.[1]
καὶ ἐν Γόησιν[2]·

ἀλίπαστον αἰεὶ τὸν θεράπον[τ]᾽ ἐπεσθίειν.

Ἐπεὶ δὲ καὶ " Σικελίας αὔχημα τροφαλὶς " ἤδ᾽
ἐστί σοι, φίλοι,[3] λέξωμέν τι καὶ περὶ ΤΥΡΩΝ.
Φιλήμων μὲν γὰρ ἐν τῷ ἐπιγραφομένῳ Σικελικῷ·

ἐγὼ πρότερον μὲν ᾠόμην[4] τὴν Σικελίαν
b   ἐν τοῦτ᾽ ἀπότακτον αὐτὸ[5] τοὺς τυροὺς ποιεῖν
καλούς. ἔτι[6] ταῦτα προσετίθην ἀκηκοώς,[7]
ἱμάτια ποικίλ᾽ εἰ λέγοι τις Σικελικά.
Β. σκεύη μὲν οὖν καὶ κτήματ᾽ ᾠόμην[8] φέρειν.

καὶ ὁ Τρομιλικὸς[9] δὲ τυρὸς ἔνδοξός ἐστι. περὶ οὗ
φησιν Δημήτριος ὁ Σκήψιος ἐν δευτέρῳ Τρωικοῦ
Διακόσμου οὕτως· "τῆς Ἀχαίας πόλις Τρομίλεια,[10]
περὶ ἣν γίνεται τυρὸς αἴγειος ἥδιστος, οὐκ ἔχων
σύγκρισιν πρὸς ἕτερον, ὁ προσαγορευόμενος Τρο-
c μιλικός[9]." οὗ καὶ Σιμωνίδης μνημονεύει ἐν Ἰάμβῳ,
οὗ ἡ ἀρχή·

ἦ[11] πολλὰ μὲν δὴ προεκπονῇ, Τηλέμβροτε,[12]
γράφων·

ἐνταῦθα μέντοι τυρὸς ἐξ Ἀχαίης

[1] κρέα added by Toup.
[2] ὁ στράβων after Γόησιν deleted by Wilamowitz: ὀστακὸν (?)
Toup (for ὁ στράβων).
[3] Σικελίας αὔχημα τροφαλὶς ἤδε τις, ὦ φίλοι Kaibel.
[4] Bentley: ὤμην A.   [5] Musurus: αυτὸν A
[6] Bentley: ἔτι τε A.
[7] After ἀκηκοὼς A has τυρὸσ σικελικὸσ ὅτι κράτιστοσ ἦν αἵ
τε περιστεραὶ σικελικαὶ: deleted by Bentley.
[8] Casaubon: ὤμην A.
[9] A: στρομιλικὸς CE.   [10] στομίλεια C.
[11] ἦ added by Hemsterhuys.   [12] τηλέμβρωτε A.

28

salt-sprinkled meats I set before you." Also in
Quacks[a] : " And on top of all, his servant is always
eating salted . . ."[b]

Cheese. Since, also, " Sicily's pride, fresh cheese,"[c]
lies here before you, friends, let us speak of cheese.
For Philemon says in the play entitled *Sicilian*[d] :
" A. I used to think before to-day that Sicily produced just this one specialty, its fine cheese. From
hearsay I further added fine clothes, when one
mentioned Sicilian embroidered garments. B. Well,
as for me, I used to think it produced furniture and
goods."[e] But the Tromilic cheese is also famous. Of
this Demetrius of Scepsis speaks as follows, in the
second book of *The Trojan Battle-Order*[f] : " Tromileia is
a city of Achaia in the neighbourhood of which is made
a goat's-milk cheese, very fine, admitting of no comparison with any other, the cheese called Tromilic."
Simonides mentions it in an *Iambic Poem* which begins
thus[g] : " Many indeed are the tasks thou hast worked
out before, Telembrotus " ; he then writes : " Here,
however, is the wonderful Tromilic cheese from

---

[a] Kock i. 691.

[b] See critical note 2. It is much more likely that the
scribe of this passage, which is clearly defective throughout,
carelessly added ὁ στράβων, here deleted, than that Aristomenes should have used a form like ὁστακός for ἀστακός.
And what could " salted lobster " be ?

[c] Part of an anonymous verse.

[d] Kock ii. 499. The title may refer to a cook, a
physician, or any product of Sicily.

[e] Torn from their original context, these last words seem
lacking in force. For σκενή . . . καὶ κτήματ' Kock proposed
ζεύγη . . . κώχήματ', "chariots and carts," see 28 a-b (vol. i.
p. 120). Kaibel: σκύτη . . . καὶ σκώμματ', " hides and
jibes."

[f] Frag. 3 Gaede, p. 18.

[g] Semonides of Amorgos, *P.L.G.*[4] ii. 456, Diehl i. 255.

Τρομιλικὸς[1] θαυμαστός, ὃν κατήγαγον.

Εὐριπίδης δ᾽ ἐν Κύκλωπι ὀπίαν καλεῖ τυρὸν τὸν δριμύν, τὸν πηγνύμενον τῷ τῆς συκῆς ὀπῷ·

καὶ τυρὸς ὀπίας ἐστὶ καὶ Διὸς[2] γάλα.

ἐπεὶ δὲ περὶ πάντων εἶπον τῶν παρακειμένων
d ἀποτράγημά τε πεποίημαι[3] τὸν Τρομιλικόν, καταπαύσω τὸν λόγον· τὸ γὰρ λείψανον τῶν τραγημάτων καὶ τρωξίμων ἀποτράγημα εἴρηκεν Εὔπολις. σκώπτων γὰρ Διδυμίαν τινὰ ἀποτράγημα αὐτὸν εἴρηκεν ἀλώπεκος ἤτοι ὡς μικρὸν τὸ σῶμα ἢ ὡς κακοήθη καὶ πανοῦργον, ὥς φησιν ὁ Ἀσκαλωνίτης Δωρόθεος. τοὺς δὲ λεπτοὺς τῶν τυρῶν καὶ πλατεῖς Κρῆτες θηλείας καλοῦσιν, ὥς φησι Σέλευκος· οὓς καὶ[4] ἐν θυσίαις τισὶν ἐναγίζουσιν. πυριέφθων δὲ μνημονεύει (οὕτω δὲ καλεῖται τὸ πρῶτον γάλα) Φιλιππίδης ἐν Αὐλοῖς·

e   τὰ δὲ πυρίεφθα[5] καὶ τὰ λάγανα[6] ταῦτ᾽ ἔχων.

καὶ ἴσως πάντα τὰ τοιαῦτα ἐπιδειπνίδας ἔλεγον Μακεδόνες. κώθωνος γὰρ ἡδύσματα ταῦτα.''

Τοιαῦτά τινα ἔτι τοῦ Οὐλπιανοῦ διαλεγομένου ἐπελθὼν εἰς ἐκείνων τῶν σοφιστῶν μαγείρων ἐκήρυσσε μῦμα. καὶ πολλῶν ξενιζομένων ἐπὶ τῷ

---

[1] Meineke: στρομίλιοσ A.
[2] διὸσ A: βοὸς Eur.
[3] Kaibel: ἀποτραγημαι επεποιημαι (sic) A.
[4] οὓς καὶ CE: οὖσ A.
[5] Schweighäuser: τοὺσ δὲ πυριεφθασ A, πυριέφθα C, πυριέφθα E, Poll. vi. 54.
[6] A: λάχανα Musurus.

Achaia, which I have brought for you." Euripides in *The Cyclops* calls by the name opias the sour cheese which is curdled by fig-juice (opos)[a]: " And here's fig-juice-cheese and milk that Zeus drank."[b] And now, having spoken about all the dishes served to us and made the Tromilic cheese the last dainty (apotragêma) of all, I will cease my discourse; for the remnant of dessert and dainty tid-bits are called apotragêma by Eupolis.[c] For, in holding up to ridicule a man named Didymias Eupolis calls him " fox's mouthful," either because he was small in body or a mischievous and rascally person, according to Dorotheus of Ascalon. The thin flat cheeses are called " female " by Cretans, according to Seleucus; these also they consecrate at certain festivals. Heat-curdled cheeses (this is a name given to the first milk) are mentioned by Philippides in *The Flutes*[d]: " He had the heat-curdled beestings and the long thin cakes."[e] And it may be that all such things as these are what the Macedonians used to call epideipnides or last courses.[f] For they are delicacies belonging to the drinking-bout.

While Ulpian was still discoursing in this vein, one of those cooks famed for learning approached and announced a " myma." And since many were

[a] *Cycl.* 136, *cf.* Aristoph. *Vesp.* 353, who puns on ὀπή, " hole."

[b] The Euripidean text has " cow's milk," which Greeks drank very seldom. G. R. Holland proposed πυός, " beestings."

[c] Kock i. 335, frag. 284, from *Etym. Magn.* 132. 12, τί γάρ ἐστ' ἐκεῖνος; ἀποπάτημ' ἀλώπεκος (fox's dung).

[d] Kock iii. 304, *cf.* Poll. i. 248 πυριάτη (beestings) τὸ ὑπὸ τῶν πολλῶν λεγόμενον πυρίεφθον. See critical note 5.

[e] For the λάγανον, Lat. tracta, *cf.* above, 647 e (vol. vi. p. 498 note a).

[f] *Cf.* Petron. 69, epidipnis.

31

κηρύγματι—οὐ γὰρ ἐδείκνυεν ὁ στιγματίας ὅ τι ἦν
—ἔφη· "ἀγνοεῖν μοι δοκεῖτε, ὦ ἄνδρες δαιταλῆς,
ὅτι καὶ Κάδμος ὁ τοῦ Διονύσου πάππος μάγειρος
ἦν." σιωπησάντων δὲ καὶ ἐπὶ τούτῳ πάντων
"Εὐήμερος, ἔφη, ὁ Κῷος ἐν τῷ τρίτῳ τῆς Ἱερᾶς
f Ἀναγραφῆς τοῦθ' ἱστορεῖ, ὡς Σιδωνίων[1] λεγόντων
τοῦτο, ὅτι Κάδμος μάγειρος ὢν τοῦ βασιλέως καὶ
παραλαβὼν τὴν Ἁρμονίαν αὐλητρίδα καὶ αὐτὴν
οὖσαν τοῦ βασιλέως ἔφυγεν σὺν αὐτῇ.

ἐγὼ δὲ φεύξομαί γ'[2] ἐλεύθερος γεγώς.

οὐδὲ γὰρ ἂν εὕροι τις[3] ὑμῶν δοῦλον μάγειρόν τινα ἐν
κωμῳδίᾳ πλὴν παρὰ Ποσειδίππῳ[4] μόνῳ. δοῦλοι
659 δ' ὀψοποιοὶ παρῆλθον ὑπὸ πρώτων Μακεδόνων τοῦτ'
ἐπιτηδευσάντων ἢ δι' ὕβριν ἢ δι' ἀτυχίαν τῶν
αἰχμαλωτισθεισῶν πόλεων. ἐκάλουν δ' οἱ[5] παλαιοὶ
τὸν μὲν πολιτικὸν μάγειρον μαίσωνα, τὸν δ' ἐκ-
τόπιον τέττιγα. Χρύσιππος δ' ὁ φιλόσοφος τὸν
μαίσωνα ἀπὸ τοῦ μασᾶσθαι οἴεται κεκλῆσθαι, οἷον
τὸν ἀμαθῆ καὶ πρὸς γαστέρα νενευκότα, ἀγνοῶν ὅτι
Μαίσων γέγονεν κωμῳδίας ὑποκριτὴς Μεγαρεὺς τὸ
γένος, ὃς καὶ τὸ προσωπεῖον εὗρε τὸ[6] ἀπ' αὐτοῦ
καλούμενον μαίσωνα, ὡς Ἀριστοφάνης φησὶν ὁ
b Βυζάντιος ἐν τῷ περὶ Προσώπων, εὑρεῖν αὐτὸν
φάσκων καὶ τὸ τοῦ θεράποντος πρόσωπον καὶ τὸ
τοῦ μαγείρου. καὶ εἰκότως καὶ τὰ τούτοις πρέ-
ποντα σκώμματα καλεῖται μαισωνικά. μάλιστα

---

[1] B, Musurus: σιδονίων A.   [2] γ' added by Schweighäuser.
[3] Musurus: ανελευθε|ροι τισ A.   [4] ποσιδίππωι A.
[5] δ' οἱ CE: οἱ A.   [6] εὗρε τὸ CE: ερευτο A.

puzzled by the announcement—for the rascal did not explain what it meant—he said : You evidently do not know, gentlemen of the banquet, that even Cadmus, the grandfather of Dionysus, was a cook. They all fell silent at this and he went on : Euhemerus of Cos, in the third book of his *Sacred Register*, tells [a] a story on the authority of the Sidonians that Cadmus was the king's cook, and that, taking Harmonia, a flute-player who also belonged to the king, he eloped with her. " I will fly, for I am freeborn." [b] Nor can any of you find a cook spoken of as a slave in comedy, except in Poseidippus alone. [c] Cooks were first represented as slaves by the Macedonians, who made a practice of this either to show their own insolence or to take advantage of the misfortunes that befell conquered cities. The ancients called a cook who was a fellow-citizen a maisôn, whereas they called a foreign cook a cicada. Now the philosopher Chrysippus thinks that maisôn is derived from masâsthai (chew), that is, an ignorant fellow intent on satisfying his belly. Chrysippus is not aware that Maisôn was a comic actor, born in Megara, who originated the rôle called from him maisôn, as Aristophanes of Byzantium declares in his work *On Masks,* [d] asserting that Maisôn invented the rôle of the servant as well as that of the cook. So, naturally, the jokes appropriate to both these personages are called maisônic.

[b] An anonymous verse, *T.G.F.*[2] 858 ; *cf.* Aristoph. *Ach.* 203 (Amphitheus speaks): ἐγὼ δὲ φεύξομαί γε τοὺς Ἀχαρνέας. For the story see Athen. 381 a (vol. iv. p. 222).

[c] Pliny, *N.H.* xviii. 108 nec cocos vero habebant in servitiis eosque ex macello conducebant.

[d] Nauck 276 ; the title refers to the stock characters of comedy. Possibly the remark of Chrysippus was quoted by Aristophanes.

γὰρ εἰσάγονται οἱ μάγειροι σκωπτικοί τινες,[1] ὡς
παρὰ Μενάνδρῳ ἐν Ἐπιτρέπουσιν. καὶ Φιλήμων
δέ πού φησιν·

σφίγγ᾽ ἄρρεν᾽, οὐ μάγειρον, εἰς τὴν οἰκίαν
εἴληφ᾽· ἁπλῶς γὰρ οὐδὲ ἕν, μὰ τοὺς θεούς,
ὧν ἂν λέγῃ[2] συνίημι· καινὰ ῥήματα

c   πεπορισμένος πάρεστιν.[3]

τὸν δὲ Μαίσωνα[4] Πολέμων ἐν τοῖς πρὸς Τίμαιον
ἐκ τῶν ἐν Σικελίᾳ φησὶν εἶναι Μεγάρων[5] καὶ οὐκ
ἐκ τῶν Νισαίων.[6] ἀλλ᾽ ὅ γε Ποσείδιππος[7] περὶ
δούλων μαγείρων ἐν Ἀποκλειομένῃ φησίν·

ταυτὶ μὲν οὖν τοιαῦτα. συμβαίνει δέ τι
νῦν μοι διακονοῦντι παρὰ τῷ δεσπότῃ
ἀστεῖον· οὐχ ἁλώσομ᾽ ἐκφέρων κρέας.

καὶ ἐν Συντρόφοις·

ἐβάδιζες ἔξω τῶν πυλῶν μάγειρος ὤν;
d Β. ἐντὸς πυλῶν γὰρ ἂν μένων[8] ἄδειπνος ἦν.
   Α. πότερ᾽ οὖν ἀφεῖσαι;[9] Β. κατ᾽ ἀγορὰν ἐργά-
      ζομαι·
ἐπρίατο γάρ τις ὁμότεχνός με γνώριμος.

Οὐδὲν οὖν ἦν παράδοξον εἰ καὶ θυτικῆς ἦσαν
ἔμπειροι οἱ παλαίτεροι μάγειροι· προΐσταντο γοῦν
καὶ γάμων καὶ θυσιῶν. διόπερ Μένανδρος ἐν

---

[1] A : τινες om. C.
[2] δσ᾽ (for ὡς) ἂν λέγῃ A at 382 c : ὧν λέγει AC, ὅσων λέγει (?)
Kaibel.
[3] 382 c : γάρ ἐστι A, γάρ ἐστιν C.
[4] μάσωνα A.   [5] Schweighäuser : μεγαρέων A.

34

For to a very great degree cooks are brought on the
stage as a kind of jester, as may be seen in Menander's
Arbitrants.[a]   And Philemon, I believe, says[b] : " I
have taken into my house a male Sphinx, not a cook.
Really, I understand absolutely not one thing, the
gods are my witnesses, of all that he says. He has
come with a stock of new-fangled expressions." As
for Maisôn, Polemon says[c] in his *Reply to Timaeus*
that he came from the Sicilian Megara, and not from
the Nisaean.[d]   But to return to the subject of slave-
cooks, Poseidippus says in *Locked Out*[e] : " So much,
then, for that. But to me to-day, while serving in
my master's house, a neat bit of luck falls to my lot :
I shall not be caught carrying meat out of doors."
Again, in *Foster-Brothers*[f] : " A. What ? Did you,
a cook, take a walk outside the gates ? B. Why, yes !
For if I'd stayed inside the gates I should have been
without a dinner. A. Then you have been freed
from slavery ? B. No, but I work in the market-
place. For an acquaintance of mine who practises
my art bought me."

It is, therefore, not to be wondered at if the
ancient cooks were also versed in the ritual of sacrifice ; for they presided, at any rate, over weddings
and festival-sacrifices. Hence Menander in *The*

[a] Kock iii. 50, *cf.* Allinson (L.C.L.) 75-77, Capps in his
edition 32-33.
[b] Kock ii. 517, *cf.* Athen. 382 b-c (vol. iv. p. 228), where
the lines are attributed to Straton's *Phoenicides*.
[c] Preller 84.   [d] In central Greece.
[e] Kock iii. 336.   [f] Kock iii. 342.

[6] νησαίων A.   [7] ποσίδιπποσ A.
    [8] γὰρ ἂν μένων Dindorf : παρμένων A.
    [9] Dobree : πότερον οὖν ἀφεισεα A.

ATHENAEUS

Κόλακι τὸν τοῖς τετραδισταῖς διακονούμενον μάγειρον ἐν τῇ τῆς Πανδήμου Ἀφροδίτης ἑορτῇ ποιεῖ
ταυτὶ λέγοντα·

σπονδή. δίδου σὺ σπλάγχν' ἀκολουθῶν. ποῖ
βλέπεις;
e σπονδή. φέρ', ὦ παῖ Σωσία.[1] σπονδή. καλῶς.[2]
ἔγχου.[3] θεοῖς Ὀλυμπίοις εὐχώμεθα
Ὀλυμπίαισι,[4] πᾶσι πάσαις· λάμβανε
τὴν γλῶτταν. ἐπὶ[5] τούτῳ διδόναι σωτηρίαν,
ὑγίειαν, ἀγαθὰ πολλὰ τῶν ὄντων τε νῦν
ἀγαθῶν ὄνησιν[6] πᾶσι. ταῦτ' εὐχώμεθα.

καὶ παρὰ Σιμωνίδῃ δέ φησιν ἕτερος·

f   χὼς ὗν ἄφευσα χὼς[7] ἐμίστυλα κρέα
ἰρωστί[8]· καὶ γὰρ οὐ κακῶς ἐπίσταμαι.

ἐμφαίνει δ' αὐτῶν τὴν ἐμπειρίαν καὶ ἡ πρὸς Ἀλέξ-
ανδρον Ὀλυμπιάδος Ἐπιστολή. προτρεπομένη
μάγειρον αὐτῇ πρίασθαι θυσιῶν ἔμπειρον ἡ μήτηρ
φησί· " Πελίγναν τὸν μάγειρον λαβὲ παρὰ τῆς
μητρός. οὗτος γὰρ οἶδε τὰ ἱερά σου τὰ πατρῷα
πάντα[9] ὃν τρόπον θύεταί καὶ τὰ Ἀργαδιστικὰ[10] καὶ
τὰ Βακχικά, ὅσα τε Ὀλυμπιὰς προθύεται οὗτος
360 οἶδεν. μὴ οὖν ἀμελήσῃς, ἀλλὰ λαβέ· καὶ ἀπό-
στειλον πρὸς ἐμὲ τὴν ταχίστην."

---

[1] Pierson: φερεω | πλειωωσια A.
[2] Musurus: καλω A.   [3] Cobet: ευχου A.
[4] Casaubon: ὀλυμπιάσι A.
[5] Meineke: ἐν A.   [6] Casaubon: ὀνησιαν A.
[7] Bourdelot: χωσα | φευσσαχωσ A.   ὗν added by Bergk.
[8] Hecker: εἰδώστι A.   [9] Musurus: παντασ A.
[10] ἀργαδιστικα A: Ἀργεαδικὰ (?) Kaibel.

36

Flatterer represents the cook who served the people at the festival of Aphrodite Pandemus on the fourth day of the month as saying, in these words [a] : " A libation ! You, there, follow me and give me the viscera. Where are your eyes ? A libation ! Come, my slave Sosias, a libation. Good. Now pour in. Let us pray to all the Olympians, gods and goddesses alike. Take the tongue.[b] For this may they grant us safety, health, and blessings many, and, for us all, enjoyment of our present blessings. Be this our prayer." And another cook says in Simonides [c] : " How I singed that hog and cut up its meat in ritual fashion ; for I understand that well." Their skill is revealed in the *Letter to Alexander* from Olympias.[d] Urging him to purchase from herself a cook versed in sacrificial rites, his mother says : " Buy Pelignas the cook from your mother. For he knows the manner in which all the sacred rites of your ancestors are carried out, both the Argadistic [e] and the Bacchic, and all the sacrifices that Olympias offers he knows. Do not neglect this, therefore, but buy him and send him to me [f] with all speed."

[a] Kock iii. 82, Allinson 394. For the title see vol. iii. p. 165 note *a*, and for the festival on the fourth day (τετράς), τετρὰς γὰρ σύνοδος ἡμῶν γίνεται . . . ἑστιάτωρ δεσπότης, Allinson 382, l. 11. *Cf.* the scene in Aristoph. *Av.* 863-881.

[b] As a special offering to Hermes.

[c] Semonides of Amorgos, *P.L.G.*[4] ii. 456, Diehl i. 255-256, Edmonds, *Elegy and Iambus* (L.C.L.) ii. 230.

[d] Rather, as the contents show, from one of the state secretaries.

[e] Either " peasant rites," *cf.* Ἀργαδεῖς or Ἀργάδεις, Poll. viii. 109, or as Kaibel conjectured, " Argeadic," from the Ἀργεάδαι, a Macedonian tribe, Thuc. viii. 53, Strabo 329, Paus. i. 38. 3.

[f] *i.e.* the secretary.

"Ότι δὲ σεμνὸν ἦν ἡ μαγειρικὴ μαθεῖν ἔστιν ἐκ
τῶν Ἀθήνησι Κηρύκων. οἶδε[1] γὰρ μαγείρων καὶ
βουτύπων[2] ἐπεῖχον τάξιν, ὥς φησιν Κλείδημος ἐν
Πρωτογονίας πρώτῳ. Ὅμηρός τε τὸ ῥέζειν ἐπὶ
τοῦ θύειν τάσσει, τὸ δὲ θύειν ἐπὶ τοῦ ψαιστὰ
μεταδόρπια θυμιᾶν· καὶ οἱ παλαιοὶ τὸ θύειν δρᾶν
ὠνόμαζον. ἔδρων δ' οἱ Κήρυκες ἄχρι πολλοῦ
βουθυτοῦντες, φησί, καὶ σκευάζοντες καὶ μιστύλ-
b λοντες, ἔτι δ' οἰνοχοοῦντες. Κήρυκας δ' αὐτοὺς
ἀπὸ τοῦ κρείττονος[3] ὠνόμαζον. ἀναγέγραπταί τε
οὐδαμοῦ μαγείρῳ μισθός, ἀλλὰ κήρυκι. καὶ
Ἀγαμέμνων δὲ παρ' Ὁμήρῳ θύει βασιλεύων·
φησὶ γὰρ ὁ ποιητής·

ἦ καὶ ἀπὸ στομάχους ἀρνῶν τάμε νηλέϊ χαλκῷ,
καὶ τοὺς μὲν κατέθηκεν ἐπὶ χθονὸς ἀσπαίροντας
θυμοῦ δευομένους· ἀπὸ γὰρ μένος εἵλετο χαλκός.

καὶ Θρασυμήδης ὁ τοῦ Νέστορος υἱὸς ἀναλαβὼν
c πέλεκυν κόπτει τὸν βοῦν, ἐπεὶ διὰ τὸ γῆρας ὁ
Νέστωρ οὐκ ἠδύνατο· συνεπόνουν δ' αὐτῷ καὶ οἱ
ἄλλοι ἀδελφοί. οὕτως ἔνδοξον ἦν καὶ μέγιστον τὸ
τῆς μαγειρικῆς τέχνης ἀξίωμα. καὶ παρὰ Ῥω-
μαίοις δ' οἱ τιμηταὶ —μεγίστη δ' αὕτη ἀρχή—τὴν

[1] Musurus: οἶδε A.   [2] Musurus: βουτύρων A.
[3] κρείοντος, "from the word for master," Capps.

---

[a] *F.H.G.* i. 362. This work was probably identical with
the Ἀτθίς, or Early History of Attica, below, 660 d.

[b] *e.g.* Il. i. 443-444, *cf.* Plut. *Qu. Conv.* 730 A ὅμως ταραττό-
μενοι καὶ δειμαίνοντες ἔρδειν μὲν ἐκάλουν καὶ ῥέζειν, ὥς τι μέγα
δρῶντες τὸ θύειν ἔμψυχον.

[c] To what occasion this alludes I do not know; ψαιστά,
which does not occur in Homer, may possibly represent the
ἄργματα of *Od.* xiv. 446 ἦ ῥα, καὶ ἄργματα θῦσε θεοῖς αἰειγε-
νέτῃσι; *cf. Il.* ix. 219-220.

And yet, that the cook's art was dignified may be learned from the case of the Heralds at Athens. For the Heralds held the office of cooks and butchers, as Cleidemus declares in the first book of his *Early Origins.*[a] And so Homer used the verb *rezein* (perform) of the act of sacrifice (*thyein*),[b] but *thyein* he uses of burning ground meal mixed with oil during the drinking[c]; the men of old after Homer also applied the word *act* to sacrificing. The Heralds, Cleidemus says, *acted* (*i.e.* sacrificed) for a long period as slayers of oxen, dressing and cutting up the meat, besides serving as wine-pourers.[d] They named them *Kerykes*, or Heralds, from the word *kreittôn*, more powerful.[e] And so there is no record anywhere of pay given to a cook, but only to a herald (*keryx*). Even Agamemnon in Homer offers sacrifice though he is a king ; for the Poet says[f] : " He spake, and cut the lambs' throats with the pitiless bronze. And he laid them upon the ground, gasping and failing of breath ; for the bronze had taken away their strength." And Thrasymedes, Nestor's son, grasped an axe and smote the ox,[g] since Nestor because of his years could not do it. His son was aided in the task by his brothers besides. So reputable and important, then, was the dignity pertaining to the cook's art. Among the Romans, also, the censors—theirs was a very high office—clad in their

---

[d] Regarded as an honourable office, Athen. 425 a-f (vol. iv. pp. 424-426).

[e] This etymology, of course, is impossible. Schweighäuser took κρείττων to refer to the eponymous ancestor of the family, Keryx, ἀπὸ τοῦ κρείττονος a prisco illo Heroë, " from that mighty man of old." This stretches the Greek too far. Harpocr., Hesych., and Suid. have ἀπὸ Κήρυκος τοῦ Ἑρμοῦ for ἀπὸ τοῦ κρείττονος. See critical note 3.

[f] *Il.* iii. 292-294.   [g] *Od.* iii. 442-446.

περιπόρφυρον ἐνδεδυκότες καὶ ἐστεφανωμένοι πε-
λέκει τὰ ἱερεῖα κατέβαλλον. οὐ παρέργως δὲ παρὰ[1]
τῷ Ὁμήρῳ καὶ τὰ ὅρκια καὶ τὰ ἱερόθυτα κήρυκες
κομίζουσιν, ὡς παλαιᾶς οὔσης καὶ προσηκούσης
αὐτοῖς τῆς λειτουργίας·

d   Ἕκτωρ δὲ προτὶ ἄστυ δύω[2] κήρυκας ἔπεμπε
   καρπαλίμως ἄρνας τε φέρειν Πρίαμόν τε κα-
      λέσσαι.[3]

καὶ πάλιν·

   αὐτὰρ ὁ Ταλθύβιον προΐει κρείων Ἀγαμέμνων
   νῆας ἐπὶ γλαφυρὰς ἰέναι ἠδ᾿ ἄρν᾿ ἐκέλευσεν
   οἰσέμεναι.

καί·

         Ταλθύβιος δὲ θεῷ[4] ἐναλίγκιος αὐδὴν
   κάπρον ἔχων ἐν χερσὶ παρίστατο ποιμένι λαῶν.

Ἐν δὲ τῷ πρώτῳ τῆς Ἀτθίδος Κλείδημος φῦλον[5]
e ἀποφαίνει μαγείρων ἐχόντων δημιουργικὰς τιμάς,
οἷς καὶ[6] τὸ πλῆθος ἀγείρειν[7] ἔργον ἦν. οὐκ ἀπεικότως δὲ καὶ Ἀθηνίων ἐν Σαμόθραξιν, ὥς φησιν
Ἰόβας, μάγειρον εἰσάγει φυσιολογοῦντα διὰ τούτων·

   οὐκ οἶσθ᾿ ὅτι πάντων ἡ μαγειρικὴ τέχνη
   πρὸς εὐσέβειαν πλεῖστα προσενήνεχθ᾿ ὅλως;
   Β. τοιοῦτόν ἐστι τοῦτο; Α. πάνυ γε, βάρβαρε.
   τοῦ θηριώδους καὶ παρασπόνδου βίου
   ἡμᾶς γὰρ ἀπολύσασα καὶ τῆς δυσχεροῦς

---

[1] Early edd.: τὰ παρὰ A.   [2] δύο A.
[3] καλέσαι A.   [4] δὲ εω A.
[5] Casaubon: καὶ | δημοσφυλον A.
[6] κατὰ τὸ πλῆθος ἐνεργεῖν Lumb.
[7] Wilamowitz   εργειν A; ὑπὲρ τοῦ πλήθους ἱερουργεῖν
Siebelis.

robes with purple border,[a] and wearing wreaths, laid low the sacrificial victims with an axe. And in Homer the heralds render no merely incidental service in taking charge of the ritual of oath and the sacrifice of victims, because this service belonged to them from ancient times. Thus [b] : " And Hector sent two heralds to the city in all haste to bring the lambs and to summon Priam." And again [c] : " And in his turn he, the lord Agamemnon, sent forth Talthybius to go to the hollow ships, and bade him bring a lamb." Also [d] : " And Talthybius, like unto a god in voice, stood beside the shepherd of the host holding a boar in his arms."

In the first book of his *History of Attica* Cleidemus [e] shows that there was a guild of cooks [f] having official rank derived from their art ; their business was to gather the multitude together.[g] It is not without reason that Athenion in *The Samothracians*, according to Juba,[h] brings on a cook haranguing on the origin of things in these words [i] : " A. Don't you know that the cook's art has contributed absolutely more than anything else to piety ? B. Is it really such a thing as that ? A. Entirely so, you ignorant foreigner. From a bestial and lawless life that art has freed

[a] The toga praetexta.   [b] *Il.* iii. 116-117.
[c] *Ibid.* 118-120.
[d] *Il.* xix. 250-251.   [e] *F.H.G.* i. 359.
[f] Or " slaughterers."
[g] The reading ἀγείρειν is not wholly satisfactory, but involves the least change in the text. Other verbs which readily occur to the mind require a different syntax.
[h] *F.H.G.* iii. 482.
[i] Kock iii. 369. This Athenion is quite unknown except for this fragment. For other learned cooks, less tedious than this, see vol. i. p. 438, vol. iii. pp. 294-296, 302-308, vol. iv. pp. 210-214.

f ἀλληλοφαγίας ἤγαγ᾽ εἰς τάξιν τινὰ
καὶ τουτονὶ περιῆψεν ὃν νυνὶ βίον
ζῶμεν. Β. τίνα τρόπον; Α. πρόσεχε, κἀγώ σοι
φράσω.
ἀλληλοφαγίας καὶ κακῶν ὄντων συχνῶν
γενόμενος ἄνθρωπός τις οὐκ ἀβέλτερος
ἔθυσ᾽ ἱερεῖον πρῶτος, ὤπτησεν κρέας.
ὡς[1] δ᾽ ἦν τὸ κρέας ἥδιον ἀνθρώπου κρεῶν,
αὑτοὺς[2] μὲν οὐκ ἐμασῶντο, τὰ δὲ βοσκήματα
θύοντες ὤπτων. ὡς δ᾽ ἅπαξ τῆς ἡδονῆς
661 ἐμπειρίαν τιν᾽ ἔλαβον, ἀρχῆς γενομένης
ἐπὶ πλεῖον ηὖξον[3] τὴν μαγειρικὴν τέχνην.
ὅθεν ἔτι καὶ νῦν τῶν πρότερον μεμνημένοι
τὰ σπλάγχνα τοῖς θεοῖσιν ὀπτῶσιν φλογὶ
ἅλας οὐ προσάγοντες· οὐ γὰρ ἦσαν οὐδέπω[4]
εἰς τὴν τοιαύτην χρῆσιν ἐξευρημένοι.
ὡς δ᾽ ἤρεσ᾽ αὐτοῖς ὕστερον,[5] καὶ τοὺς ἅλας
προσάγουσιν ἤδη, τῶν ἱερῶν γε δρωμένων[6]
τὰ πάτρια διατηροῦντες. ἅπερ ἡμῖν μόνα
ἅπασιν ἀρχὴ γέγονε τῆς σωτηρίας,
b τὸ προσφιλοτεχνεῖν, διά τε τῶν ἡδυσμάτων
ἐπὶ πλεῖον αὔξειν τὴν μαγειρικὴν τέχνην.
Β. καινὸς γάρ ἐστιν οὑτοσὶ Παλαίφατος.
Α. μετὰ ταῦτα γαστρίον τις ὠνθυλευμένον

---

[1] Porson, Casaubon: κρέα· ἴσωσ AC.

[2] αὑτοὺσ A, εἶτ᾽ αὐτοὺς C: αὐτοὺς ἔτ᾽ Meineke.

[3] Dindorf: πλεῖον τινην | ξον A, πλεῖον τινὲς ηὖξον CE.

[4] A: οὐδὲ γὰρ ἦσαν ἔτι C.

[5] A: ὡς δ᾽ ἤρεσεν αὐτοῖς, ὕστερον C.

[6] γε δρωμένων Gulick: γε· γραμμένων A.

42

us ; from disgusting cannibalism she has led us to
discipline, and has adorned us with this life we now
lead. B. But how ? A. Pay close attention and I
will explain it to you. At a time when cannibalism
and all sorts of evils existed, a man arose who was no
simpleton, the first to sacrifice a victim and roast the
meat. And since the meat was nicer than human
flesh, they no longer chewed one another, but sacrificed and roasted sheep. And once they had experi-
enced that pleasure, with the beginning thus made,
they advanced the cook's art further. But, mindful
to this day of the earlier customs, they roast in the
flame the entrails in honour of the gods without adding salt. For they had not as yet discovered its
application to that use. But since it pleased them
later to do so, they added salt from that time on,
although, when holy rites are performed, they still
observe the ancestral custom.[a] But the principles
which alone proved to be the salvation of all of us were
our zeal in adding to our skill, and the use of sauces
and seasonings advancing still further the cook's art.
B. This fellow is Palaephatus come to life again ![b]
A. Then, with the progress of time some one intro-

---

[a] Of abstaining from salt. The priests of Egypt were not
permitted to use sea salt during their days of consecration, Plut. 729 A ἁγνεύοντες δὲ καὶ τὸν ἅλα φεύγουσιν ὡς μήτ'
ὄψον προσφέρεσθαι μήτ' ἄλλο τι ἅλεσι θαλαττίοις μεμιγμένον, cf.
552 F, 685 A. There is no reason to doubt that this primitive
prohibition obtained also in Greece, see Hermes xxix. 627-629,
xxxii. 235. Salt was permitted in the cult of Aphrodite,
Nilsson, Griech. Feste 365, 381.

[b] The proper name Palaephatus is here used as a compound
with active meaning, " speaking of ancient and incredible
things." Suidas mentions four writers of this name ; one
in particular, of Paros or Priene, who wrote five books of
Ἀπίστων, Incredibilium. The others wrote on ancient history.

προϊόντος εἰσηνέγκατ᾽ ἤδη τοῦ χρόνου·
ἐρίφιον[1] ἐτακέρωσε, πνικτῷ διέλαβεν
περικομματίῳ, διεγίγγρασ᾽[2] ὑποκρούσας γλυκεῖ,
ἰχθὺν παρεισεκύκλησεν οὐδ᾽ ὁρώμενον,[3]

c λάχανον, τάριχος πολυτελές,[4] χόνδρον, μέλι.
ὡς πολὺ δὲ[5] διὰ τὰς ἡδονὰς ἃς νῦν λέγω
ἀπεῖχ᾽ ἕκαστος τοῦ φαγεῖν ἂν ἔτι νεκροῦ·
αὐτοῖς ἅπαντες ἠξίουν συζῆν, ὄχλος
ἠθροίζετ᾽, ἐγένονθ᾽ αἱ πόλεις οἰκούμεναι
διὰ τὴν τέχνην, ὅπερ εἶπα, τὴν μαγειρικήν.
Β. ἄνθρωπε χαῖρε, περὶ πόδ᾽ εἶ τῷ δεσπότῃ.
Α. καταρχόμεθ᾽ ἡμεῖς οἱ μάγειροι, θύομεν,
σπονδὰς ποιοῦμεν, τῷ μάλιστα τοὺς θεοὺς
ἡμῖν ὑπακούειν διὰ τὸ ταῦθ᾽ εὑρηκέναι[6]

d τὰ μάλιστα συντείνοντα πρὸς τὸ ζῆν καλῶς.
Β. ὑπὲρ εὐσεβείας οὖν ἀφεὶς[7] παῦσαι λέγων.
Α. ἥμαρτον. Β. ἀλλὰ δεῦρο νῦν[8] συνείσιθι
ἐμοί,[9] τά τ᾽ ἔνδον εὐπρεπῆ[10] πόει λαβών.

Καὶ Ἄλεξις δ᾽ ἐν Λεβητίῳ δηλοῖ ὅτι ἡ μαγειρικὴ
τέχνη ἐπιτήδευμα ἦν ἐλευθέρων· πολίτης γάρ τις
e οὐ ταπεινὸς[11] ἐν αὐτῷ δείκνυται ὁ μάγειρος. καὶ οἱ
τὰ Ὀψαρτυτικὰ δὲ συγγράψαντες Ἡρακλείδης τε
καὶ Γλαῦκος ὁ Λοκρὸς οὐχ ἁρμόττειν φασὶ

---

[1] Dobree: ἀκριβῶς ἐρίφιον A.
[2] Dobree: διεπιγγρασ A.
[3] ἑωραμένον (?) Kaibel.   [4] πουλύποδας Kock.
[5] δὲ added by Meineke.   [6] Musurus: εἰρηκέναι A.
[7] Jacobs: ἄφεσ A.   [8] νῦν added by Cobet.
[9] Dobree: συνέσθιέ μοι A.
[10] sic A: εὐτρεπῆ edd., perhaps rightly.

44

duced the stuffed paunch, cooked a kid so that it melted in the mouth, gave it distinction with fine trimmings of meat smothered in it, gave it a nice tone with the gentle touch [a] of grape-syrup, smuggled in a bit of fish that couldn't even be seen, some greens, rich smoked-fish, groats, honey. Wherefore, because of the delights I am telling you of now, every one kept aloof from eating a man's corpse any longer. All consented now to live with one another, a populace came together, cities became civilized, all through this art, I repeat, of cookery. B. Hail, my good fellow! You come pat to my master's need.[b] A. It is we cooks who perform the rites of consecration; we offer sacrifice, pour libations, because the gods hearken more to us than to all the others for having discovered those things which pertain most to the good life. B. Quit the subject of piety and stop your talk. A. My error! B. Just come into the house now with me, and with your utensils make everything inside nice and proper."

Alexis, also, makes it clear in *The Melting Pot* [c] that the art of cookery was a profession belonging to free-born persons; for in that play the cook is shown to be a citizen of no lowly station. Further, the compilers of cookery-books, Heracleides and Glaucus of Locris assert that the cook's art is not appropriate " to slaves,

[a] The terms are taken from music. For the γίγγρας see 618 c (vol. vi. p. 331), and see also vol. i. p. 441.

[b] For the proverb *cf.* Plat. Com. (Kock i. 656) ὡς ἔστι μοι τὸ χρῆμα τοῦτο περὶ πόδα, explained by Suid. *s. περὶ πόδα·* οἷον ἁρμόττον σφόδρα, ὡς τὰ ὑποδήματα τοῖς ποσίν.

[c] Kock ii. 343. Elsewhere the title is given as Λέβης, not Λεβήτιον.

---

[11] οὐ ταπεινὸς Gulick : οὐκ ἀπίνησ (*sic*) A, κακοπινὴς Schoenemann.

δούλοισι[1] τὴν μαγειρικήν,
ἀλλ' οὐδὲ τοῖς τυχοῦσι τῶν ἐλευθέρων.

ἐκσεμνύνει δὲ τὴν τέχνην καὶ ὁ νεώτερος Κρατῖνος
ἐν τοῖς Γίγασι λέγων·

ἐνθυμεῖ[2] δὲ τῆς γῆς ὡς γλυκὺ
ὄζει καπνός τ' ἐξέρχετ' εὐωδέ·ιτερος;[3]
οἰκεῖ τις, ὡς ἔοικεν, ἐν[4] τῷ χάσματι
λιβανωτοπώλης ἢ μάγειρος Σικελικός.

f   B. παραπλησίαν ὀσμὴν λέγεις ἀμφοῖν;[5] . . .

καὶ Ἀντιφάνης[6] δ' ἐν Δυσπράτῳ ἐπαινῶν τοὺς
Σικελικοὺς μαγείρους λέγει·

Σικελῶν δὲ τέχναις ἡδυνθεῖσαι
δαιτὸς διαθρυμματίδες.[7]

καὶ Μένανδρος ἐν Φάσματι·

ἐπισημαίνεσθ' ἐὰν[8]
ἡ σκευασία καθάρειος[9] ᾖ καὶ ποικίλη.

Ποσείδιππος[10] ἐν Ἀναβλέποντι·

ἐγὼ μάγειρον λαμβάνων[11] ἀκήκοα
662 τὰ τῶν μαγείρων πάνθ' ἃ[12] καθ' ἕκαστον κακὰ
ἀντεργολαβοῦντος ἔλεγον· ὁ μὲν[13] ὡς οὐκ ἔχει
ῥῖνα κριτικὴν[14] πρὸς τοὔψον, ὁ δ' ὅτι τὸ[15] στόμα
πονηρόν, ὁ δὲ τὴν γλῶτταν εἰς ἀσχήμονας
ἐπιθυμίας ἐμίαινε[16] τῶν ἡδυσμάτων,
κάθαλος, κάτοξος,[17] χναυστικός, προσκαυστικός,

---

[1] δούλοισι added by Kaibel.   [2] ἐνθυμει A.
[3] ACE: εὐωδέστατος Bergk.
[4] ἐν added by Musurus.
[5] ἀμφοῖν C: ἀμφοῖν γλυκύς A.
[6] καὶ ὁ γλυκὺς Ἀντιφάνης Dobree; see preceding note.

46

or even to merely ordinary freemen." [a] The younger
Cratinus also magnifies the art when in *The Giants* he
says [b] : " A. Do you note how sweet the earth smells,
and the steam is coming forth with greater fragrance ?
It would seem that some seller of frankincense
dwells in the chasm, or else a Sicilian cook. B. Do
you mean that both can have the same smell . . . ? "
And Antiphanes, too, says in praise of the Sicilian
cooks in *Hard to Sell* [c] : " Cakes for a banquet,
spiced by Sicilian arts." Menander, also, in *The
Ghost* [d] : " Indicate your approval if you find my
receipts dainty and varied." Poseidippus in *Recover-
ing his Sight* [e] : " I, when buying a cook, have heard
all the abuses uttered by cooks against every one of
their competitors ; against one, that he hasn't a nose
sensitive to dainty cooking ; that another has a viti-
ated taste, still another has fouled his tongue in
unseemly desires for seasoning—too much salt, too
much vinegar, too much nibbling here and there, too
much given to searing the meat ; one can't stand the

[a] An anonymous verse, as recognized by Dindorf ; Kock
iii. 442.
[b] Kock ii. 289.   [c] Kock ii. 48.
[d] Kock iii. 144, Allinson 454 ; a cook speaks to a party at
dinner.
[e] Kock iii. 335. For λαμβάνων, " buy," cf. 658 f, where
it is said that Poseidippus represents cooks as slaves.

---

7 διὰ θριμματιδεσ A.
8 Bentley : ἐπισημαίνεσθαι ἀν A.
9 καθάριοσ A.   10 ποσίδιπποσ A.
11 Meineke : ἀναλαβὼν A.   12 Kock : πάντα A.
13 Grotius : ἐλεγο | μεν A.   14 B : κρητικὴν A.
15 τὸ added by Grotius.
16 Cobet : ἐπιθυμίασ· ἔνιά τε A. Dindorf marked a lacuna
after ἐπιθυμίας.
17 Grotius : κατοξουσ A.

47

καπνὸν οὐ φέρων, πῦρ οὐ φέρων. ἐκ[1] τοῦ πυρὸς
εἰς τὰς μαχαίρας ἦλθον· ὧν εἷς οὑτοσὶ
b διὰ τῶν μαχαιρῶν τοῦ πυρός τ᾽ ἐλήλυθεν.

Ἀντιφάνης δ᾽ ἐν Φιλώτιδι τὴν σοφίαν τῶν μαγείρων ἐμφανίζων φησίν·

οὐκοῦν τὸ μὲν γλαυκίδιον,[2] ὥσπερ ἄλλοτε,
ἕψειν[3] ἐν ἅλμῃ φημί. Β. τὸ δὲ λαβράκιον;
Α. ὀπτᾶν ὅλον. Β. τὸν γαλεόν; Α. ἐν ὑπο-
τρίμματι
ζέσαι.[4] Β. τὸ δ᾽ ἐγχέλειον; Α. ἅλες,[5] ὀρί-
γανον,
ὕδωρ. Β. ὁ γόγγρος; Α. ταὐτόν. Β. ἡ βατίς;
Α. χλόη.
Β. πρόσεστι θύννου τέμαχος. Α. ὀπτήσεις.[6] Β.
κρέας
ἐρίφειον;[7] Α. ὀπτόν. Β. θάτερον; Α. τἀ-
ναντία.
c Β. ὁ σπλήν; Α. σεσάχθω. Β. νῆστις; Α.
ἀπολεῖ μ᾽ οὑτοσί.

ἀοιδίμων δ᾽ ὀψαρτυτῶν ὀνόματα καταλέγει Βάτων
ἐν Εὐεργέταις οὕτως·

εὖ γ᾽, ὦ Σιβύνη, τὰς νύκτας οὐ καθεύδομεν
οὐδ᾽ ἀνατετράμμεθ᾽,[8] ἀλλὰ καίεται λύχνος,
καὶ βιβλίον ἐν[9] ταῖς χερσί, καὶ φροντίζομεν
τί Σόφων καταλέλοιπ᾽ ἢ τί Σημωνακτίδης[10]
d ὁ Χῖος ἢ Τυνδάριχος[11] ὁ Σικυώνιος,
ἢ Ζωπυρῖνος. Β. αὐτὸς εὕρηκας δὲ τί;

Grotius: οὐ πῦρ οὐ φέρων δ᾽ ἐκ Α.
[2] 295 d: γλυκιδον (sic) Α.   [3] ἑλεῖν Α.

48

smoke, another the fire; from the fire they took to
knifing; out of all these, my man here has alone come
safely through the knives and the fire." But Antiphanes reveals the erudition of cooks when he says in
Philotis [a] : " A. Very well, I tell you to cook the little
grey-fish in salt water, as at other times. B. And
the little bass? A. Bake whole. B. The dog-fish?
A. Should boil in a sour sauce. B. The little eel?
A. Salt, marjoram, and water. B. The conger-eel?
A. Same way. B. The ray? A. Green herbs. B.
We've got besides a cutlet of tunny. A. You will
broil that. B. Kid meat? A. Broil. B. The other
meat? A. Just the opposite—boil. B. The spleen?
A. Stuff it well. B. The empty intestine? A. This
fellow will be the death of me." Baton enumerates
the names of famous fancy-cooks thus in *Benefactors* [b] :
" A. Good, Sibynê! We don't get to sleep o' nights,
or so much as lie on our backs [c]; no, the lamp burns
while we, with cookery-book in hand, study to see
what Sophôn [d] has bequeathed us, or Semonactides
of Chios, or Tyndarichus of Sicyon, or Zopyrinus.
B. And what have you yourself invented? A. The

---

[a] Kock ii. 109, Athen. 295 d (vol. iii. p. 324).
[b] Kock iii. 327 ; a cook addresses his female assistant.
[c] *Cf.* Aristoph. *Ran.* 542 ἐν στρώμασιν Μιλησίοις ἀνα-
τετραμμένος ; see critical note 8.
[d] Sophôn of Acarnania, famous cook, is mentioned vol. iv.
pp. 328, 330, *cf.* 622 e (vol. vi. p. 355), Pollux vi. 70-71.

---

⁴ Casaubon: ὑποτριμματί | ζεσθαι A.
⁵ ἐγχέλιον ἄλας A.
⁶ ὀπτῆσ εἰσ A.   ⁷ ἐρίφιον A.
⁸ Bothe: ἀναγεγραμμεθα A, ἀναπεπαύμεθ' Cobet.
⁹ ἐν added by Bothe.
¹⁰ Porson: σοφῶν καταλέλοιπεν· ητισ ἡμωνακτειδησο A.
¹¹ Porson: τυνδαρικὸσ A.

ATHENAEUS

A. τὰ μέγιστα. B. ποῖα[1] ταῦτα; A. τοὺς τεθνηκότας . . .

Ἐγὼ δὲ τοιουτονὶ βρῶμα ὑμῖν, ἄνδρες φίλοι, τὸ μῦμα φέρω. περὶ οὗ Ἀρτεμίδωρος μὲν ὁ Ἀριστοφάνειος ἐν Ὀψαρτυτικαῖς Γλώσσαις φησὶν ὅτι σκευάζεται ἐκ κρεῶν καὶ αἵματος, πολλῶν ἀρτυμάτων συνεμβαλλομένων. Ἐπαίνετος δ᾽ ἐν Ὀψαρτυτικῷ λέγει ταῦτα· "μῦμα δὲ παντὸς ἱερείου, καὶ ὄρνιθος δὲ χρὴ ποιεῖν τὰ ἁπαλὰ τῶν κρεῶν μικρὰ
e συντεμόντα καὶ τὰ σπλάγχνα καὶ τὸ ἔντερον καὶ τὸ αἷμα διαθρύψαντα καὶ ἀρτύσαντα ὄξει, τυρῷ ὀπτῷ, σιλφίῳ, κυμίνῳ, θύμῳ χλωρῷ καὶ ξηρῷ, θύμβρᾳ, κοριάννῳ χλωρῷ τε καὶ ξηρῷ, καὶ γητείῳ[2] καὶ κρομμύῳ καθαρῷ πεφωσμένῳ ἢ μήκωνι καὶ σταφίδι ἢ μέλιτι καὶ ῥόας ὀξείας κόκκοις. εἶναι δέ σοι τὸ αὐτὸ μῦμα[3] καὶ ὄψου[4]."

Τοσαῦτα καὶ τούτου κατακόψαντος οὐ μόνον τὰ προειρημένα ἀλλὰ καὶ ἡμᾶς, ἄλλος ἐπεισῆλθεν τὴν
f ματτύην κομίζων. ὑπὲρ ἧς καὶ ζητήσεως γενομένης καὶ τοῦ Οὐλπιανοῦ εἰπόντος τὰ ἐκ τῶν Ὀψαρτυτικῶν Γλωσσῶν τοῦ προειρημένου Ἀρτεμιδώρου, Αἰμιλιανὸς Δωροθέῳ ἔφη τῷ Ἀσκαλωνίτῃ σύγγραμμα ἐκδεδόσθαι ἐπιγραφόμενον Περὶ Ἀντιφάνους καὶ περὶ τῆς παρὰ τοῖς νεωτέροις

---

[1] Schweighäuser: πόσα A.   [2] γητίωι A.
[3] μῦμα deleted by Kaibel.   [4] Schweighäuser: ὄψον A.

[a] Sc. "I can bring to life again by the smell of my food." For the thought to be supplied here cf. the cook's boast in Philemon's *Soldier*, 289 a (vol. iii. p. 296):—

ἀθανασίαν εὕρηκα· τοὺς ἤδη νεκροὺς
ὅταν μόνον ὀσφρανθῶσι ποιῶ ζῆν πάλιν.

greatest of all. B. And what are they? A. Dead
men . . ."ᵃ

That kind of dish, my dear sirs, I offer you now in
the "myma" here.ᵇ Concerning this Artemidorus,
the disciple of Aristophanes,ᶜ says in his *Glossary of
Cookery* that it is prepared with meat and blood and
the addition of many condiments. And Epaenetus
in his *Art of Cookery* gives this receipt : "A myma of
any kind of meat, including fowl, should be made by
cutting up the tender parts of the meat into small
pieces, mashing in the viscera, intestine, and blood,
and spicing with vinegar, toasted cheese, silphium,
cummin, fresh and dried thyme, savory, fresh and
dried coriander, horn onion, common peeled onion
roasted, or poppy-head and raisins, or honey, or the
pips of an acid pomegranate. You may also have
the same myma with fish."

After this speaker had crushed not only all the
things herein mentioned but also ourselves as well,
another cook entered bringing the *mattyê*.ᵈ A de-
bate arose as to the nature of this, and after Ulpian
had quoted passages from the *Glossary of Cookery*
by the above-mentioned Artemidorus, Aemilianus
said that Dorotheus of Ascalon had published a
treatise entitled *Concerning Antiphanes*, including an
account of the *mattyê* mentioned in the later comic

ᵇ Returning to the subject introduced above, 658 e (p. 31).
ᶜ Of Byzantium. *Cf.* 5 b, 387 d (vol. i. p. 20, vol. iv.
p. 250).
ᵈ A general term for any delicacy, 141 d-e (vol. ii. pp. 144-
146), below, 663 c (p. 53). For the slang use of κατακόπτω
"crush," "din," see Pollux vi. 119 κόπτων τὰ ὦτα = μακρολόγος.

κωμικοῖς¹ ματτύης· ἦν Θετταλῶν φησιν εἶναι
εὕρημα, ἐπιχωριάσαι δὲ² κἀν ταῖς Ἀθήναις κατὰ
τὴν Μακεδόνων ἐπικράτειαν. ὁμολογοῦνται δ' οἱ
663 Θετταλοὶ πολυτελέστατοι τῶν Ἑλλήνων γεγενῆ-
σθαι περί τε τὰς ἐσθῆτας καὶ τὴν δίαιταν· ὅπερ
αὐτοῖς αἴτιον ἐγένετο καὶ τοῦ κατὰ τῆς Ἑλλάδος
ἐπαγαγεῖν τοὺς Πέρσας, ἐζηλωκόσι τὴν τούτων
τρυφὴν καὶ πολυτέλειαν. ἱστορεῖ δὲ περὶ τῆς
πολυτελείας αὐτῶν καὶ Κριτίας³ ἐν τῇ Πολιτείᾳ
αὐτῶν. ὠνομάσθη⁴ δὲ ἡ ματτύη, ὡς μὲν ὁ Ἀθη-
ναῖος Ἀπολλόδωρός φησιν ἐν τῷ πρώτῳ τῶν
b Ἐτυμολογουμένων, ἀπὸ τοῦ μασᾶσθαι, ὥσπερ καὶ
ἡ μαστίχη καὶ ἡ μάσταξ⁵· ἡμεῖς δέ φαμεν ἀπὸ τοῦ
μάττειν, ἀφ' οὗ καὶ ἡ μᾶζα αὐτὴ ὠνομάσθη καὶ ἡ
παρὰ Κυπρίοις καλουμένη μαγίς, καὶ τὸ τρυφᾶν
καθ' ὑπερβολὴν ὑπερμαζᾶν. κατ' ἀρχὰς μὲν οὖν
τὴν δημοτικὴν καὶ κοινὴν ταύτην τροφὴν τὴν ἐκ
τῶν ἀλφίτων μᾶζαν ὠνόμαζον καὶ μάττειν τὸ
παρασκευάζειν αὐτήν. ὕστερον δὲ ποικίλλοντες⁶
τὴν ἀναγκαίαν τροφὴν ἀκολάστως καὶ περιέργως
c μικρὸν παραγαγόντες⁷ τοὔνομα τῆς μάζης ματτύην
ὠνόμαζον πᾶν τὸ πολυτελὲς ἔδεσμα, τὸ δὲ ματ-
τυάζειν τὸ παρασκευάζειν αὐτά, εἴτε ἰχθὺς εἴη εἴτε
ὄρνις εἴτε λάχανον εἴτε ἱερεῖον εἴτε πεμμάτιον.
τοῦτο δὲ δῆλόν ἐστιν ἐξ οὗ καὶ ὁ Ἀρτεμίδωρος

---

¹ Musurus: κωμικῆσ A.   ² CE: τε A.
      ³ Casaubon: κρατῖνοσ A.
      ⁴ A: ὠνόμασται CE.
   ⁵ Kaibel: ἡ μαστίχη καὶ τὰ μάλιστα A.
  ⁶ A: ποικίλαντες CE.   ⁷ παράγοντες C.

ᵃ This phrase is included by Kock ii. 11 in his argument
for rejecting the term " Middle Comedy." *Cf.* Aristot. *Eth.*

poets.[a] It is, he says, an invention of the Thessalians, but it became popular in Athens as well during the Macedonian domination. Now the Thessalians are generally admitted to have been the most extravagant of all the Greeks in the matter both of clothing and food ; this in fact was their reason for bringing the Persians into Greece, since they emulated Persian luxury and extravagance. Critias gives an account of their extravagance in his work on their *Constitution*.[b] Now the *mattyê* was so named, according to Apollodorus of Athens in the first book of his *Etymologies*,[c] from the verb *masâsthai* (chew), like *mastiché* and *mastax* (jaw) ; but we assert that it comes from *mattein* (mould), from which verb the barley-cake (*maza*) itself got its name, as also the *magis*,[d] as it is called by the Cyprians, and just as to be very luxurious is called *hypermazân*.[e] In early times, that is, they called this food which was made from barley-meal and was in general use among the common people *maza*, and the preparation of it *mattein*. But later they began to vary their daily food with extravagant refinements, and by a slight lengthening of the word *maza* they called every rich delicacy a *mattyê*, while the preparation of it was described by the verb *mattyazein*, be it fish, fowl, vegetable, meat, or sweet cake. This is made clear from the testi-

Nic. 1128 a 22 (κωμῳδίαν) τὴν τῶν παλαιῶν, τὴν τῶν καινῶν. It is, however, used by Athenaeus, as we have seen.

[b] See 527 a-b (vol. v. p. 379 and note *b*), *F.H.G.* ii. 69, Diels 622.

[c] J. 2 B 1108. The same derivation is given above for *maisôn*, 659 a-b (p. 33).

[d] Lump, cake, pudding, referring to the round mould in which it was made or served.

[e] *i.e.* "to be stuffed with barley-cakes."

παρέθετο μαρτυρίου 'Αλέξιδος· συνεμφῆναι γὰρ
βουλόμενος ὁ "Αλεξις τὴν ἀκολασίαν τῆς παρα-
σκευῆς προσέθηκε τὸ λέπεσθαι. ἔχει δ' οὕτως[1] ἡ
σύμπασα ἐκλογὴ οὖσα ἐκ τοῦ διεσκευασμένου
δράματος ὃ ἐπιγράφεται Δημήτριος·

> τοὔψον λαβούσαι τοῦτο τοὐπεσταλμένον[2]
> σκευάζετ', εὐωχεῖσθε, προπόσεις πίνετε,
d   λέπεσθε, ματτυάζετε.

τῷ[3] δὲ λέπεσθαι χρῶνται οἱ 'Αθηναῖοι ἐπ' ἀσελγοῦς
καὶ φορτικῆς δι' ἀφροδισίων ἡδονῆς.

Καὶ ὁ 'Αρτεμίδωρος ἐν ταῖς 'Οψαρτυτικαῖς
Γλώτταις[4] τὴν ματτύην ἀποφαίνει κοινὸν εἶναι
πάντων ὄνομα τῶν πολυτελῶν ἐδεσμάτων,[5] γράφων
οὕτως· " ἔστι τις[6] ὄρνιθος ματτύης. ἐσφάχθω μὲν
διὰ τοῦ στόματος εἰς τὴν κεφαλήν. ἔστω δὲ ἔωλος
καθάπερ ὁ πέρδιξ· ἐὰν δὲ θέλῃς, ὡς ἔχει αὐτοῖς[7]
πτεροῖς ἐᾶν, μὴ τετιλμένην."[8] εἶτα τὸν τρόπον
ἐκθεὶς τῆς ἀρτύσεως καὶ τῆς ἑψήσεως ἐπιφέρει
e εὐθύς· " καὶ νομάδα παχεῖαν ἔψε καὶ νεοσσοὺς τῶν
ἤδη κοκκυζόντων, ἐὰν θέλῃς παρὰ πότον χρῆσθαι.
εἶτ' ἐξελὼν τὰ λάχανα[9] εἰς τρυβλίον καὶ τῆς ὄρνιθος

---

[1] οὕτως added by Kaibel here: ἐκλογὴ οὕτως Schweighäuser.
[2] Hirschig (τἀπεσταλμένον B, Musurus): ταπεταλμενον A.
[3] CE: τὸ A.   [4] sic A here.
[5] Kaibel: ἡδυσμάτων ACE.
[6] Kaibel (ἔστι καί τις Schweighäuser): εἴ τισ τῆσ A.
[7] Kaibel: τοῖσ A.
[8] πτεροῖς ἐᾶν μὴ τετιλμένην Dalechamps: πτεροῖς ἐᾶν τε
τιλμένην A.
[9] λάχανα A: λάγανα Hesychius.

---

[a] This word (λέπω) had various slang meanings (vol. ii.

mony of Alexis cited by Artemidorus. For Alexis, wishing to emphasize still further the extravagance of their equipment, added the accusation of " peeling." *a* The complete quotation, which comes from the revised edition of the play entitled *Demetrius*, is as follows *b* : " When you women have got this delicacy that has been prescribed, you make ready, have a grand feast, drink toasts, play at peeling, have fancy dishes." Now the Athenians use the word " peel " of perverted and vulgar indulgence in sexual affairs.

Artemidorus, in his *Glossary of Cookery*, further declares that the word *mattyê* is a general term for all rich foods ; he writes as follows : " There is a *mattyês* *c* made with a fowl. Let the bird be killed by thrusting the knife through the beak into the head. Let it hang for a day, as in the case of partridges, just as it is, if you prefer, feathers and all, leaving the bird unplucked." *d* He then explains the method of seasoning and cooking it and immediately continues : " Also cook a fat guinea-hen and young cockerels *e* if you want to use them during the drinking.*f* Then taking the vegetables *g* from the pot and putting them into a bowl, lay them over the meat of

p. 233 and note *c*, iii. 111 note *c*). Artemidorus here takes it *sens. obsc.*, as at 403 a (vol. iv. p. 324).

b Kock ii. 315.　　　　　　　*c* Masculine form.

d The reading in A, ὡς ἔχει τοῖς πτεροῖς ἐᾶν τετιλμένην, is ungrammatical and unintelligible. Wilamowitz assumed a lacuna between ἐᾶν and τετιλμένην.

e Lit. " young which have already begun to crow."

f *i.e.* at the " second tables," above, 641 c (vol. vi. p. 461).

g Hesychius has λάγανα, the thin wafer-like cakes (Lat. *tracta*) mentioned above, p. 31, *cf.* 110 a (vol. ii. p. 16). He says *s.v.* ματτύης· ἡ μὲν φωνὴ Μακεδονική. ὄρνις καὶ τὰ ἐκ τοῦ ζωμοῦ αὐτοῦ λάγανα περιφορήματα (περιφερόμενα). Hence τὸ λάγανον κατάθρυπτε below.

τῶν κρεῶν ἐπιθεὶς παρατίθει· τοῦ θέρους ἀντὶ τοῦ
ὄξους τῆς ὄμφακος ἐμβαλὼν εἰς τὸν ζωμὸν ὡς ἔχει
τοὺς βότρυς· ἐπειδὰν δὲ ἑφθὴ γένηται, ἔξελε μετὰ
τοῦ βοτρυδίου πρὸ τοῦ τὸ γίγαρτον ἐξαφεῖναι, εἶθ᾽
οὕτως τὸ λάγανον κατάθρυπτε. οὗτος[1] ματτύης ἐν
τοῖς ἡδίστοις.'' ὅτι μὲν οὖν κοινὸν ἦν τοὔνομα τῶν
f πολυτελεστάτων ἐδεσμάτων φανερόν· ὅτι δὲ καὶ
ὁ τρόπος τῆς τοιαύτης εὐωχίας ὁμοίως ἐλέγετο
Φιλήμων φησὶν ἐν ʽΑρπαζομένῳ·

> γυμνῷ φυλακὴν ἐπίταττε, καὶ διὰ τριῶν[2]
> ποτηρίων με ματτύης εὐφραινέτω.

καὶ ἐν ᾽Ανδροφόνῳ·

> πιεῖν τις ἡμῖν ἐγχεάτω καὶ ματτύην
> ποιεῖτε θᾶττον.

῎Αλεξις δ᾽ ἐν Πυραύνῳ ἀμφιβόλως εἴρηκεν·

664
> ἐγὼ δ᾽ ἐπειδὰν ἀσχολουμένους λάβω,
> ἀνέκραγον '' οὐ δώσει τις ἡμῖν ματτύην;''

ὥσπερ ἂν εἰ τὸ δεῖπνον ἔλεγεν· πιθανὸν δὲ καὶ
ἰδίως ἐπί τι[3] τῶν ἐδεσμάτων ἀναφέρειν.

Μάχων δ᾽ ὁ Σικυώνιος τῶν μὲν κατὰ ᾽Απολ-
λόδωρον τὸν Καρύστιον κωμῳδιοποιῶν[4] εἷς ἐστι
καὶ αὐτός· οὐκ ἐδίδαξεν δ᾽ ᾽Αθήνησι τὰς κωμῳδίας
τὰς ἑαυτοῦ, ἀλλ᾽ ἐν ᾽Αλεξανδρείᾳ. ἦν δ᾽ ἀγαθὸς[5]
ποιητὴς εἴ τις ἄλλος τῶν μετὰ τοὺς ἑπτά· διόπερ ὁ
γραμματικὸς ᾽Αριστοφάνης ἐσπούδασε συσχολάσαι

---

[1] οὗτος ὁ Kaibel unnecessarily.
[2] ἐπίταττε καὶ διατριῶν A : ἐπίτάττετ· ἀλλὰ μετὰ τριῶν Kock,
ἐπίταττε καί τις διὰ τριῶν Kaibel.
[3] τι added by Kaibel.
[4] Musurus : κωμωιδιοποιοῦ A.
[5] CE : ἀλλ᾽ ἀλεξανδρείην δ᾽ ἀγαθὸσ A.

the bird and serve ; in summer, instead of using vinegar, put into the broth the grapes from the unripe cluster, just as it is ; when it [a] is done, take it from the pot along with the grape-cluster before the seeds have cooked out of it, and then crumble the wafer-bread into it. Here you have a *mattyês* of the very nicest sort." That, therefore, the word is a general term for the richest foods is plain ; but that the spirit of revelry accompanying a rich feast was likewise called *mattyês* is shown by Philemon in *Kidnapped* [b] : " ' Enjoin caution upon an unarmed man,' and with every three cups let a *mattyês* give me cheer." So in *The Murderer* [c] : " Somebody pour me out a drink and quickly make a *mattyês*." But Alexis in *The Fire-Lighter* uses the word ambiguously [d] : " But when I find them busy I cry out ' Is no one going to give us a party (*mattyês*) ? ' " Here he might mean the whole dinner ; but it is also probable that it refers specifically to one dish on the *menu*.

Now Machon of Sicyon is also one of the comic poets who lived at the same time as Apollodorus of Carystus ; he did not bring out his comedies at Athens, but in Alexandria. He was a good poet, if ever there was one, next to the Seven [e] ; hence the grammarian Aristophanes, when a young man, was eager to study

---

[a] The bird ? Schweighäuser understood ἐφθή to refer to the unripe grapes, which can hardly be right.

[b] Kock ii. 482. The proverb at the beginning is explained by Hesychius : ἐπὶ τῶν μὴ δεομένων προστάξεως, " said of those who do not require urging " ; Zenobius ii. 98.

[c] Kock ii. 480.

[d] *Ibid.* 372 ; spoken by a parasite.

[e] The Alexandrian Pleiad : Lycophron, Alexander of Aetolia, Sosiphanes, Sositheus from Alexandria in the Troad, Dionysiades, Homerus of Byzantium, Philiscus.

b αὐτῷ νέος ὤν. ἐποίησε δὲ καὶ οὗτος ἐν δράματι
'Αγνοίᾳ ταυτί·

> ἥδιον οὐδέν ἐστί μοι τῆς ματτύης,
> τοῦτ' εἴτε πρῶτοι Μακεδόνες τοῖς 'Αττικοῖς
> κατέδειξαν¹ ἡμῖν εἴτε πάντες οἱ θεοί·
> οὐκ οἶδα· πλήν γ' ὅτι² μουσικωτάτου τινός . . .

Ὅτι δὲ ὕστατον καὶ ἐπὶ πᾶσιν εἰσεφέρετο Νικό-
στρατός φησιν ἐν 'Απελαυνομένῳ. μάγειρος δ'
ἐστὶν ὁ διηγούμενος ὡς λαμπρὰν καὶ εὔτακτον
παρεσκεύασεν εὐωχίαν· προδιηγησάμενός τε οἷον ἦν
c τὸ ἄριστον καὶ τὸ δεῖπνον καὶ τρίτης μνησθεὶς
παραθέσεως ἐπιφέρει·

> εὖ γ',³ ἄνδρες, εὖ σφόδρ'⁴· ἀλλὰ μὴν τῇ ματτύῃ
> οὕτω διαθήσω τὰ μετὰ ταῦθ' ὥστ' οἴομαι
> οὐδ' αὐτὸν ἡμῖν τοῦτον⁵ ἀντερεῖν ἔτι.

καὶ ἐν Μαγείρῳ·

> θρῖον δὲ καὶ κάνδαυλον⁶ ἢ τούτων τι τῶν
> εἰς ματτύην οὐδέτερος⁷ εἶδε πώποτε.

ἄλλος δέ τίς φησιν·

> περιφέρειν ματτύην καὶ⁸ ποδάριον
d καὶ γαστρίον τακερόν τι καὶ μήτρας ἴσως.

Διονύσιος δ' ἐν 'Ακοντιζομένῳ· μάγειρος δ' ἐστὶν
ὁ λέγων·

> ὥστ' ἐνίοτ' ἂν τούτοισι⁹ ποιῶν ματτύην

---

¹ Casaubon: κατεδίδαξαν ACE.
² Schweighäuser: πλὴν ἐστιν γε A, πλὴν ἔστι γε C.
³ Casaubon: ἐυγετ' A. ⁴ σφόδρα A.
⁵ Μῶμον (?) Kock. ⁶ 517 a: κάνδυλον A.

58

with him.[a] Machon wrote the following in his play, *The Mistake*[b] : " There's nothing nicer for me than the *mattyê*, whether it was the Macedonians that first taught the receipt for it to us Athenians, or all the gods of heaven ; I know not ; but that it came from a very great genius. . . ."

That, however, the *mattyê* was brought in as the last dish to cap all the others is shown by Nicostratus in *Driven Out*. A cook appears who describes what a brilliant, well-ordered feast he had prepared ; and having described first the nature of the luncheon and the dinner, he then mentions the third service and continues[c] : " Fine, gentlemen, very fine indeed ! But more ! With my *mattyê* I am going to put you in such a frame of mind in a moment that I fancy not even this man here[d] will have a word to say against me any longer." Again, in *The Cook*[e] : " But an omelette or a pilaf or one of those things that go into a *mattyê* neither one of them has ever yet seen." And another comedian says[f] : " To carry around a *mattyê* or pig's foot or tender bit of paunch or matrix[g] perhaps." Dionysius in *Hit by a Javelin* ; a cook is the speaker[h] : " Wherefore sometimes, when making a

---

[a] Cf. 354 e (vol. iv. p. 104) and 168 a (vol. ii. p. 262), τοῖς φιλοσόφοις συσχολάζοντες.

[b] Kock iii. 324.

[c] Kock ii. 221.

[d] Or, reading αὐτὸν . . . Μῶμον with Kock (see critical note 5), " not even Momus himself (the god of blame)."

[e] Kock ii. 224, Athen. 517 a (vol. v. p. 326).

[f] Kock iii. 482 ; the author is unknown.

[g] See 96 e (vol. i. p. 414).　　　　　　[h] Kock ii. 423.

---

[7] Wilamowitz: οὐδετερον A.

[8] καὶ added by Meineke.

[9] Musurus: τούτου τοῖσι A.

σπεύδων ἅμ᾽ εἰσήνεγκα διαμαρτὼν μίαν
ἄκων περιφορὰν τῶν νεκρῶν ὡς τὸν νεκρόν.

Φιλήμων ἐν Πτωχῇ·

ἐξὸν ἀποσάττεσθαι δ᾽ ὅλην τὴν ἡμέραν,
ποιοῦντα καὶ διδόντα ματτύας ἐκεῖ.

e Μόλπις δ᾽ ὁ Λάκων τὰ παρὰ τοῖς Σπαρτιάταις
ἐπαίκλεια, ὃ σημαίνει[1] τὰς ἐπιδειπνίδας, ματτύας
φησὶ λέγεσθαι παρὰ τοῖς ἄλλοις. ὁ δὲ κυνικὸς
Μένιππος ἐν τῷ ἐπιγραφομένῳ Ἀρκεσιλάῳ γράφει
οὕτως· '' πότος ἦν ἐπικωμασάντων τινῶν καὶ ματτύην ἐκέλευσεν εἰσφέρειν Λάκαινάν τις[2]· καὶ εὐθέως
περιεφέρετο περδίκεια[3] ὀλίγα καὶ χήνεια[4] ὀπτὰ καὶ
τρύφη πλακούντων.'' τὸ δὲ τοιοῦτον δεῖπνον οἱ μὲν
f Ἀττικοὶ προσηγόρευον ἐπιδόρπισμα, οἱ δὲ Δωριεῖς
ἐπάικλον, τῶν δ᾽ ἄλλων Ἑλλήνων οἱ πλεῖστοι
ἐπιδειπνίδα.[5]

Τοσούτων καὶ περὶ τῆς ματτύης λεχθέντων
ἔδοξεν ἀπιέναι· καὶ γὰρ ἑσπέρα ἦν ἤδη. διελύ-
θημεν οὖν οὕτως.

ΙΔ

---

[1] ἐπαικλεια σημαίνει A, ἐπαίκλεια ὅ ἐστιν C, ἐπαίκλεια (or
ἐπάικλα?) ἃ σημαίνει Kaibel.
[2] Kaibel: λάκαινά τισ ACE.

mattyê for these fellows here, in my haste and unconsciously I have made a mistake and brought in a dish of—the dead to the dead." Philemon in *Beggar Woman* [a] : " When he might have been stuffing himself all day long, making and giving out *mattyês* over there." Again, Molpis of Lacedaemon says [b] that the *epaikleia* of the Spartans, a word which means " eaten after dinner (*epideipnis*)," are called *mattyês* among other peoples. The Cynic Menippus, however, writes in the work entitled *Arcesilaus* as follows : " There was a drinking-party of some revellers, and one ordered a Lacedaemonian *mattyê* to be brought in ; and immediately there were carried around a few slices of partridge and roast goose and pieces of different kinds of cake." [c] Such a collation as this was called by the Athenians an *epidorpisma* or after-supper ; by the Dorians, an *epaïklon* ; but most other Greeks called it an *epideipnis*.

After all this had been said on the subject of the *mattyê* we decided to leave ; for by this time it was evening. So at this point we dissolved the meeting.

[a] Kock ii. 496.
[b] *F.H.G.* iv. 454, *cf.* Athen. 141 d (vol. ii. p. 144), 642 e (vol. vi. p. 469).
[c] For these see vol. vi. pp. 496-498.

---

[3] E: περδίκια C, περδίκ̇ια A.

[4] CE: χηνία A.   [5] Kaibel: ἐπίδειπνα ACE.

IE

665 Εἴ μοι τὸ Νεστόρειον εὔγλωσσον μέλος
Ἀντήνορός τε τοῦ Φρυγὸς δοίη θεός,

κατὰ τὸν πάνσοφον Εὐριπίδην, ἑταῖρε Τιμόκρατες,
οὐκ ἂν δυναίμην ἀπομνημονεύειν ἔτι σοι τῶν πολλάκις λεχθέντων ἐν τοῖς περισπουδάστοις τούτοις
συμποσίοις διά τε[1] τὴν ποικιλίαν καὶ τὴν ὁμοιό-
τητα[2] τῶν ἀεὶ καινῶς προσευρισκομένων. καὶ
b γὰρ καὶ περὶ τάξεως τῶν περιφορῶν πολλάκις
ἐλέχθη καὶ περὶ τῶν μετὰ τὸ δεῖπνον ἐπιτελουμένων,
ἅπερ καὶ μόλις ἀναπεμπάζομαι, εἰπόντος τινὸς τῶν
ἑταίρων τὰ ἐκ τῶν Λακώνων Πλάτωνος ἰαμβεῖα[3]·

ἄνδρες δεδειπνήκασιν ἤδη; Β. σχεδὸν ἅπαντες.
   Α. εὖ γε·
τί οὐ τρέχων σὺ[4] τὰς τραπέζας ἐκφέρεις; ἐγὼ δὲ
λίτρον[5] παραχέων ἔρχομαι.[6] Β. κἀγὼ δὲ παρα-
   κορήσων.
σπονδὰς δ' ἔπειτα παραχέας τὸν κότταβον
   παροίσω·
c τῇ παιδὶ τοὺς αὐλοὺς ἐχρῆν ἤδη πρὸ χειρὸς[7] εἶναι

---

[1] Musurus: γε Α.
[2] ἀνομοιότητα "dissimilarity" Dalechamps.
[3] ἴαμβια Α.   [4] σὺ added by Musurus.
[5] νίπτρον Casaubon.   [6] Hermann: εἰσέρχομαι Α.
[7] Hermann: προχείρουσ Α, διὰ χειρὸς (?) Kock.

BOOK XV

" If some god," as the all-wise Euripides says,[a]
" should give me the sweet-tongued melodiousness
of Nestor or Trojan Antenor,"[b] I should be quite
unable, friend Timocrates, further to recall for you
the things that were said so often in these banquets
of ours, to which we came with eager zest; not only
the diversity, but even the similarity of the novel
devices brought forth from time to time, are my
excuse. For even the proper order of the dinner-
courses was discussed many times, as well as the
festivities introduced after dinner, so many that
I can hardly count them. One of our company,
for example, quoted the iambic verses of Plato's
Laconians[c]: " A. Have the gentlemen finished dinner
already? B. Nearly all. A. Good news! Run then,
won't you, and carry away the tables, while I will
go and pour out soda.[d] B. And I to sweep up the
floor.[e] Then, after I have poured out for them wine
for libations, I will set up the cottabos beside them.
The flutes must be ready for the girl by this time, and

---

[a] *T.G.F.*[2] 649, *cf.* Eust. 1301. 33, who interpreted εἴ μοι
as εἴθε μοι, " would that."

[b] The two are joined together in an enumeration of
eloquent men by Plato, *Symp.* 221 c.

[c] Kock i. 620; two slaves are conversing, *cf.* Philyllius,
Athen. 408 e (vol. iv. p. 350).

[d] For the hand-washing.

[e] *Cf.* the model banquet of Xenophanes, 462 c (vol. v. p. 16).

καὶ προαναφυσᾶν.[1] τὸ μῦρον ἤδη παράχεον[2]
βαδίζων
Αἰγύπτιον κᾆτ᾽ ἴρινον· στέφανον δ᾽ ἔπειθ᾽
ἑκάστῳ
δώσω φέρων τῶν ξυμποτῶν. νεοκρᾶτά τις
ποιείτω.
A. καὶ δὴ κέκραται. B. τὸν λιβανωτὸν ἐπι-
τίθει σὺ . . .

εἶτ᾽ ἐπάγει[3]·

d σπονδὴ μὲν[4] ἤδη γέγονε καὶ πίνοντές εἰσι[5]
πόρρω·
καὶ σκόλιον ᾖσται, κότταβος δ᾽ ἐξοίχεται θύραζε.
αὐλοὺς δ᾽ ἔχουσά τις κορίσκη Καρικὸν μέλος τι[6]
μελίζεται τοῖς συμπόταις· κἄλλην[7] τρίγωνον
εἶδον
ἔχουσαν, εἶτ᾽ ᾖδεν[8] πρὸς αὐτὸ μέλος Ἰωνικόν τι.

Μετὰ ταῦτ᾽, οἶμαι, καὶ περὶ κοττάβων ζήτησις
e ἦν καὶ τῶν ἀποκοτταβιζόντων. οὓς οἰηθείς τις
τῶν παρόντων ἰατρῶν εἶναι τούτων οἳ ἀπὸ βαλα-
νείου καθάρσεως ἕνεκα τοῦ στομάχου πίνοντες
ἄμυστιν ἀποβλύζουσιν, ἔφη οὐκ εἶναι παλαιὰν
ταύτην παράδοσιν οὐδ᾽ εἰδέναι τινὰ τῶν ἀρχαίων
ταύτῃ τῇ καθάρσει χρησάμενον. δι᾽ ὃ καὶ Ἐρασί-
666 στρατον τὸν Ἰουλιήτην ἐν τῇ περὶ τῶν Καθόλου
πραγματείᾳ ἐπιτιμᾶν τοῖς τοῦτο ποιοῦσιν, βλαπ-
τικὸν ὀφθαλμῶν τὸ ἐπιχείρημα δεικνύων καὶ τῆς

---

[1] Cobet: προσαναφυσᾶν A.
[2] Musurus: παράχεων A.
[3] Meineke: ἐπιτιθεῖσ εἶ|πε A.
[4] Schweighäuser: σπονδημε A.
[5] Porson: ἤδη A.   [6] τι added by Hermann.
[7] Schweighäuser: καλὴν A.

she should be warming them up [a] beforehand. Go at once and pour the perfume for them, Egyptian [b] and orris both. After that, I will fetch wreaths to give to each of the banqueters. Let somebody mix up a fresh bowl of wine. A. It's mixed already. B. Put the frankincense on the altar. . . ." He then continues : "A. Libation has been made already, and they are far along in their drinking ; they've sung a round, and the cottabos is coming out now. A little wench with flutes is playing an outlandish tune for the banqueters ; I saw another girl with a triangular harp, and she was singing to its accompaniment a bawdy song."

After this, as I remember, there was a discussion of the cottabos and those who play the game.[c] As to these, one of the physicians present understood them to be those persons who after the bath, and to purge the stomach, drink off wine at a single gulp and spew it forth ; he said, however, that this was not an ancient tradition, and he did not know of anyone in old times who had used this method of purging. Hence also, he said, Erasistratus of Iulis in his treatise *On General Practice* condemns those who do this, showing that this practice is harmful to the eyes and is apt to block the intestines. In

---

[a] Lit. " blow up beforehand," an exact description of the process of warming up a wind-instrument before it can be played ; " play a prelude " (L. & S.) is incorrect.

[b] Below, 689 b, and 66 c (vol. i. p. 288).

[c] The word ἀποκοτταβίζειν has two senses, " dash off the last drops of wine " in the game, and " vomit," as understood by the next speaker. *Etym. Mag.* 533. 15 κοτταβίζειν, τὸ τῷ κοττάβῳ χρῆσθαι φασὶν οἱ Ἀττικοί, οὐχὶ τὸ ἐμεῖν, ὥσπερ οἱ νῦν λέγουσιν.

---

[8] Schweighäuser: ειτηδε A.

κάτω κοιλίας ἐπισχετικόν. πρὸς ὃν Οὐλπιανὸς
ἔφη·

ὅρσ' 'Ασκληπιάδη, καλέει κρείων σε Χαρωνεύς.

οὐ γὰρ κακῶς τινι τῶν ἑταίρων ἡμῶν ἐλέχθη τὸ
" εἰ μὴ ἰατροὶ ἦσαν, οὐδὲν ἂν ἦν τῶν γραμματικῶν
μωρότερον." τίς γὰρ ἡμῶν οὐκ οἶδεν ὅτι οὐκ ἦν
οὗτος ὁ ἀποκοτταβισμὸς ἀρχαῖος; εἰ μή τι σὺ
καὶ τοὺς 'Αμειψίου 'Αποκοτταβίζοντας[1] ἀποβλύζειν
ὑπολαμβάνεις. ἐπεὶ οὖν ἄπειρος εἶ τῆς τοιαύτης
b θεωρίας, μάθε παρ' ἐμοῦ ὅτι πρῶτον μὲν ἡ τῶν
κοττάβων εὕρεσις Σικελική ἐστιν παιδιά, ταύτην[2]
πρώτων εὑρόντων Σικελῶν, ὡς Κριτίας φησὶν ὁ
Καλλαίσχρου ἐν τοῖς 'Ελεγείοις διὰ τούτων·

κότταβος ἐκ Σικελῆς ἐστι χθονὸς ἐκπρεπὲς
ἔργον,
ὃν σκοπὸν ἐς λατάγων[3] τόξα καθιστάμεθα.

Δικαίαρχος δ'[4] ὁ Μεσσήνιος, 'Αριστοτέλους μαθητής, ἐν τῷ περὶ 'Αλκαίου καὶ τὴν λατάγην[5] φησὶν
c εἶναι Σικελικὸν ὄνομα. λατάγη δ' ἐστὶν τὸ ὑπο-
λειπόμενον ἀπὸ τοῦ ἐκποθέντος ποτηρίου ὑγρόν, ὃ
συνεστραμμένῃ τῇ χειρὶ ἄνωθεν ἐρρίπτουν οἱ παί-

---

[1] 'Αποκοτταβίζοντας added by Meineke.
[2] ταύτην omitted in Schol. Aristoph. Pac. 1244.
[3] 28 b: ἐκλαταγῶν A.
[4] δ' added from Schol. Ar.
[5] τὴν λάταγα αὐτὴν Schol. Ar.

---

[a] Timon, Wachsmuth frag. 27, see Diels, P.P.G. iii. 1.
202 : Il. iv. 204 ὅρσ' 'Ασκληπιάδη (Machaon), καλέει κρείων
'Αγαμέμνων.
[b] Alluding to physicians as sons of Asclepius, cf. Il. iv.
193-194.
[c] This name seems to occur only here, and is suspected.

answer to him Ulpian quoted [a]: "Rise up, Asclepiades,[b] the lord Charoneus [c] calls thee." The remark
of one of our companions wasn't half bad, "Were
it not for the doctors, there wouldn't be anything
stupider than the professors." Who among us,
in fact, does not know that this use of the word
"cottabos-shooting"[d] was not ancient? Unless, of
course, you assume that the title *Playing at Cottabos*
of Ameipsias refers to spewing. Since, then, you
are unfamiliar with this branch of study, let me
inform you that the game of cottabos, in the first
place, is a Sicilian invention, the Sicels being the
first to devise it, as Critias, the son of Callaeschrus,
makes clear in his *Elegiac Verses* in these words [e]:
"The cottabos is the chief product of Sicily; we
set it up as a mark to shoot at with drops of wine
(*latages*)." Dicaearchus of Messenê, pupil of Aristotle, says [f] in his book *On Alcaeus* that the word
latagê [g] is likewise Sicilian. It means the drop of
moisture which is left in the cup after it has been
drunk out, and which the players tossed up into the

But it may be a paragogic form of Χάρων, like Ἀιδωνεύς for
Ἀίδης, and the satirical line, in the form given to it by Timon,
may allude to the inability of physicians to heal themselves,
as if he said, "Bestir yourself, for Charon is likely to get
you." For καλεῖ used of the last summons *cf.* Socrates'
words ἐμὲ δὲ νῦν ἤδη καλεῖ, φαίη ἂν ἀνὴρ τραγικός, ἡ εἱμαρμένη,
Plato, *Phaedo* 115 ᴀ (Athen. vol. iv. p. 49 note *a*): so Aristoph.
Lys. 606.   [d] In the sense of vomiting.

[e] Athen. 28 b (vol. i. p. 122), *P.L.G.*[4] ii. 279, Diehl i. 81. On
the game, which seems to have been popular for three centuries, see Schol. Aristoph. *Pac.* 1241 (*cf.* 342), Schol. Lucian,
Lexiph. 3, Pollux vi. 109-111, H. W. Hayley in *H.S.C.P.*
v. 73-82.

[f] *F.H.G.* ii. 247, *cf.* Athen. 479 d, 487 c-d (vol. v. pp. 122,
166).

[g] Both forms, λάταξ (plur. λάταγες) and λατάγη, are attested.

ζοντες εἰς τὸ κοττάβιον.[1] Κλείταρχος δ' ἐν τῇ
περὶ Γλωττῶν πραγματείᾳ λατάγην[2] Θεσσαλοὺς
καὶ Ῥοδίους τὸν ἀπὸ τῶν ποτηρίων κότταβον
λέγειν.

Κότταβος δ' ἐκαλεῖτο καὶ[3] τὸ τιθέμενον ἆθλον
τοῖς νικῶσιν ἐν τῷ πότῳ, ὡς Εὐριπίδης παρίστησιν
ἐν Οἰνεῖ λέγων οὕτως·

πυκνοῖς δ' ἔβαλλον Βακχίου[4] τοξεύμασιν
κάρα γέροντος· τὸν βαλόντα δὲ στέφειν
ἐγὼ 'τετάγμην, ἆθλα κοττάβων[5] διδούς.

d ἐκαλεῖτο δὲ κότταβος καὶ τὸ ἄγγος εἰς ὃ ἔβαλλον[6]
τὰς λάταγας, ὡς Κρατῖνος ἐν Νεμέσει δείκνυσιν·
ὅτι δὲ καὶ χαλκοῦν ἦν, Εὔπολις ἐν Βάπταις λέγει·
" χαλκῷ περὶ κοττάβῳ."[7] Πλάτων δὲ ἐν Διὶ
Κακουμένῳ παιδιᾶς εἶδος[8] παροίνιον τὸν κότταβον
εἶναι ἀποδίδωσιν, ἐν ᾗ ἐξίσταντο καὶ τῶν σκευα-
ρίων οἱ δυσκυβοῦντες.[9] λέγει δ' οὕτως·

ΠΟΡΝ. πρὸς κότταβον παίζειν, ἕως ἂν σφῶν ἐγὼ

---

[1] κοττάβιον CE, Schol. Ar.: κοτταβειον A.
[2] ACE: λάταγα Kaibel.   [3] καὶ CE, Schol. Ar.: om. A.
[4] Musurus: βακχείου ACE.
[5] κοτταβων ACE, κοσσάβων Nauck: κότταβον Casaubon.
[6] A: ἐνέβαλλον Schol. Ar.
[7] ὅτι δὲ καὶ . . . κοττάβῳ added by Kaibel from Schol. Ar.
[8] Schol. Ar.: οἶνος A.
[9] A: διακυβεύοντες Schol. Ar.

---

[a] This meaning of κότταβος seems to be attested by
Hesychius s. λατάγη· τῷ ἀπορριπτομένῳ ἀπὸ τῶν ποτηρίων καὶ
ἦχον ἀποτελοῦντι, and s. λάταξ· ψόφος, κότταβος, ὁ ἀπὸ ποτηρίου
γενόμενος, and is so understood by Schweighäuser (" sonitus,"
" strepitus"). Cf. Anon. Rhet iii. 210 (Spengel's ed.) who, in
giving examples of onomatopoeia, cites κότταβος ἀσπίδων καὶ
πάταγος ἀνέμου. Here κόναβος is proposed for κότταβος, but

basin with a twist of the hand. Cleitarchus, however, in his treatise *On Glosses* says that Thessalians and Rhodians call the clatter (cottabos) arising from the cups [a] *latagê*.

Cottabos was also a name given to the prize offered for victory in the drinking-bout, as Euripides testifies in *Oeneus* when he speaks as follows [b] : " With frequent arrows of wine they tried to hit the old man's head ; and I was appointed to wreath him who succeeded, offering the prizes of cottabos-games." The vessel into which they tossed the wine-drops was also called cottabos, as Cratinus shows in *Nemesis* [c] ; that it was made of bronze Eupolis tells us in *The Dyers* [d] : " On the bronze cottabos." Plato in *Zeus Outraged* represents the cottabos as a kind of game played at drinking-parties, in which those who were unlucky with their throw lost their shirts. He speaks as follows [e] : " *Leno.* You can play at cottabos until I have made the dinner ready for you two in

in the absence of any satisfactory etymology of κότταβος (see Prellwitz *s.v.*) it is as likely to be onomatopoetic as anything else. The noisy clatter of the game distinguished it especially; below, 668 b (p. 79).

[b] *T.G.F.*[2] 537. Athenaeus's statement that cottabos was the name of the prize is based on a mis-reading of the last line, κότταβον for κοττάβων (see critical note 5). The scene described may represent an indignity laid upon the aged Oeneus, as indeed the game itself may have originated in the use of a slave as target for the wine, *cf.* Hayley, *op. cit.* 81 and below, 667 c-d (p. 75).

[c] Below, 667 f, Kock i. 50.

[d] *Ibid.* 278.

[e] *Ibid.* 612 ; a conversation between a brothel-keeper and Heracles. In the kind of cottabos here played (κότταβος δι' ὀξυβάφων), the object was to sink small cups (ποτήρια, ὀξύβαφα), floating in a basin of water, by flipping wine-drops at them ; below, 667 e-f (p. 77).

τὸ δεῖπνον ἔνδον[1] σκευάσω.   ΗΡ. πάνυ βούλομαι·
ἀλλ' ἄγγος[2] ἔστ';   Π. ἀλλ' εἰς θυΐαν παιστέον.[3]
ΗΡ. φέρε τὴν θυΐαν, αἶρ' ὕδωρ, τὰ[4] ποτήρια
e παράθετε. παίζωμεν δὲ περὶ φιλημάτων.
Π. ποίων φιλημάτων;[5] ἀγεννῶς οὐκ ἐῶ
παίζειν. τίθημι[6] κοττάβεια σφῶν ἐγὼ
τασδί τε[7] τὰς κρηπῖδας ἃς αὕτη[8] φορεῖ,
καὶ τὸν κότυλον τὸν σόν.   ΗΡ. βαβαιάξ· οὑτοσὶ[9]
μείζων ἀγὼν τῆς[10] Ἰσθμιάδος ἐπέρχεται.

Ἐκάλουν δὲ καὶ κατακτούς τινας κοττάβους.
ἐστὶν δὲ λυχνία ἀναγόμενα πάλιν τε συμπίπτοντα.
Εὔβουλος Βελλεροφόντῃ·

τίς ἂν λάβοιτο τοῦ σκέλους κάτωθέ μοι;[11]
f ἄνω γὰρ ὥσπερ κοττάβειον αἴρομαι.

Ἀντιφάνης δ' ἐν Ἀφροδίτης Γοναῖς·

τονδὶ[12] λέγω, σὺ δ' οὐ συνιεῖς;[13] κότταβος
τὸ λυχνίον ἐστί. πρόσεχε τὸν νοῦν· ᾠὰ μὲν

---

[1] Jacobs, Dindorf: ὃν ἐν A.
[2] ἀλλ' ἄγγος Kock : αλλα νεμοσ A.
[3] Hermann (who read ἃ νόμος ἔστ'): ἐσταλλεισ θυΐαν παῖσ τεον A.
[4] τὰ added by Kock.
[5] ποίων φιλημάτων; added by Dobree; ἰδοὺ φιλημάτων Cobet, σφὼ περὶ φιλημάτων Kock.
[6] Cobet: τίθεμαι A.   [7] Elmsley: γε A.
[8] Elmsley: αὐτη A.   [9] Casaubon: ουτοισῖ A.
[10] Casaubon: μιζω|νιάγωνιστὴσ A.
[11] Musurus: κάτω θέμενοι A, κάτω θέμενος CE, κάτωθέ μου Kaibel.
[12] Schweighäuser: τονδει A.

the house. *Heracles.* I'd like to very much ; but have you got a basin ? L. No, you can play into a mortar. H. Bring out the mortar, fetch water, set ready the cups. Let's play for kisses. L. Kisses indeed ! I won't let you play for vulgar stakes. Rather, I propose as prizes for you two these fancy boots that the girl here wears, and your own cup.[a] H. Bless my soul ! Here's a contest coming on that's bigger than the Isthmian Games."

Certain kinds of cottabos were called " descending." They require lampstands which can be raised and lowered again.[b] Eubulus in *Bellerophon*[c] : " Who will catch hold of my leg down below ? Indeed I am lifted aloft like a cottabos shaft." Antiphanes in *Birth of Aphrodite*[d] : " A. This here is the thing I mean. Don't you understand ? The lampstand is a cottabos. Pay close attention. The prize is eggs

[a] This cup seems to have figured conspicuously in this play, *cf.* 478 c (vol. v. p. 116). It was probably of gold or silver or set with jewels, *cf.* 482 a-b (vol. v. p. 136), certainly of greater worth than the girl's boots.

[b] This vague and inaccurate paragraph is out of place, belonging rather to 667 d-e below. The term κατακτός (" capable of being lowered ") is variously interpreted. Pollux vi. 109 thought it referred to a disk suspended from the ceiling : τὸ μὲν κοτταβεῖον ἐκρέματο ἀπὸ τοῦ ὀρόφου ὕπτιόν τε καὶ λεῖον, χαλκοῦ πεποιημένον, ὥσπερ λυχνίου τὸ ἐπίθεμα ὃ τὸν λύχνον ὑπʼ αὐτοῦ φέρει. Others think of the lampstand itself, and explain that this was made in two shafts, one sliding up and down in the other. But while such lampstands may have existed (Hayley, *op. cit.* 76-77), they were not essential to the game, in spite of the quotation immediately following.

[c] Kock ii. 171 ; the speaker seems to be Bellerophon mounted on Pegasus.

[d] Kock ii. 33, *cf.* Athen. 487 d (vol. v. p. 168).

---

[13] Early edd. : συνιεισ A.

° ° ° ° ° ° ° ° .¹ πέντε νικητήριον.

Β. περὶ τοῦ; γελοῖον. κοτταβιεῖ δὲ τίνα² τρόπον;
Α. ἐγὼ διδάξω³ καθ' ἕν· ὃς⁴ ἂν τὸν κότταβον
ἀφεὶς ἐπὶ τὴν πλάστιγγα ποιήσῃ πεσεῖν—
Β. πλάστιγγα⁵ ποίαν; τοῦτο τοὐπικείμενον
ἄνω τὸ μικρόν, τὸ πινακίσκιον λέγεις;

667 Α. τοῦτ' ἐστὶ πλάστιγξ—οὗτος ὁ κρατῶν γίγνεται.

Β. πῶς δ' εἴσεταί τις τοῦτ'; Α. ἐὰν⁶ τύχῃ⁷ μόνον
αὐτῆς, ἐπὶ τὸν μάνην πεσεῖται καὶ ψόφος
ἔσται πάνυ πολύς. Β. πρὸς θεῶν, τῷ κοττάβῳ
πρόσεστι καὶ Μάνης τις ὥσπερ οἰκέτης;

καὶ μετ' ὀλίγα·

ᾧ δεῖ λαβὼν τὸ ποτήριον δεῖξον νόμῳ.
Α. αὐλητικῶς δεῖ καρκινοῦν⁸ τοὺς δακτύλους
οἶνόν τε μικρὸν ἐγχέαι καὶ μὴ πολύν·
b ἔπειτ' ἀφήσεις.⁹ Β. τίνα τρόπον; Α. δεῦρο¹⁰ βλέπε·
τοιουτονί.¹¹ Β. Πόσειδον, ὡς ὑψοῦ¹² σφόδρα.
Α. οὕτω ποιήσεις. Β. ἀλλ' ἐγὼ μὲν σφενδόνῃ
οὐκ ἂν ἐφικοίμην αὐτός'. Α. ἀλλὰ μάνθανε.

Ἀγκυλοῦντα γὰρ δεῖ σφόδρα τὴν χεῖρα εὐρύθμως
πέμπειν τὸν κότταβον, ὡς Δικαίαρχός φησιν καὶ
Πλάτων δ' ἐν τῷ Διὶ¹³ Κακουμένῳ. παρακελεύεται

---

¹ Supply καὶ μῆλα θήσω?
² Kaibel (κοτταβιῇ): κοτταβιει τε τινα A, κοτταβιῇ τινα CE.
³ 'πιδείξω 487 d.   ⁴ Kaibel: καθ' ὅσον ACE.
⁵ ποιήσῃ . . . πλάστιγγα added by Toup (cf. Schol. Luc.
Lexiph. 3).   ⁶ 487 e: τοῦτο ἂν ACE.
⁷ ACE, Schol. Luc.: θίγῃ Jacobs.
⁸ CE: δικαρκινοῦν A.   ⁹ CE: ἔπειτα φήσεις A.
¹⁰ δεῦρο om. C.   ¹¹ Kaibel: τοιοῦτον ACE.
¹² CE: ὑψους A.
¹³ τῷ repeated after Διὶ deleted by Kaibel.

and five . . .[a] B. But what for ? It seems silly.
How will you ' shoot cottabos ' ? A. I will show you
step by step ; whoever when he shoots at the pan
causes the cottabos to fall— B. The pan ? What
pan ? Do you mean that little thing that lies up
there on top, the tiny platter ? A. Yes, that's the
pan—he becomes the winner. B. How is one going
to know that ? A. Why, if he just hits it, it will
fall on the *Manês*,[b] and there will be a very loud
clatter. B. In the gods' name, tell me, has the
cottabos got a *Manês*, attending it like any slave ? "
And after a few lines he goes on : " B. Take the
cup and show me how you do it. A. Like a good
flute-player, you've got to curl your fingers round the
handle, pour in a little wine—not too much !—and
then shoot. B. But how ? A. Watch me. Like
this. B. Poseidon, what a high shot you've made ! [c]
A. That's the way you must do it. B. But I
couldn't get as high as that with a sling. A. Then
practise it."

One must, indeed, bend the wrist very gracefully
in shooting the cottabos, as Dicaearchus says,[d] and
Plato, too, in *Zeus Outraged*.[e] In that play someone

---

[a] Schweighäuser, comparing 667 d (p. 74), deleted πέντε and
filled out the line with καὶ πέμμα καὶ τράγημα, " a cake and
dessert." See Eubulus below, 668 d (p. 82), from which
one may possibly render here " I will set up five eggs and
apples as a prize." See the story of Aenesidemus, who
ironically sent cottabos prizes to Gelon, tyrant of Syracuse,
for anticipating him in the conquest of a neighbouring city,
Aristot. *Rhet.* i. 12. 30 and Cope's note.

[b] A small statuette representing a slave; vol. v. p. 169
note b; above, p. 69 note b.

[c] Apparently Antiphanes had in mind a pan suspended
from the ceiling (above, p. 71 note b).

[d] F.H.G. ii. 247.

[e] Kock i. 613.

δέ τις τῷ Ἡρακλεῖ μὴ σκληρὰν ἔχειν τὴν χεῖρα
c μέλλοντα κοτταβίζειν. ἐκάλουν δ' ἀπ' ἀγκύλης
τὴν τοῦ κοττάβου πρόεσιν διὰ τὸ ἐπαγκυλοῦν[1] τὴν
δεξιὰν χεῖρα ἐν τοῖς ἀποκοτταβισμοῖς. οἱ δὲ
ποτηρίου εἶδος τὴν ἀγκύλην φασί.[2] Βακχυλίδης ἐν
Ἐρωτικοῖς·

εὖτε τὴν ἀπ' ἀγκύλης ἵησι τοῖσδε τοῖς νεανίαις,
λευκὸν ἀντείνασα πῆχυν.

καὶ Αἰσχύλος δ' ἐν Ὀστολόγοις ἀγκυλητοὺς λέγει
κοττάβους διὰ τούτων·

Εὐρύμαχος, οὔ τις ἄλλος,[3] οὐδὲν ἥσσονας[4]
ὕβριζ' ὑβρισμοὺς οὐκ ἐναισίους[5] ἐμοί.
ἦν μὲν γὰρ αὐτῷ σκοπὸς[6] ἀεὶ τοὐμὸν[7] κάρα,
d τοῦ δ' ἀγκυλητοὺς κοσσάβους ἐπίσκοπος[8]
†ἐκτεμῶν†[9] ἡβῶσα χεὶρ ἐφίετο.

ὅτι δὲ ἆθλον προὔκειτο τῷ εὖ προεμένῳ τὸν κότταβον προείρηκε μὲν καὶ ὁ Ἀντιφάνης· ᾠὰ γάρ
ἐστι καὶ πεμμάτια καὶ τραγήματα. ὁμοίως δὲ
διεξέρχονται Κηφισόδωρος ἐν Τροφωνίῳ καὶ Καλ-
λίας ἢ Διοκλῆς ἐν Κύκλωπι καὶ Εὔπολις Ἕρμιππός

---

[1] Schol. Ar.: ἀπαγκυλοῦν ACE.　　　　[2] CE: φησι A.
[3] Sidgwick: οὐκάλλοσ A.
[4] Musurus: ἧσσον A, ἡσσόνως Nauck, ἧσσον αὖ Kaibel.
[5] Porson: αινεσιουσ A.　　　[6] Dobree: κότταβος A.
[7] Petit: τοῦ μεν A.
[8] Kaibel: του δ' ἀγκυλητοῦ κοσσάβιόσ εστινσκοπος A, τοῖς
δ' ἀγκυλητοῖς κοσσάβοις ἐπίσκοπα Dobree.
[9] ἔκτεμων A: ὅσσων ἐμῶν Dobree.

74

directs Heracles not to hold his wrist stiffly when he
is going to shoot. And so they spoke of the throw-
ing of the cottabos as " the bend-toss " (*ankylê*)
because in playing cottabos-games they bent the
right wrist.[a] But others say that *ankylê* is a kind
of cup. Bacchylides in his *Love-Songs* [b] : " When,
raising high her white arm, she makes the ' bend-
toss ' for these young men." And Aeschylus in *The
Bone-Collectors* even speaks of " bended cottabi " in
these lines [c] : " Eurymachus—'twas no one else—
laid just as strong and outrageous insults upon me.
For my head was ever his target, and at it with sure
aim his lusty arm let fly bended cottabi. . . ."[d] That
a prize was offered for skilful tossing of the cottabos
has already been stated by Antiphanes [e] ; they are
eggs, cakes, nuts, and raisins. Similar details are
given by Cephisodorus in *Trophonius*,[f] Callias (or
Diocles) in *The Cyclopes*,[g] Eupolis,[h] and Hermippus

---

[a] *Cf.* 782 d-e (vol. v. pp. 42-44).

[b] *P.L.G.*⁴ iii. 577-578, Edmonds iii. 214, *cf.* vol. v. p. 44.

[c] *T.G.F.*² 58 ; from a satyric drama. For Eurymachus,
one of Penelope's suitors often mentioned, see *Od.* xviii. 349,
xxii. 69-88, Athen. 17 b (vol. i. p. 74).

[d] *i.e.* he tossed the missiles with the same form that
cottabos-players employed. Dobree's emendation would
mean " With the bended cottabos-toss his lusty arm let fly
missiles that hit my eyes with sure aim." But ὅσσων ἐμῶν,
which Sidgwick adopts, seems a rather violent change for
ἐκτεμών (*sic*) (see critical note 9). Perhaps καὶ ἐπὶ γέλωτι or
ἐπὶ γέλῳ lurks here, *cf. Od.* xviii. 349-350 Εὐρύμαχος . . .
κερτομέων 'Οδυσῆα· γέλω δ' ἑτάροισιν ἔτευχε.

[e] *Cf.* above, 666 f (p. 73 and note *a*), where, unfortun-
ately, the pertinent words are missing.

[f] Kock i. 801.

[g] *Ibid.* 696.

[h] *Ibid.* 278, from *The Dyers*, Βάπται, according to Runkel
and Kock ; *cf.* Schol. Aristoph. *Peace* 1244 Εὔπολις ἐν
Βάπταις λέγει " χαλκῷ περὶ κοττάβῳ," above, p. 68.

τε ἐν τοῖς Ἰάμβοις. τὸ δὲ καλούμενον κατακτὸν
e κοττάβιον τοιοῦτόν ἐστιν· λυχνίον ἐστὶν ὑψηλόν,
ἔχον τὸν μάνην καλούμενον, ἐφ᾽ ὃν[1] τὴν καταβαλ-
λομένην ἔδει πεσεῖν πλάστιγγα· ἐντεῦθεν δὲ πίπτειν[2]
εἰς λεκάνην ὑποκειμένην πληγεῖσαν τῷ κοττάβῳ[3]·
" καί τις ἦν ἀκριβὴς εὐχέρεια[4] τῆς βολῆς." μνημονεύει δὲ τοῦ μάνου Νικοχάρης ἐν Λάκωσιν.

Ἕτερον δ᾽ ἐστὶν εἶδος παιδιᾶς τῆς ἐν λεκάνῃ.
αὕτη δ᾽ ὕδατος πληροῦται, ἐπινεῖ δὲ[5] ἐπ᾽ αὐτῆς[5]
ὀξύβαφα κενά, ἐφ᾽ ἃ βάλλοντες τὰς λατάγας ἐκ
καρχησίων ἐπειρῶντο καταδύειν· ἀνῃρεῖτο δὲ τὰ
f κοττάβια[6] ὁ πλείω καταδύσας. Ἀμειψίας Ἀποκοτ-
ταβίζουσιν·

ἡ Μανία, φέρ᾽ ὀξύβαφα καὶ κανθάρους
καὶ τὸν ποδανιπτῆρ᾽, ἐγχέασα θὔδατος.

Κρατῖνος ἐν Νεμέσει·

τὸ δὲ κοττάβιον[7] προθέντα συμποτικοῖσι[8] νόμοις
τοῖς ἐπινέουσιν ὀξυβάφοισιν[9] ἐμβάλλειν ποτόν,
τῷ[10] δὲ βαλόντι[11] πλεῖστα νέμειν[12] τύχης τόδ᾽ ἆθλον.[13]

Ἀριστοφάνης Δαιταλεῦσιν·

[1] οὗ Schol. Luc., ᾧ Schol. Aristoph.
[2] δὲ πίπτειν Kaibel, δ᾽ ἐμπίπτειν Schol. Aristoph.: δ᾽
ἔπιπτεν A.
[3] πληγεῖσαν τῷ κοττάβῳ placed above, after πλάστιγγα, by
Dobree and Meineke.
[4] Schol. Aristoph.: εὐχειρία A.
[5] δὲ Kaibel: τε A. ἐπέκειτο δὲ ἐπ᾽ αὐτῇ Schol. Aristoph.
[6] CE: κοττάβεια corrected to κοττάβια A.
[7] Gulick: κοττάβῳ A.
[8] Kaibel: προθέντασ ἐν πατρικοῖσι A.
[9] Herwerden: τὸ κεινεου ὀξυβάφοισ A.
[10] Kock (βάλλειν τῷ ποτῷ Bothe): βάλλειν μὲν τῷ πόντῳ A.
[11] Meineke: βάλλοντι A.   [12] Kock: νέμω πλεῖστα A.
[13] Dalechamps, Kaibel: τὸ δ᾽ ἆθλον A.

In his *Iambic Verses.*[a] Now the " descending " cottabos, as it is called, is of the following sort[b] : it is a high lampstand[c] holding the so-called *Manês,*[d] upon which the descending scale-pan[e] was designed to fall; thence the scale-pan, when struck by the cottabos-throw, fell into a basin lying beneath. " And an accurate dexterity was needed for the throw." [f] The *Manês* is mentioned by Nicochares in *Laconians.*[g]

There is, however, another variety of the game, played with a basin. This basin is filled with water, and empty cruets float on the surface; these they would try to sink by tossing the wine-drops upon them from their cups ; the player who sank the most won the prizes. Ameipsias in *Playing at Cottabos*[h] : " You, Mania, hand me vinegar-cruets and wine-cups and the foot-basin after you have poured into it some water." Cratinus in *Nemesis*[i] : " Setting up the cottabos-prize according to the rules of the symposium, toss the wine on the floating cruets, and to the man who hits the most award this prize of good luck." Aristophanes in *Men of Dinner-*

[a] Kock i. 247-248.
[b] *Cf.* Schol. Lucian, *Lexiph.* 3.
[c] Supply " which can be raised and lowered," *cf.* 666 e ἀναγόμενα πάλιν τε συμπίπτοντα, Schol. Aristoph. λυχνίον ἀγόμενον (*sic*) πάλιν τε συμπίπτον.
[d] Page 73 note *b*, Hayley, *op. cit.* p. 77, *cf.* p. 79, Athen. 487 d (vol. v. p. 166).
[e] Or disk which, according to Hayley, was balanced on the top of the rod.
[f] An anonymous trochaic verse, reading εὐχέρεια for εὐχειρία, *cf.* Luc. *Amores* 11 τῆς Πραξιτέλους εὐχερείας.
[g] Kock i. 772.
[h] Kock i. 670 ; see vol. v. p. 89 note *h*.
[i] Kock i. 50. The garbled text offers but a faint glimmer of sense.

"ἔγνωκ'· ἐγὼ δὲ χαλκίον¹ (τοῦτ' ἐστὶν κοτ-
668   τάβειον ἱστάναι) καὶ μυρρίνας."

Ἕρμιππος Μοίραις·

χλανίδες δ' οὖλαι καταβέβληνται,
θώρακα δ' ἅπας ἐμπερονᾶται,
κνημὶς δὲ περὶ σφυρὸν ἀρθροῦται,²
βλαύτης δ' οὐδεὶς ἔτ' ἔρως³ λευκῆς,
ῥάβδον δ' ὄψει τὴν κοτταβικὴν
ἐν τοῖς ἀχύροισι κυλινδομένην,
μάνης δ' οὐδὲν⁴ λατάγων ἀίει·⁵
τὴν δὲ τάλαιναν πλάστιγγ' ἂν⁶ ἴδοις
παρὰ τὸν στροφέα τῆς κηπαίας
ἐν τοῖσι κορήμασιν οὖσαν.

Ἀχαιὸς δ' ἐν Λίνῳ περὶ τῶν Σατύρων λέγων
φησίν·

ῥιπτοῦντες, ἐκβάλλοντες, ἀγνύντες, τί μ' οὐ⁷
b   λέγοντες; "ὦ κάλλιστον Ἡρακλεῖ λάταξ."

τοῦτο δὲ "λέγοντες" παρ' ὅσον τῶν ἐρωμένων
ἐμέμνηντο ἀφιέντες ἐπ' αὐτοῖς τοὺς λεγομένους
κοσσάβους. διὸ καὶ Σοφοκλῆς ἐν Ἰνάχῳ Ἀφρο-
δισίαν εἴρηκε τὴν λάταγα·

ξανθὴ δ' Ἀφροδισία λάταξ⁸
πᾶσιν⁹ ἐπεκτύπει¹⁰ δόμοις.

καὶ Εὐριπίδης ἐν Πλεισθένει·

¹ Musurus: χάλκειον A.
² Porson: κνημιδεσ δὲ . . . ἀρθροῦνται A.
³ Jacobs: ἐτέρωσ A.   ⁴ Cf. 487 e: οὐδε A.
⁵ Jacobs: αει A.   ⁶ ἂν om. A: cf. 487 e.
⁷ τί μου A.   ⁸ Musurus: αλάταξ A.
⁹ Heath: παισιν A.
¹⁰ Nauck: ἐπεκύπτει A, ἐπικτυπεῖ Meineke.

ville [a] : " That's all *he* knows ; but *I* know the bronze rod " (this means setting up the cottabos-stand) " and the myrtle-boughs." Hermippus in *The Fates* [b] : " Woolly cloaks are now laid aside and every man is buckling on his breastplate ; the greave is fitted round the shin, and there's no desire left for the white-polished shoe ; you will see the shaft of the cottabos rolling neglected in the chaff, and *Manês* pays no attention to wine-drops tossed at him ; as for the unhappy pan, you may see that resting beside the socket of the back door in a pile of sweepings." Achaeus, speaking of the satyrs in *Linus*, says [c] : " Hurling, tossing, crashing—what did they not say of me ? ' Nicely, now, oh wine-drop, for Heracles.' " This phrase, " say of me," is used because the players mentioned the names of their lovers when they tossed the so-called cossabi for them.[d] Hence Sophocles in *Inachus* connects the wine-drop with Aphrodite [e] : " Aphrodite's golden wine-drop echoed through the whole house." So Euripides in *Pleisthenes* [f] : " The

[a] Kock i. 444. A boy who prefers the gay life contrasts that with the ways of his virtuous brother (Kock). Myrtleboughs were placed round the basin (λεκάνη), perhaps to prevent the floor from becoming too sloppy ; Schol. Aristoph. *Pac.* 1243 καὶ κύκλῳ τῆς λεκάνης μυρσίνας.

[b] Kock i. 237, *cf.* Athen. 487 e (vol. v. p. 168).

[c] *T.G.F.*[2] 752, from a satyric drama ; the quotation is obviously incomplete, and none of the proposed emendations are convincing. Heracles seems to be the darling of the satyrs, who are playing at cottabos for his favours.

[d] Or, " to win them." *Cf.* Theocr. xiv. 18-20 (though the cottabos does not enter into the picture) ἤδη δὲ προϊόντος (*sc.* τοῦ πότου) ἔδοξ᾽ ἐπιχεῖσθαι ἄκρατον ὦτινος εἰπεῖν. ἀμὲς μὲν φωνεῦντες (=λέγοντες above) ἐπίνομες. Callim. *Epigr.* 31 (L.C.L. 158) ἔγχει καὶ πάλιν εἰπὲ " Διοκλέος."

[e] *T.G.F.*[2] 190.

[f] *T.G.F.*[2] 557.

πολὺς δὲ κοσσάβων ἀραγμὸς Κύπριδος
προσῳδὸν ἀχεῖ μέλος ἐν δόμοισιν.

καὶ Καλλίμαχος δέ φησι·

πολλοὶ καὶ φιλέοντες 'Ακόντιον ἧκαν ἔραζε[1]
c   οἰνοπόται Σικελὰς ἐκ κυλίκων λάταγας.

῏Ην δέ τι καὶ ἄλλο κοτταβίων εἶδος προτιθέμενον
ἐν ταῖς παννυχίσιν, οὗ μνημονεύει Καλλίμαχος[2] ἐν
Παννυχίδι διὰ τούτων·

ὁ δ' ἀγρυπνήσας . . . μέχρι τῆς κορώνης[3]
τὸν πυραμοῦντα λήψεται καὶ[3] τὰ κοττάβεια
καὶ τῶν παρουσῶν ἣν θέλει χὸν θέλει[3] φιλήσει.

ἐγίνετο δὲ καὶ πεμμάτιά τινα ἐν ταῖς παννυχίσιν, ἐν
αἷς πλεῖστον ὅσον χρόνον διηγρύπνουν χορεύοντες·
καὶ διωνομάζετο τὰ πεμμάτια τότε χαρίσιοι[4] ἀπὸ
d τῆς τῶν ἀναιρουμένων χαρᾶς. μνημονεύει Εὔβουλος ἐν 'Αγκυλίωνι λέγων οὑτωσί·

καὶ γὰρ πάλαι πέττει[5] τὰ νικητήρια.

εἶθ' ἑξῆς φησιν·

ἐξεπήδησ'[6] ἀρτίως πέττουσα τὸν χαρίσιον.

---

[1] Schol. Aristoph.: ἔργαζε A.
[2] Wilamowitz: καλλιποσ A (sic).
[3] μέχρι τῆς κορώνης, καὶ, χὸν θέλει added from Berl. Pap.
13417 B.
[4] Schweighäuser (cf. 646 b, Suid. s. ἀνάστατοι and χαρίσιον):
χαρισιαι A, χαρίσια CE.
[5] πεττι A.   [6] ἐξεπήδησα A (so C, om. ἀρτίως).

---

[a] Schneider frag. 102, A. W. Mair (L.C.L.) 214 ; cf.
Schol. Aristoph. Pac. 1243, Athen. 479 d (vol. v. p. 122),
666 b, 668 e.

loud clattering of Cypris's cossabi rings out their
harmonious tune in the house." And Callimachus
says also [a] : " Many were the drinkers of wine who
in their love of Acontius let fall from their cups the
Sicilian wine-drops upon the ground."

But there was still another class of prizes, called
cottabia, which were set up at the night-festivals, and
are mentioned by Callimachus in *The Vigil* in these
lines [b] : " He that stays awake until the very end [c]
shall receive the cake and the prizes and shall kiss
anyone he likes of the girls in the party and any
man he likes." Certain kinds of small cakes were
to be had at the night-festivals, in which they used
to keep themselves awake the longest possible time
by dancing ; and these cakes were widely known
at that time as *charisioi* [d] because the winners were
glad to get them. Eubulus mentions them in
Ancylion, speaking as follows [e] : " Why ! She has
been baking the prizes for victory a long time."
And farther along Eubulus says : " I jumped just
now when I was baking the glad-to-get-it." And

---

[b] Frag. 2 Pfeiffer. The metre is the syncopated iambic
trimeter. Kock iii. 378, assigning the verses to a very shadowy
figure, Callippus (critical note 2). Porson had already proposed to read καὶ Ἵππαρχος, *cf.* below, 691 c (p. 202). It would
appear that in Callimachus's time cottabia had become a
general term for " favours " given at a party. The game itself
seems to have been no longer played, at least in Alexandria,
Smith, *Dict. Ant.* i. 558.

[c] Lit. " up to the crown " or " limit," Hesych. *s.* κορώνη·
καὶ τὸ ἄκρον τοῦ τόξου. Poseidippus *ap.* Athen. 414 d-e
(vol. iv. p. 376) plays on these two senses of κορώνη: τὸν
φαγεῖν βορόν, οἷα κορώνην παννυχικήν. Did the word also
suggest satiety ? *Cf.* the tag ἄχρι κόρου, Demosth. xix. 187.

[d] " Glad-to-get-'em," Athen. 646 b (vol. vi. p. 489 note c).

[e] Kock ii. 165 ; Athen. 646 b.

ὅτι δὲ καὶ φίλημα ἦν ἆθλον ἑξῆς λέγει ὁ Εὔβουλος·

εἶεν, γυναῖκες· νῦν ὅπως τὴν νύχθ' ὅλην
ἐν τῇ δεκάτῃ τοῦ παιδίου χορεύσετε·
θήσω δὲ νικητήριον τρεῖς ταινίας
καὶ μῆλα πέντε καὶ φιλήματ' ἐννέα.

"Ότι δὲ ἐσπούδαστο[1] παρὰ τοῖς Σικελιώταις ὁ
e κότταβος δῆλον ἐκ τοῦ καὶ οἰκήματα ἐπιτήδεια τῇ
παιδιᾷ κατασκευάζεσθαι, ὡς ἱστορεῖ Δικαίαρχος ἐν
τῷ περὶ Ἀλκαίου. οὐκ ἀπεικότως οὖν οὐδ' ὁ
Καλλίμαχος Σικελὴν τὴν λάταγα προσηγόρευσεν.
μνημονεύει τῶν λατάγων[2] καὶ τῶν κοττάβων καὶ ὁ
Χαλκοῦς[3] καλούμενος Διονύσιος ἐν τοῖς Ἐλεγείοις
διὰ τούτων·

κότταβον ἐνθάδε σοι τρίτον ἑστάναι οἱ δυσέρωτες
f   ἡμεῖς προστίθεμεν γυμνασίῳ Βρομίου,
κώρυκον.   οἱ δὲ παρόντες ἐνείρετε[4] χεῖρας
    ἅπαντες
ἐς σφαίρας[5] κυλίκων· καὶ πρὶν ἐκεῖνον ἰδεῖν,[6]
ὄμματι βηματίσαισθε[7] τὸν αἰθέρα τὸν κατὰ
    κλίνην,[8]
εἰς ὅσον αἱ λάταγες χωρίον ἐκτατέαι.[9]

Ἐπὶ τούτοις ὁ Οὐλπιανὸς ᾔτει πιεῖν μεγάλῃ
κύλικι, ἐπιλέγων ἐκ τῶν αὐτῶν ἐλεγείων καὶ τόδε·

---

[1] A : ἐσπούδασται σφόδρα Schol. Aristoph.
[2] λαταγῶν A.   [3] Musurus, C: χαλκὸς A.
[4] Musurus: ενειρεται A.   [5] εσφαίρασ A.
[6] ἀπ' οἴνον ἰεῖν (?) Bergk.

that a kiss was also the prize Eubulus says farther along : " Now then, ladies ; be sure you dance the livelong night on this, the baby's tenth day.ª I will set up, as prize for victory, three ribbons,ᵇ five apples, and nine kisses."

That the cottabos was popular among the Sicilian Greeks is proved by the custom of constructing rooms especially designed for the game ; this is recorded by Dicaearchus in his treatise *On Alcaeus.*ᶜ And so, with good reason, too, Callimachus has called the wine-drop " Sicilian." Dionysius Chalcûs (" the Bronze ") in his *Elegies* mentions the wine-drops and the cottabos-games in these lines ᵈ : " We, the love-sick, add a third cottabos prize to stand for you here in the Wine-god's gymnasium ᵉ; a punching-bag it is. All of you in the company must insert your hands in the cups you use as balls ; and before you see it,ᶠ measure with your eyes the air by your couch and see over how much space the wine-drops must reach."

Upon this Ulpian demanded a drink from a large cup,ᵍ capping from the same elegies with the follow-

---

ª The child received his name at a family festival ten days after birth.

ᵇ Or possibly, ribbon-fish, Athen. 325 f (vol. iii. p. 464).

ᶜ *F.H.G.* ii. 246.

ᵈ *P.L.G.*⁴ ii. 263, Diehl i. 75, Buecheler, *Jahrb. f. Phil.* 1875, 125. For the name Dionysius Chalcûs see below, 669 d.

ᵉ *i.e.* the symposium, here likened to the part of the gymnasium used for ball-playing (σφαιριστήριον). The prize is a sack of wine, suggesting a punching-bag.

ᶠ The bag? Bergk's conjecture is plausible (critical note 5): " before tossing the wine."

ᵍ See vol. iii. p. 145, vol. v. p. 251.

---

⁷ A : βηματίσασθε Musurus. ⁸ κλεινην Α.

⁹ Buecheler : ἐκτέταται Α.

669 " ὕμνους οἰνοχοεῖν ἐπιδέξια σοί τε καὶ ἡμῖν
τόν τε[1] σὸν[2] ἀρχαῖον τηλεδαπόν[3] τε φίλον
εἰρεσίῃ γλώσσης ἀποπέμψομεν εἰς μέγαν αἶνον
τοῦδ᾽ ἐπὶ συμποσίου· δεξιότης τε[4] λόγου
Φαίακος Μουσῶν ἐρέτας ἐπὶ σέλματα πέμπει.

—κατὰ γὰρ τὸν νεώτερον Κρατῖνον, ὃς ἐν Ὀμφάλ
φησίν·

πίνειν μένοντα τὸν καλῶς εὐδαίμονα
b κρεῖττον· μάχαι δ᾽ ἄλλοισι καὶ πόνοι μέλοι."—

πρὸς ὃν ὁ Κύνουλκος ἀεὶ τῷ Σύρῳ ἀντικορυσσό
μενος καὶ οὐδέποτε τῆς φιλονεικίας παυόμενος ἧ
εἶχε πρὸς αὐτόν, ἐπεὶ θόρυβος κατεῖχεν τὸ συμπό
σιον, ἔφη· " τίς οὗτος ὁ τῶν συρβηνέων[5] χορός
καὶ αὐτὸς δὲ τούτων τῶν ἐπῶν μεμνημένος τινα
ἐρῶ, ἵνα μὴ ὁ Οὐλπιανὸς βρενθύηται ὡς ἐκ τα
ἀποθέτων τοῖς Ὁμηρίδαις μόνος ἀνασπάσας τ
κοττάβεια·

ἀγγελίας ἀγαθῆς δεῦρ᾽ ἴτε πευσόμενοι[6]
c καὶ κυλίκων ἔριδας διαλύσατε καὶ κατάθεσθε
τὴν ξύνεσιν παρ᾽ ἐμοὶ καὶ τάδε μανθάνετε,

εἰς τὴν παροῦσαν ζήτησιν ἐπιτήδεια ὄντα. ὁρ

[1] A : τόνδε Musurus.
[2] σον A : τὸν (with τόνδε) Bergk.
[3] Casaubon : τηλεπαδον A.   [4] A : δὲ Bergk.
[5] Meineke (cf. Hesych. s.v.): συρβηναίων A here an
671 c.   [6] Casaubon : πεσσόμενοι A.

[a] P.L.G.[4] ii. 263, Diehl i. 75.
[b] See, on the clockwise practice in drinking and singing
152 d note a (vol. ii. p. 194), 432 e (vol. iv. p. 460), 463 f (vol.
p. 22).
[c] Cf. Dionysius Chalcûs in Athen. 443 d (vol. iv. p. 50

84

ing [a] : " Pour out like wine songs of praise for you and for us from left to right.[b] We shall send forth thine old friend, him from overseas, to high praise with the oarage of our tongues [c] at this symposium ; readiness of speech Phaeacian sends the Muses' oarsmen to the thwarts."—For, as the younger Cratinus says in Omphalê [d] : " It's better for him who is happily at ease to stay at home and drink ; let fights and fusses [e] worry other people." — In answer to Ulpian Cynulcus, who was always butting against the Syrian [f] and never gave up the malice which he bore toward him, said, after uproar began to prevail in the symposium : What is this cater-wauling band ? [g] I too remember some of these verses and will recite them, in order that Ulpian may not give himself airs for being the only one to snatch the prizes from the Homeridae in their recital of mysteries [h] : " Come hither and learn the good news, stop your quarrels over the cups, give your attention to me,[i] and learn what is to come "—for it fits in well with our present inquiry. For I see that the

οἶνον ἄγοντες ἐν εἰρεσίᾳ Διονύσου. On the allusion in " Phaea-cian " see the Index s.v.

[d] Kock ii. 290. This quotation is out of place. It should come after ὁ τῶν συρβηνέων χορός.

[e] Cf. Aristoph. Ach. 1071 ἰὼ πόνοι τε καὶ μάχαι καὶ Λάμαχοι! Bergk's πόνος for πόνοι, adopted by Kaibel, is wholly gratuitous.

[f] Ulpian came from Tyre, Introd. vol. i. p. xii.

[g] Lit. " band of pipers "; Hesych. s. συρβηνεύς· ἤτοι αὐλητής· σύρβη γὰρ ἡ αὐλοθήκη (flute-case). Below, 671 c, 697 e.

[h] Alluding to Plato, Phaedr. 252 B λέγουσι δὲ οἶμαί τινες Ὁμηριδῶν ἐκ τῶν ἀποθέτων ἐπῶν δύο ἔπη εἰς τὸν Ἔρωτα. Jowett rendered ἀποθέτων by " apocryphal." P.L.G.⁴ ii. 262, Diehl i. 74.

[i] Lit. " deposit your minds with me."

γὰρ καὶ τοὺς παῖδας ἤδη φέροντας ἡμῖν στεφάνους
καὶ μύρα. διὰ τί δὲ λέγονται, τῶν ἐστεφανωμένων
ἐὰν λύωνται οἱ στέφανοι, ὅτι ἐρῶσιν; τοῦτο γὰρ
ἐν παισὶ τὰ Καλλιμάχου ἀναγινώσκων ἐπιγράμ-
ματα, ὧν ἐστι καὶ τοῦτο, ἐπεζήτουν μαθεῖν, εἰπόντος τοῦ Κυρηναίου·

d   τὰ δὲ ῥόδα φυλλοβολεῦντα
τῶνδρὸς ἀπὸ στεφάνων πάντ' ἐγένοντο χαμαί.

σὸν οὖν ἐστιν, ὦ μουσικώτατε, τὴν χιλιέτη μου
ταύτην ζήτησιν ἀπολύσασθαι, Δημόκριτε, καὶ διὰ
τί οἱ ἐρῶντες στεφανοῦσι τὰς τῶν ἐρωμένων θύρας."

Καὶ ὁ Δημόκριτος " ἀλλ' ἵνα κἀγώ, φησίν, μνη-
μονεύσω τῶν τοῦ Χαλκοῦ ποιητοῦ καὶ ῥήτορος
Διονυσίου—Χαλκοῦς δὲ προσηγορεύθη διὰ τὸ
συμβουλεῦσαι Ἀθηναίοις χαλκῷ νομίσματι χρῆσα-
e σθαι, καὶ τὸν λόγον τοῦτον ἀνέγραψε Καλλίμαχος
ἐν τῇ τῶν Ῥητορικῶν Ἀναγραφῇ[1]—λέξω τι καὶ
αὐτὸς ἐκ τῶν Ἐλεγείων· σὺ δέ, ὦ Θεόδωρε (τοῦτο
γάρ σου τὸ κύριον ὄνομα),

          δέχου τήνδε προπινομένην
τὴν ἀπ' ἐμοῦ ποίησιν. ἐγὼ δ' ἐπιδέξια πέμπω
σοὶ πρώτῳ Χαρίτων ἐγκεράσας χάριτας.
καὶ σὺ λαβὼν τόδε δῶρον ἀοιδὰς[2] ἀντιπρόπιθι,
συμπόσιον κοσμῶν καὶ τὸ σὸν εὖ θέμενος.

---

¹ Musurus : απογραφῇ A.   ² δωροσαοιδασ A.

ᵃ Anth. Pal. xii. 134, Wilam. 64, A. W. Mair (L.C.L.)
166 (of a guest) ἕλκος ἔχω, " had a wound," i.e. unhappy
love.
  ᵇ Perhaps said in allusion to Plato, Rep. 621 D ἐν τῇ
χιλιέτει πορείᾳ.
  ᶜ Frag. 100 d 24, see A. W. Mair (L.C.L.) 12. Phot. s.
Θουριομάντεις calls him Χαλκιδεύς, " from Chalcis."
86

slaves are by this time bringing us wreaths and perfumes. Why do people say that if the wreaths on
people who wear them are broken up, they must
be in love ? For I was very eager to learn the meaning of this when I was a boy in school reading the
epigrams of Callimachus, among which is the following ; for the poet of Cyrene says [a] : " And the roses,
shedding their petals, all fell from his wreaths to the
ground." It is therefore your task, Democritus,
most devoted servant of the Muses, to free me from
this thousand-year inquiry [b] of mine, and explain
why people in love place wreaths on their lovers'
doors.

And Democritus said : In order that I, also, may
mention the verses of the poet and orator Dionysius
Chalcûs—he was called Chalcûs because he advised
the Athenians to adopt a bronze (*chalcos*) currency,
and this statement is recorded [c] by Callimachus in his
Register of Oratory—I will in my turn quote from
the *Elegies* [d] : " Receive," Theodorus (for that is
indeed your true name [e]), " this poem pledged as a
toast from me. I send it on its right course [f] to thee
first of our company, mixing in the cup of the
Graces the graces of friendship.[g] Take this gift
and pledge us with answering songs, adorning our
symposium and ordering well thine own prosperity."

[d] *P.L.G.*[4] ii. 263, Diehl i. 74.
[e] His nickname throughout has been Cynulcus, Dog
(Cynic)-Leader, 692 b.
[f] Lit. " from left to right." On songs and the capping of
verses see Reitzenstein, *Epigram u. Skolion* 24-28, and vol. vi.
p. 246 note *a*. For the cup (ᾠδός) which accompanied the
song see Athen. 503 e (vol. v. p. 256).
[g] *Cf.* Simias Rhod. (*Anth. Pal.* vii. 22) ἦν ὁ μελιχρὸς
(Sophocles) ἤσκησεν Μουσῶν ἄμμιγα καὶ Χαρίτων.

f φὴς οὖν " διὰ τί, τῶν ἐστεφανωμένων ἐὰν λύηται ὁ
στέφανος, ἐρᾶν λέγονται ; " " πότερον ὅτι ὁ ἔρως
τοῦ τῶν ἐρώντων ἤθους περιαιρεῖται τὸν κόσμον,
διὰ τοῦτο τὴν[1] τοῦ ἐπιφανοῦς κόσμου περιαίρεσιν
φρυκτόν τινα," φησὶ Κλέαρχος ἐν πρώτῳ Ἐρωτικῶν, " καὶ σημεῖον νομίζουσιν τοῦ καὶ τὸν τοῦ
ἤθους κόσμον περιῃρῆσθαι τοὺς τοιούτους. ἢ
670 καθάπερ ἐπὶ τῆς μαντικῆς ἄλλα πολλά, καὶ τοῦτο
σημειοῦνταί τινες; ὁ γὰρ ἐκ τοῦ στεφάνου κόσμος
οὐδὲν ἔχων μόνιμον σημεῖόν ἐστι πάθους ἀβεβαίου
μὲν κεκαλλωπισμένου δέ. τοιοῦτος δ' ἐστὶν ὁ
ἔρως· οὐδένες γὰρ μᾶλλον τῶν ἐν τῷ ἐρᾶν ὄντων
καλλωπίζονται· εἰ μὴ ἄρα ἡ φύσις οἱονεί τι δαι-
μόνιον δικαίως βραβεύουσα τῶν πραγμάτων ἕκαστον οἴεται δεῖν τοὺς ἐρῶντας μὴ στεφανοῦσθαι
πρὶν κρατήσωσιν τοῦ ἔρωτος· τοῦτο δ' ἐστὶν ὅταν
κατεργασάμενοι τὸν ἐρώμενον ἀπαλλαγῶσιν τῆς
ἐπιθυμίας. τὴν ἀφαίρεσιν οὖν τοῦ στεφάνου σημεῖον τοῦ ἔτι ἐν τῷ διαγωνίζεσθαι εἶναι ποιούμεθα.
b ἢ ὁ Ἔρως αὐτὸς οὐκ ἐῶν καθ' αὑτοῦ στεφανοῦσθαι
καὶ ἀνακηρύττεσθαι τῶν μὲν τὸν στέφανον περιαι-
ρεῖ,[2] τοῖς δὲ λοιποῖς ἐνδίδωσιν αἴσθησιν μηνύων ὅτι
ἡττῶνται ὑπὸ αὐτοῦ· δι' ὃ ἐρᾶν οἱ λοιποὶ τοὺς
τοιούτους φασίν. ἢ ὅτι λύεται μὲν πᾶν τὸ δεδε-

---

[1] Schweighäuser: διὰ τὸ πρὸς τὴν Α.
[2] CE: περιαιρεῖσθαι Α.

---

[a] Rohde, *Gr. Roman*[3], 62-63 note 2.
[b] *F.H.G.* ii. 315 ; for similar balderdash see Athen.
553 e (vol. v. p. 514).

You ask, then, why is it that if the wreath of those who wear them is broken, they are said to be in love ? [a] " Is it," says Clearchus in the first book of his *Amatoria*,[b] " for this reason : that just as love strips from the lover's character its orderly beauty, so, men believe, the stripping off of the visible beauty [c] becomes a kind of beacon and sign that lovers have had their beauty of character stripped off ? In other words, as in augury there are many signs to denote different things, so here certain persons are clearly marked as being in love ? For the beauty of a wreath, which has no abiding power, is the symbol of an emotion which, however adorned, is inconstant. Love is like that, since there are no persons in the world more given to adornment than those in love ; unless, of course, Nature, like some divine power giving righteous judgement in all things, believes that lovers ought not to put on wreaths before they have won their victory in love ; that is to say, when they have completed the conquest of the loved one and are freed from their desire. The withering [d] of the wreath, therefore, we regard as a sign that the struggle is still going on. Or can it be that the god of love himself, not suffering any to be crowned and proclaimed as victor over him,[e] strips the wreath from the lovers, while to all the rest he reveals their condition by disclosing that they have been overcome by him ; hence they are declared by these others to be in love. Or is it because

[c] Of the wreath ; κόσμος is used in two senses : (a) the order and composure of the soul (ἦθος) when undisturbed by emotion ; (b) the beauty of a wreath when fresh and untorn.

[d] Lit. " removal," " loss."

[e] *i.e.* Eros τύραννος θεῶν τε κἀνθρώπων (vol. vi. p. 32).

μένον,¹ ὁ δὲ ἔρως στεφανουμένων τινῶν δεσμός
ἐστιν (οὐθένες γὰρ ἄλλοι τῶν δεδεμένων περὶ τὸ
στεφανοῦσθαι σπουδάζουσιν πλὴν οἱ ἐρῶντες²), τὴν
τοῦ στεφάνου δὴ λύσιν³ σημεῖον τοῦ περὶ τὸν ἔρωτα
δεσμοῦ νομίζοντες ἐρᾶν φασιν τοὺς τοιούτους; ἢ
e διὰ τὸ πολλάκις τοὺς ἐρῶντας διὰ τὴν πτοίησιν, ὡς
ἔοικεν,⁴ στεφανουμένους περιρρεῖν⁵ αὐτῶν⁶ τὸν στέφανον, ἀντιστρέφομεν τῇ ὑπονοίᾳ τὸ πάθος, ὡς οὐκ
ἄν ποτε τοῦ στεφάνου περιρρέοντος εἰ μὴ ἤρων; ἢ
ὅτι ἀναλύσεις περὶ μόνους μάλιστα τοὺς ἐρῶντας
καὶ καταδεδεμένους γίνονται, τὴν δὲ τοῦ στεφάνου
ἀνάλυσιν καταδεδεμένων τινῶν εἶναι νομίζοντες
ἐρᾶν φασι τοὺς τοιούτους; καταδέδενται γὰρ οἱ
d ἐρῶντες. εἰ μὴ ἄρα διὰ τὸ κατεστέφθαι τῷ Ἔρωτι
τοὺς ἐρῶντας οὐκ ἐπίμονος αὐτῶν ὁ στέφανος γί-
νεται· χαλεπὸν γὰρ ἐπὶ μεγάλῳ⁷ καὶ θείῳ στεφάνῳ
μικρὸν καὶ τὸν τυχόντα μεῖναι.⁸ στεφανοῦσιν δὲ
τὰς τῶν ἐρωμένων θύρας ἤτοι τιμῆς χάριν, καθ-
απερεί τινος θεοῦ τὰ πρόθυρα,⁹ ἢ οὐ τοῖς ἐρωμένοις
ἀλλὰ τῷ Ἔρωτι ποιούμενοι τὴν τῶν στεφάνων
ἀνάθεσιν, ὡς¹⁰ τοῦ μὲν Ἔρωτος τὸν ἐρώμενον

---

¹ λύεται μὲν μόνον τὸ πρὶν δεδεμένον Rohde, λύεται μὲν οὐδὲν
πλὴν τὸ δεδεμένον Kaibel.
² ὁρῶντες C.
³ δὴ λύσιν Musurus: δήλωσιν ACE.
⁴ Here στεφάνου δήλωσιν σημεῖον . . . ὡς ἔοικεν repeated in A.
⁵ CE: περιρεῖν A, περιαιρεῖν Musurus.
⁶ A: αὐτῶν Rohde.   ⁷ μεγάλωι AE: γλώσσει C.
⁸ Meineke: θεῖναι ACE.
⁹ στεφανοῦσιν αὐτῶν after τὰ πρόθυρα in A deleted by
Meineke.
¹⁰ ὡς added by Rohde.

ᵃ Plato, Tim. 41 A (cited by Rohde) τὸ μὲν οὖν δεθὲν πᾶν

everything that is bound together can be broken up,[a] and just as love is a binding of certain persons wearing wreaths (for no other persons in bonds are so particular in wearing wreaths as those who are in love), so people regard the dissolution of the wreath as a sign of the love-bond, and assert that such persons are in love ? Or can it be, since lovers wearing wreaths often permit their wreaths to fall away, apparently in passionate excitement, that we suspect them of the passion, reasoning conversely, since we infer that the wreath would never drop its leaves if they were not in love ? Or is it because dissolution occurs chiefly in the case of lovers only, and persons bound by a spell, and so, believing the dissolution of the wreath is connected with persons who are, in a manner of speaking, bound by a spell, people assert that such persons are in love ?[b] For certainly lovers are spell-bound. Maybe it is because lovers are enwreathed by Eros that their wreath cannot last long ; for it would be difficult, of course, for any small creature, even, to stay long on a wreath that was portentously large. Further, they put wreaths on the doors of their beloved, either to do them honour, just as they wreath the portals of a god, or by way of dedicating the wreath, not to the beloved, but to

λυτόν. But Clearchus in his muddled logic means to say : " only that which has been bound can be broken apart," or better " what is broken apart must have been previously bound." See critical note 1.

[b] Rohde regarded this sentence as a mere repetition of the thought expressed above in c. But the change from δεδεμένοι to καταδεδεμένοι, of persons bound by a witch's spell, injects a new suspicion of magic. In the next sentence, the text of which is uncertain, the meaning seems to be that if a wreath, however large, cannot bear the weight of anything small, much less will it bear the heavy weight of Eros.

ἄγαλμα, τούτου δὲ ναὸν ὄντα τὴν οἴκησιν στεφανοῦσιν.[1] διὰ ταῦτα δὲ καὶ θύουσιν ἔνιοι ἐπὶ ταῖς τῶν
e ἐρωμένων θύραις· ἢ μᾶλλον ὑφ' ὧν οἴονταί τε καὶ
πρὸς ἀλήθειαν τὸν τῆς ψυχῆς κόσμον ἐσκύλευνται,
καὶ τούτοις καὶ τὸν τοῦ σώματος κόσμον ὑπὸ τοῦ
πάθους ἐξαγόμενοι, καὶ σκυλεύοντες ἑαυτούς, ἀνα-
τιθέασιν. πᾶς δ' ὁ ἐρῶν τοῦτο δρᾷ μὲν παρόντος,[2]
μὴ παρόντος δὲ τοῦ ἐρωμένου τῷ[3] ἐμποδὼν ποιεῖται
τὴν ἀνάθεσιν. ὅθεν Λυκοφρονίδης τὸν ἐρῶντα
ἐκεῖνον αἰπόλον ἐποίησε λέγοντα·

τόδ' ἀνατίθημί σοι ῥόδον,
καλὸν ἀνάθημα[4] καὶ πέδιλα καὶ κυνέαν
καὶ τὰν θηροφόνον λογχίδ', ἐπεί μοι νόος ἄλλᾳ
    κέχυται
f ἐπὶ τὰν Χάρισι φίλαν παῖδα καὶ καλάν."[5]

Ἀλλὰ μὴν καὶ ὁ ἱερώτατος Πλάτων ἐν ἑβδόμῳ
Νόμων πρόβλημά τι προβάλλει[6] στεφανωτικόν,
ὅπερ ἄξιόν ἐστιν ἐπιλύσασθαι, οὕτως λέγοντος τοῦ
φιλοσόφου· "μήλων τέ τινων διανομαὶ καὶ[7] στεφάνων πλείοσιν ἅμα καὶ ἐλάττοσιν ἁρμοττόντων
τῶν ἀριθμῶν τῶν αὐτῶν." ὁ μὲν Πλάτων οὕτως

---

[1] στεφανοῦσι(ν) Musurus: στεφάνου A. τὰ τῶν ἐρωμένων
πρόθυρα deleted by Wilamowitz after στεφανοῦσιν.
[2] παρόντος added by Dalechamps.
[3] τῷ Edmonds: τοῦ A.
[4] Bergk (ἄνθημα Casaubon): νόημα A.
[5] παῖδ' Ἀκακαλλίδα Wilamowitz.
[6] CE: προβάλλω A.   [7] καὶ Plato, CE: om. A.

---

[a] ἄγαλμα, image, statue, also means delight, darling.
[b] See critical note 3. Dalechamps read (with A) τοῦ

92

Eros, since the beloved is the image [a] of Eros, and so they wreath their dwelling as being his temple. For this reason some also offer sacrifice at the doors of their beloved. Or perhaps, rather, they think they have been robbed by their beloved, and as a matter of fact they *have* been stripped of their soul's adornment ; and so, to grace their beloved, and carried away by passion, they strip themselves of their bodily adornment as well, and dedicate it to them. Now every lover does this if his beloved be there ; if not, he makes the dedication to anyone who is.[b] Hence Lycophronides made his passionate goatherd say [c] : ' This rose I dedicate to thee—an offering fair—and my shoes and cap and this beast-slaying javelin ; for my thoughts stream elsewhere, to the maid dear to the Graces, and so fair.' "

But more : the most saintly Plato, in the seventh book of *Laws*,[d] propounds a problem relating to wreaths which is worth solving ; the philosopher says : " They distribute apples and wreaths, the same number being used to fit a larger or smaller number of persons." These are Plato's words.

ἐμποδών, and understood Clearchus to mean : The lover dedicates himself and his wreath to the beloved by his side ; if he is absent, he makes a dedication to him in some public place—taking τοῦ ἐμποδών equal to ἐμποδών alone. But this does not explain the last verse of Lycophronides. σοί may refer to a wayside Herm, but the story of Aesop in Philostr. *Vit. Apollon.* v. 15 does not help much : τί γὰρ δεῖ, ὦ Ἑρμῆ, ἔλεγε, στεφάνους πλέκειν καὶ ἀμελεῖν τῶν προβάτων, " what good does it do to plait wreaths while I neglect my sheep ? "

[c] *P.L.G.*⁴ iii. 634, Diehl ii. 157, Edmonds iii. 414. Clearchus has quoted Lycophronides before, 564 a-b (vol. vi. p. 46).

[d] 819 B, of arithmetical games in Egyptian education.

εἶπεν. ἐστὶν δ' ὃ λέγει τοιοῦτον· ἕνα βούλεσθαι
671 ἀριθμὸν εὑρεῖν, ᾧ[1] ἕως τοῦ τελευταίου εἰσελθόντος
ἐξ ἴσου πάντες ἕξουσιν ἤτοι μῆλα ἢ στεφάνους.
φημὶ οὖν τὸν τῶν ἑξήκοντα ἀριθμὸν εἰς ἓξ συμπότας
δύνασθαι τὴν ἰσότητα πληροῦν. οἶδα γὰρ ὅτι κατ'
ἀρχὰς ἐλέγομεν μὴ συνδειπνεῖν[2] τῶν πέντε γε
πλείους· ὅτι δ' ἡμεῖς ψαμμακόσιοι ἐσμὲν δῆλον. ὁ
οὖν τῶν[3] ἑξήκοντα ἀριθμὸς εἰς ἓξ συμπληρωθέντος[4]
τοῦ συμποσίου ἀρκέσει[5] οὕτως. εἰσῆλθεν εἰς τὸ
συμπόσιον ὁ πρῶτος καὶ ἔλαβεν στεφάνους ἑξή-
κοντα· ἐπεισελθόντι τῷ δευτέρῳ δίδωσιν τοὺς
b ἡμίσεις καὶ ἑκατέρῳ γίνονται τριάκοντα· καὶ τρίτῳ
ἐπεισελθόντι συνδιαιρούμενοι τοὺς πάντας ἐξ[6] εἴκοσιν ἔχουσι, τετάρτῳ πάλιν ὁμοίως κοινωνή-
σαντες ἐκ δεκαπέντε,[7] πέμπτῳ δὲ ἐκ δώδεκα καὶ
τῷ ἕκτῳ ἐκ δέκα. καὶ οὕτως ἰσότης ἀναπληροῦται
τῶν στεφάνων."

Ταῦτ' εἰπόντος τοῦ Δημοκρίτου ὁ Οὐλπιανὸς
ἀποβλέψας πρὸς τὸν Κύνουλκον

" οἵῳ μ' ὁ δαίμων, ἔφη, φιλοσόφῳ συνῴκισεν[8]·

—κατὰ τὸ Θεογνήτου τοῦ κωμῳδιοποιοῦ Φάσμα—

ἐπαρίστερ' ἔμαθες, ὦ πόνηρε, γράμματα·
3 ἀνέστροφέν[9] σου τὸν βίον τὰ βιβλία·

---

[1] CE: ὃσ A.
[2] A: οἶδα γὰρ ὅτι οὐκ ἐξῆν συνδειπνεῖν CE.
[3] τῶν added by Kaibel. *Cf.* above and Plato, *Legg.* 771 c.
[4] CE: τοὺσ συμπληρωθέντασ A.
[5] Rohde: ἄρξεται ACE.   [6] Casaubon: ξ A.
[7] γίνονται after δεκαπέντε in A deleted by Kaibel. κοινω-
νήσασιν ἐκ ιε γίνεται CE.
[8] Corrected in A from συνῴκησεν.
[9] Porson: ἀντέστροφέν A as at 104 c (vol. i. p. 446, where
critical note 1 should be corrected).

What he means is something like this : One number, of apples or of wreaths, is to be found such that all shall have an equal quantity down to the last person who enters. I mean, that is to say, that if we take the number sixty, it can be divided amongst six banqueters in such a way as to fulfil the condition of equality. I remember, to be sure, that at the beginning we said that no more than five persons should dine together [a] ; but everybody knows that we dine in numbers as the sand. Now the number sixty, if the banquet is manned to the number of six, will satisfy the condition just stated : the first man to enter the banquet receives sixty wreaths ; he, when the second man comes in, gives him half the number, so that each has thirty ; then, when the third enters, they divide up the whole number among themselves, and have twenty apiece ; with the fourth, in turn, they share likewise, fifteen apiece, with the fifth twelve apiece, and with the sixth ten. In this way equality in the number of wreaths is achieved.

After these words of Democritus,[b] Ulpian, glancing at Cynulcus spoke : To quote the comic poet Theognetus's *Ghost*[c] : " Alas, that I am compelled by fate to live with such a philosopher ! You, poor fool, must have learned your letters backwards ; books have turned your life upside-down.[d] You

---

[a] Vol. i. p. 18, quoting Archestratus.
[b] Begun at 669 d (p. 86). Rohde, I think wrongly, believed the passage from Clearchus extended to this point.
[c] Kock iii. 364. See Athen. 104 b (vol. i. p. 446) for the beginning of the quotation.
[d] For ἀνέστροφεν Hirschig conjectured ἀνατέτροφεν " have fed you up." But the context here inevitably calls to mind Acts xxvi. 24 τὰ πολλά σε γράμματα εἰς μανίαν περιτρέπει " much learning makes thee mad."

πεφιλοσόφηκας γῇ τε κοὐρανῷ λαλῶν,
οἷς οὐδέν[1] ἐστιν ἐπιμελὲς τῶν σῶν λόγων.

πόθεν γάρ σοι καὶ ὁ τῶν συρβηνέων[2] ἐπῆλθεν χορός;
τίς τῶν ἀξίων λόγου μέμνηται τοῦ μουσικοῦ τούτου
χοροῦ;" καὶ ὃς " οὐ πρότερον, ἔφη, ὦ οὗτος,
διδάξω σε πρὶν ἂν τὸν ἄξιον παρὰ σοῦ λάβω
μισθόν. οὐ γὰρ ἐγὼ τὰς ἐκ τῶν βιβλίων ἀκάνθας
ὥσπερ σὺ ἀναγινώσκων ἐκλέγω, ἀλλὰ τὰ χρησι-
d μώτατα καὶ ἀκοῆς ἄξια." ἐπὶ τούτοις ὁ Οὐλπιανὸς
δυσχεράνας ἀνεβόησεν τὰ ἐξ Ὕπνου[3] Ἀλέξιδος·

" οὐδ' ἐν Τριβαλλοῖς ταῦτά γ' ἐστὶν ἔννομα·
οὗ φασι τὸν θύοντα τοῖς κεκλημένοις
δείξαντ' ἰδεῖν[4] τὸ δεῖπνον εἰς τὴν αὔριον
πωλεῖν ἀδείπνοις ἃ παρέθηκ' αὐτοῖς ἰδεῖν.

τὰ αὐτὰ ἰαμβεῖα[5] φέρεται καὶ παρὰ Ἀντιφάνει ἐν
Ὕπνῳ." καὶ ὁ Κύνουλκος· " ἐπεὶ περὶ στεφάνων
e ζητήσεις ἤδη γεγόνασιν, εἰπὲ ἡμῖν τίς ἐστιν ὁ παρὰ
τῷ χαρίεντι Ἀνακρέοντι Ναυκρατίτης στέφανος,
ὦ Οὐλπιανέ. φησὶν γὰρ οὕτως ὁ μελιχρὸς[6]
ποιητής·

στεφάνους δ'[7] ἀνὴρ τρὶς[8] ἕκαστος εἶχεν,
τοὺς μὲν ῥοδίνους, τὸν δὲ Ναυκρατίτην.

καὶ διὰ τί παρὰ τῷ αὐτῷ ποιητῇ λύγῳ τινὲς

---

[1] οὐδέν A.   [2] συρβηναίων A, see 669 b.
[3] Schweighäuser: ὑπονοίασ A.
[4] δείξαντα ἰδεῖν A : δείξαντα δεῖν Kaibel.
[5] ἰαμβια A.   [6] μελίχροσ A.
[7] Musurus: στεφάνου· ὁδ' A.
[8] Meister (cf. 430 d): τρεῖσ A.

have gabbled your silly philosophy to earth and
heaven, which pay no heed whatever to your words." [a]
Whence has this caterwauling band [b] swarmed in
upon you ? What authority worth quoting has ever
mentioned this musical band ? To which he replied :
I'll not tell you, my man, until I get from you my
appropriate reward. For I do not select thorny
questions read in books, like you, but matters that are
most useful and worth hearing. Ulpian, in irritation
at this, cried out the lines from Alexis in *Sleep* [c] :
" Not even amongst the Triballians [d] would such acts
as these be considered lawful ; there, it is said, the
man who offers sacrifice of meat shows the feast for
his invited guests to gaze at, and next morning offers
for sale to the dinnerless all that he had set before
the others to see." The same iambic verses occur
also in Antiphanes' *Sleep.* [e] Then Cynulcus said :
Now that queries about wreaths have come up,
tell us, Ulpian, what the " wreath of Naucratis " is
in the charming Anacreon. For that delightful poet
says [f] : " Each man had three wreaths—two of roses,
the other a wreath of Naucratis." And why, in the
same poet, are some persons wreathed with withes ? [g]

---

[a] The nurse in Eur. *Med.* 57 seeks to relieve her sorrow
by telling it forth to earth and heaven ; parodied by Philemon,
Athen. 288 d (vol. iii. p. 294).

[b] Above, 669 b (p. 85 note *g*).

[c] Kock ii. 385.

[d] For the uncivilized Triballians see Aristoph. *Av.* 1567,
Athen. vol. vi. p. 85 note *c*.

[e] Kock ii. 104.

[f] *P.L.G.*[4] iii. 277, Diehl i. 466, Edmonds ii. 186. Pollux
vi. 107 Ναυκρατίτῃ στεφάνῳ· σάμψυχος (of marjoram) οὗτος
ἦν. See below, 675 f.

[g] Of the *agnus castus*, Athen. 515 f (vol. v. p. 320 and note
a) ; cf. Pliny, *N.H.* xxiv. 9. 38 ; below, 673 d.

στεφανοῦνται; φησὶν γὰρ ἐν τῷ δευτέρῳ τῶν
Μελῶν·

f   ὁ[1] Μεγίστης δ' ὁ φιλόφρων δέκα δὴ μῆνες ἐπείτε
στεφανοῦται[2] τε λύγῳ καὶ τρύγα πίνει[2] μελιηδέα.

ὁ γὰρ τῆς λύγου στέφανος ἄτοπος· πρὸς δεσμοὺς
γὰρ καὶ πλέγματα ἡ λύγος ἐπιτήδειος. εἰπὲ οὖν
ἡμῖν τι περὶ τούτων, ζητήσεως ἀξίων ὄντων, καὶ
μὴ ὀνόματα[3] θήρα, φιλότης.''

Σιωπῶντος δ' αὐτοῦ καὶ ἀναζητεῖν προσποιου-
μένου ὁ Δημόκριτος ἔφη· ''Ἀρίσταρχος ὁ γραμ-
672 ματικώτατος, ἑταῖρε, ἐξηγούμενος τὸ χωρίον ἔφη
ὅτι καὶ λύγοις ἐστεφανοῦντο οἱ ἀρχαῖοι. Ταίναρος[4]
δὲ ἀγροίκων εἶναι λέγει στεφάνωμα τὴν λύγον. καὶ
οἱ ἄλλοι δὲ[5] ἐξηγηταὶ ἀπροσδιόνυσά τινα εἰρήκασιν περὶ τοῦ προκειμένου. ἐγὼ δ' ἐντυχὼν τῷ
Μηνοδότου τοῦ Σαμίου συγγράμματι, ὅπερ ἐπιγράφεται Τῶν κατὰ τὴν Σάμον ἐνδόξων ἀναγραφή,
εὗρον τὸ ζητούμενον. Ἀδμήτην γάρ φησιν τὴν
Εὐρυσθέως ἐξ Ἄργους φυγοῦσαν ἐλθεῖν εἰς Σάμον,
θεασαμένην δὲ τὴν τῆς Ἥρας ἐπιφάνειαν καὶ τῆς
b οἴκοθεν σωτηρίας χαριστήριον βουλομένην ἀποδοῦναι ἐπιμεληθῆναι τοῦ ἱεροῦ τοῦ καὶ νῦν ὑπάρ-
χοντος, πρότερον δὲ ὑπὸ Λελέγων καὶ Νυμφῶν[6]
καθιδρυμένου· τοὺς δ' Ἀργείους πυθομένους καὶ
χαλεπαίνοντας πεῖσαι χρημάτων ὑποσχέσει Τυρ-

---

[1] ὁ added by Gaisford.
[2] 673 d: στεφανοῦνται, πίνουσιν A.
[3] Schweighäuser: ονοματων A.
[4] Ταίναρος Meineke: τεναρος A.
[5] Meineke: ἀλλοί γε A.   [6] νυμφῶν A.

---

[a] P.L.G.[4] iii. 267, Diehl i. 453, Edmonds ii. 160.
[b] This name for a writer is otherwise unknown.

For in the second book of his *Lyrics* he says [a] : " Our Megistês, that good-natured one, has now for ten months wreathed himself with withes, and has been drinking honey-sweet must." Of course a wreath of withes is absurd, since they are suitable only for roping and wicker-work. Tell us then, my dear, something about these things, since they are worth inquiry, and don't hunt down mere names.

Ulpian, however, was silent, and while he was pretending to search for an answer Democritus said : Aristarchus, that most eminent grammarian, expounded the passage, my friend, and said that the ancients used withes for wreaths. Taenarus [b] says that the withe was used for wreaths by peasants. And the other interpreters, also, have advanced irrelevant [c] ideas on the subject. But I have lighted on the treatise of Menodotus of Samos, entitled *Register of Notable Things in Samos*, and have found the object of our search.[d] He says that Admetê, the daughter of Eurystheus, went in flight from Argos to Samos, and after seeing Hera in a vision she wished to render a thank-offering for her escape from home, and so undertook the care of the temple which is there to-day, founded earlier by the Leleges and the Nymphs [e] ; but the Argives, hearing of this, in their anger promised money to the Tyrrhenians, who lived

---

[c] For the adjective ἀπροσδιόννσα see vol. v. p. 201 note *b*. C summarizes the story of the λύγος briefly, ἔστι δὲ περὶ αὐτῶν ἀπεραντολογία τις μυθική.

[d] *F.H.G.* iii. 103.

[e] Hesych. *s. ἄστυ νυμφέων* says that Samos was called the city of the Nymphs by Anacreon. P.-W. *s. Nymphai* col. 1564. Meineke conjectured Μιλνῶν, the original inhabitants of Lycia ; but there is no need to question the reading Νυμφῶν. On the worship of Hera at Samos *cf.* 525 e (vol. v. p. 370).

ρηνοὺς ληστρικῷ τῷ[1] βίῳ χρωμένους ἁρπάσαι
τὸ βρέτας, πεπεισμένους αὐτοὺς[2] ὡς, εἰ τοῦτο
γένοιτο, πάντως τι κακὸν πρὸς τῶν τὴν Σάμον
κατοικούντων ἡ Ἀδμήτη πείσεται. τοὺς δὲ Τυρ-
ρηνοὺς ἐλθόντας εἰς τὸν Ἡραΐτην ὅρμον καὶ ἀπο-
c βάντας[3] εὐθέως ἔχεσθαι τῆς πράξεως. ἀθύρου δὲ
ὄντος τότε τοῦ νεὼ ταχέως ἀνελέσθαι τὸ βρέτας
καὶ διακομίσαντας ἐπὶ θάλασσαν εἰς τὸ σκάφος
ἐμβαλέσθαι· λυσαμένους δ᾽ αὐτοὺς τὰ πρυμνήσια
καὶ τὰς ἀγκύρας[4] ἀνελομένους εἰρεσίᾳ τε πάσῃ
χρωμένους ἀπαίρειν οὐ δύνασθαι. ἡγησαμένους
οὖν θεῖόν τι τοῦτ᾽ εἶναι πάλιν ἐξενεγκαμένους τῆς
νεὼς τὸ βρέτας ἀποθέσθαι παρὰ τὸν αἰγιαλόν· καὶ
ψαιστὰ αὐτῷ παραθέντας[5] περιδεεῖς ἀπαλλάττε-
σθαι. τῆς δὲ Ἀδμήτης ἔωθεν δηλωσάσης ὅτι τὸ
βρέτας ἠφανίσθη καὶ ζητήσεως γενομένης εὑρεῖν
d μὲν αὐτὸ τοὺς ζητοῦντας ἐπὶ τῆς ἠόνος, ὡς δὲ δὴ[6]
βαρβάρους Κᾶρας ὑπονοήσαντας αὐτόματον ἀπο-
δεδρακέναι, πρός τι λύγου θωράκιον ἀπερείσασθαι,
καὶ τοὺς εὐμηκεστάτους τῶν κλάδων ἑκατέρωθεν
ἐπισπασαμένους περιειλῆσαι πάντοθεν. τὴν δὲ
Ἀδμήτην λύσασαν αὐτὸ ἁγνίσαι καὶ στῆσαι πάλιν
ἐπὶ τοῦ βάθρου, καθάπερ πρότερον ἵδρυτο. διόπερ
ἐξ ἐκείνου καθ᾽ ἕκαστον ἔτος ἀποκομίζεσθαι τὸ
βρέτας εἰς τὴν ἠόνα καὶ ἀφαγνίζεσθαι ψαιστά τε
αὐτῷ παρατίθεσθαι· καὶ καλεῖσθαι Τόναια[7] τὴν
e ἑορτήν, ὅτι συντόνως συνέβη περιειληθῆναι τὸ
βρέτας ὑπὸ τῶν τὴν πρώτην αὐτοῦ ζήτησιν ποιη-
σαμένων.

    [1] Kaibel : τε A.
    [2] Capps : τοὺ ἀργείουσ A.
    [3] Kaibel : διαβάντασ A.
    [4] αγκύλασ A.

the life of pirates, if they would carry off the image of Hera, being themselves convinced that if that happened Admetê would surely suffer some harm at the hands of the people of Samos. So the Tyrrhenians made for the port of Hera, and disembarking set to work at once. Since the temple had no door at that time, they soon picked up the image and carried it to the sea, where they placed it in their ship ; but though they loosed the cables, pulled up the anchors, and rowed with all their might, they could not get under way. Thinking, therefore, that this was a divine portent, they carried the image out of the ship again and deposited it on the shore ; and setting barley-cakes beside it they departed in great fear. Next morning Admetê disclosed that the image had disappeared, and starting in search the seekers found it on the beach ; but the Carians, as one would expect of barbarians, surmised that the image had run away of its own accord, and so they fastened it to a mat of withes, pulling the longest branches tightly on both sides of it, and so wrapping it round. Admetê unfastened the image and purified it and set it once more on its pedestal, just as it had stood before. Wherefore, ever since, they have carried the image every year to the sea-beach and purged it and set offerings of barley-cakes beside it ; the festival is called the Tonaia,[a] because the image, as it happened, had been so tightly wrapped about by the men who made the first search for it.

[a] Lit. " The Tight-pulling," Nilsson, *Gr. Feste* 47-48.

---

[b] Gulick : ποιήσαντασ A, παρανήσαντας Wilamowitz, στορέσαντας Lumb.

[6] Kaibel : ὡσ δ᾽ ἀν A.   [7] Casaubon : τόνεα A.

'Ιστορεῖται δ' ὑπ' αὐτὸν ἐκεῖνον τὸν χρόνον τῶν
Καρῶν δεισιδαιμονίᾳ περισχεθέντων ἐπὶ τὸ μαν-
τεῖον τοῦ θεοῦ παραγενομένων εἰς Ὕβλαν[1] καὶ
πυνθανομένων περὶ τῶν ἀπηντημένων, θεσπίσαι
τὸν Ἀπόλλωνα ποινὴν αὐτοὺς ἀποδοῦναι τῇ θεῷ
δι' ἑαυτῶν ἑκούσιον καὶ χωρὶς δυσχεροῦς συμφορᾶς·
f ἣν ἐν τοῖς ἔμπροσθεν χρόνοις ἀφώρισεν ὁ Ζεὺς τῷ
Προμηθεῖ χάριν τῆς κλοπῆς τοῦ πυρός, λύσας αὐτὸν
ἐκ τῶν χαλεπωτάτων δεσμῶν· καὶ τίσιν ἑκούσιον
ἐν ἀλυπίᾳ κειμένην δοῦναι θελήσαντος, ταύτην ἔχειν[2]
ἐπιτάξαι τὸν καθηγούμενον τῶν θεῶν. ὅθεν ἀπ'
ἐκείνου[3] τὸν δεδηλωμένον στέφανον τῷ Προμηθεῖ
περιγενέσθαι καὶ μετ' οὐ πολὺ τοῖς εὐεργετηθεῖσιν
ἀνθρώποις ὑπ' αὐτοῦ κατὰ τὴν τοῦ πυρὸς δωρεάν.
διόπερ καὶ τοῖς Καρσὶ κατὰ τὸ παραπλήσιον ἔθος[4]
παρεκελεύσατο Ἀπόλλων[5] στεφανώματι χρωμένοις
τῇ λύγῳ καταδεῖν τὴν ἑαυτῶν κεφαλὴν τοῖς κλάδοις
673 οἷς αὐτοὶ κατέλαβον τὴν θεόν. καταλῦσαι δὲ καὶ
τἆλλα γένη τῶν στεφάνων ἐπέταξε χωρὶς τῆς
δάφνης· ταύτην[6] δ' αὐτὸς ἔφη τοῖς τὴν Ἥραν[7]
θεραπεύουσι μόνοις ἀπονέμειν δῶρον. τοῖς τε
χρησθεῖσιν ἐκ τῆς μαντείας κατακολουθήσαντας αὐτοὺς ἀβλαβεῖς ἔσεσθαι, δίκην[8] ἐν εὐωχίαις ἀπο-
διδόντας τῇ θεῷ τὴν προσήκουσαν. ὅθεν τοὺς

---

[1] Ὑλλούαλα (?) Kaibel.
[2] A: ἐκείνῳ Kaibel.   [3] Heyne: οὔτ' ἐκείνου A.
[4] ἔθος ACE: ὁ θεὸς Kaibel.
[5] CE: om. A.   [6] CE: τὴν A.
[7] CE: θεὸν (θν) A.
[8] καὶ before δίκην deleted by Wilamowitz.

---

[a] There were three cities in Sicily so named, but they
were far distant, and no oracle seems to be associated with

102

It is recorded, too, that about the same time the Carians, completely given over to superstition as they were, went to the god's oracle at Hybla [a] and inquired about these occurrences. Apollo returned answer that they must render to the goddess in their own persons a penance of their own choice and without any grave harm; this penance Zeus had in early times laid upon Prometheus for stealing fire after he had loosed him from his cruel bonds ; and when Prometheus consented to make the requital, involving no pain to himself, we are told that the chief of all the gods ordained he should undergo this. [b] And so, from that circumstance, the wreath revealed to Prometheus soon came to prevail also amongst human beings, who had profited by his gift of fire. Hence for the Carians, too, Apollo similarly prescribed the custom of using withes in making wreaths, binding up their heads with the kind of branches by which they had held fast the goddess. But he also directed them to do away with all other kinds of wreath except the laurel ; this, he said, he himself assigned as a privilege solely to those who worshipped Hera. Further, those, he said, who observed the ordinances given forth by the oracle would be unscathed, provided they rendered to the goddess at their feasts the proper penance. And

[a] them. Kaibel's conjecture Hyllouala, a Carian city (Steph. Byz. *s.v.*), is attractive. Nevertheless Steph. Byz. *s.* Γαλεῶται says there was a μάντεων εἶδος Σικελῶν, inhabiting Hybla. So Hesychius, *s.* Γαλεοί· μάντεις. οὗτοι κατὰ τὴν Σικελίαν ᾤκησαν.

[b] *Cf.* Hyginus, *Poet. astr.* i. 15 p. 54 Bunte : (Promethea) nonnulli etiam coronam habuisse dixerunt, ut se victorem impune peccasse diceret ; itaque homines in maxima laetitia victoriisque coronas habere instituerunt.

Κᾶρας ὑπακοῦσαι βουλομένους τοῖς ἐκ τοῦ χρη-
στηρίου καταλῦσαι τὰς ἔμπροσθεν εἰθισμένας στε-
φανώσεις αὐτούς τε κατὰ πλῆθος χρῆσθαι μὲν τῇ
b λύγῳ, τοῖς δὲ θεραπεύουσιν τὴν θεὸν ἐπιτρέψαι
φορεῖν τὸν καὶ νῦν ἔτι διαμένοντα τῆς δάφνης
στέφανον.

Μνημονεύειν δ᾽ ἔοικεν ἐπὶ ποσόν τι τῆς κατὰ τὴν
λύγον[1] στεφανώσεως καὶ Νικαίνετος ὁ ἐποποιὸς ἐν
τοῖς Ἐπιγράμμασιν, ποιητὴς ὑπάρχων ἐπιχώριος
καὶ τὴν ἐπιχώριον ἱστορίαν ἠγαπηκὼς[2] ἐν πλείοσιν.
λέγει δ᾽ οὕτως·

οὐκ ἐθέλω, Φιλόθηρε, κατὰ πτόλιν, ἀλλὰ παρ᾽
  Ἥρῃ
δαίνυσθαι ζεφύρου πνεύμασι τερπόμενος.
ἀρκεῖ μοι λιτὴ[3] μὲν ὑπὸ πλευροῖσι χαμευνάς,[4]
  ἐγγύθι[5] πὰρ[6] προμάλου δέμνιον ἐνδαπίης,
καὶ λύγος, ἀρχαῖον Καρῶν στέφος. ἀλλὰ
  φερέσθω
οἶνος καὶ Μουσῶν ἡ χαρίεσσα λύρη,
θυμῆρες πίνοντες ὅπως Διὸς εὐκλέα[7] νύμφην
  μέλπωμεν, νήσου δεσπότιν ἡμετέρης.

ἐν τούτοις γὰρ ἀμφιβόλως εἰρηκὼς ὁ Νικαίνετος
πότερον στρωμνῆς ἕνεκεν ἢ στεφανώσεως ἀρκεῖται
d τῇ λύγῳ, τῷ λέγειν[8] αὐτὴν τῶν Καρῶν ἀρχαῖον
στέφος πρόδηλον καθίστησι τὸ ζητούμενον. συνέβη
δὲ τὴν τῆς λύγου στεφάνωσιν καὶ μέχρι τῶν κατὰ
Πολυκράτην χρόνων, ὡς ἄν τις εἰκάσειεν, ἐν[9] τῇ

---

[1] Casaubon: τον λυγον A. [2] ἠρευνηκὼς Rohde.
[3] Dindorf: αιτη A. [4] Dindorf: χαμμευνα A.
[5] Dindorf: ἔγγυοι A. [6] Kaibel: γὰρ A.
[7] εὐκλεᾶ A. [8] Musurus: τῷ δὲ λέγειν A.
[9] ἐν added by Kaibel (εἰκάσειετῇ A).

so the Carians, eager to heed the oracle's ordinances, did away with the kinds of wreath which had been customary before, and used the withe as a general practice, but permitted the special worshippers of the goddess to wear the wreath of laurel which remains in use even to this day.

The epic poet Nicaenetus in his *Epigrams* reminds us, it would seem, that the withe was used in wreaths to some extent; he was a poet of that region,[a] who often expresses his love of [b] its history. He says [c]: " My wish, Philotherus,[d] is not to feast in the city, but rather beside the shrine of Hera, enjoying the breath of the west wind. Sufficient for me is a simple pallet on the ground beneath my body,[e]—a bed close beside a native willow, and a withe, ancient wreathing of the Carians. But let wine be brought and the Muses' charming lyre, that, drinking to our hearts' delight, we may celebrate the glorious bride of Zeus, the mistress of our isle." Although in these verses Nicaenetus leaves us in doubt whether he is satisfied with the withe as bedding or for making a wreath, yet by speaking of it as the " ancient wreathing of the Carians " he establishes quite clearly the answer to our question.[f] Further, it happened that the use of the withe in making wreaths, as one may infer, was rather common in the island even down to the

---

[a] Athen. 590 b (vol. **vi.** p. 182) Νικαινέτου τοῦ Σαμίου ἢ Ἀβδηρίτου.

[b] Or, reading ἠρευνηκὼς for ἠγαπηκὼς, "has made wide research into."

[c] Powell 3, *Anthol. app. ep.* iv. 40 Cougny.

[d] Though a man's name, it may be translated " Lover-of-the-chase."

[e] Lit. " my ribs."

[f] Whether or not withes were used in making wreaths, above, p. 99.

νήσῳ συνηθεστέραν ὑπάρχειν. ὁ γοῦν Ἀνακρέων
φησίν·

ὁ[1] Μεγίστης ὁ φιλόφρων δέκα δὴ μῆνες ἐπειδὴ[2]
στεφανοῦταί τε λύγῳ καὶ τρύγα πίνει μελιηδέα."

Ταῦτα ἴσασιν οἱ θεοὶ ὡς πρῶτος αὐτὸς ἐν τῇ
καλῇ Ἀλεξανδρείᾳ εὗρον κτησάμενος τὸ τοῦ Μηνοδότου συγγραμμάτιον καὶ ἐπιδείξας πολλοῖς ἐξ
e αὐτοῦ τὸ παρὰ τῷ Ἀνακρέοντι ζητούμενον. λαβὼν
δὲ παρ' ἐμοῦ ὁ πᾶσιν κλοπὴν ὀνειδίζων Ἡφαιστίων
ἐξιδιοποιήσατο τὴν λύσιν καὶ σύγγραμμα ἐξέδωκεν
ἐπιγράψας Περὶ[3] τοῦ παρ' Ἀνακρέοντι λυγίνου
στεφάνου· ὅπερ νῦν ἐν τῇ Ῥώμῃ εὕρομεν παρὰ τῇ
ἀντικοττυραι Δημητρίῳ. τοιοῦτος δέ τις καὶ[4] περὶ
τὸν καλὸν ἡμῶν Ἄδραστον[5] ἐγένετο. ἐκδόντος γὰρ
τούτου πέντε μὲν βιβλία Περὶ τῶν παρὰ Θεο-
φράστῳ ἐν τοῖς περὶ Ἠθῶν καθ' ἱστορίαν καὶ λέξιν
ζητουμένων, ἕκτον δὲ περὶ τῶν ἐν τοῖς Ἠθικοῖς
f Νικομαχείοις[6] Ἀριστοτέλους, ἐννοίας ἀμφιλαφῶς
παραθεμένου περὶ τοῦ παρὰ Ἀντιφῶντι τῷ τραγῳ-
διοποιῷ Πληξίππου καὶ πλεῖστα ὅσα καὶ περὶ

---

[1] ὁ added by Gaisford. [2] So A here: ἐπείτε 671 f.
[3] Musurus: παρα A.
[4] After καὶ the words ὁ Ἡφαιστίων συγγραφεὺς καὶ deleted
by Casaubon.
[5] Casaubon: ἄδραντον A. [6] νικομαχίοισ A.

---

[a] i.e. the last third of the sixth century B.C. For Anacreon's relations with Polycrates in Samos see 540 e (vol. v.
p. 444).
[b] Above, 671 e-f (pp. 96-98).
[c] The words παρὰ τῇ ἀντικοττυραι Δημητρίῳ as written
in A make neither sense nor syntax. Most editors change
τῇ (τῇ in A) to τῷ, and understand either a temple of Ceres,

time of Polycrates.[a] At any rate Anacreon says [b] :
" Our Megistês, that good-natured one, has for ten
months now wreathed himself with withes, and has
been drinking honey-sweet must."

The gods are my witness that I was the first to
discover all this in our beautiful Alexandria, when
I acquired the little treatise of Menodotus and
showed from it to many persons the thing we
are looking for in Anacreon. But Hephaestion, who
accuses everybody of plagiarism, took the solution from
me and ascribed it to himself, publishing a treatise
entitled *On the Wreath of Withes in Anacreon* ; this
book we found lately in Rome at the . . . Demetrius.[c]
And Hephaestion proved to be the same thieving
sort in the case of our noble Adrastus.[d] For Adrastus
had published five books *On Questions of History and
Style in the Morals of Theophrastus*, and a sixth book
On the Nicomachean Ethics of Aristotle, abundantly
setting forth ideas on the character of Plexippus [e]
in the play of Antiphon the tragic poet, as well as

or a bookseller (ἀντικυαρίῳ = καλλιγράφῳ Schweighäuser, *cf.*
Lydus, *De Mens.* i. 33 Wuensch) named Demetrius. Kaibel
proposed παρὰ τῇ ἐν οὐίκῳ Τυραρίῳ Δήμητρι " beside the (altar
of) Ceres in the Turarius quarter," comparing Hor. *Epist.*
ii. 1. 269 deferar in vicum vendentem tus et odores. But
there is no evidence of an altar of Ceres there, nor of a form
οὖικος, or even οἶκος = Lat. vicus in sense.

    [d] Peripatetic philosopher in the time of the Antonines,
possibly a teacher of Athenaeus.

    [e] Maternal uncle of Meleager who figured in Antiphon's
play *Meleager* ; *T.G.F.*[2] 792. Aristotle does not mention
him in the *Ethics*, but in *Rhet.* ii. 2. 19 (vol. ii. p. 28 Cope),
when discussing anger, he says: τοῖς δὲ φίλοις (ὀργίζονται)
. . . ἐὰν μὴ αἰσθάνωνται δεομένων, ὥσπερ ὁ Ἀντιφῶντος Πλή-
ξιππος τῷ Μελεάγρῳ " people are angry at friends if they
fail to notice that something is wanted of them, like Antiphon's Plexippus in his *Meleager*."

αὐτοῦ τοῦ Ἀντιφῶντος εἰπόντος, σφετερισάμενος
καὶ ταῦτα ἐπέγραψέν τι βιβλίον Περὶ τοῦ παρὰ
Ξενοφῶντι ἐν τοῖς Ἀπομνημονεύμασιν Ἀντιφῶντος, οὐδὲν ἴδιον προσεξευρών, ὥσπερ κἂν τῷ Περὶ
τοῦ λυγίνου στεφάνου. μόνον γὰρ τοῦτ' ἴδιον
εἴρηκεν ὅτι Φύλαρχος ἐν τῇ ἑβδόμῃ τῶν Ἱστοριῶν
674 οἶδεν τὴν κατὰ τὴν¹ λύγον ἱστορίαν καὶ ὅτι οὔτε τὰ
Νικαινέτου οἶδεν οὔτε τὰ Ἀνακρέοντος ὁ συγ-
γραφεύς· ἀπέδειξε δὲ² καὶ διαφωνοῦντα αὐτὸν κατ'
ἔνια τῶν ἱστορηθέντων παρὰ τῷ Μηνοδότῳ. δύναται δέ τις λέγειν περὶ τῆς λύγου ἁπλούστερον,
ὅτι ὁ Μεγίστης τῇ λύγῳ ἐστεφανοῦτο,³ ὡς παρα-
κειμένης ἐκ τοῦ δαψιλοῦς ἐν ᾧ εὐωχεῖτο τόπῳ,
συνδέσεως ἕνεκα τῶν κροτάφων. καὶ γὰρ καὶ
Λακεδαιμόνιοι καλάμῳ στεφανοῦνται ἐν τῇ τῶν
Προμαχείων⁴ ἑορτῇ, ὥς φησι Σωσίβιος ἐν τοῖς
περὶ τῶν ἐν Λακεδαίμονι Θυσιῶν γράφων οὕτως·
b " ἐν ταύτῃ συμβαίνει τοὺς μὲν ἀπὸ τῆς χώρας
καλάμοις στεφανοῦσθαι ἢ στλεγγίδι, τοὺς δ' ἐκ τῆς
ἀγωγῆς παῖδας ἀστεφανώτους ἀκολουθεῖν."

Ἀριστοτέλης δ' ἐν δευτέρῳ Ἐρωτικῶν καὶ Ἀρί-
στων⁵ ὁ περιπατητικός, Κεῖος⁶ δὲ τὸ γένος, ἐν β'
Ἐρωτικῶν Ὁμοίων⁷ φασὶν ὅτι οἱ ἀρχαῖοι διὰ τοὺς
περὶ τὸν οἶνον πόνους τῶν κεφαλαλγιῶν δεσμοὺς
εὕρισκον τοὺς τυχόντας, τῆς τῶν κροτάφων συν-

---

¹ τὴν added by Wilamowitz.
² Wilamowitz: απεδειξετε A.
³ Schweighäuser: λυγωσ στεφανουτο A.
⁴ προμαχιων AC.   ⁵ ἀρίσταρχος C.
⁶ κιοσ A: κῖος C.
⁷ Casaubon (cf. 419 c, 563 f): ομοίωσ A.

ᵃ Mem. i. 6. 1.   This Antiphon was a Sophist.

saying a very great deal about Antiphon himself; but Hephaestion appropriated this also and wrote a book entitled *On the Antiphon of Xenophon's Memorabilia,*[a] although he had discovered nothing additional of his own, any more than he had in his work *On the Wreath of Withes.* To be sure he does say this one thing of his own, namely that Phylarchus, in the seventh book of his *Histories,*[b] knows the story of the withe, but that the historian knows neither the verses of Nicaenetus nor those of Anacreon ; he showed, too, that Phylarchus was at variance in some details with the account found in Menodotus. One may possibly say of the withe more simply, that Megistês used the withe as a wreath to bind his temples because it lay at hand in rich abundance in the place where he feasted. For the Lacedaemonians even use reeds for wreaths in the festival of the Promacheia, as Sosibius asserts in his work *On the Sacrifices in Lacedaemon,* writing as follows [c] : " At this festival the boys from the countryside wreathe themselves with reeds or with the tiara,[d] but the boys reared in the strict discipline follow without wreaths."

Aristotle, in the second book of his *Erotics,*[e] and Ariston the Peripatetic, born in Ceos, in the second book of his *Erotic Likenesses,* say that " the men of old, in the pangs of headaches caused by wine, devised as bandages whatever they could find, since the tight binding of the temples was regarded as

---

[b] *F.H.G.* i. 336, J. 2 A 165.

[c] *F.H.G.* ii. 626. This appears to be the sole mention of the Promacheia, or Festival of the Champions. *Cf.* below, 678 b (p. 130 and note *b*).

[d] For these metal head-coverings see 128 e (vol. ii. p. 92), Xen. *An.* i. 2. 10.

[e] Frag. 95 Rose.

ATHENAEUS

δέσεως ὠφελεῖν¹ δοκούσης· οἱ δ' ὕστερον ἅμα τῷ
κροτάφῳ προσέβαλόν τινα καὶ κόσμον οἰκεῖον τῇ
παρὰ τὸν οἶνον διαγωγῇ, μηχανησάμενοι τὸν στέ-
c φανον. βέλτιον δὲ διὰ τὸ πάσας τὰς αἰσθήσεις ἐν
τῇ κεφαλῇ εἶναι ταύτην στεφανοῦσθαι ἢ διὰ τὸ
συμφέρειν ἐσκεπάσθαι καὶ συνδεδέσθαι τοὺς κρο-
τάφους πρὸς τὸν οἶνον. ἐστεφανοῦντο δὲ καὶ τὸ
μέτωπον, ὡς ὁ καλὸς Ἀνακρέων ἔφη·

> ἐπὶ² δ' ὀφρύσιν σελίνων στεφανίσκους
> θέμενοι θάλειαν³ ἑορτὴν⁴ ἀγάγωμεν⁵
> Διονύσῳ.

ἐστεφανοῦντο δὲ καὶ τὰ στήθη καὶ ἐμύρουν ταῦτα,
ἐπεὶ αὐτόθι ἡ καρδία. ἐκάλουν δὲ καὶ οἷς περι-
εδέοντο τὸν τράχηλον στεφάνους ὑποθυμίδας,⁶ ὡς
Ἀλκαῖος ἐν τούτοις·

d
> ἀλλ' ἀνήτω⁷ μὲν περὶ ταῖς δέραισι⁸
> περθέτω πλεκτὰς ὑποθυμίδας⁹ τις.

καὶ Σαπφώ·

> καὶ πολλαὶς ὑποθυμίδας¹⁰
> πλεκταὶς ἀμπ' ἀπαλᾷ¹¹ δέρᾳ.

καὶ Ἀνακρέων·

> πλεκτὰς δ'
> ὑποθυμίδας¹² περὶ στήθεσι¹³ λωτίνας ἔθεντο.

---

¹ CE: ὀφελεῖν A.   ² CE: ἐπει A.
³ CE: θαλιαν A.
⁴ ACE. Anacreon pronounced it ὀρτὴν or ἑορτὴν.
⁵ CE: αγαγωμε A.
⁶ Blomfield, confirmed (for Sappho) by Berlin Pap. 9722. 2:
ὑποθυμιάδασ ACE.
⁷ Casaubon: ἀννητω A.   ⁸ Ahrens: δεραιο A.

110

beneficial; but the men of later date added, with
the binding of the temples, some adornment appropriate to the entertainment afforded by the wine,
and so contrived the wreath. And it is better, since
all our sensations are in the head, to wreathe that,
than to have our temples covered and tightly bound
as an expedient against the wine." But they also
wreathed the forehead, as the beautiful Anacreon
has said [a] : " Upon our foreheads let us place little
wreaths of celery and celebrate a rich feast in honour
of Dionysus." Further, they wreathed their breasts
and put perfumes on them, because the heart is
there. Then there were the wreaths which they
bound round the neck and called *hypothymides*,[b] as
Alcaeus shows in these verses [c] : " Up, then! Let
one place wreaths (*hypothymidas*) plaited with anise
about our necks." And Sappho [d] : " (Thou hast
placed) many plaited wreaths about thy tender
neck." So Anacreon [e] : " And plaited wreaths of
lotus they placed about their breasts."

[a] *P.L.G.*⁴ iii. 270, Diehl i. 457, Edmonds ii. 166.
[b] Lit. " sweet-scents-under." Plut. *Qu. Conv.* 647 ε, citing
the form ὑποθυμίδας (see critical note 6) explains it: διὰ τὴν
ἀποφορὰν (effluvium) καὶ ὑποθυμίασιν (fumigation). Below,
678 d (pp. 130-132).
[c] *P.L.G.*⁴ iii. 162, Diehl i. 429, Edmonds i. 416 ; further
vss. below, 687 d (p. 180).
[d] *P.L.G.*⁴ iii. 105, Diehl i. 370, Edmonds i. 242.
[e] *P.L.G.*⁴ iii. 266, Diehl i. 456, Edmonds ii. 158.

⁹ Blomfield: ὑποθυμιαδασ A.
¹⁰ πολλαισ ὑποθυμιάδαισ A.
¹¹ Dindorf, following Schweighäuser: πλεκταισ ἀντιαπαλαι
A, πλεκ . . . απαλαι Berl. Pap.
¹² Dindorf: ὑποθυμιάδασ ACE.
¹³ CE: στηθεσσιν A.

111

Αἰσχύλος δ᾽ ἐν τῷ Λυομένῳ Προμηθεῖ σαφῶς
φησιν ὅτι ἐπὶ[1] τιμῇ τοῦ Προμηθέως τὸν στέφανον
περιτίθεμεν τῇ κεφαλῇ, ἀντίποινα τοῦ ἐκείνου
δεσμοῦ, καίτοι ἐν τῇ ἐπιγραφομένῃ Σφιγγὶ εἰπών·

τῷ δὲ ξένῳ γε στέφανον,[2] ἀρχαῖον στέφος·
e δεσμῶν ἄριστος ἐκ Προμηθέως[3] λόγου.

Σαπφὼ δ᾽ ἁπλούστερον τὴν αἰτίαν ἀποδίδωσιν τοῦ
στεφανοῦσθαι ἡμᾶς, λέγουσα τάδε·

σὺ δὲ στεφάνοις, ὦ Δίκα,[4] περθέσθ᾽[5] ἐραταῖς[6]
φόβαισιν

ὄρπακας ἀνήτοιο[7] συνέρραισ᾽ ἀπαλαῖσι[8] χερσίν.
εὐανθέα γὰρ πέλεται καὶ[9] Χάριτες μάκαιραι[10]
μᾶλλον προτόρην,[11] ἀστεφανώτοισι δ᾽ ἀπυ-
στρέφονται.

ὡς εὐανθέστερον γὰρ καὶ κεχαρισμένον μᾶλλον τοῖς
θεοῖς παραγγέλλει στεφανοῦσθαι τοὺς θύοντας.
f Ἀριστοτέλης δ᾽ ἐν τῷ Συμποσίῳ φησὶν ὅτι οὐδὲν
κολοβὸν προσφέρομεν πρὸς τοὺς θεούς, ἀλλὰ τέλεια
καὶ ὅλα. τὸ δὲ πλῆρες τέλειόν ἐστιν, τὸ δὲ στέφειν
πλήρωσίν τινα σημαίνει. Ὅμηρος·

κοῦροι δὲ κρητῆρας ἐπεστέψαντο ποτοῖο.
καί·

ἀλλὰ θεὸς μορφὴν ἔπεσι στέφει.

" τοὺς γὰρ αὖ τὴν ὄψιν ἀμόρφους, φησίν, ἀνα-
675 πληροῖ ἡ τοῦ λέγειν πιθανότης· ἔοικεν οὖν ὁ

---

[1] CE: επι τε A.   [2] A: στέφανος Grotius.
[3] προμηθέος A.   [4] Welcker: ωδικα A.
[5] Seidler: παρθεσθ A. ερθεσ. Pap.
[6] εραταισ A: ἐράτοις (with στεφάνοις) Wilamowitz.
[7] Ahrens: αννητωι A.   [8] Casaubon: ἀπαλλαγιση A.
[9] πελεται και A: παῖδ᾽ ἐθέλησαν Wilamowitz.

112

Aeschylus in *Prometheus Unbound* distinctly says [a]
that we place the wreath on the head in honour of
Prometheus, in requital for his bonds ; and yet in
the play entitled *The Sphinx* he says [b] : " And to the
guest a wreath, the ancient mode of wreathing ; the
best of bonds, according to Prometheus's reasoning." But Sappho gives more simply the reason why
we wreathe ourselves when she says [c] : " Bind together
with your dainty hands, my Dica, sprays of anise,
and place them as a wreath on your lovely hair. For
'tis so : the blessed Graces look with more favour on
the lass that is decked with flowers, but turn with
aversion from all that are unwreathed." Obviously
she enjoins the wearing of wreaths by those who offer
sacrifice, because the more decked with flowers, the
more acceptable a thing is in the sight of the gods.
Aristotle in his *Symposium* [d] says that we never bring
anything disfigured as an offering to the gods, but
only things complete and whole. But fullness is com-
pleteness, and wreathing implies a kind of fullness.
Thus Homer [e] : " And the young men wreathed the
mixing-bowls with wine." And again [f] : " But still
the god wreathes his words with beauty." " For,"
Aristotle explains, " the eloquence of their words
fills up the void in those who are of ugly appearance.

---

[a] *T.G.F.*[2] 68.　　　　　　　　　　[b] *T.G.F.*[2] 76.

[c] *P.L.G.*[4] iii. 115, Diehl i. 364, Edmonds i. 264, *cf. Ox.
Pap.* 1787 (vol. xv. p. 38, frag. 33), where, however, only
three syllables of this quotation are recoverable ; the context
makes the general sense clear.

[d] Frag. 101 Rose.

[e] *Il.* i. 470 ; the verb for " wreathed " meant also " filled
to the brim."

[f] *Od.* viii. 170.

---

[10] Wilamowitz: μακαιρα A.　　　　[11] Seidler: προτερην A.

στέφανος τοῦτο ποιεῖν βούλεσθαι. διὸ καὶ περὶ τὰ
πένθη τοὐναντίον παρασκευάζομεν. ὁμοπαθείᾳ γὰρ
τοῦ κεκμηκότος κολοβοῦμεν ἡμᾶς αὐτοὺς τῇ τε
κουρᾷ τῶν τριχῶν καὶ τῇ τῶν στεφάνων ἀφαιρέσει."

Φιλωνίδης δ' ὁ ἰατρὸς ἐν τῷ περὶ Μύρων καὶ
Στεφάνων " ἐκ τῆς Ἐρυθρᾶς, φησίν, θαλάσσης ὑπὸ
Διονύσου μετενεχθείσης εἰς τὴν Ἑλλάδα τῆς ἀμπέλου καὶ πρὸς ἄμετρον ἀπόλαυσιν τῶν πολλῶν
ἐκτρεπομένων ἄκρατόν τε προσφερομένων αὐτόν,[1]
b οἱ μὲν μανιωδῶς ἐκτρεπόμενοι[2] παρέπαιον,[3] οἱ δὲ
νεκροῖς ἐῴκεσαν ἀπὸ τῆς καρώσεως. ἐπ' ἀκτῆς δέ
τινων πινόντων ἐπιπεσὼν ὄμβρος τὸ μὲν συμπόσιον
διέλυσεν, τὸν δὲ κρατῆρα, ὃς εἶχεν ὀλίγον οἶνον
ὑπολελειμμένον,[4] ἐπλήρωσεν ὕδατος. γενομένης δ'
αἰθρίας εἰς τὸν αὐτὸν ὑποστρέψαντες[5] τόπον, γευσά-
μενοι τοῦ μίγματος προσηνῆ καὶ ἄλυπον ἔσχον
ἀπόλαυσιν. καὶ διὰ τοῦθ' οἱ Ἕλληνες τῷ μὲν παρὰ
δεῖπνον ἀκράτῳ προσδιδομένῳ τὸν Ἀγαθὸν ἐπι-
φωνοῦσι Δαίμονα, τιμῶντες τὸν εὑρόντα δαίμονα·
c ἦν δ' οὗτος ὁ Διόνυσος.[6] τῷ δὲ μετὰ δεῖπνον
κεκραμένῳ πρώτῳ προσδιδομένῳ ποτηρίῳ[7] Δία
Σωτῆρα ἐπιλέγουσι,[8] τῆς ἐκ τοῦ μίγματος ἀλύπου
κράσεως τὸν καὶ τῶν ὄμβρων ἀρχηγὸν αἴτιον
ὑπολαβόντες. ἔδει μὲν[9] οὖν βοηθημάτων τοῖς ἐν
τῷ πότῳ κεφαλὴν ἐπιθλιβεῖσιν, ἣν δὲ δεσμὸς ἐξ
αὐτῶν προχειρότατος καὶ τῆς φύσεως ἐπὶ τοῦτο

---

[1] αὐτόν CE: αυτων A. [2] A: om. CE.
[3] CE: παρέπεον A.
[4] C: ὑπολελιμμένον A, ὑπολελεμμένον E.
[5] CE: ἐπιστρέψαντεσ A.

It would seem, then, that the purpose of the wreath is to do this. Hence, also, when we are in mourning we arrange just the opposite. For in our sympathy for the dead we disfigure ourselves, not only by cutting the hair but also by doing away with wreaths."

The physician Philonides says in his work *On Perfumes and Wreaths*: "After the vine had been brought by Dionysus from the Red Sea into Greece, most men perversely turned to unmeasured enjoyment of it, and drank it unmixed; some, in their insane perversity, became delirious, others became like corpses in their stupor. But once upon a time, when some men were drinking at the seashore, a rain-storm fell upon them and broke up the party, but filled up the bowl, which still had a little wine left in it. After the weather cleared they returned to the same place, and tasting the mixture of wine and water they found pleasant and painless enjoyment. For this reason, when the unmixed wine is poured during the dinner, the Greeks call upon the name of the Good Divinity, doing honour to the divinity who discovered the wine; he was Dionysus. But with the first cup of mixed wine given after the dinner they call upon Zeus the Saviour, because they assume that he, as the originator of rain-storms, was the author of the painless mixture derived from the mingling of wine and rain. There was need, to be sure, of some means of aiding those whose heads were oppressed by the wine, and of all these aids a bandage was the readiest at hand, Nature herself

---

⁶ A : τιμῶντας τὸν εὑρόντα Διόνυσον CE, δαίμονα deleted by Meineke.

⁷ ποτέρῳ C.   ⁸ CE : ἐπιλεγουσα A.

⁹ ἔδει μὲν Nauck : ἐδέησεν ACE.

ὁδηγούσης. ἀλγήσας γάρ τις κεφαλήν, ὥς φησιν
Ἀνδρέας, εἶτα πιέσας καὶ κουφισθεὶς εὗρεν κεφαλαλγίας δεσμὸν φάρμακον. τούτῳ οὖν βοηθήματι
πρὸς τοὺς πότους[1] χρώμενοι τοῖς παραπίπτουσι[2] τὴν
κεφαλὴν ἐδέσμευον· καὶ ἐπὶ τὸν κίσσινον στέφανον
ἦλθον αὐτόματόν τε καὶ πολὺν ὄντα καὶ κατὰ πάντα
τόπον γεννώμενον, ἔχοντα καὶ πρόσοψιν οὐκ
ἀτερπῆ, χλωροῖς πετάλοις καὶ κορύμβοις σκιάζοντα
τὸ μέτωπον καὶ τοὺς ἐν τῷ σφίγγειν τόνους[3] ὑπο-
μένοντα, προσέτι δὲ ψύχοντα χωρὶς ὀδμῆς καρού-
σης. καὶ ταύτῃ μοι δοκεῖ Διονύσῳ ὁ βίος ἀνεῖναι
τὸ στέφος, τὸν εὑρετὴν τοῦ πώματος καὶ τῶν δι᾽
αὐτὸ ἐλασσωμάτων ἀλεξητῆρα βουλόμενος εἶναι.
ἐντεῦθεν δὲ εἰς ἡδονὴν τραπέντες τὸ μὲν συμφέρον[4]
καὶ τοῖς ἐκ μέθης παραβοηθοῦν[5] ἐλαττώμασιν ἀφ-
ῆκαν,[6] τοῦ δὲ[7] πρὸς ὄψιν ἢ πρὸς ὀσμὴν ἐπιτερποῦς
ἐφρόντισαν. διὸ μυρσίνης μὲν στέφανον στύφοντα
καὶ τὴν οἴνων ἀναθυμίασιν ἀποκρουόμενον, ἔτι δὲ
ῥόδινον ἔχοντά τι καὶ κεφαλαλγίας παρηγορικὸν
σὺν τῷ καὶ κατὰ ποσὸν ψύχειν, πρὸς δὲ τοῖς δάφ-
νινον οὐκ ἀλλότριον πότου[8] ἡγητέον. λευκόϊνον[9]
δὲ κινητικὸν ὄντα κεφαλῆς καὶ ἀμαράκινον καὶ
ἅπαντας τοὺς καροῦν δυναμένους ἢ βαρύνειν ἄλλως
κεφαλὴν περιστατέον[10].᾽᾽ τὰ αὐτὰ εἴρηκεν καὶ

---

[1] CE: προσποτουσ A. [2] παραπίνουσι C.
[3] CE: τονοσ A.   [4] Early edd.: εἰσ συμφερον A.
[5] E: παραβοηθων A, παραβοηθεῖ C.
[6] CE: ο στέφανοσ A.   [7] τοῦ δὲ CE: τοῦ A.
[8] αλλοτριον ποτοισ A, ἀλλότρια ποτοῦ CE.
[9] Schweighäuser: λευκόϊον ACE.
[10] A: παραιτητέον CE.

guiding them to this device. For, as Andreas [a] says, a man with a pain in his head finds relief by pressing it with his hands, and so discovers the bandage as a remedy for headache. With this, then, as an aid in their drinking-bouts, they bandaged the head with the best means that fell to hand; and so they resorted to the wreath of ivy, which grows without cultivation everywhere in abundance and has a pleasing appearance, with its green leaves and clusters of berries shading the brow, and is able to withstand the strain of tight binding, besides having a cooling effect, without any overpowering fragrance. And so, I think, it is for this reason that our civilization has dedicated the wreath to Dionysus, meaning that he is the discoverer of wine and may also be protector against its disadvantages. But from that point on, given over as men were only to pleasure, they neglected the merely expedient object and the means to aid them against the disadvantages of drunkenness, and took thought only for what afforded delight in its appearance or fragrance. And so a myrtle wreath, which is astringent and can dispel the fumes of wine; or again a wreath of roses, which has a sedative power against headache and is to a certain extent cooling; or, besides these, a laurel wreath may be deemed not inappropriate to a drinking-bout. But a wreath of gillyflowers, which excite the nerves of the head,[b] or one of marjoram, in fact all that are capable of stupefying or otherwise oppressing the head, must be avoided." The same remarks, word

[a] For this physician (Andron below, 680 d) cf. 115 e (vol. ii. p. 42), 312 d (vol. iii. p. 402).
[b] Theocr. vii. 63-65 does not agree: κἠγὼ τῆνο κατ' ἄμαρ ἀνήτινον ἢ ῥοδόεντα | ἢ καὶ λευκοΐων στέφανον περὶ κρατὶ φυλάσσων | τὸν Πτελεατικὸν οἶνον ἀπὸ κρατῆρος ἀφυξῶ.

Ἀπολλόδωρος ἐν τῷ περὶ Μύρων καὶ Στεφάνων
ἱ αὐταῖς λέξεσιν. καὶ περὶ μὲν τούτων, ὦ ἑταῖροι,
ταῦτα.

Περὶ δὲ τοῦ Ναυκρατίτου στεφάνου τίς ἐστι τὴν
ἄνθην πολλὰ ἀναζητήσας καὶ πολλῶν πυθόμενος,
ὡς οὐδὲν ἐμάνθανον, ἐνέτυχον ὀψέ ποτε Πολυ-
χάρμου Ναυκρατίτου ἐπιγραφομένῳ βιβλίῳ Περὶ
Ἀφροδίτης, ἐν ᾧ ταυτὶ γέγραπται· " κατὰ δὲ τὴν
τρίτην πρὸς ταῖς εἴκοσιν Ὀλυμπιάδα ὁ Ἡρόστρατος, πολίτης ἡμέτερος ἐμπορίᾳ[1] χρώμενος καὶ
χώραν πολλὴν περιπλέων, προσσχών[2] ποτε καὶ
676 Πάφῳ τῆς Κύπρου ἀγαλμάτιον Ἀφροδίτης σπι-
θαμιαῖον, ἀρχαῖον τῇ τέχνῃ, ὠνησάμενος ᾔει φέρων
εἰς τὴν Ναύκρατιν. καὶ αὐτῷ πλησίον φερομένῳ
τῆς Αἰγύπτου ἐπεὶ χειμὼν αἰφνίδιον ἐπέπεσεν καὶ
συνιδεῖν οὐκ ἦν ὅπου[3] γῆς ἦσαν, κατέφυγον ἅπαντες
ἐπὶ τὸ τῆς Ἀφροδίτης ἄγαλμα σώζειν αὐτοὺς
αὐτὴν δεόμενοι. ἡ δὲ θεὸς (προσφιλὴς γὰρ τοῖς
Ναυκρατίταις ἦν) αἰφνίδιον ἐποίησε πάντα τὰ
b παρακείμενα αὐτῇ μυρρίνης χλωρᾶς[4] πλήρη ὀδμῆς
τε ἡδίστης ἐπλήρωσεν τὴν ναῦν ἤδη ἀπειρηκόσι
τοῖς ἐμπλέουσιν τὴν σωτηρίαν διὰ τὴν πολλὴν
ναυτίαν γενομένου τε ἐμέτου πολλοῦ· καὶ ἡλίου
ἐκλάμψαντος κατιδόντες τοὺς ὅρμους[5] ἧκον εἰς τὴν
Ναύκρατιν. καὶ ὁ Ἡρόστρατος ἐξορμήσας τῆς

---

[1] ἐμπορείαι corrected in A.   [2] προσχων A.
[3] Early edd.: οὐ συνιδεῖν ουκην ὅποι A.
[4] Meineke: μυρρίνασ χλωρᾶσ A.
[5] Meineke: τοῦσ ὅρουσ A.

---

[a] Above, 671 e. Pollux vi. 107, Hesych. s. Ναυκρατίτης
στέφανος.
[b] F.H.G. iv. 480.
[c] 688-685 B.C. This date, according to Kahrstedt (P.-W.

for word, are made by Apollodorus in his work *On Perfumes and Wreaths*. So much, then, my comrades, for that.

Now about the Naucratite wreath [a] and what flowers it bears, after much research, and inquiring of many persons without learning anything, I at last lighted on a book by Polycharmus of Naucratis entitled *On Aphrodite*, wherein the following stands written [b] : " During the twenty-third Olympiad [c] Herostratus, a citizen of our town engaged in trade, was voyaging far and wide when he landed once at Paphos, in Cyprus, and bought a statuette of Aphrodite nine inches high, of ancient workmanship [d] ; departing, he carried it to Naucratis. As he approached Egypt a storm suddenly broke upon him and it was impossible to see where in the world they were ; so they all took refuge at the statue of Aphrodite, begging her to save them. The goddess, being friendly to the Naucratites, suddenly caused everything that lay beside her to be covered with fresh green myrtle, filling the ship with a most pleasant odour, when the men sailing in her were by this time despairing of their safety, for they were very seasick and there was much vomiting [e] ; then the sun shone forth and they could see their anchorage, and so arrived in Naucratis. Herostratus, setting forth

viii. 1145), is too early, since the settlement of Naucratis by Miletus seems to have taken place *ca.* 570–550 B.C. See How and Wells on Herodotus ii. 178 ; Athen. 283 d-e (vol. iii. p. 272).

[d] On the Babylonian-Cyprian idols of this type see Furtwängler in Roscher, *Lex. d. Myth. s. Aphrodite*, 407-408.

[e] This last clause would stand better after κατέφυγον above (" took refuge "), but may be justified by the double meaning of ἀπειρηκόσι " despairing of " and " being worn out."

νεὼς μετὰ τοῦ ἀγάλματος, ἔχων καὶ τὰς αἰφνίδιον
αὐτῷ ἀναφανείσας χλωρὰς μυρρίνας, ἀνέθηκεν ἐν
τῷ τῆς Ἀφροδίτης ἱερῷ· θύσας[1] δὲ[2] τῇ θεῷ καὶ
ἀναθεὶς τῇ Ἀφροδίτῃ τἄγαλμα,[3] καλέσας δὲ[4] καὶ
c ἐφ᾽ ἑστίασιν ἐν αὐτῷ τῷ ἱερῷ τοὺς προσήκοντας
καὶ τοὺς οἰκειοτάτους ἔδωκεν ἑκάστῳ καὶ στέφανον ἐκ τῆς μυρρίνης, ὃν καὶ τότε ἐκάλεσε Ναυκρατίτην.'' ὁ μὲν οὖν Πολύχαρμος ταῦτα. οἷς
κἀγὼ πείθομαι, ἡγούμενος οὐκ ἄλλον τινὰ εἶναι
Ναυκρατίτην[5] στέφανον ἢ τὸν ἐκ τῆς μυρρίνης,
τῷ καὶ μετὰ τῶν ῥόδων ὑπὸ τοῦ Ἀνακρέοντος
φορεῖσθαι.

Καὶ ὁ Φιλωνίδης δὲ εἴρηκεν ὡς ὁ τῆς μυρρίνης
στέφανος τὴν ἐκ τῶν οἴνων ἀναθυμίασιν ἀπο-
κρούεται καὶ ὁ τῶν ῥόδων ἔχει τι κεφαλαλγίας
παρηγορικὸν πρὸς τῷ καὶ ἐμψύχειν. γελοῖοι οὖν
εἰσιν[6] οἱ λέγοντες Ναυκρατίτην εἶναι στέφανον τὸν
ἐκ τῆς βύβλου[7] τῆς στεφανωτρίδος καλουμένης παρ᾽
d Αἰγυπτίοις,[8] παρατιθέμενοι Θεοπόμπου ἐκ τῆς
τρι(σκαιδεκάτης τῶν Φιλιππικῶν καὶ ἑνδεκά)της
τῶν Ἑλληνικῶν,[9] ὅς φησιν Ἀγησιλάῳ τῷ Λάκωνι
παραγενομένῳ εἰς Αἴγυπτον δῶρα πέμψαι τοὺς
Αἰγυπτίους ἄλλα τέ τινα καὶ δὴ καὶ τὴν στε-
φανωτρίδα βύβλον.[10] ἐγὼ δὲ οὐκ οἶδα τίνα ὠφέ-
λειαν ἢ ἡδονὴν ἔχει τὸ βύβλῳ[11] στεφανοῦσθαι μετὰ
ῥόδων, πλὴν εἰ μή τι οἱ τούτοις χαίροντες στέ-

---

[1] Canter: θυσιάσ A (ι apparently corrected).
[2] Kaibel: τὲ A.   [3] Kaibel: ἀγαλμα A.
[4] Kaibel: τε A.   [5] Early edd.: εἰναικρατίτην A.
[6] CE: εισιν καὶ A.   [7] E: βίβλου AC.
[8] στεφόμενον after Αἰγυπτίοις (A) deleted by Kaibel: καὶ ἐκ
ῥόδων added after Αἰγυπτίοις in C.
[9] G. and H. (cf. above, p. 22): ἐκ τῆσ τρίτησ τῶν ἑλληνικῶν A.

from the ship with the statue and the green myrtle-branches that had so suddenly appeared to him, dedicated them in Aphrodite's temple. And having sacrificed to the goddess and dedicated the statue to Aphrodite, he invited his relations and closest friends to a feast in the temple itself, giving to each a wreath made from the myrtle, which even at that time he called a Naucratite wreath." So much, then, for what Polycharmus says. I believe it, too, for I think that a Naucratite wreath is none other than one made of myrtle, since it is worn by Anacreon along with the roses.[a]

And Philonides,[b] also, agrees that the wreath of myrtle dispels the fumes arising from wine, and the wreath of roses has a sedative power against headache, besides a cooling effect. It is absurd, therefore, for people to say that the Naucratite wreath is the one made from the flowering tops of papyrus, called " wreath-papyrus " among the Egyptians, though they quote from the thirteenth book of Theopompus's *History of Philip* and the eleventh book of his *History of Greece* [c]; he says that when Agesilaus, the Lacedaemonian king, arrived in Egypt the Egyptians sent presents to him, including amongst other things the wreath of papyrus-tops. For myself, I do not know what benefit or pleasure is found in wreathing oneself in papyrus with roses, except that people who like that kind of thing would join

---

[a] Above, 671 e (p. 96).
[b] Above, 675 a (p. 114).
[c] *F.H.G.* i. 279, J. 2 B 560, G. and H. 22 (c), Plut. *Ages.* 36. On Agesilaus in Egypt *cf.* above, 657 b (p. 22) and vol. iv. p. 234.

---

[10] βίβλον A. [11] βύβλω A.

ψονται ὁμοῦ σκορόδοις καὶ ῥόδοις.[1] παμπόλλους
δὲ οἶδα λέγοντας τὸν ἐκ τῆς σαμψούχου[2] στέφανον
εἶναι τὸν Ναυκρατίτην· πολὺ δὲ τὸ ἄνθος τοῦτο
e κατὰ τὴν Αἴγυπτον. διάφορος δὲ γίνεται κατὰ τὴν
ὀδμὴν ἡ ἐν Αἰγύπτῳ μυρρίνη παρὰ τὰς ἐν ἄλλαις
χώραις, ὡς καὶ Θεόφραστος ἱστορεῖ.

Ἔτι τούτων λεγομένων ἐπεισῆλθον παῖδες στεφάνους φέροντες τῶν ἀκμαζόντων κατὰ τοὺς
καιρούς. καὶ ὁ Μυρτίλος " λέγε, καλέ, εἶπεν,
Οὐλπιανέ, στεφάνων ὀνόματα. οἱ γὰρ παῖδες,
κατὰ τὸν Χαιρήμονος Κένταυρον,

στεφάνους ἑτοιμάζουσιν, οὓς εὐφημίας
κήρυκας εὐχαῖς[3] προυβάλοντο[4] δαιμόνων.

f καὶ ἐν τῷ Διονύσῳ δὲ ὁ αὐτὸς ἔφη ποιητής·

στεφάνους τεμόντες, ἀγγέλους εὐφημίας.

σὺ δὲ μὴ τὰ ἐκ τῶν ἐπιγραφομένων Αἰλίου
Ἀσκληπιάδου Στεφάνων φέρε ἡμῖν ὡς ἀνηκόοις
αὐτῶν, ἀλλ' ἄλλο τι παρ' ἐκεῖνα λέγε. δεῖξαι
γὰρ οὐκ ἔχεις ὅτι διαλελυμένως τις εἴρηκε ῥόδων
στέφανον καὶ ἴων στέφανον· τὸ γὰρ παρὰ Κρατίνῳ
κατὰ παιδιὰν εἴρηται· ' ναρκισσίνους ὀλίσβους.[5] '"
καὶ ὃς γελάσας " πρῶτον[6] ἐν τοῖς Ἕλλησι στέφανος ὠνομάσθη, ὥς φησι Σῆμος ὁ Δήλιος ἐν δ'

---

[1] σκορόδοις καὶ ῥόδα C: σκορόδοισ καὶ ῥόδα AE, ῥόδοις καὶ
σκόροδα Kaibel.   [2] 681 b: σαμψύχου ACE.
[3] Dalechamps: εὐχαὶ A.   [4] Canter: προυβάλλοντο A.
[5] Schweighäuser: ὀλίσκουσ A.
[6] Kaibel: πρῶτοσ ACE.

---

[a] *Hist. Plant.* vi. 8. 5 θαυμασταὶ τῇ εὐοσμίᾳ.   Here end
the remarks by Democritus, begun at 671 f (p. 98).

garlic and roses to make a wreath! Again, I know
that very many writers explain the Naucratite wreath
as the one made of marjoram, and it is true that this
flower is abundant in Egypt. Further, the myrtle
of Egypt is especially distinguished for its fragrance
compared with the myrtle of other countries, as
Theophrastus records.[a]

While this talk was still going on, there entered
boys carrying wreaths of flowers which were at the
height of their season. And Myrtilus spoke: Tell
us, my noble Ulpian, said he, some names of wreaths.
For it is as Chaeremon says in *The Centaur* [b]: "The
boys make ready the wreaths which, as heralds of
holy silence,[c] they throw as a protection upon our
prayers to the gods." And in his *Dionysus* the same
poet says [d]: "Having cut wreaths, as messengers of
holy silence." But don't keep bringing us material
taken from the work entitled *Wreaths*, by Aelius
Asclepiades, as if we had never heard of it; rather,
tell us of anything else but that. You cannot, indeed,
show that any writer speaks of a "wreath of roses"
or a "wreath of violets" in a loose way [e]; of course
the phrase "narcissus-*olisbos*" in Cratinus [f] is a jest.
And Ulpian with a laugh replied: At first, as Semus
of Delos says in the fourth book of his *History of*

[b] *T.G.F.*[2] 785. On this play see Bywater, *Aristot. Poet.*
p. 110; Athen. vol. vi. p. 279 note f.

[c] *i.e.* proclaiming a religious ceremony.

[d] *T.G.F.*[2] 783.

[e] The meaning, despaired of by Casaubon and Schweighäuser, may be that the specific mention of a flower is to be
taken literally, and not as in the quotation from Cratinus
immediately following.

[f] Kock i. 113, referring to the *penis coriaceus*, Aristoph.
Lys. 109; *cf.* Athen. vol. v. p. 502 note c, Nairn, *Herodas* vi.
introductory note.

677 Δηλιάδος, τὸ παρὰ μὲν ἡμῖν στέφος,[1] παρὰ δέ τισι
στέμμα προσαγορευόμενον, διὸ καὶ τούτῳ πρώτῳ
στεφανωσάμενοι δεύτερον περιτιθέμεθα τὸν δάφ-
νινον. κέκληται δὲ στέφανος ἀπὸ τοῦ στέφειν.
σὺ δὲ οἴει με, ἔφη, Θετταλὲ ποικιλόμυθε, τῶν
κοινῶν τούτων καὶ κατημαξευμένων ἐρεῖν τι; διὰ
δὲ τὴν σὴν γλῶσσαν τῆς ΥΠΟΓΛΩΤΤΙΔΟΣ μνησθήσομαι, ἧς Πλάτων ἐμνήσθη ἐν Διὶ Κακουμένῳ·

καίτοι φορεῖτε γλῶσσαν ἐν ὑποδήμασι,
στεφανοῦσθ'[2] ὑπογλωττίσιν ὅταν[3] πίνητέ[4] που·
b κἂν[5] καλλιερῆτε γλῶτταν ἀγαθὴν πέμπετε.[6]

Θεόδωρος δ' ἐν ταῖς Ἀττικαῖς Φωναῖς, ὥς φησιν
Πάμφιλος ἐν τοῖς περὶ Ὀνομάτων, πλοκῆς στεφάνων γένος τι τὴν ὑπογλωττίδα ἀποδίδωσιν. λαβὲ
οὖν καὶ παρ' ἐμοῦ κατὰ τὸν Εὐριπίδην·

ἐκ παντὸς (γὰρ)[7] ἄν τις πράγματος δισσῶν λόγων
ἀγῶνα θεῖτ' ἄν, εἰ λέγειν εἴη σοφός.

ΙΣΘΜΙΑΚΟΝ. οὕτως τοῦτον καλούμενον στέφανον[8]
Ἀριστοφάνης μνήμης ἠξίωσεν ἐν Ταγηνισταῖς
λέγων οὕτως·

c τί οὖν ποιῶμεν; χλανίδ' ἐχρῆν λευκὴν λαβεῖν·
εἶτ' Ἰσθμιακὰ λαβόντες ὥσπερ οἱ χοροὶ
ᾄδωμεν εἰς τὸν δεσπότην ἐγκώμιον.

[1] Canter: στέφανος ACE.
[2] Porson: στεφάνουσδ' (sic) A.
[3] Schweighäuser: οτε A.   [4] πεινητε A.
[5] Casaubon: καὶ A.   [6] πέμπεται A.
[7] γὰρ belongs to Ulpian's prose.
[8] τὸν στέφανον (?) Kaibel.

124

Delos,[a] the term *stephanos* (wreath) was used among the Greeks for what with us is called a *stephos* (wreath) but with others a *stemma* (fillet), hence, after wreathing ourselves first with this fillet, we then put on the laurel. The word *stephanos* comes from the verb *stepho* (put round). As for you,[b] you Thessalian of intricate speech, do you suppose I am going to tell you anything commonplace and trite ? Because of your own tongue I will mention first the wreath of tongue-leaves,[c] mentioned by Plato in *Zeus Outraged*[d] : " And yet you wear a ' tongue ' in your shoes, you wreathe yourselves with ' tongue '-plants when you drink ; and if you find the omens at sacrifice favourable you send forth a brave ' tongue.' " And Theodorus in his *Attic Dialect,*[e] according to Pamphilus in his work *On Names*, defines the tongue-leaf as a kind of wreath-twining. So take from me also the words of Euripides, who says[f] : " In everything one might set up a contest between two arguments, if one were clever enough at speaking."

Isthmian. This is a wreath, so named, which Aristophanes thought worth mentioning in *Masters of the Frying-Pan*, thus[g] : " What, then, are we to do ? We ought to get white cloaks, and then putting on Isthmians as the choruses do, let us sing a hymn of praise to our master." Silenus in his *Glossary* says :

---

[a] *F.H.G.* iv. 493.

[b] Cynulcus ; see Introd. vol. i. p. xiii.

[c] Seemingly made of the ὑπόγλωσσον or ἱππόγλωσσον, butcher's broom or kneeholly, *Ruscus aculeatus.* Pliny, *N.H.* xxvii. 11. 67.

[d] Kock i. 614.

[e] Called *Attic Glossary* below, 678 d, and 646 c (vol. vi. p. 490).

[f] *T.G.F.*[2] 416 from *Antiope.*   [g] Kock i. 518.

Σιληνὸς δ' ἐν ταῖς Γλώσσαις φησίν· "Ἴσθμιον στέφανον." Φιλίτας δέ φησι· "Ἴσθμιος[1] στέφανος ἤγουν ὁμωνυμία ἀμφοτέρωθι οἷον τῆς κεφαλῆς καὶ τοῦ πρώτου κόσμος.[2] λέγω δὲ τὸ ἐπὶ τοῦ φρέατος καὶ τοῦ ἐγχειριδίου ἴσθμιον[3]." Τιμαχίδας δὲ καὶ Σιμμίας οἱ Ῥόδιοι ἀποδιδόασιν ἓν ἀνθ' ἑνὸς "Ἴσθμιον, στέφανον." οὗ μνημονεύει καὶ Καλλίξεινος ὁ Ῥόδιος καὶ αὐτὸς γένος ἐν τοῖς περὶ Ἀλεξανδρείας γράφων οὕτως. . . .

Ἐπεὶ δὲ Ἀλεξανδρείας ἐμνημόνευσα, οἶδά τινα ἐν τῇ καλῇ ταύτῃ πόλει καλούμενον στέφανον ANTINOEION[4] γινόμενον ἐκ τοῦ αὐτόθι καλουμένου λωτοῦ. φύεται δ' οὗτος ἐν λίμναις θέρους ὥρᾳ, καὶ εἰσὶν αὐτοῦ χροιαὶ δύο, ἡ μὲν τῷ ῥόδῳ ἐοικυῖα· ἐκ τούτου δὲ ὁ πλεκόμενος στέφανος κυρίως Ἀντινόειος καλεῖται· ὁ δὲ ἕτερος λώτινος ὀνομάζεται, κυανέαν ἔχων τὴν χροιάν. καὶ Παγκράτης τις τῶν ἐπιχωρίων ποιητὴς ὃν καὶ ἡμεῖς ἔγνωμεν, Ἀδριανῷ τῷ αὐτοκράτορι ἐπιδημήσαντι τῇ Ἀλεξανδρείᾳ μετὰ πολλῆς τερατείας ἐπέδειξεν τὸν ῥοδίζοντα λωτόν, φάσκων αὐτὸν δεῖν καλεῖν Ἀντινόειον, ἀναπεμφθέντα[5] ὑπὸ τῆς γῆς ὅτε τὸ αἷμα ἐδέξατο τοῦ Μαυρουσίου λέοντος, ὃν κατὰ τὴν πλησίον τῇ Ἀλεξανδρείᾳ Λιβύην ἐν κυνηγίῳ καταβεβλήκει ὁ Ἀδριανός, μέγα χρῆμα ὄντα καὶ πολλῷ χρόνῳ κατανεμηθέντα πᾶσαν τὴν Λιβύην, ἧς καὶ πολλὰ

---

[1] Ἴσθμιος added by Kaibel.   [2] Lumb: κόσμου A.
[3] ἴσθιον A.   [4] CE: αντινόϊον A.
[5] CE: ἀντινόϊον ἀναπεφθέντα A.

---

[a] Bach frag. 46, Kuchenmüller 100.
[b] Referring to a well *isthmion* (" neck ") must mean the

" Isthmion, a wreath." And Philitas says [a] : " Isthmian wreath ; that is, a homonym with double meaning, as for example, an ornament for the head and a prize for the winner. I mention, too, the *isthmion* of a well and of a dagger." [b] Timachidas, also, and Simmias,[c] both of Rhodes, define one by the other : " Isthmion, wreath." And Callixeinus, who also was a Rhodian by birth, mentions it in his work *On Alexandria*, writing as follows [d] : . . .

Speaking of Alexandria, I know that in that fair city there is a wreath called *Antinoeios* made from the lotus bearing that name there. This grows in marshes in the summer season ; there are two colours, one resembling the rose ; it is from this that the wreath properly called Antinoeios is twined ; the other is called lotus, and its colour is blue. Pancrates, a poet of those regions whom we knew,[e] showed the Emperor Hadrian when he visited Alexandria the rosy lotus as a great wonder, alleging that it was the one which should be called Antinoeios,[f] since it sprang, so he said, from the earth when it received the blood of the Mauritanian lion which Hadrian had killed when hunting in the part of Libya near Alexandria ; it was a huge creature that for a long time had ravaged the whole of Libya, of which this lion had

masonry above ground just under the kerb (στόμιον). In the dagger it is probably the tang connecting the blade with the hilt. [c] Powell 120.

[d] *F.H.G.* iii. 65 ; the quotation is lost, although the scribe of A puts the following seven lines in quotation marks.

[e] On Pancrates see Plut. *De Mus.* 1137 F, *Ox. Pap.* viii. 73 (fragment of the poem in which Pancrates described the lion-hunt), Athen. 478 a (vol. v. p. 114).

[f] From Antinoüs, Hadrian's favourite. For the festival in memory of " Antinoüs infelix " (Tertullian, *De Cor.* 13), held at Athens and Eleusis, see *I.G.* iii. 1129, 1147.

ἀοίκητα ἐπεποιήκει οὗτος ὁ λέων. ἡσθεὶς οὖν ἐπὶ
τῇ τῆς ἐννοίας εὑρέσει καὶ καινότητι τὴν ἐν Μου-
f σῶν[1] αὐτῷ σίτησιν ἔχειν ἐχαρίσατο. καὶ Κρατῖνος
δ' ὁ κωμῳδιοποιὸς ἐν ᾿Οδυσσεῦσι κέκληκεν τὸν[2]
λωτὸν στεφάνωμα διὰ τὸ πάντα τὰ φυλλώδη ὑπὸ
τῶν ᾿Αθηναίων στεφανώματα λέγεσθαι. ὁ δὲ
Παγκράτης ἐν τῷ ποιήματι οὐκ ἀγλαφύρως
εἴρηκεν·

οὔλην ἔρπυλλον, λευκὸν κρίνον ἠδ' ὑάκινθον
πορφυρέην γλαυκοῦ[3] τε[4] χελιδονίοιο πέτηλα
καὶ ῥόδον εἰαρινοῖσιν ἀνοιγόμενον ζεφύροισιν·
οὔπω γὰρ φύεν ἄνθος ἐπώνυμον ᾿Αντινόοιο.

678 ΠΥΛΕΩΝ. οὕτως καλεῖται ὁ στέφανος ὃν τῇ
῞Ηρᾳ περιτιθέασιν Λάκωνες, ὥς φησιν Πάμφιλος.
᾿Αλλὰ μὴν καὶ ιακχαν τινὰ καλούμενον οἶδα
στέφανον ὑπὸ Σικυωνίων, ὥς φησι Τιμαχίδας ἐν
ταῖς Γλώσσαις. Φιλίτας δ' οὕτως γράφει· ''Ἰάκχα,
ἐν τῇ Σικυωνίᾳ, στεφάνωμα εὐῶδες·

ἔστηκ' ἀμφὶ κόμας[5] εὐώδεας ἀγχόθι πατρὸς
καλὸν ᾿Ιακχαῖον θηκαμένη στέφανον.''

Σέλευκος δ' ἐν ταῖς Γλώσσαις ΕΛΛΩΤΙΔΑ καλεῖσθαί φησι τὸν ἐκ μυρρίνης πλεκόμενον στέφανον,
b ὄντα τὴν περίμετρον πηχῶν κ', πομπεύειν τε ἐν
τῇ τῶν ῾Ελλωτίων ἑορτῇ. φασὶ δ' ἐν αὐτῷ τὰ τῆς
Εὐρώπης ὀστᾶ κομίζεσθαι, ἣν ἐκάλουν ῾Ελλωτίδα.
ἄγεσθαι δὲ καὶ ἐν Κορίνθῳ τὰ ῾Ελλώτια.

---

[1] ἐν Μουσείῳ Casaubon.   [2] Hesychius: τὸ A.
[3] Schweighäuser: λευκοῦ ACE.   [4] CE: δὲ A.
[5] Schweighäuser: αμφίκομα A.

---

[a] i.e. in the Museum at Alexandria.   [b] Kock i. 60.

made many places uninhabitable. Hadrian, therefore, pleased at the originality and novelty of his
thought, granted him the favour of maintenance in
the temple of the Muses.[a] The comic poet Cratinus,
also, calls [b] the lotus a wreath-plant in *Odysseis*, since
all leafy [c] plants are spoken of as wreath-plants by
the Athenians. So Pancrates in his poem says, not
without elegance : " The thyme with its woolly
tufts, the white lily, the purple hyacinth, the
flowers of blue celandine, yes, and the rose which
unfolds to the zephyrs of spring ; but not before,
surely, has the earth brought to bloom the flower
named for Antinoüs."

Pyleôn. This name is given to the wreath which
Lacedaemonians place on the image of Hera, according to Pamphilus.[d]

But more : I know of a wreath called *Iaccha*
by the people of Sicyon, according to Timachidas
in his *Glossary*. Philitas writes [e] : " Iaccha, in the
Sicyonian Register, is a fragrant kind of wreath.
' She stands close to her father after placing a fair
Iaccha-wreath on her fragrant locks.' "

Seleucus in his *Glossary* says that *Hellotis* is the
name given to the wreath twined with myrtle, having
a circumference of thirty feet, and carried in the
procession at the festival of the Hellotia.[f] They say
that the bones of Europa, whom they called Hellotis,
are carried with due care in the wreath. The
Hellotia were held also in Corinth.

---

[c] Hesych. *s.* στεφάνωμα adds καὶ ποώδη, " and herbaceous."

[d] Below, 681 a (p. 146).

[e] Bach frag. 45, Powell 95, Kuchenmüller 99. With τῇ
Σικυωνίᾳ supply 'Αναγραφῇ.

[f] For this festival, originally Cretan, see Pind. *Ol.* xiii.
40 (Sandys, L.C.L. 137), Nilsson, *Gr. Feste* 96.

ΘΥΡΕΑΤΙΚΟΙ. οὕτω καλοῦνταί τινες στέφανοι παρὰ
Λακεδαιμονίοις, ὥς φησι Σωσίβιος ἐν τοῖς περὶ
Θυσιῶν, ψιλίνους αὐτοὺς φάσκων νῦν ὀνομάζεσθαι,
ὄντας ἐκ φοινίκων. φέρειν δ' αὐτοὺς ὑπόμνημα
τῆς ἐν Θυρέᾳ[1] γενομένης νίκης τοὺς προστάτας τῶν
c ἀγομένων χορῶν ἐν τῇ ἑορτῇ ταύτῃ, ὅτε καὶ τὰς
Γυμνοπαιδιὰς ἐπιτελοῦσιν. χοροὶ δ' εἰσὶν γ', ὁ μὲν
πρόσω παίδων, ὁ δ' ἐκ δεξιοῦ γερόντων, ὁ δ' ἐξ
ἀριστεροῦ ἀνδρῶν,[2] γυμνῶν ὀρχουμένων καὶ ᾀδόν-
των Θαλήτα[3] καὶ Ἀλκμᾶνος ᾄσματα καὶ τοὺς
Διονυσοδότου τοῦ Λάκωνος παιᾶνας.

ΜΕΛΙΛΩΤΙΝΩΝ δὲ στεφάνων μνημονεύει Ἄλεξις ἐν
Κρατείᾳ[4] ἢ Φαρμακοπώλῃ οὕτως·

στεφάνους τε πολλοὺς κρεμαμένους μελιλωτίνους.

ΕΠΙΘΥΜΙΣ.[5] Σέλευκός φησι " τὰ πάντα στεφανώματα." Τιμαχίδας δέ φησιν τὰ παντοδαπὰ
στεφανώματα ἃ τὰς γυναῖκας φορεῖν οὕτως καλεῖσθαι.

d ΥΠΟΘΥΜΙΣ δὲ καὶ ὑποθυμίδες[6] στέφανοι παρ'
Αἰολεῦσιν καὶ Ἴωσιν, οὓς περὶ τοὺς τραχήλους
περιετίθεντο, ὡς σαφῶς ἔστιν μαθεῖν ἐκ τῆς Ἀλκαίου καὶ Ἀνακρέοντος ποιήσεως. Φιλίτας[7] δ' ἐν
τοῖς Ἀτάκτοις ὑποθυμίδα[8] Λεσβίους φησὶν καλεῖν

---

[1] C: θυρεᾶι A.
[2] Wyttenbach, Kaibel: εἰσὶν τὸ μὲν πρόσω παίδων τὸ δ'
ἐξ ἀρίστου ἀνδρῶν A.
[3] θάλητα A.   [4] κρατίαι A.
[5] ἐπιθυμεῖσ A.   [6] ὑποθυμιάδες A.
[7] A: φιλίτας CE.   [8] Kaibel: ὑποθυμίδασ ACE.

---

[a] F.H.G. ii. 626.
[b] Probably the famous battle of the 300 champions of
Argos and Sparta (ca. 547 B.C.), Herod. i. 82. The territory

Thyreatikoi. This is the name given to certain wreaths by the Lacedaemonians, as Sosibius says in his work *On Sacrifices,*[a] alleging that they are to day called *psilinoi,* being made of palm branches. They are carried, he says, as a memorial of the victory won at Thyrea,[b] by the leaders of the choruses which perform during that festival wherein they carry out the Naked-boy-dances.[c] The choruses number three, the one at the head consisting of boys, that on the right of old men, and that on the left of men in their prime, dancing naked and singing songs by Thaletas and Alcman, and the paeans of Dionysodotus the Lacedaemonian.

Melilot wreaths are mentioned by Alexis in *Crateias* r *The Apothecary* thus[d]: " And many wreaths of melilot a-hanging."

Epithymis. Seleucus defines as " all materials used in wreaths."[e] But Timachidas says that wreaths of all sorts worn by women are so called.

Hypothymis and *hypothymis*-wreaths are mentioned as used by Aeolians and Ionians ; they were placed round the neck, as one may clearly learn from the poetry of Alcaeus and Anacreon.[f] And Philitas in *Irregular Words* says[g] that the Lesbians call a

---

[b] of Cynuria, of which Thyrea was a part, was long disputed. Thuc. v. 41 ἧς αἰεὶ πέρι διαφέρονται, μεθορίας οὔσης, *i.e.* being on the border. *Cf.* above on the Promacheia festival, p. 108.

[c] Athen. 630 e (vol. vi. p. 402), Suid. *s.* γυμνοπαιδία, Nilsson, *Gr. Feste* 141-142.

[d] Kock ii. 337. A kind of sweet clover is meant.

[e] *Cf.* Hesych. *s.* ἐπιθυμίδες, who has τὰ παντοδαπὰ for τὰ πάντα. Distinguished from ὑποθυμίδες, Plut. *Qu. Conv.* 647 D-E.

[f] Above, 674 c-d (p. 110).

[g] Bach frag. 58, Kuchenmüller 102.

μυρσίνης κλῶνα, περὶ ὃν πλέκειν ἴα καὶ ἄλλα
ἄνθη.

Καὶ ΥΠΟΓΛΩΤΤΙΣ δὲ στεφάνου ἐστὶν εἶδος. Θεόδωρος δ' ἐν Ἀττικαῖς Γλώσσαις στεφάνων πλοκῆς
γένος παρὰ Πλάτωνι ἐν Διὶ Κακουμένῳ.

e Εὑρίσκω δὲ καὶ παρὰ τοῖς κωμικοῖς ΚΥΛΙΣΤΟΝ
τινα καλούμενον στέφανον καὶ μνημονεύοντα αὐτοῦ
Ἀρχιππον ἐν Ῥίνωνι διὰ τούτων·

ἀθῶος ἀποδοὺς[1] θοἰμάτιον ἀπέρχεται,
στέφανον ἔχων τῶν ἐκκυλίστων οἴκαδε.

Ἄλεξις δ' ἐν μὲν Ἀγωνίδι ἢ Ἱππίσκῳ·

ὁ τρίτος οὗτος δ'[2] ἔχει
σύκων κυλιστὸν στέφανον. ἀλλ' ἔχαιρε καὶ
ζῶν τοῖς τοιούτοις.

ἐν δὲ τῷ Σκίρωνι[3] φησι·

ὥσπερ κυλιστὸς στέφανος αἰωρούμενος.

μνημονεύει δ' αὐτοῦ καὶ Ἀντιφάνης ἐν Ἑαυτοῦ
f Ἐρῶντι, Εὔβουλος δ' ἐν Οἰνομάῳ ἢ Πέλοπι·

περιφοραῖς κυκλούμενος
ὥσπερ κυλιστὸς στέφανος.

τίς οὖν οὗτος ὁ κυλιστός; οἶδα γὰρ τὸν Θυατει-
ρηνὸν Νίκανδρον ἐν τοῖς Ἀττικοῖς Ὀνόμασι λέγοντα τάδε· " ἐκκύλιστοι[4] στέφανοι, καὶ μάλιστα
οἱ ἐκ ῥόδων." καὶ τὸ εἶδος ὁποῖον ζητῶ, ὦ

---

[1] A: ἀποδὺς Canter, Toup.
[2] Meineke: δ' οὗτοσ A.　　　　　　[3] σκείρωνι A.

132

myrtle-spray *hypothymis*, round which are twined violets and other flowers.

Hypoglottis [a] also is a variety of wreath. Theodorus in his *Attic Glossary* defines it as a kind of wreath-twining mentioned by Plato in *Zeus Outraged*.[b]

I find also in the comic poets a kind of wreath called *kylistos* (rolled or tossed out); Archippus mentions it in *Rhinon* in these lines [c] : " He gave up [d] his cloak but got away unhurt, wearing a wreath of the 'rolled-out' on his way home." And Alexis in *Agonis*, or *The Scarf* [e] : " This one, the third man he, has a rolled wreath of figs. Still, he was glad enough to live on that kind of thing." Again, in *Sciron* he says [f] : " Swinging high like a rolled-out wreath." Antiphanes, also, mentions it in *In Love with Himself*,[g] as does Eubulus in *Oenomaus* or *Pelops* [h] : " Rolling round and round in twists, like a rolled-out wreath." What, then, is this wreath? I know, to be sure, that Nicander of Thyateira says in his *Attic Vocabulary* : " ' Rolled-outs ' are wreaths, particularly those made with roses." I want to know

---

[a] This paragraph is an echo of 677 b (p. 124).

[b] Kock i. 614.

[c] Kock i. 687, Pollux vii. 199 ; κυλιστός and ἐκκύλιστος mean "tightly rolled " or " rolled out." Hesych. *s.* ἐκκύλιστοι· στέφανοι μεγάλοι, ἁδροί " large and thick." But Archippus puns on the other meaning, " rolled out headlong," " forcibly ejected "; probably an adulterer is meant.

[d] Or, reading ἀποδὺς for ἀποδοὺς, " was stripped of."

[e] Kock ii. 298.

[f] Kock ii. 373 ; probably alluding to Sinis, " the pine-tree bender " (ὁ πιτυοκάμπτης).

[g] Kock ii. 31.

[h] Kock ii. 190 ; referring to Oenomaus, tossed from his chariot in the race with Pelops.

---

[*] Schweighäuser : ἐκκυλίσιοι AE, ἐκκλισίοι C.

Κύνουλκε, καὶ μή μοι εἴπῃς ὅτι δεῖ τοὺς ἁδροὺς
ἀκούειν. σὺ γὰρ εἶ ὁ τὰ ἐν τοῖς βιβλίοις οὐ μόνον
ἀπόρρητα[1] ἐκλέγων ἀλλὰ καὶ διορύττων,[2] καθάπερ
οἱ παρὰ Βάτωνι τῷ κωμῳδιοποιῷ ἐν Συνεξ-
απατῶντι φιλόσοφοι, περὶ ὧν καὶ Σοφοκλῆς Συν-
679 δείπνοις[3] φησίν, οὐσί σοι παραπλησίοις·

> οὗτοι γένειον ὧδε χρὴ διηλιφὲς[4]
> φοροῦντα κἀντίπαιδα καὶ γένει μέγαν
> γαστρὸς καλεῖσθαι παῖδα, τοῦ πατρὸς παρόν.

ἐπειδὴ οὖν ἤδη καὶ σὺ πεπλήρωσαι[5] οὐ μόνον τῶν
τοῦ γλαύκου κρανίων ἀλλὰ καὶ τῆς ἀειζώου[6] βο-
τάνης, ἧς ὁ Ἀνθηδόνιος ἐκεῖνος δαίμων ἐμφορηθεὶς
ἀθάνατος πάλιν †ητις†[7] γέγονε, λέγε ἡμῖν περὶ τοῦ
προκειμένου, ἵνα μὴ κατὰ τὸν θεῖον Πλάτωνα
ὑπολάβωμέν σε ἀποθανόντα μεταμορφωθῆναι[8]· τοὺς
μὲν γὰρ τὰς γαστριμαργίας τε καὶ ὕβρεις καὶ
b φιλοποσίας μεμελετηκότας καὶ μὴ διευλαβουμένους
εἰς τὰ τῶν ὄνων γένη καὶ τῶν τοιούτων θηρίων
εἰκὸς ἐνδύεσθαι."

---

[1] ACE: ἀπόρρητα οὐ μόνον Meineke.
[2] ACE: ἐξορύττων Meineke.
[3] Musurus (cf. 685 f): συνδείπνοι A, συνδείπνῳ Casaubon.
[4] Casaubon: διήλειφεσ A.
[5] Early edd.: συμπεπλήρωσαι A.
[6] ἀϊζώου A.
[7] πάλιν ητια A: πλανητὴς Schweighäuser, πολύμητις Kaibel,
ἀλινηχὴς Adam, παλιγγενής τις Capps. Read πολυειδὴς? Cf.
Plato, Rep. 612 a and μεταμορφωθῆναι below.
[8] The gloss ἐν τῷ περὶ ψυχῆς at this point deleted by
Schweighäuser.

---

[a] See Hesychius, quoted in note c, p. 133.
[b] Kock iii. 329. See Athen. 103 b (vol. i. p. 442).
[c] T.G.F.[2] 162. For the title of this satyric drama cf. 17 d
(vol. i. p. 76), 365 b (vol. iv. p. 152). Cynulcus, Ulpian sneers,

what kind it is, Cynulcus, and don't tell me that we must simply understand those that are thick.[a] You are one who not only picks out, but even digs up, secrets in books, like the philosophers in *The Fellow-Cheater* of Baton, the comic poet [b]; of them Sophocles says in his *Dinner-Guests* (who, by the way, were like you) [c]: "Surely it is not right for you, now past your childhood and of so great a family, to carry about a chin so greasy and be known as the son of the belly, when you might bear your father's name." Since, then, you too have already gorged yourself not only with the heads of the grey-fish (*glaucus*) but also with that everlasting plant of which the well-known divinity of Anthedon took his fill and so became an immortal . . .,[d] explain to us the matter in hand, that we may not imagine, as the divine Plato would put it,[e] that you have died and been transformed; for he says that men who have indulged in acts of gluttony and wantonness and drunkenness instead of avoiding them with care naturally slip into the family of asses [f] and such beasts.

is a dinner-guest who is also a cheat. The obscure quotation seems to describe a gluttonous lout at the feast. γαστρός "belly" is said by surprise for μητρός "mother," which Nauck wrongly reads; *cf.* vol. iv. p. 525 and note *g*. See *Berl. Klass. Texte* v. 64, 72 note 2.

[d] One of the many divinities named Glaucus belonged to Anthedon, on the coast of Boeotia. Athen. 316 a (vol. iii. p. 418), *Am. J. Arch.* vi. (1890), 96. The town was named from the tree ἀνθηδών, either a medlar or hawthorn. P.-W. vii. 1416 (*cf.* 1411) distinguishes this Glaucus from the one whose story is told Athen. 296 a (vol. iii. p. 326). See Plato, *Rep.* 611 E, and critical note 7.

[e] *Phaedo* 81 E, on re-incarnation.

[f] *Cf.* the ὕβριν ὀρθίαν "rampant lewdness" of the asses which excited Apollo's laughter, Pind. *Pyth.* x. 36 (Sandys, L.C.L. 290).

Ἀπορ* οῦντος δ' αὐτοῦ " ἐπὶ ἕτερον," φησί, " στέφανον μεταβήσομαι," ὁ Οὐλπιανός, " τὸν ΣΤΡΟΥ-
ΘΙΝΟΝ καλούμενον, οὗ μέμνηται μὲν ὁ Ἀσκλη-
πιάδης, παρατιθέμενος τὰ ἐκ τῶν Εὐβούλου
Στεφανοπωλίδων ταῦτα·

> ὦ μάκαρ, ἥτις ἔχουσ' ἐνὶ[1] δωματίῳ στρούθιον[2]
> ἀεροφόρητον[3]
> λεπτότατον περὶ σῶμα συνίλλεται[4]
> ἡδύπνοον[5] περὶ νυμφίον εὔτριχα,
> Κισσὸς ὅπως Καλάμῳ περιφύεται
> c αὐξόμενος ἔαρος[6] ὀλολυγόνος
> ἔρωτι κατατετηκώς.

πλέκεται δ' οὗτος ἐκ τοῦ στρουθίου καλουμένου
ἄνθους, οὗ μνημονεύει Θεόφραστος ἐν ἕκτω Φυ-
τικῆς Ἱστορίας ἐν τούτοις· " ἀνθεῖ δὲ καὶ ἡ ἶρις
τοῦ θέρους καὶ τὸ στρούθιον καλούμενον, ὃ τῇ
μὲν ὄψει καλὸν ἄνθος, ἄοσμον δέ." Γαλήνη δ' ἡ
Σμυρναία στρούθιον[7] αὐτὸν ὀνομάζει.

ΠΟΘΟΣ. οὕτως τις στέφανος ὀνομάζεται, ὡς
Νίκανδρός φησιν ὁ Κολοφώνιος ἐν Γλώσσαις· καὶ
ἴσως ὁ ἀπὸ τοῦ οὕτω καλουμένου ἄνθους[8] πλεκόμενος, οὗ μνημονεύει ὁ αὐτὸς Θεόφραστος ἐν τῷ
d ἕκτῳ τῶν Φυτικῶν γράφων ὧδε· " τὰ δὲ θερινὰ
μᾶλλον, ἥ τε λυχνὶς καὶ τὸ Διὸς ἄνθος[9] καὶ τὸ
κρίνον καὶ τὸ[9] ἴφυον καὶ ἀμάρακος ὁ Φρύγιος, ἔτι

---

[1] Kock: ἐν A.   [2] στρουθιον A: στρουθίον Kaibel.
[3] A: ἀβροφόρητον Meineke, αὐριφόρητον Wilamowitz.
[4] Schweighäuser: ἴλλεταιτε A.
[5] Kock, joining it with περίδημα, which he reads for περὶ
σῶμα.   [6] ὄαρος "song" Kaibel.
[7] στρουθιον A. The right word is lost.
[8] πόθου before ἄνθους deleted by Kaibel.
[9] ἄνθος and τὸ added by Kaibel.

Since Cynulcus had no answer, Ulpian continued: I will pass to another wreath, that called *struthinos*,[a] which Asclepiades mentions, citing these lines from *The Wreath-sellers* of Eubulus [b]: "Ah, happy she, that in her bower, with wreath of soapwort waving in the breeze, presses her lithe body to her bridegroom of the sweet breath and beautiful hair, even as Cissus (Ivy) clings to Calamus (Reed), waxing strong in the spring-time, melting with love for the tree toad." This wreath is twined from the flower of the *struthion*, as it is called, which Theophrastus mentions in the sixth book of his *Enquiry into Plants*, in these words [c]: "The iris blooms in summer, as does also the so-called *struthion*, which is a beautiful flower in appearance but lacks fragrance." Galene of Smyrna calls it . . .[d]

Pothos.[e] Thus is denominated a kind of wreath, as Nicander of Colophon says in his *Glossary* [f]; perhaps also a wreath twined from the flower of this name, which the same Theophrastus mentions in the sixth book of his *Plants*, writing as follows [c]: "Those that belong rather to summer are the rose-campion, the carnation, the lily, the spike-lavender, the Phrygian sweet marjoram, and again the *pothos*, as

---

[a] Of soapwort, fuller's herb.

[b] Kock ii. 199; the text is very uncertain. This " pulcherrima ecloga " (Kock) is best understood as a mock lyric, mostly dactylic, in the style of Aristoph. *Ran.* 1264-1295 (also dactylic). For romantic stories of plants see Rohde, *Gr. Rom.*³ 168-169, note 2.

[c] Theophr. *Hist. Plant.* vi. 8. 3, Hort (L.C.L. ii. 50), below. 680 f (p. 144).

[d] See critical note 7. No writer named Galene is otherwise known; an hetaera of the name Athen. 587 f (vol. vi. p. 168).

[e] Lit. " Desire," or " Regret " (Hort).

[f] Frag. 144, p. 206 Schneider.

δὲ ὁ πόθος καλούμενος. οὗτος δέ ἐστι διττός, ὁ
μὲν ἔχων τὸ ἄνθος ὅμοιον ὑακίνθῳ, ὁ δ' ἕτερος
ἄχρως, ἔκλευκος,[1] ᾧ χρῶνται πρὸς τοὺς τάφους."
καταλέγει δὲ Εὔβουλος καὶ ἄλλους στεφάνους·

> Αἰγίδιον, σὺ δὲ τόνδε φορήσεις
> στέφανον πολυποίκιλον ἀνθέων,
> ὑγρότατον,[2] χαριέστατον, ὦ Ζεῦ·
> τί γάρ; αὐτὸν[3] ἔχουσα φιλήσει.

e κἀν τοῖς ἑξῆς τάδε φησί·

> στεφάνους ἴσως βούλεσθε· πότερ'[4] ἑρπυλλίνους
> ἢ μυρτίνους ἢ τῶν διηνθεμισμένων;[5]
> Β. τῶν μυρτίνων βουλόμεθα τουτωνί· σὺ δὲ[6]
> τά γ'[7] ἄλλα πώλει πάντα πλὴν τῶν μυρτίνων.

ΦΙΛΤΡΙΝΟΣ. Ξέναρχος Στρατιώτῃ·

> φιλύρας εἶχε γὰρ
> ὁ παῖς ἀφύλλου στέφανον ἀμφικείμενον.

Καλοῦνται δέ τινες καὶ ΕΛΙΚΤΟΙ στέφανοι, ὥσπερ
f παρὰ 'Αλεξανδρεῦσι μέχρι καὶ νῦν. μνημονεύει δ'
αὐτῶν Χαιρήμων ὁ τραγῳδιοποιὸς ἐν Διονύσῳ διὰ
τούτων·

> κισσῷ τε ναρκίσσῳ τε τριέλικας κύκλῳ
> στεφάνων ἑλικτῶν ὁρμαθούς[8] . . .

Περὶ δὲ τῶν ἐν Αἰγύπτῳ αἰεὶ ἀνθούντων στε-

---

[1] AC: εὔλευκος E, λευκὸς Theophr.
[2] Hirschig: γρυπότατον A.
[6] τί γάρ; αὐτὸν Bergk: τίο γαρ αὐτὸν A.
[4] Canter: πότερον A.　　　[5] Kock: διηνθημένων A.
[6] τουτωνί· σὺ δὲ Dobree: τούτῳ οὐ A.

it is called. This name is applied in two senses, the one with a flower like that of the larkspur, the other [a] being colourless, whitish, which they use at funerals."

Eubulus gives a list of other wreaths besides [b]: " Aegidium (Kid), you shall wear this wreath varied with many flowers, most pliant and full of charm, Zeus knows! What, indeed? With it you'll find a lover." And in the verses coming after these he says [c]: " A. Perhaps you'd like some wreaths; shall they be of tufted thyme, or myrtle, or some of these with flowers throughout? B. We want some of these myrtle-wreaths here; you may keep and sell all the others, but not the myrtles."

Linden. Xenarchus in *The Soldier* [d]: " For the lad had a wreath of leafless linden [e] round his head."

Heliktoi [f] is an epithet applied to some wreaths, as among the Alexandrians to this very day. They are mentioned by the tragic poet Chaeremon, in *Dionysus*, in these lines [g]: " Chains of twisted wreaths thrice-coiled all about with ivy and narcissus . . ."

Concerning the ever-flowering wreaths of Egypt

[a] Asphodel.
[b] Kock ii. 200 : addressed to a girl, possibly an hetaera. *cf.* Αἴξ " goat," 587 a (vol. vi. p. 164).
[c] Kock ii. 198.
[d] Kock ii. 473.
[e] The inner bark of the linden furnished the twine for tying the wreath together : Hor. *Od.* i. 38 Persicos odi, puer, apparatus, | displicent nexae philyra (or philyris) coronae.
[f] " Twisted," merely a poetic epithet, not the name of a new variety.
[g] *T.G.F.*[2] 784. For the narcissus in wreaths *cf.* Soph. *O.C.* 682-684 ὁ καλλίβοτρυς . . . νάρκισσος, μεγάλαιν θεαῖν ἀρχαῖον στεφάνωμα.

---

[7] τά γ' ἄλλα Hermann : τ' ἄλλα A.
[8] ὁρμαθούς added conjecturally by Kaibel.

φάνων Ἑλλάνικος ἐν τοῖς Αἰγυπτιακοῖς οὕτως
γράφει· "πόλις ἐπιποταμίη, Τίνδιον ὄνομα· αὕτη[1]
θεῶν ὁμήγυρις καὶ ἱερὸν μέγα καὶ ἁγνὸν ἐν μέσῃ
τῇ πόλει λίθινον καὶ θύρετρα λίθινα. ἔσω τοῦ
ἱεροῦ ἄκανθαι πεφύκασι λευκαὶ καὶ μέλαιναι. ἐπ'
680 αὐτῆσι[2] στέφανοι ἐπιβέβληνται ἄνω, τῆς ἀκάνθου
τοῦ ἄνθεος[3] καὶ ῥοιῆς[4] καὶ ἀμπέλου πεπλεγμένοι·
καὶ οὗτοι αἰεὶ ἀνθέουσι· τοὺς[5] ἀπέθεντο οἱ θεοὶ
ἐν Αἰγύπτῳ πυθόμενοι βασιλεύειν τὸν Βάβυν, ὅς
ἐστι Τυφών." Δημήτριος δ' ἐν τῷ Περὶ τῶν κατ'
Αἴγυπτον περὶ Ἄβυδον[6] πόλιν τὰς ἀκάνθας ταύτας
εἶναί φησιν γράφων οὕτως· "ἔχει δὲ ὁ κάτω τόπος
καὶ ἄκανθάν τινα δένδρον, ὃ τὸν καρπὸν φέρει
b στρογγύλον ἐπί τινων κλωνίων περιφερῶν. ἀνθεῖ
δ' οὗτος ὅταν ὥρα ᾖ, καὶ ἐστὶ τῷ χρώματι τὸ ἄνθος
καλὸν[7] καὶ εὐφεγγές. λέγεται δέ τις μῦθος ὑπὸ
τῶν Αἰγυπτίων ὅτι οἱ Αἰθίοπες στελλόμενοι εἰς
Τροίαν ὑπὸ τοῦ Τιθωνοῦ, ἐπεὶ ἤκουσαν τὸν Μέ-
μνονα τετελευτηκέναι, ἐν τούτῳ τῷ[8] τόπῳ τοὺς
στεφάνους ἀνέβαλον ἐπὶ τὰς ἀκάνθας· ἐστὶ δὲ
παραπλήσια τὰ κλωνία στεφάνοις, ἐφ'[9] ὧν τὸ
ἄνθος φύεται." ὁ δὲ προειρημένος Ἑλλάνικος καὶ
Ἄμασιν Αἰγύπτου βασιλεῦσαι, ἰδιώτην ὄντα καὶ
c τῶν τυχόντων κατὰ τὸν πρῶτον βίον, διὰ στε-

---

[1] Kaibel: τινδιον ονομα ἀυτη A.
[2] Meineke: ἀυτοῖσ οἱ A.　　　　　[3] ἄνθουσ A.
[4] Meineke: ροιῆσ ἄνθοσ A.
[5] στεφάνους after τοὺς deleted by Kaibel.
[6] Berkel: ἄβυλον A.
[7] καλὸν added by Gulick: τὸ ἄνθοσ καὶ εὔφεγγεσ A, καλλι-
φεγγές Salmasius.
[8] τῷ added by early edd.　　　　　[9] Kaibel: ἀφ' A.
140

Hellanicus in his *History of Egypt* writes as follows [a] : A city by the river named Tindium ; this is a meeting-place of all the gods, and there is a large and holy temple of stone in the middle of the city, with stone portals. Within the temple grow acacias, white and black.[b] Upon them wreaths are laid high above, twined with blossoms of the acanthus, pomegranate, and grape-vine ; they are ever-flowering ; these the gods deposited in Egypt when they learned that Babys, who is Typhôn, was king." But Demetrius in his work *On Egypt* says that these acacias are found near the city of Abydus [c] ; he writes as follows [d] : " The region below has a kind of acacia, a tree bearing globose fruit on small circling stems. It blooms in spring, and the flower is of a beautiful brilliant colour.[e] There is a story told by the Egyptians that after the Ethiopians, dispatched to Troy by Tithonus, heard that Memnon had died, they placed their wreaths on the acacia-trees in this region; for the stems on which the flowers grow do resemble wreaths." Hellanicus, whom we have just quoted, says [f] also that Amasis, who was an ordinary man of humble rank in the first part of his career, came to

---

[a] *F.H.G.* i. 66, J. 1. 121. Steph. Byz. places the city in Libya, and the entire story seems to have been transplanted by Hellanicus from the Thracian Chalcidice to Egypt. Babys is more correctly Βέβων = Τυφὼν-Σήθ, Plut. *Is. et Os.* 62 576 A-B), P.-W. ii. 2718-2719.

[b] *Acacia albida*, *A. arabica*.

[c] In Upper Egypt.

[d] *F.H.G.* iv. 383.

[e] *Cf.* Theophr. *H.P.* iv. 2. 8 (Hort i. 298) τὸ δ' ἄνθος καὶ τῇ ὄψει καλόν, ὥστε καὶ στεφάνους ποιεῖν ἐξ αὐτοῦ, of the black acacia, or gum arabic. See critical note 7.

[f] *F.H.G.* i. 66, J. 1. 122. On Amasis see Athen. 560 d (vol. vi. p. 29 and note *i*).

φάνου δωρεὰν ὃν ἔπεμψεν ἀνθέων πλεξάμενος τ
ὥρᾳ περικαλλεστάτων γενέθλια ἐπιτελοῦντι Πατάρ
μιδι τῷ τῆς Αἰγύπτου τότε βασιλεύοντι. τοῦτο
γὰρ ἡσθέντα τῷ κάλλει τοῦ στεφάνου καὶ ἐπ
δεῖπνον καλέσαι τὸν Ἄμασιν καὶ μετὰ ταῦτ
τῶν φίλων ἕνα αὐτὸν ἔχοντα ἐκπέμψαι ποτὲ κα
στρατηγόν, Αἰγυπτίων αὐτῷ πολεμούντων· ὑφ
ὧν διὰ τὸ τοῦ Πατάρμιδος μῖσος ἀποφανθῆνα
βασιλέα.

ΣΥΝΘΗΜΑΤΙΑΙΟΙ[1] στέφανοι, ἠργολαβημένοι κα
ἐκδόσιμοι. Ἀριστοφάνης ἐν Θεσμοφοριαζούσαις·

d   πλέξαι στεφάνους συνθηματιαίους[2] εἴκοσιν.

ΧΟΡΩΝΟΝ.[3] Ἀπίων ἐν τῷ περὶ τῆς Ῥωμαϊκῆς
Διαλέκτου φησὶν τὸν στέφανον πάλαι χορωνὸν
καλούμενον ἀπὸ τοῦ τοὺς χορευτὰς ἐν τοῖς θεάτροις
αὐτῷ χρῆσθαι, αὐτούς τε περικειμένους καὶ ἐπὶ τὸν
στέφανον ἀγωνιζομένους, καθὼς ἐν τοῖς Σιμωνίδου
Ἐπιγράμμασιν ἰδεῖν ἔστιν οὕτως καλούμενον[4]·

Φοῖβον, ὃς ἀγεῖται[5] τοῖς[6] Τυνδαρίδῃσιν ἀοιδᾶν[7]
ἁμέτεροι[8] τέττιγες[9] ἐπεστέψαντο χορωνῷ.

ΑΚΙΝΙΝΟΙ.[10] Στέφανοί τινες καλοῦνται οὕτως οἱ
τῆς ἀκίνου[11] τοῦ φυτοῦ πλεκόμενοι, ὥς φησιν

---

[1] CE: συνθηματιαῖοι A.   [2] sic A.
[3] χορωνον A: χορωνός Casaubon.
[4] Pursan: καλουμένου A.
[5] Wilamowitz: φοῖβον ἐσαγειται A.
[6] τοῖς added by Bergk.   [7] Bergk: αοιδησαν A.
[8] ἁμέτεροι Hartung: αμετροι A.   [9] τέτιγεσ A.
[10] Kaibel: ἀκίννι· οι A.   [11] Canter: ακιδοσ A.

---

[a] Or " of spring."
[b] This account of the rise of Amasis to the throne differs

...e ruler over Egypt through the gift of a wreath
which he had sent, after having it twined with the
most beautiful flowers of the season,[a] in observance
of the birthday of Patarmis, who was ruling over
Egypt at that time.[b] For he, delighted with the
beauty of the wreath, invited Amasis to dinner, and
treating him thereafter as one of his friends, sent him
out on one occasion as commander of his forces when
the Egyptians went to war against him ; and they,
in their hatred of Patarmis, proclaimed Amasis king.

Contractual wreaths are those that have been accepted or supplied by contract. Thus Aristophanes
in *Thesmophoriazusae* [c] : " For I must twine twenty
wreaths already contracted for."

Chorônon.[d] Apion in his work *On the Latin Language*
says that the wreath was in times past called *chorônon*
because the *choreutae* [e] used it in the theatre, not
only putting it on them but also contending for it
as a prize ; thus one may see it so called in the
Epigrams of Simonides [f] : " Phoebus, who guides the
sons of Tyndareus in their songs, is wreathed with a
crown (*chorônos*) by our cicadas." [g]

Akininoi. Certain wreaths are so called, those
twined with the plant *akinos*,[h] according to the

greatly from that in Herod. ii. 162-169 ; see How and Wells
i. 252. Patarmis may be the same as Patarbemis, Herod. ii. 162.

[c] *Thesm.* 457-458, a woman speaks : ἀλλ' εἰς ἀγορὰν ἄπειμι·
δεῖ γὰρ ἀνδράσιν πλέξαι, κτλ. Pollux vii. 200.

[d] *i.e.* κορώνη, Hesych, *s.v.* εἶδος στεφάνου. Quintil. i. 5. 20
cites older Lat. chorona for corona, *cf.* Cic. *Orat.* 48.

[e] Dancers and singers of the chorus; but the etymology
given is incorrect.

[f] *P.L.G.*[4] iii. 507, Diehl ii. 87, Edmonds ii. 402.

[g] For cicada, term jestingly applied to the singing Spartan,
see 633 a (vol. vi. p. 415 and note *f*).

[h] Wild basil, calamint.

143

Ἄνδρων ὁ ἰατρός. παρέθετο δ' αὐτοῦ τὴν λέξ‹
e Παρθένιος ὁ τοῦ Διονυσίου ἐν τῷ πρώτῳ τῶν παρ‹
τοῖς ἱστορικοῖς Λέξεων.

Στεφανωματικὰ δὲ ἄνθη καταλέγει Θεόφραστ‹
τάδε· "ἴον,[1] Διὸς ἄνθος, ἴφυον, φλόγα, ἡμερο
καλλές. πρῶτόν τε τῶν ἀνθέων ἐκφαίνεσθαί φησ‹
τὸ λευκόιον, ἅμα δὲ αὐτῷ καὶ τὸ φλόγινον[2] καλού
μενον τὸ[3] ἄγριον, ἔπειτα νάρκισσον καὶ λείριον κ‹
τῶν ἀγρίων ἀνεμώνης[4] γένος τὸ καλούμενον ὄρειο‹
καὶ τὸ τοῦ βολβοῦ κώδυον. συμπλέκουσι[6] γὰρ κ‹
τοῦτ' ἔνιοι εἰς τοὺς στεφάνους. ἐπὶ τούτοις ἥ τ
οἰνάνθη καὶ τὸ μέλαν ἴον καὶ τῶν ἀγρίων ὅ τ
f ἐλίχρυσος[7] καὶ τῆς ἀνεμώνης ἡ λειμωνία[8] καλουμέν‹
καὶ ξίφιον καὶ ὑάκινθος. τὸ δὲ ῥόδον ὑστερε‹
τούτων καὶ τελευταῖον μὲν φαίνεται, πρῶτον δ
παύεται. τὰ δὲ θερινὰ μᾶλλον, ἥ τε λυχνὶς καὶ τ
Διὸς ἄνθος καὶ τὸ κρίνον καὶ τὸ ἴφυον καὶ ἀμάρακο‹
ὁ[9] Φρύγιος, ἔτι δὲ ὁ πόθος καλούμενος." ἐν δὲ τ‹
θ' ὁ αὐτὸς Θεόφραστός φησιν· "ἐάν τις το‹
ΕΛΙΧΡΥΣΟΥ τῷ ἄνθει στεφανῶται,[10] εὔκλειαν ἴσχε‹
μύρῳ ῥαίνων.[11]" μνημονεύει αὐτοῦ Ἀλκμὰν ‹‹
τούτοις·

[1] ἰωνία (nom.) Theophr.　　[2] τὸν φλόνον A.
[3] τὸν A.　　[4] αιριον καὶ τῶν οριων μανεμωνην ἦσ A.‹
[5] ὅριον A.　　[6] ἐμπλέκουσι Theophr.
[7] ἐλείχ- or ἐλειόχρυσος Theophr.
[8] λιμωνία A.　　[9] ὁ 679 d : om. A.
[10] στεφάνωτε A.　　[11] ῥαίων A.

[a] Or Andreas, 675 c (p. 116).
[b] Meineke, Anal. Alex. 293.

physician Andron.[a] His statement is quoted by Parthenius, the disciple of Dionysius, in the first book of his *Vocabulary of the Historians.*[b]

Theophrastus gives a list of flowers used in wreaths as follows [c] : " Gilliflower, carnation, spike-lavender, wallflower, and day-lily. Of the flowers the first to appear, he says,[d] is the gilliflower ; but with it also [e] the one called the wild wallflower, next pheasant's eye and *polyanthus narcissus,* and among wild plants the kind of anemone which is called the mountain-anemone, and the head of the purse-tassel.[f] For even this some interweave in their wreaths. After these come the drop-wort and the violet, and among wild plants the gold-flower, the meadow-anemone so-called, corn-flag,[g] and squill. The rose is later than these, being the last to appear and the first to cease blooming. Those [h] that belong rather to summer are the rose-campion, the carnation, the lily, spike-lavender, the Phrygian sweet marjoram, also the plant called ' desire.' " And in the ninth book, again, Theophrastus says [i] : " And if a man wreathes himself with the flower of gold-flower, sprinkling it with perfume, he keeps his good name." Alcman mentions it in these verses [j] : " To thee as

[c] *Hist. Pl.* vi. 6. 11 (Hort ii. 44).   [d] vi. 8. 1 (Hort ii. 48).

[e] Theophrastus adds " or a little later."

[f] Lit. " bulb," often mentioned in Athenaeus as a viand. See S. C. Atchley, *Wild Flowers of Attica,* p. 54.

[g] Or gladiolus.

[h] *Cf.* above, 679 d (p. 136).

[i] ix. 19. 3 (Hort ii. 312), with interesting folk-lore omitted by Athenaeus. Hort's rendering " gold-flower " for helichrysum is given above ; it seems to be related to one of the varieties of everlastings or immortelles.

[j] *P.L.G.*[4] iii. 21, Diehl ii. 20, Edmonds i. 68, a girl's song to Hera ; see above, 678 a (p. 128), for the wreath πυλεών.

681

καὶ τὶν εὔχομαι φέροισα
τόνδ᾽ ἑλιχρύσω πυλεῶνα
κῆράτω¹ κυπαίρω.²

καὶ Ἴβυκος·

μύρτα τε καὶ ἴα καὶ ἑλίχρυσος,
μᾶλά³ τε καὶ ῥόδα καὶ τέρεινα δάφνα.⁴

Κρατῖνος δὲ ἐν Μαλθακοῖς φησιν·

ἑρπύλλῳ, κρόκοις, ὑακίνθοις, ἑλιχρύσου⁵ κλάδοις.

ἐστὶ δὲ τὸ ἄνθος ὅμοιον λωτῷ. Θεμισταγόρας δ᾽ ὁ
Ἐφέσιος ἐν τῇ ἐπιγραφομένῃ Χρυσέῃ Βύβλῳ ἀπὸ
b τῆς πρώτης δρεψαμένης νύμφης Ἑλιχρύσης ὄνομα
τὸ ἄνθος ὀνομασθῆναι. τὰ δὲ κρίνα φησὶν ὁ
Θεόφραστος εἶναι καὶ πορφυρανθῆ.

Φιλῖνος δὲ τὸ ΚΡΙΝΟΝ ὑφ᾽ ὧν μὲν λείριον, ὑφ᾽ ὧν
δὲ ἴον καλεῖσθαι. Κορίνθιοι δ᾽ αὐτὸ ἀμβροσίαν
καλοῦσιν, ὥς φησι Νίκανδρος ἐν Γλώσσαις.

Διοκλῆς δ᾽ ἐν τῷ περὶ Θανασίμων Φαρμάκων
"ΑΜΑΡΑΚΟΝ, φησίν, ὃν σάμψουχόν τινες καλοῦσιν."

ΚΟΣΜΟΣΑΝΔΑΛΩΝ δὲ μνημονεύει Κρατῖνος ἐν Μαλθακοῖς διὰ τούτων·

κεφαλὴν ἀνθέμοις ἐρέπτομαι,
λειρίοις, ῥόδοις, κρίνεσιν,⁶ κοσμοσανδάλοις.⁷

c Κλέαρχος δ᾽ ἐν β΄ Βίων " ὅρα, φησίν, τοὺς τὸ

¹ Boissonade: πυλεω ακηράτων A.

² Welcker: κυπερω A.   ³ μᾶλα A.

⁴ Canter: τερινα δαφηα A.

⁵ A: ἐλειχρύσου Meineke.

⁶ Porson: κρίνοισι A.   ⁷ κοσμοσάνδαλλοσ A.

ᵃ Doric for *kypeiron*, mentioned among aromatic plants
Theophr. *H.P.* ix. 7. 3, and identified by Hort (Index) with
Cyperus rotundus.

146

I pray I bring this wreath of gold-flower and lovely *kypairon.*[a] " Also Ibycus [b] : " Myrtles, gilliflowers, and gold-flower, apple-blossoms and roses and delicate bay." And Cratinus in *Mollycoddles* says [c] : " With tufted thyme, saffron crocus, squills, and sprays of gold-flower." The flower is like that of the lotus.[d] Themistagoras of Ephesus in his *Golden Book,* as it is entitled, says [e] that the flower was called *helichrysus* from the nymph, Helichrysê by name, who first gathered it. As for the lilies, Theophrastus says [f] that they even have purple flowers.

Philinus asserts that the lily is called *leirion* by some, *ion* by others. The Corinthians call it *ambrosia,* according to Nicander in his *Glossary.*[g]

Diocles in his treatise *On Deadly Drugs* says [h] : " *Amaracus* (sweet marjoram), which some call *sampsûchus.*"

Cosmosandala are mentioned by Cratinus in *Mollycoddles* in these lines [c] : " I crown my head with flowers—narcissus, roses, lilies, larkspur." Clearchus in the second book of his *Lives* says [i] : " Look at the

---

[b] *P.L.G.*[4] iii. 238, Diehl ii. 56, Edmonds ii. 88.

[c] Kock i. 43, below, 685 b-c (p. 168).

[d] Indeterminate ; of this word Theophr. *H.P.* vii. **15. 3** says " some plants are found in several forms which have almost the same name, as the lotus " (Hort ii. 139).

[e] *F.H.G.* iv. 512.

[f] *H.P.* vi. 6. 3. He apparently had not seen them himself : εἴπερ δή, καθάπερ φασίν, ἔνια καὶ πορφυρᾶ ἐστι.

[g] Frag. 126 Schneider, p. 204. Below, 683 d (p. 160).

[h] Wellmann 195 ; above, 676 d (p. 122).

[i] *F.H.G.* ii. 303 ; the moralist plays on the word κόσμος, order, adornment, in cosmosandalon. See Paus. ii. 35. 5 for the Spartan use of larkspur at the festival of Demeter Chthonia ; on the humiliating treatment of the Spartans by Alexander and Antipater, Aeschin. iii. 133, Diod. xvii. 73, Plut. 235 B.

κοσμοσάνδαλον ἀνείροντας[1] Λακεδαιμονίους, οἳ τὸν
παλαιότατον τῆς πολιτικῆς κόσμον συμπατήσαν-
τες ἐξετραχηλίσθησαν. διόπερ καλῶς περὶ αὐτῶν
εἴρηκεν ὁ κωμῳδιοποιὸς ᾿Αντιφάνης ἐν Κιθαριστῇ·

οὐκ ἐφύσων οἱ Λάκωνες ὡς ἀπόρθητοί ποτε;
νῦν δ᾿ ὁμηρεύουσ᾿ ἔχοντες πορφυροῦς κεκρυ-
φάλους;"

᾿Ικέσιος δ᾿ ἐν δευτέρῳ περὶ ῞Υλης τὸ ΛΕΥΚΟΙΟΝ
φησι μεσότητά τινα ἔχειν ἐν τῷ στύφειν, πολὺ δ᾿
d ἀρίστην εὐωδίαν καὶ δυναμένην τέρπειν, ἀλλὰ πρὸς
ὀλίγιστον. " τὸ δὲ μέλαν, φησί, τὴν μὲν αὐτὴν
θεωρίαν ἔχει, εὐῶδες δ᾿ ἐστὶ πολὺ μᾶλλον." ᾿Απολ-
λόδωρος δὲ ἐν τῷ περὶ Θηρίων φησί· " χαμαίπιτυν,
οἱ δὲ ὁλόκυρον, οἱ δὲ ᾿Αθήνησιν ἰωνιάν, οἱ δὲ κατ᾿
Εὔβοιαν σιδηρῖτιν." Νίκανδρος δ᾿ ἐν δευτέρῳ
Γεωργικῶν (τὰ δὲ ἔπη ὀλίγον ὕστερον παρα-
θήσομαι, ὅταν περὶ πάντων τῶν στεφανωματικῶν
ἀνθῶν διεξέρχωμαι) τὸ ἴον, φησίν, ᾿Ιωνιάδες[2] τινὲς
νύμφαι ῎Ιωνι ἐχαρίσαντο πρώτῳ.[3]

e Τὸν δὲ ΝΑΡΚΙΣΣΟΝ ἐν τῷ ς´ περὶ Φυτῶν ᾿Ιστορίας
ὁ Θεόφραστος καλεῖσθαί φησι καὶ λείριον. εἶθ᾿
ὑποβὰς ὡς διαλλάσσοντα τίθησιν νάρκισσον καὶ

---

[1] Natalis Comes: ἀνευρόντασ A.
[2] A: ἰάδες C.   [3] C adds ὅθεν καὶ ἐκλήθη.

---

[a] Kock ii. 57.   [b] i.e. they are no better than women.
[c] From the point of view of a physician writing on diet
as well as materia medica; cf. 118 b (vol. ii. p. 50).
[d] Frag. 10 in Schneider's *Nicander*, p. 195.
[e] Diosc. i. 158 says *holokyron* was the name given to the
ionia in Pontus. Perhaps οἱ ἐν Πόντῳ should be read above
(Kaibel).   [f] Below, 683 a (p. 156).
[g] The white *ion* is the gilliflower, the dark the violet.

larkspur-twining Lacedaemonians, who, trampling under foot the most ancient adornment of their commonwealth, took a toss to their utter ruin. Hence the comic poet Antiphanes has well said of them in his *Harp Player* [a] : ' Did not the Lacedaemonians use to swell about as if they should never be ravaged ? Yet to-day they give hostages while they wear their purple bandannas.' " [b]

Hicesius in the second book of his work *On Materials for Food* [c] says that the *leukoion* (gilliflower) has a moderately astringent effect, but much the best fragrance and power to delight, though lasting a very short while. "The violet," he says, "may be regarded in the same way, but it is much more fragrant." Apollodorus in his book *On Wild Creatures* says [d] : "Some speak of *chamaipitys* (ground-pine), others [e] call it *holokyron*; the men at Athens call it *ionia* (gilli-flower), those in Euboea *sideritis*." Nicander in the second book of his work *On Farming* (I will cite the verses a little later, [f] after I have treated successively all the flowers used in wreaths) says that the *ion* [g] was conferred first on Ion by certain Ioniad [h] nymphs.

The *narcissus*, Theophrastus says in the sixth book of his *Enquiry into Plants*, [i] is called also *leirion*. But later he treats narcissus and *leirion* as distinct. [j]

[h] The form Ἰωνιάδες (om. L. & S.; below, 683 a, p. 156) occurs also in Strabo 356, who says that these nymphs had a shrine beside the Cytherius (or Cytherus) River in Elis, noted for its healing waters; so Paus. vi. 22. 7. *Cf.* the story of the babe Iamus, hidden by his mother Evadne in a bed of " yellow and crimson gilliflowers," Pind. *Ol.* vi. 54-55.

[i] *H.P.* vi. 6. 9; Hort ii. 466 (Index) identifies with *narcissus serotinus.*

[j] *H.P.* vi. 8. 1 pheasant's eye and *polyanthus narcissus* (Hort ii. 51), above, 680 e (p. 144).

149

λείριον.[1] Εὔμαχος[2] δ᾽ ὁ Κορκυραῖος ἐν ῾Ριζο-
τομικῷ καὶ ἀκακαλλίδα φησὶ καλεῖσθαι τὸν νάρκισσον καὶ κρόταλον. τοῦ δὲ ἡμεροκαλλοῦς
καλουμένου ἄνθους, ὃ τὴν μὲν νύκτα μαραίνεται,
ἅμα δὲ τῷ ἡλίῳ ἀνατέλλοντι θάλλει, μνημονεύει
Κρατῖνος ἐν Μαλθακοῖς λέγων οὕτως·

> ἡμεροκαλλεῖ τε τῷ φιλουμένῳ.

Τῆς δ᾽ ΕΡΠΥΛΛΟΥ, φησὶ Θεόφραστος, τὴν ἄ-
f γριον[3] κομίζοντες ἐκ τῶν ὁρῶν[4] φυτεύουσιν ἐν
Σικυῶνι καὶ ᾿Αθήνησιν ἐκ τοῦ ῾Υμηττοῦ. παρ᾽
ἄλλοις δὲ ὅλα[5] ὄρη πλήρη ἐστὶ τοῦ ἄνθους, καθάπερ ἐν Θράκῃ. Φιλῖνος δέ φησιν αὐτὴν ζυγίδα
καλεῖσθαι. περὶ δὲ τῆς ΛΥΧΝΙΔΟΣ λέγων ᾿Αμερίας ὁ
Μακεδὼν ἐν τῷ ῾Ριζοτομικῷ φησιν ἀναφῦναι αὐτὴν
ἐκ τῶν ᾿Αφροδίτης λουτρῶν ὅτε ῾Ηφαίστῳ συγ-
κοιμηθεῖσα ἡ ᾿Αφροδίτη λούοιτο.[6] εἶναι δ᾽ ἀρίστην
ἐν Κύπρῳ καὶ Λήμνῳ, ἔτι δὲ Στρογγύλῃ καὶ ῎Ερυκι
καὶ Κυθήροις. ἡ δ᾽ ΙΡΙΣ,[7] φησὶ Θεόφραστος, ἀνθεῖ
τοῦ θέρους μόνη τε τῶν Εὐρωπαίων ἀνθέων εὔ-
οσμός ἐστιν. ἀρίστη δ᾽ ἐστὶν ἐν ᾿Ιλλυριοῖς τοῖς
682 ἀνωκισμένοις τῆς θαλάσσης. Φιλῖνος δέ φησι τὰ
ἄνθη τῆς ἴριδος[8] λέγεσθαι λύκους διὰ τὸ ἐμφερῆ
εἶναι λύκου χείλεσι. Νικόλαος δ᾽ ὁ Δαμασκηνὸς ἐν
τῇ ὀγδόῃ τῶν ᾿Ιστοριῶν πρὸς ταῖς ἑκατὸν περὶ τὰς

---

1 αιριον A.   2 εὔμοχος A.
3 A (ἔρπυλλος ἄγριος Theophr.): ἀγρίαν CE.
4 Theophr: ἀγρῶν A.
5 ὅλα added by Meineke (ὅλως Theophr.).
6 A: λούεται CE, ἐλούσατο Kaibel.   7 CE: ἱερισ A.
8 τῆς ἴριδος E: τῆσ ἱεριδοσ A, ταύτης C.

---

a Kock i. 43, below, 685 c (p. 168).

Eumachus of Corcyra in his *Root-Gathering* declares that the narcissus is called both *akakallis* and *krotalon* (rattle). The so-called *hemerocalles*, day-lily, which droops during the night but revives at sunrise, is mentioned by Cratinus in *Mollycoddles* thus[a] : "And with the day-lily so much beloved."

The wild variety of *herpyllus* (thyme), as Theophrastus says,[b] is brought from the mountains and planted at Sicyon, or from Hymettus and planted at Athens. And in other districts entire mountains are covered with the flower, for instance in Thrace. Philinus says it is called *zygis*.[c] And speaking of the *lychnis* (rose campion), Amerias of Macedonia in his book *On Root-Gathering* says that it sprang up from Aphrodite's bath whenever she, after lying with Hephaestus,[d] bathed herself. The best is found in Cyprus and Lemnos, also in Strongylê,[e] Eryx, and Cythera. The *iris*, according to Theophrastus,[f] blooms in summer, and is the only one of the European flowers having a fragrant perfume.[g] The best is found in the parts of Illyria inland from the sea. Philinus says that iris flowers are called " wolves " because they resemble the lips of a wolf. Nicolas of Damascus in the one hundred and eighth book of his *Histories*[h] says that near the Alps is a lake covering

[b] *H.P.* vi. 7. 2 (Hort ii. 44).
[c] So Diosc. iii. 38.
[d] Aphrodite is his wife in *Od.* viii. 268-270.
[e] Stromboli.   [f] *H.P.* vi. 8. 3.
[g] *Ibid.* ix. 7. 3, where Theophrastus says that the iris is the only European plant used for perfumes ; all others come " from Asia and sunny regions," *e.g.* spikenard and myrrh. *Cf. H.P.* iv. 5. 2 τῶν δὲ εὐωδῶν οὐδὲν ἐν ταύταις (Greek countries) πλὴν ἴρις ἐν τῇ Ἰλλυρίδι καὶ περὶ τὸν Ἀδρίαν. Doubtless this is *iris dalmatica*.
[h] *F.H.G.* iii. 416, J. 2 A 377.

Ἄλπεις λίμνην τινά φησιν εἶναι πολλῶν σταδίων
οὖσαν, ἧς περὶ τὸν κύκλον πεφυκέναι δι' ἔτους ἄνθη
ἥδιστα καὶ εὐχρούστατα, ὅμοια ταῖς καλουμέναις
ΚΑΛΧΑΙΣ. τῶν δὲ καλχῶν μέμνηται καὶ Ἀλκμὰν ἐν
τούτοις·

χρύσιον[1] ὅρμον ἔχων ῥαδινᾶν πετάλοισι καλχᾶν.[2]

b μνημονεύει αὐτῶν καὶ Ἐπίχαρμος ἐν Ἀγρωστίνῳ.[3]
" Τῶν δὲ ΡΟΔΩΝ, φησὶ Θεόφραστος ἐν τῷ ἕκτῳ,
πολλαί εἰσι διαφοραί. τὰ μὲν γὰρ πλεῖστα αὐτῶν[4]
πεντάφυλλα, τὰ δὲ δωδεκάφυλλα, ἔνια δ' ἐστὶ καὶ
ἑκατοντάφυλλα περὶ Φιλίππους. λαμβάνοντες γὰρ
ἐκ τοῦ Παγγαίου φυτεύουσιν· ἐκεῖ γὰρ γίγνεται[5]
πολλά. μικρὰ δὲ σφόδρα τὰ ἐντὸς φύλλα· ἡ γὰρ
ἔκφυσις αὐτῶν οὕτως ἐστὶν ὥστ' εἶναι τὰ μὲν
ἐντός, τὰ δὲ ἐκτός· οὐκ εὔοσμα δὲ οὐδὲ μεγάλα
τοῖς μεγέθεσιν. τὰ δὲ πεντάφυλλα εὐώδη μᾶλλον
c ὧν τραχὺ τὸ κάτω. εὐοσμότατα δὲ τὰ ἐν Κυρήνῃ,
διὸ καὶ τὸ μύρον ἥδιστον. καὶ τῶν ἴων δὲ καὶ τῶν
ἄλλων ἀνθέων ἄκρατοι μάλιστα καὶ θεῖαι[6] αἱ ὀσμαί·
διαφερόντως δὲ ἡ τοῦ κρόκου." Τιμαχίδας δὲ ἐν
τοῖς Δείπνοις τὸ ῥόδον φησὶ τοὺς Ἀρκάδας καλεῖν
εὔομφον[7] ἀντὶ τοῦ εὔοσμον. Ἀπολλόδωρος δ' ἐν

---

[1] Early edd.: χρυσειον A.
[2] Dalechamps: ραδιναν πεταλοισι καλχαν ACE.
[3] αγρωστεινωι A.
[4] εἰσὶν after αὐτῶν deleted by Meineke. αὐτῶν εἰσιν om. Theophr.   [5] γίνονται C.
[6] καὶ θεῖαι ACE: ἐκεῖ Theophr., ἐκεῖθι Schneider following Saracenus, Hort.
[7] Nauck: εὐόμφαλον ACE.

---

[a] Said to be a kind of chrysanthemum; Hesych. s.v. calls it vaguely a βοτάνιον ἀνθοφόρον.

many stadia, round the circuit of which grow the
year through very lovely and beautifully-coloured
flowers similar to the *calchai*,[a] as they are called.
The *calchai* are mentioned by Alcman in these
words [b] : " He wore a golden chain of *calchai* with
soft petals." They are mentioned by Epicharmus
also in *The Rustic*.[c]

" Among *roses*," says Theophrastus in the sixth
book,[d] " there are many differences. Most of them
have five petals, others twelve, and some even a
hundred, in the neighbourhood of Philippi. For the
Philippians get them on Mount Pangaeus and plant
them in gardens, since they are abundant in that
region. The inner petals are very small ; for their
manner of growth is such that some are inside, some
outside ; they are not especially fragrant nor of large
size. Those with five petals of which the part [e]
below is rough are more fragrant. The most fragrant
are those of Cyrene, hence the perfume made from
them is most delightful. In fact the fragrance from
gilliflowers and other flowers too is most pure and
heavenly [f] ; and especially so is that of the saffron
crocus." Timachidas in *The Banquets* says that the
Arcadians call the rose *euomphos* [g] for *euosmos*
(fragrant). Apollodorus in the fourth book of his

[b] *P.L.G.*[4] iii. 52, Diehl ii. 37, Edmonds i. 88.
[c] Kaibel 91.   [d] *H.P.* vi. 6. 4.
[e] According to Hort (ii. 38 note 5) the " hip," called
μῆλον (apple), *H.P.* vi. 6. 6, or ὀμφαλός, Aristot. *Probl.*
xii. 8 διὰ τί ἥδιον ὄζει τῶν ῥόδων ὧν ὁ ὀμφαλὸς τραχύς ἐστιν
ἢ ὧν λεῖος;
[f] So wrote Athenaeus, meaning, of course, the flowers of
Cyrene. See critical note 6.
[g] Or, reading εὐόμφαλον, " well-hipped," *cf.* note *e* and
critical note 7. In favour of Nauck's conjecture is Hesych.
ὀμφά· ὀσμή, and ὀμφή . . . πνοή.

δ΄ Παρθικῶν ἄνθος τι ἀναγράφει καλούμενον
ΦΙΛΑΔΕΛΦΟΝ κατὰ τὴν Παρθικὴν χώραν, περὶ οὗ
τάδε φησίν· " καὶ μυρσίνης γένη ποικίλα μῖλάξ τε
καὶ τὸ καλούμενον φιλάδελφον, ὃ τὴν ἐπωνυμίαν
d ἔλαβε τῇ φύσει πρόσφορον. ἐπειδὰν γὰρ ἐκ δια-
στήματος αὐτομάτως κράδαι συμπέσωσι, ἐμψύχων
περιπλοκῇ ἐν τῷ . . . μένουσιν[1] ἡνωμέναι καθάπερ
ἀπὸ ῥίζης μιᾶς, καὶ τὸ λοιπὸν ἀνατρέχουσιν καὶ
ζῳοφυτοῦσιν· διὸ καὶ τοῖς ἡμέροις φυλακὴν ἀπ᾿
αὐτῶν κατασκευάζουσιν. ἀφαιροῦντες γὰρ τῶν
ῥάβδων τὰς λεπτοτάτας καὶ διαπλέξαντες[2] δικτύου
τρόπῳ φυτεύουσιν κύκλῳ τῶν κηπευμάτων· καὶ
ταῦτα συμπλεκόμενα περιβόλου παρέχεται δυσπάρ-
οδον ἀσφάλειαν."

Ἀνθῶν δὲ στεφανωτικῶν μέμνηται ὁ μὲν τὰ
e Κύπρια Ἔπη πεποιηκὼς Ἡγησίας ἢ Στασῖνος·
Δημοδάμας γὰρ ὁ Ἁλικαρνασσεὺς ἢ Μιλήσιος ἐν
τῷ περὶ Ἁλικαρνασσοῦ Κυπρία[3] Ἁλικαρνασσέως
αὐτὰ[4] εἶναί φησι ποιήματα. λέγει δ᾿ οὖν ὅστις ἐστὶν
ὁ ποιήσας αὐτὰ ἐν τῷ α΄ οὑτωσί·

εἵματα[5] μὲν χροῒ ἔστο τά[6] οἱ Χάριτές τε καὶ Ὧραι
ποίησαν καὶ ἔβαψαν ἐν ἄνθεσιν εἰαρινοῖσιν,
οἷα φοροῦσ᾿[7] ὧραι, ἔν τε κρόκῳ ἔν θ᾿ ὑακίνθῳ
ἔν τε ἴῳ θαλέθοντι ῥόδου τ᾿ ἐνὶ ἄνθεϊ καλῷ,

---

[1] περιπλοκῇ μένουσιν CE: περιπλοκὴν ἐν τῶι μένουσιν A.
[2] Schweighäuser: διαπλέξαντέστε A.
[3] Hecker: κύπρια A.
[4] δ᾿ before αὐτὰ deleted by Hecker.
[5] Canter: ἱμάτια A.   [6] Meineke: χροιᾶσ τότε A.
[7] A: ὅσσα φέρουσ᾿ Hecker.

---

[a] F.H.G. iv. 309, Behr frag. 8, p. 39. Possibly jasmine
is meant, though the shrub called *philadelphus* in America

Parthian History records a flower called *philadelphum*
in the Parthian country, of which he says [a] : " And
there are various kinds of myrtle such as *smilax*
(bindweed) and the so-called *philadelphum,* which got
its name as being appropriate to its nature. For
whenever separate sprays of it meet accidentally,
they remain united in an embrace like that of
animate creatures,[b] as though sprung from a single
root, and then continue to run on and put out new
shoots ; hence men contrive from them a protection
for their cultivated plants. For taking the lightest
shoots, they interweave them like a net and plant
them round about their garden-plots ; and thus en-
twined together they provide a fence of impenetrable
security."

Flowers used in wreaths are mentioned by the
author of the *Cyprian Lays,* Hegesias or Stasinus ;
Demodamas of Halicarnassus or Miletus, to be sure,
in his book *On Halicarnassus* says [c] that they are the
work of Cyprias of Halicarnassus. Be that as it may,
whoever the writer of them is says in the first book [d] :
" She robed her body in the garments which the
Graces and Seasons had made and dyed with the
flowers of spring, even such as the seasons bring [e]—
with saffron crocus and larkspur, with the lush violet

and Britain is the mock-orange or syringa. Philadelphus,
of course, means " loving one's brother or sister."

[b] The lacuna (see critical note 1) has been filled in various
ways, none quite satisfactory. Perhaps we should read
ἐμψύχων περιπλοκῆς ἐγγυτάτω " most closely like the embrace
of animate creatures."

[c] *F.H.G.* ii. 444.

[d] *Frag. ep.* pp. 16, 22. Welcker, *Ep. Cyclus* ii. 88 explains the verses as a description of Aphrodite preparing
for the judgement of Paris. *Cf. h. Hom.* vi.

[e] For this meaning of φοροῦσι cf. below, 686 a and note d.

ἡδέϊ[1] νεκταρέῳ, ἔν τ' ἀμβροσίαις καλύκεσσιν
f ναρκίσσου[2] . . . καὶ λειρίου[3]. . .
. . . . δϊ"[4] 'Αφροδίτη
ὥραις παντοίαις τεθυωμένα εἵματα ἔστο.

οὗτος ὁ ποιητὴς καὶ τὴν τῶν στεφάνων χρῆσιν
εἰδὼς φαίνεται δι' ὧν λέγει·

ἡ δὲ σὺν ἀμφιπόλοισι φιλομμειδὴς[5] 'Αφροδίτη . . .[6]
πλεξάμεναι στεφάνους εὐώδεας ἄνθεα γαίης
ἂν κεφαλαῖσιν ἔθεντο θεαὶ λιπαροκρήδεμνοι,
Νύμφαι καὶ Χάριτες, ἅμα δὲ χρυσῆ 'Αφροδίτη,
καλὸν ἀείδουσαι κατ' ὄρος πολυπιδάκου Ἴδης.

683 Νίκανδρος δ' ἐν δευτέρῳ Γεωργικῶν καταλέγων
καὶ αὐτὸς στεφανωτικὰ ἄνθη καὶ περὶ Ἰωνιάδων[7]
Νυμφῶν καὶ περὶ ῥόδων τάδε λέγει·

ἀλλὰ τὰ μὲν σπείροις τε καὶ ὅσσ'[8] ὡραῖα φυ-
τεύοις,
ἄνθε'[9] Ἰαονίηθε· γένη γε μὲν ἴασι[10] δισσά,
ὠχρόν τε χρυσῷ τε φυὴν εἰς ὦπα προσειδές,[11]
ἄσσα τ' Ἰωνιάδες Νύμφαι στέφος ἁγνὸν Ἴωνι
Πισαίοις ποθέσασαι ἐνὶ κλήροισιν ὄρεξαν.
ἤνυσε γὰρ χλούνηνδε[12] μετεσσύμενος σκυλάκεσσιν,
b Ἀλφειῷ[13] καὶ λύθρον ἑῶν ἐπλύνατο γυίων
ἑσπέριος Νύμφαισιν Ἰαονίδεσσι νυχεύσων.—

[1] ἡδεῖ Λ.
[2] ἄνθεσι (gloss) ναρκίσσου A. Lacunae indicated by Koechly and Meineke.
[3] καὶ λειρίου Meineke: καλιρρόου A.
[4] Casaubon: δ οια A. [5] φιλομειδὴς A.
[6] Lacuna marked by Meineke.
[7] Kaibel (cf. above, 681 d, notes 2 and h, pp. 148, 149): τῶν ἰάδων A.
[8] Schneider: ὠσ A. [9] Schneider: ἄνθη A.

and the fair blossom of the rose, sweet and nectarous, and with the ambrosial cups of narcissus and lily . . . divine Aphrodite robed herself in garments scented with all the seasons." This poet is also plainly aware of the use of wreaths from what he says in the following [a] : " And she, the laughter-loving Aphrodite, with her handmaids. . . . The goddesses of the glossy veils, twining fragrant wreaths of earth's flowers, placed them on their heads,—Nymphs and Graces, and with them golden Aphrodite, the while they sang beautifully on Mount Ida with its many springs."

Nicander in the second book of his *Farming*, giving likewise a list of flowers used in wreaths, has the following concerning the Ioniad Nymphs as well as roses [b] : " But some thou may'st sow and all that mature transplant, the flowers which came from Ionia ; the kinds of Iad-flowers [c] are twain, yellow or like unto gold in appearance, and those again which the Ioniad Nymphs [d] in their yearning offered as a chaste wreath to Ion in the glebes of Pisa. For he had made a kill when he went in pursuit of a boar with his hounds, and in the Alpheius River at eventide, with the aid of the Ioniad Nymphs,[e] he washed away the gore from his limbs as he prepared

---

[a] *Frag. ep.* 23.
[b] Frag. 74 Schneider. pp. 91-112.
[c] ἰάδες = ἴα, gilliflowers and violets.
[d] Above, 681 d (p. 149 note *h*).
[e] So Schneider, rightly joining Νύμφαισιν with ἐπλύνατο, against Meineke, who construed Νύμφαισιν with νυχεύσων (so L. & S.).

---

[10] Ἰάδι Meineke, εἰδόσι Ludwich.
[11] Schweighäuser : εισῶπατροσειδεσ A.
[12] Schneider : χλοῦν ἦν δὲ A.   [13] αλφιω A.

αὐτὰρ ἀκανθοβόλοιο ῥόδου κατατέμνεο βλάστας
τάφροις τ' ἐμπήξειας, ὅσον¹ διπάλαιστα τε-
λέσκων²·
πρῶτα μὲν Ὠδονίηθε Μίδης³ ἅπερ Ἀσίδος ἀρχὴν
λείπων ἐν κλήροισιν ἀνέτρεφεν Ἡμαθίοισιν,⁴
αἰὲν ἐς ἑξήκοντα πέριξ κομόωντα πετήλοις·
δεύτερα Νισαίης⁵ Μεγαρηίδος, οὐδὲ Φάσηλις

c   οὐδ' αὐτὴ Λεύκοφρυν ἀγασσαμένη⁶ ἐπιμεμφής,
Ληθαίου Μάγνητος ἐφ' ὕδασιν εὐθαλέουσα.—
κισσοῦ δ' ἄλλοτε κλῶν' εὐρυρρίζου⁷ καπέτοισιν,
πολλάκι δὲ στέφος αὐτὸ κορυμβήλοιο⁸ φυτεύσαις
Θρασκίω ἢ ἀργωπὸν ἠὲ⁹ κλαδέεσσι πλανήτην·
βλαστοδρεπῆ δὲ χυτοῖο καεὶς¹⁰ μίαν ὄρσεο
κόρσην,¹¹
ὑπείραν ὑπὸ σπυρίδεσσι νεοπλέκτοισι καθάπτων,
ὄρρα δύο κροκόωντες ἐπιζυγέοντε κόρυμβοι¹²
μέσφα¹³ συνωρίζωσιν ὑπερφιάλοιο μετώπου,
χλωροῖς ἀμφοτέρωθεν ἐπηρεφέες πετάλοισιν.—

---

¹ Meineke: οδον A.   ² Scaliger: διπαλεστατε λεσχων A.
³ Schweighäuser: ωδονιησθεμιδησ A.
⁴ Weston: ηματίοισιν A.   ⁵ Canter: νισέησ A.
⁶ Schweighäuser: ἀγασσαμένησ A.
⁷ κλῶν' εὐρυρρίζου Schneider: κλῶνεα εὐρίζου A.
⁸ κορυμβηλοιο A (sic).
⁹ Schneider: θρασκιον η αργωπονηε A.
¹⁰ Ludwich: βλαστοδρεπιδεχυτοιο καὶ εισ A.
¹¹ J. G. Schneider: ορεοκορσην A.
¹² Canter: κορύμβοισ A.   ¹³ Meineke: μέσσα A.

ᵃ So Theophr. *H.P.* vi. 6. 6 advises the propagating of
roses from slips rather than by the slow process of growing
them from seed.

to pass the night.—Then, cut scions ^a of the thorny
rose and set them firmly in trenches, making them
about two hand-breadths high.^b First, roses which
Midas of Odonia, when he left his realm in Asia,
grew in the Emathian glebes, roses ever luxuriant
with sixty petals all round.^c Secondly, roses from
Nisaea in Megara ; nor is Phaselis ^d to be spurned,
nor again the city which reveres the goddess of the
White Brow, flourishing beside the waters of the
Lethaeus River in Magnesia.^e—At another time plant
a slip of wide-rooting ivy ^f in trenches ; often, again,
you may make a festoon by itself ^g of white-berried
ivy, when spring comes,^h either the white or the kind
with sprawling tendrils ⁱ ; set upright a single head
of it pruned from a spreading vine ^j by singeing,
fastening a cord to freshly-plaited wicker-lattices, so
that two clusters, weaving and yoking together, may
unite the while in a proud head shaded on each side

^b Varro, *De re rust.* i. 35 says the slips should be one hand-
breadth long. Meineke took διπάλαιστα to mean the space
between them.

^c So Herod. viii. 138.

^d In Pamphylia, famous for its attar of roses, below, 688 e
(p. 186).

^e On the Maeander, where there was a celebrated temple
of Artemis Λευκόφρυς or Λευκοφρυηνή.

^f *H.P.* iii. 18. 9 : " All ivies have numerous close roots
tangled together " (Hort). See critical note 7.

^g *i.e.* the mature and already rooted plant as opposed to
a spray. It must, however, be " cut back " or singed.
Cf. H.P. vi. 6. 6.

^h Lit. " At the time of the N.W wind " (Θρασκίας).

ⁱ Perhaps the *helix*, *H.P.* iii. 18. 6 (Hort i. 273).

^j The reading and meaning are much disputed, χυτοῖο
being specially difficult. Perhaps it is the same as χώματος
(*H.P.* ii. 5. 2), the " hill " or mass of soil in which the plant
is set.

σπέρματι μὴν[1] κάλυκες κεφαλήγονοι[2] ἀντελέουσιν,
ἀργήεις πετάλοισι, κρόκῳ μέσα χροισθεῖσαι[3]·
ἃ κρίνα, λείρια δ' ἄλλοι ἐπιφθέγγονται ἀοιδῶν,
οἱ δὲ καὶ ἀμβροσίην, πολέες δέ τε[4] χάρμ' Ἀ-
    φροδίτης·
ἤρισε γὰρ χροιῇ. τὸ δέ που ἐπὶ μέσσον ὄνειδος

e ὅπλον βρωμήταο διεκτέλλον πεφάτισται.
ἶρις δ' ἐν ῥίζῃσιν ἀγαλλιὰς ἤ θ'[5] ὑακίνθῳ
αἰαστῇ προσέοικε, χελιδονίοισι δὲ τέλλει[6]
ἄνθεσιν, ἰσοδρομεῦσα χελιδόσιν, αἵ τ'[7] ἀνὰ κόλπῳ[8]
φυλλάδα νηλείην ἐκχεύετον,[9] ἀρτίγονοι δὲ
εἴδοντ'[10] ἠμύουσαι ἀεὶ κάλυκες στομίοισιν.
σὺν καὶ ἄπερ[11] τ' ὀξεῖα[12] χροιῇ λυχνὶς οὐδὲ θρυ-
    αλλίς,
οὐδὲ μὲν ἀνθεμίδων κενεὴ γηρύσεται ἀκμή,
οὐδὲ βοάνθεμα κεῖνα τά τ' αἰπύτατον κάρη[13] ὑψοῖ,[14]
φλόξ τε[15] θεοῦ αὐγῇσιν ἀνερχομένης γανάουσα.[16]

---

[1] Schneider: σπερματινην A.
[2] κεφαληγονοι A: κεφαληγόνοι Schneider.
[3] χροϊσθεῖσαι A.   [4] δέ τε Schneider: δεγε A.
[5] Schneider: αγαλλιασηδ' A.   [6] Canter: τιλλει A.
[7] χελιδόσιν ἤ τε Schneider.   [8] καυλῷ "stalk"?
[9] Early edd.: ἐγχευε τὸν A.
[10] Casaubon: αρτιγονον δε ειδοντετ' A.
[11] καὶ ἄπερ Schneider: καιπερ A.   [12] Meineke: τοξια A.
[13] Schweighäuser: τατεπυτατον κορη A.
[14] Casaubon: ὑψοῦ A.   [15] Schweighäuser: δὲ A.
[16] Schneider: αουσα A.

---

[a] Passing now to the lily. μὴν after σπέρματι implies
that growing lilies from seed is possible though not so desir-
able, whereas the iris must always be grown from roots.

[b] Above, 681 b (p. 146).

[c] Sarcastic, as shown by the next verse and Nicander

with green leaves.[a]—The ' cups ' which grow at the
head will, it is true, grow from seed, those cups
whose petals are white tinged with saffron inside ;
these some bards call *krina*, others *leiria*, others
ambrosia,[b] and many *Aphrodite's delight* [c] ; for the
lily rivalled her in complexion. And haply, as it is
said, that object of shame in the middle, the bray-
ing ass's member, springs up.[d]—The iris, however,
is grown from roots, the dwarf iris and that which
resembles the mourning hyacinth,[e] and it rises in
reddish-brown flowers coming at the time of the
swallows,[f] and they put forth a pitiless [g] leafage from
their womb, while the new-born ' cups ' appear to
let their hollows droop ever downward.—With them,
too, comes the rose campion dazzling in colour, nor
is the plantain-lily nor again the camomile at its
height to be called worthless, nor the ox-eyes, those
flowers which raise their heads so very high aloft,
and the wallflower rejoicing in the mounting [h] rays of

again in *Alex.* 406-407 : λειριόεν τε κάρη, τό τ᾿ ἀπέστυγεν ᾿Αφρὼ
οὔνεκ᾿ ἐριδμαίνεσκε χροῆς ὕπερ.

[d] So Nic. *Alex.* 407-409 ἐν δέ νυ θρίοις (petals) ἀργαλέην
μεσάτοισιν ὀνειδείην ἐπέλασσε δεινὴν βρωμήεντος (brayer) ἐναν-
θήσασα κορύνην (club, *sens. obsc.* = ὅπλον).

[e] " That sanguine flower inscribed with woe." Theocr.
x. 28 ἁ γραπτὰ ὑάκινθος. Markings on this " iris " were
supposed to be αἲ αἴ, expressing grief for the death of
Hyacinthus or of Ajax (Αἴας).

[f] Or " competing in their russet hues with the swallow's
throat." So the russet figs are called χελιδονίαι (vol. vi.
p. 527) ; but see below, 684 e (p. 166), where it appears
that Athenaeus took χελιδονίοισι and χελιδόσιν to mean
" swallow-plants " (greater celandine) (*H.P.* vii. 15. 1, Hort
ii. 137).

[g] Referring to the sharp sword-like leaves. *Cf.* the name
gladiolus and the plant called yucca or Spanish sword.

[h] Or " returning," *i.e.* with the spring, *cf.* 680 e (p. 144).

161

f ἔρπυλλον δ' ἐφύδροισιν ἐπ' ἀμβώνεσσι[1] φυ-
    τεύσεις,
ὄφρα κλάδοις μακροῖσιν ἐφερπύζων διάηται
ἠὲ κατακρεμάησιν ἐφιμείρων[2] ποτὰ Νυμφέων.
καὶ δ' αὐτῆς μήκωνος ἄπο πλαταγώνια βάλλοις,
ἄβρωτον κώδειαν[3] ὄφρα κνώπεσσι φυλάξῃ·
φυλάσιν[4] ἢ γὰρ πάντα διοιγομέναισιν ἐφίζει
ἑρπετά, τὴν δὲ δρόσοισιν[5] εἰσκομένην βοτέονται
684 κώδειαν,[3] καρποῖο μελιχροτέρου πλήθουσαν.
θρίων δ' οἰχομένων[6] ῥέα μὲν φλόγες, ἄλλοτε ῥιπαὶ[7]
πῆξαν[8] σάρκα τυπῆσι[9]· τὰ δ' οὐ βάσιν ἐστήριξαν,
(θρῖα δ' οὐ λέγει τὰ τῆς συκῆς, ἀλλὰ τὰ τῆς
    μήκωνος)

οὔτε τί παι[10] βρώμην ποτιδέγμενα· πολλάκι δ' ἴχνη
στιφροῖς ὠλίσθηναν[11] ἐνιχρίμψαντε καρείοις.[12]
ἁδρύνει δὲ βλάστα βαθεῖ ἐν τεύχεϊ κόπρος[13]
b σαμψύχου λιβάνου τε νέας κλάδας ἠδ' ὅσα κῆποι
ἀνδράσιν[14] ἐργοπόνοις στεφάνους ἔπι πορσαί-
    νουσιν.[15]

ἢ γὰρ καὶ λεπταὶ πτερίδες καὶ παιδὸς ἔρωτες
λεύκη ἰσαιόμενοι, ἐν καὶ κρόκος εἴαρι μύων,[16]
κύπρος τ' ὀσμηρόν[17] τε σισύμβριον ὅσσα τε
    κοίλοις[18]
ἄσπορα ναιομένοισι τόποις[19] ἀνεθρέψατο λειμών

---

[1] Schneider (ἐφύδροισιν Casaubon): ἔρπυλλον δεφριαλευσοτεν βωλοισι A.   [2] Scaliger: ἐφ' μιρων A.
[3] κωδιαν A.   [4] Schweighäuser: φυλασσιν A.
[5] δροσιαν A.   [6] Schweighäuser: διοιχομένων A.
[7] J. G. Schneider: ρειπη A.   [8] O. Schneider: πληξαν A.
[9] J. G. Schneider: σαρκοτυπησι A.
[10] A: οὐδ' ἔμπα Wilamowitz.   [11] O. Schneider: ωλισθησαν A.
[12] καρεί οισ (one letter erased) A, καρήνοις Schweighäuser.
[13] O. Schneider: βαθει εντευχεῖ καρπὸν A.

the sun-god.—You will plant tufted thyme on moist
terraces, so that as it spreads its long branches it may
be blown in the breeze and hang over as it seeks the
waters of the Nymphs.—From the poppy itself[a] throw
away the broad petals, that you may keep its head
uneaten by caterpillars; for all creeping pests like
to rest upon the leaves as they unfold, and they
batten on the head, which seems like some tender
young creature, filled as it is with honey-sweet fruit.
But when the leaves[b] are gone, the flames easily kill,
or at another time cold blasts freeze their flesh with
their blows; and they have no firm resting-place (by
' leaves ' he means not those of the fig, but of the
poppy), and they can nowhere find food; and often
they slip in their tracks when they approach the
solid heads.—[c] Shoots of marjoram, set deep in a pot,
may be forced by manure, so too young sprouts of
the frankincense-tree and all other plants that our
gardens provide to make wreaths for toiling men.
Ay, there are slender ferns, and holm-oak resembling
white poplar,[d] and the crocus closing[e] in spring-time,
henna, too, and bergamot-mint with pungent smell
and all the beauties which a meadow rears without

[a] The meaning is not clear, and Schneider assumed a
lacuna of at least a verse and a half.
[b] θρῖα are almost always fig-leaves, hence the explanatory
parenthesis in prose below.
[c] Potted plants are treated next.
[d] Paus. ii. 10. 6 of the παιδέρως: φύλλοις δ' ἂν λεύκης
μάλιστα εἰκάζοις τὴν χροιάν.
[e] In Greece the crocus blooms in winter and quickly passes,
H.P. vii. 7. 4, Atchley, Wild Flowers of Attica 45-47.

---

[14] κηποπανδρασιν A.   [15] Meineke: ἐπιπορσαινουσιν A.
[16] Casaubon: ἴαριμινίων A.   [17] A: ὀσμαρὸν C.
[18] Porson: κ' οἴαισ A.
[19] Casaubon, Schweighäuser: νεομενοισι ποτοισ A.

κάλλεϊ βουφθαλμόν τε καὶ εὐῶδες¹ Διὸς ἄνθος,
c χάλκας, σὺν δ' ὑάκινθον ἰωνιάδας² τε χαμηλὰς
ὀρφνοτέρας, ἃς στύξε μετ' ἄνθεσι Φερσεφόνεια.³
σὺν δὲ καὶ ὑψῆέν τε πανόσμεον⁴ ὅσσα τε τύμβοι
φάσγανα παρθενικαῖς νεοδουπέσιν⁵ ἀμφιχέονται,
αὐταί τ' ἠιθέας⁶ ἀνεμωνίδες ἀστράπτουσαι
τηλόθεν ὀξυτέρῃσιν ἐφελκόμεναι χροιῇσιν.

(ἐν ἐνίοις δὲ γράφεται '' ἐφελκόμεναι φιλοχροιαῖς.'')

d πᾶς δέ τις ἢ ἐλένειον ἢ ἀστέρα φωτίζοντα
δρέψας εἰνοδίοισι⁷ θεῶν παρακάββαλε σηκοῖς
ἢ αὐτοῖς βρετάεσσιν, ὅτε⁸ πρώτιστον ἴδωνται·
πολλάκι θέρμια⁹ καλά, τοτὲ¹⁰ χρυσανθὲς ἀμέργων
λείριά τε¹¹ στήλαισιν¹² ἐπιφθίνοντα καμόντων
καὶ γεραὸν πώγωνα καὶ ἐντραπέας κυκλαμίνους
σαύρην θ', ἢ χθονίου πέφαται στέφος Ἡγεσι-
λάου.¹³

Ἐκ τούτων τῶν ἐπῶν δῆλον γίνεται ὅτι ἕτερόν

¹ A : εὐειδὲς Schneider.
² Scaliger : ἰωνιδασ A.   ³ φερσεφονεία A.
⁴ Meineke following Casaubon : ὑψήεντα ταπανοσ μεον A.
⁵ Meineke : νεοχουπαιων A.   ⁶ Schneider : ἠίθειαι A.
⁷ δρεψασ' εινοδιοισιν A.   ⁸ Meineke : ἅτε A.
⁹ Wilamowitz (θερμία) : θελ μια (one letter erased) A.
¹⁰ Schweighäuser : τό τε A.   ¹¹ Canter : λιριαστε A (sic).
¹² στήλεσιν A.   ¹³ Salmasius : ηγεσιλιου A.

ᵃ O. Schneider, followed by Meineke and Kaibel, changed
εὐῶδες "fragrant" to εὐειδές "beautiful" because Theoph.
H.P. vi. 6. 2 calls the Διὸς ἄνθος and the φλόξ (wallflower)
ἄνοσμον "scentless." Some varieties of pink are odourless,
others not. Hort (ii. 36 note 2) accepts the reading given
above.
ᵇ The violet is the flower most often mentioned in connexion with the rape of Persephone, Aristot. *Ausc. Mirab.*
82, Diod. v. 3, Ovid, *Metam.* v. 392. Against this Pamphôs

cultivation in hollow watered places, ox-eye and
fragrant [a] pink, chrysanthemums and hyacinth withal,
and dark violets close to the ground, which Persephone loathed [b] amongst flowers. And with them
are the towering all-scent, and the corn-flags that
spread round the tombs of maidens newly dead,
while the brightly-flashing anemones, in their turn,
lure virgins from afar by their dazzling colours. [c] (In
some copies is written ' lure by dazzling love-
colours.') And every passer-by plucks calamint or
glowing daisy, and sets them beside the wayside
shrines of the gods or at the very images, so soon
as they see them; often he gathers fair lupins,[d] or
another time the marigold, or lilies that fade on the
gravestones of the dead, and the reverend [e] goat's-
beard and modest [f] cyclamens and nose-smart, which
is called the wreath of the underworld Leader of the
People." [g]

From these verses it is clear that the " swallow-

---

[a] Paus. ix. 31. 9 says (Κόρην) ἁρπασθῆναι δὲ οὐκ ἴοις
ἀπατηθεῖσαν ἀλλὰ ναρκίσσοις. στύξε may be rendered " caused
to be hated," since the violet, like the πόθος, was associated
with funerals. See Halliday's note on h. Hom. Cer. 8 (p. 130).

[c] A scholiastic note merged with the poem.

[d] What Nicander wrote here is not known. Wilamowitz's
conjecture is adopted as a makeshift (critical note 9).

[e] The seed-heads are grey, H.P. vii. 7. 1 (ἔχει) τὴν κάλυκα
μεγάλην καὶ ἐξ ἄκρου μέγαν τὸν πάππον, ἀφ' οὗ καλεῖται τραγο-
πώγων.

[f] ἐντραπέας occurs only here, like so many other words
in this poem. Schneider, rightly retaining it, derived it
from τέρπω. But " well-pleasing " is weak. I prefer to
connect it with ἐντρέπομαι " feel shame "; cf. " born to blush
unseen," which well describes the field-cyclamen of Greece.

[g] The form Ἡγεσίλαος, epithet of Hades, does not occur
elsewhere. Casaubon read Ἀγεσιλάου, cf. Athen. 99 b (vol. i.
p. 426), Callim. v. 103 (Mair, L.C.L. 122).

e ἐστιν τὸ χελιδόνιον τῆς ἀνεμώνης· τινὲς γὰρ ταὐτὸ
εἶναί φασι. Θεόφραστος δέ φησι· " τὰς δ' ἀνθήσεις
λαμβάνειν δεῖ συνακολουθοῦντα[1] τοῖς ἄστροις τὸ
ἡλιοτρόπιον καλούμενον καὶ τὸ χελιδόνιον· καὶ γὰρ
τοῦτο ἅμα τῇ χελιδόνι ἀνθεῖ." καὶ ἀμβροσίαν δὲ
ἄνθος τι ἀναγράφει ὁ Καρύστιος ἐν Ἱστορικοῖς
Ὑπομνήμασι λέγων οὕτως· " Νίκανδρός φησιν ἐξ
ἀνδριάντος τῆς κεφαλῆς Ἀλεξάνδρου τὴν καλουμένην ἀμβροσίαν φύεσθαι ἐν Κῷ." προείρηται δ'
f ἄνω περὶ αὐτῆς ὅτι τὸ κρίνον οὕτω λέγουσι. Τιμαχίδας δ' ἐν τετάρτῳ Δείπνου καὶ θήσειόν τι
ἀναγράφει καλούμενον ἄνθος·

θήσειόν θ' ἁπαλὸν μήλῳ ἐναλίγκιον ἄνθος,
Λευκερέης ἱερὸν περικαλλέος, ὅ ῥα[2] μάλιστα
φίλατο.

ἀπὸ τούτου δέ φησι τοῦ ἄνθους καὶ τὸν τῆς Ἀρι-
άδνης καλούμενον στέφανον πεπλέχθαι. καὶ ὁ
685 Φερεκράτης δὲ ἢ ὁ πεποιηκὼς τὸ δρᾶμα τοὺς
Πέρσας μνημονεύων καὶ αὐτὸς ἀνθῶν τινων στεφανωτικῶν φησιν·

ὦ μαλάχας μὲν ἐξερῶν, ἀναπνέων δ' ὑάκινθον,
καὶ μελιλώτινον λαλῶν καὶ ῥόδα προσσεσηρώς·

---

[1] λαμβάνειν δεῖ συνακολουθοῦντα A : λαμβάνουσι ἀκολουθοῦντα
Theophr., Θ. φησὶ λαμβάνειν συνακ. C. λαμβάνει ἀεὶ συνακ. (?)
Kaibel.
[2] Casaubon : περικαλλὲς ὅν ρα A.

---

[a] Above, 683 e, 684 c, and 680 e (pp. 160, 164, 144). The
anemone blooms earlier.
[b] H.P. vii. 15. 1 (Hort ii. 136). The text of Theophrastus
differs from the above ; both are corrupt in some particulars.

166

plant " is different from the anemone ^a; some, to
be sure, say it is the same.   Theophrastus says ^b:
" Some must take their flowering-time in close de-
pendence on the heavenly bodies, as the plant called
heliotropion and the swallow-plant; this, in fact,
blooms when the swallow comes." ^c   A flower called
ambrosia is recorded by Carystius in *Historical Notes*
as follows ^d: " Nicander says ^e that the so-called
ambrosia grows from the head of Alexander's statue
on the island of Cos."   It has already been said of
it above ^f that some call the *krinon* (lily) by this name,
ambrosia.   Timachidas, again, records in the fourth
book of his *Banquet* ^g a flower called *theseion* ^h: " And
the delicate *theseion*, with blossom like that of the
apple, sacred to fair Leucerea, ⁱ for that she especially
loved it."   He says also that Ariadne's wreath was
twined with this flower.   And Pherecrates, or whoever wrote the play called *The Persians*, in mentioning on his own account some flowers suitable for
wreaths, says ^j: " O you, that belch mallows, that
breathe hyacinth, whose speech is melilot, whose
grin is roses ! ^k O you, whose kiss is sweet marjoram,

---

^c Theophrastus says " when the swallow-wind (χελιδονία)
blows."   Pliny, *N.H.* ii. 47. 122 Favonium quidam . . .
chelidonian vocant ab hirundinis visu.   For the swallow-
plant (greater celandine) *cf.* 372 c (vol. iv. p. 186).

^d *F.H.G.* iv. 357.   ^e Frag. 127, p. 204 Schneider.

^f 681 b (p. 146).

^g Perhaps " in the fourth of his *Banquets*," *cf.* p. 152 (682 c).

^h Holewort, *H.P.* vii. 12. 3.

ⁱ Mentioned only here; perhaps an attendant nymph of
Artemis, since the root of the plant was thought to be
emmenagogic.

^j Kock i. 183.   *Cf.* Nicomachus χρυσοῦς ἐμῶν (vol. v. p. 38),
Eupolis καλλαβίδας βαίνει (vol. vi. p. 492).

^k *Cf.* Aristoph. *Nub.* 910 ῥόδα μ' εἴρηκας.

ὦ φιλῶν μὲν ἀμάρακον, προσκινῶν[1] δὲ σέλινα,
γελῶν δ' ἱπποσέλινα καὶ κοσμοσάνδαλα[2] βαίνων,
ἔγχει κἀπιβόα τρίτον παιῶν',[3] ὡς νόμος ἐστίν.

ὁ δὲ πεποιηκὼς τοὺς εἰς αὐτὸν ἀναφερομένους
Μεταλλεῖς φησιν·

b 　ὑπ' ἀναδενδράδων ἁπαλὰς ἀσπαλάθους πατοῦντες
ἐν λειμῶνι λωτοφόρῳ κύπειρόν τε δροσώδη
κἀνθρύσκου μαλακῶν τ' ἴων λείμακα[4] καὶ τρι-
　φύλλου.

ἐν τούτοις ζητῶ τί τὸ τρίφυλλον. καὶ γὰρ εἰς Δη-
μαρέτην ἀναφέρεταί τι ποιημάτιον ὃ ἐπιγράφεται
Τρίφυλλον κἀν τοῖς ἐπιγραφομένοις δὲ Ἀγαθοῖς ὁ
Φερεκράτης ἢ Στράττις φησίν·

　λουσάμενοι δὲ πρὸ λαμπρᾶς
ἡμέρας ἐν τοῖς στεφανώμασιν, οἱ δ' ἐν τῷ μύρῳ
λαλεῖτε[5] περὶ σισυμβρίων κοσμοσανδάλων τε.

καὶ Κρατῖνος ἐν Μαλθακοῖς·

　παντοίοις γε μὴν κεφαλὴν ἀνθέμοις ἐρέπτομαι,
c λειρίοις ῥόδοις κρίνεσιν[6] κοσμοσανδάλοις ἴοις
καὶ σισυμβρίοις ἀνεμωνῶν[7] κάλυξί τ' ἠριναῖς
ἑρπύλλῳ κρόκοις ὑακίνθοις ἑλειχρύσου[8] κλάδοις
οἰνάνθησιν ἡμεροκαλλεῖ τε τῷ φιλουμένῳ,
ἀνθρύσκου . . . . ναρκίσσου[9] φόβῃ
τῷ τ' ἀειφρούρῳ μελιλώτῳ κάρα πυκάζομαι·

---

[1] A : προσκυνῶν CE.
[2] CE : κοσμοσάνδαλλα A.
[3] κἀπιβόα παίων C. 　　　[4] λιμακα A.
[5] Dobree : λαλεῖται A. 　　　[6] Porson : κρίνοισ A.
[7] ἀνέμων ὧν A, corrected by later hand.

168

whose embrace is celery,[a] whose laugh is alexanders,[b] whose walk is larkspur ![c] Fill up a cup and raise the shout of the triple paean, as our custom is." And the writer of *The Miners*, attributed to Pherecrates, says[d] : " Beneath the branches of the clinging vine they tread on tender[e] nettles in a lotus-bearing meadow, on dewy grass in a field of chervil and soft violets and trefoil." In these lines, what, I ask, is the trefoil ? There is, indeed, a little poem attributed to Demaretê, entitled *Trefoil* ; and in *Nice People*, as it is entitled, Pherecrates or Strattis says[f] : " Some of you, all bathed, babble before it is bright daylight in the wreath market, while others of you gabble at the perfume-booths over bergamot-mint and larkspur." And Cratinus in *Mollycoddles*[g] : " I crown my head, to be sure, with all sorts of flowers—narcissus, roses, lilies, larkspur, gilliflowers, bergamot-mint too, and the cups of spring anemones, tufted thyme, crocus, squills, and sprays of gold-flower, drop-wort and day-lily so well beloved, chervil too . . . tufts of narcissus, and with the perennial

[a] προσκινῶν σέλινα *sens. obsc.* cf. Aristoph. *Lys.* 227 προσκινήσομαι, and for σέλινα=τὸ γυναικεῖον αἰδοῖον cf. vol. iv. pp. 500-501, notes 5 and f, Schol. Theocr. xi. 10.
[b] Lit. "horse-celery," olusatrum, ἱππο- being used *sens. obsc.*, vol. v. p. 405 note f.
[c] Lit. "fancy-sandals" ; above, p. 146. The triple paean is the thrice-repeated ἰὴ παιάν at a dinner-party, below, 701 e (p. 268). [d] Kock i. 177.
[e] The adjective and noun have been wrongly suspected ; the scene is in Elysium. ἀσπάλαθοι may here=sweet broom.
[f] Kock i. 145 (Pherecrates).
[g] Kock i. 43 ; above, p. 146.

[8] Meineke: ἐλιχρύσου A.
[9] ἀνθρύσκου . . . ναρκίσσου Bergk: ανθρυσκισσου A.

καὶ . . . κύτισος αὐτόματος παρὰ Μέδοντος
ἔρχεται.

Ἡ δὲ τῶν στεφάνων καὶ μύρων πρότερον εἴσοδος
εἰς τὰ συμπόσια ἡγεῖτο τῆς δευτέρας τραπέζης, ὡς
παρίστησι Νικόστρατος ἐν Ψευδοστιγματίᾳ διὰ
τούτων.

d   καὶ σὺ μὲν
τὴν δευτέραν τράπεζαν εὐτρεπῆ ποίει,
κόσμησον αὐτὴν παντοδαποῖς τραγήμασιν,
μύρον, στεφάνους, λιβανωτόν, αὐλητρίδα λαβέ.

Φιλόξενος δ᾿ ὁ διθυραμβοποιὸς ἐν τῷ ἐπιγραφομένῳ
Δείπνῳ ἀρχὴν ποιεῖται τὸν στέφανον τῆς εὐωχίας
οὑτωσὶ λέγων·

                 κατὰ χειρὸς δ᾿
ἤλυθ᾿ ὕδωρ· ἁπαλὸς παιδίσκος ἐν ἀργυρέᾳ φέρων
    προχόῳ[1] ἐπέχευεν.
εἶτ᾿ ἔφερεν[2] στέφανον λεπτᾶς ἀπὸ μυρτίδος[3]
    εὐγνήτων κλάδων δισύναπτον.

e Εὔβουλος Τίτθαις[4]·

ὡς γὰρ εἰσῆλθε τὰ γερόντια τότ᾿ εἰς δόμους,
εὐθὺς ἀνεκλίνετο· παρῆν στέφανος[5] ἐν τάχει,
ᾖρετο τράπεζα, παρέκειθ᾿ ἅμα τετριμμένη
μᾶζα χαριτοβλέφαρος.

τοῦτο δ᾿ ἦν ἔθος καὶ παρ᾿ Αἰγυπτίοις, ὡς Νικό-
στρατός φησιν ἐν Τοκιστῇ. Αἰγύπτιον γὰρ ὑπο-
στησάμενος τὸν τοκιστὴν φησιν·

καταλαμβάνομεν τὸν πορνοβοσκὸν καὶ δύο[6]
f ἑτέρους κατὰ χειρὸς ἀρτίως εἰληφότας

---

    [1] προχοω φέρων A.   [2] ἔφερε Bergk.
    [3] Grotefend: στεφανολεπτασ ἀπὸ μυρτίδων A.
  [4] τιτθαῖσ A.   [5] Erfurdt: ὁ στέφανοσ A.   [6] δυ᾿ A.

melilot I deck my head, . . . and wild medick comes
from Medon." [a]

In earlier times the fetching of wreaths and perfumes into symposia preceded the " second table,"
as Nicostratus shows in these lines from *The Sham
Scoundrel* [b] : " Do you make ready the second table,
grace it with all kinds of sweetmeats, buy perfume,
wreaths, frankincense, and hire a flute girl." Philoxenus, the dithyrambic poet, in his work entitled
The Banquet, makes the wreath the signal for the
beginning of the feast in these words [c] : " Over the
hand came lustral water [d] ; a tender lad brought it
in a silver jug and poured it out. Then he brought
a wreath doubly-plaited from lush sprays of delicate
myrtle." Eubulus in *The Nurses* [e] : " For so soon
as the old fellows entered the house they straight-
way took their places on the couch ; wreaths were
brought with speed, tables were carried in, and withal
kneaded barley-cakes lovely to the eye." [f] This was
also the practice in Egypt, as Nicostratus says in *The
Money Lender*. For he brings on an Egyptian as the
money-lender, and makes him say [g] : " A. There we
found the whoremaster and two other men, who had
just received the water over the hands, and wreaths.

[a] Unknown ; nor is the text certain. The plant medick,
or lucerne, is related to alfalfa.

[b] Kock ii. 227.

[c] *P.L.G.*[4] iii. 601, Diehl i. 314, Edmonds iii. 348.

[d] See 408 b-d (vol. iv. p. 348) ; *Od.* i. 136-137 χέρνιβα δ'
ἀμφίπολος προχόῳ ἐπέχευε φέρουσα | καλῇ χρυσείῃ, ὑπὲρ ἀργυ-
ρέοιο λέβητος.

[e] Kock ii. 204.

[f] Lit. " with eyes like those of the Graces," a comic
misuse of the compound adjective.

[g] Kock ii. 226. For the parasite Chaerephon see vol. iii.
pp. 92-97.

καὶ στέφανον. Β. εἶεν· καλὸς ὁ καιρός, Χαιρεφῶν.

σὺ δὲ γαστρίζου, Κύνουλκε· καὶ μετὰ ταῦτα ἡμῖν εἰπὲ διὰ τί Κρατῖνος εἴρηκε τὸν μελίλωτον " τῷ τ᾽ ἀειφρούρῳ μελιλώτῳ." ἐπεὶ δέ σε ὁρῶ ἔξοινον ἤδη γεγενημένον—οὕτως δ᾽ εἴρηκε τὸν μεθύσην Ἄλεξις ἐν Εἰσοικιζομένῳ—παύσομαί σε ἐρεσχηλῶν καὶ τοῖς παισὶ παρακελεύομαι κατὰ τὸν Σοφοκλέα, ὃς ἐν Συνδείπνοις φησί·

686   φορεῖτε, μασσέτω τις, ἐγχείτω βαθὺν
    κρατῆρ᾽[1]· ὅδ᾽ ἀνὴρ οὐ πρὶν ἂν φάγῃ[2] καλῶς
    ὅμοια καὶ βοῦς ἐργάτης ἐργάζεται.

καὶ κατὰ τὸν Φλιάσιον δὲ Ἀριστίαν· καὶ γὰρ οὗτος ἐν ταῖς ἐπιγραφομέναις Κηρσὶν ἔφη·

    σύνδειπνος ἢ ᾽πίκωμος[3] ἢ μαζαγρέτας,
    Ἅιδου[4] τραπεζεύς, ἀκρατέα[5] νηδὺν ἔχων.

ἐπεὶ δὲ τοσούτων λεχθέντων μηδὲν ἀποκρίνεται, κελεύω αὐτὸν κατὰ τοὺς Ἀλέξιδος Διδύμους χυδαίοις στεφανωθέντα στεφάνοις ἐξάγεσθαι τοῦ b συμποσίου. τῶν δὲ χυδαίων στεφάνων μνημονεύων ὁ κωμῳδιοποιός φησιν·

    στεφάνων τε τούτων τῶν[6] χύδην πεπλεγμένων.

κἀγὼ δ᾽ ἐπὶ τούτοις τοῦ λέγειν ἤδη παύσομαι τὸ τήμερον, παραχωρῶν[7] τε τὸν περὶ τῶν μύρων λόγον τοῖς βουλομένοις διεξέρχεσθαι τῷ τε παιδὶ προσ-

B. Well! You were in the nick of time, Chaerephon!"
But you, Cynulcus, are eating like a pig [a]; next I
would have you tell us why Cratinus says [b] of melilot,
"with the everlasting melilot." However, since I see
that you are by this time *exoinos* (quite wined)—for
that is how Alexis describes the drunken man in
The New Tenant [c]—I will stop teasing you, and I
exhort the slaves in the words of Sophocles, who says
in *Dinner-Guests* [d]: "Bring the things on! Knead
the barley-cakes, somebody, fill up a deep bowl!
This man won't do his work well, any more than a
working ox, until he has eaten." Again, in the
words of Aristias of Phlius, who says in the play
entitled *Spirits of Doom* [e]: "Dinner-guest or reveller
or barley-cake-beggar, Hades' trencherman [f] with
insatiable belly." But since to all that I have said
he answers not a word, I order that he be wreathed
with "confused" wreaths, to imitate Alexis in *The
Twins*, and be shipped out of our symposium. For,
mentioning these "confused" wreaths the comic
poet says [g]: "And these wreaths confusedly plaited."
As for myself, I shall at this point stop speaking for
to-day, yielding the discussion of perfumes to those
who want to carry it on, and requiring the slave,

---

[a] Resuming the reproach in 678 f (p. 134).
[b] Above, p. 168.
[c] Vol. vi. p. 304 ; see vol. i. p. 6 note c.
[d] *T.G.F.*[2] 161. For φορεῖτε, wrongly altered by Meineke
and Bergk to φυρᾶτε, cf. *Od.* ix. 9 (ὅτε) μέθυ δ' ἐκ κρατῆρος
ἀφύσσων οἰνοχόος φορέῃσι.
[e] *T.G.F.*[2] 727.   [f] Or " parasite."   [g] Kock ii. 315.

---

[1] κρατῆρα A : κρητῆρα C.   [2] φάγοι C.
[3] L. Dindorf: 'πίκωποσ AC (ἢ C).
[4] A: αἰδοῖ CE.   [5] CE: ακραταιαν A.
[6] τῶν added by Meineke.   [7] Kaibel: παραχωρῶ A.

τάττων ἐπὶ τῇ στεφανηφόρῳ ταύτῃ μου διαλέξει
κατὰ τὸν Ἀντιφάνη·

στεφάνους ἐνεγκεῖν[1] δεῦρο τῶν χρηστῶν[2] δύο

c καὶ δᾷδα χρηστὴν ἡμμένην χρηστῷ πυρί.

οὕτω γὰρ τὴν τῶν λόγων ἔξοδον[3] ὥσπερ δράματος
ποιήσομαι."

Καὶ μετ' οὐ πολλὰς ἡμέρας ὥσπερ αὐτὸς[4] αὑτοῦ
σιωπὴν καταμαντευσάμενος ἀπέθανεν εὐτυχῶς,
οὐδένα καιρὸν νόσῳ παραδούς, πολλὰ δὲ λυπήσας
ἡμᾶς τοὺς ἑταίρους.

Περιενεγκόντων δὲ τῶν παίδων ἐν ἀλαβάστοις
καὶ ἄλλοις χρυσοῖς σκεύεσιν μύρα, νυστάζοντα[5] τὸν
Κύνουλκον θεασάμενός τις πολλῷ τῷ μύρῳ τὸ
πρόσωπον ἐπέχρισεν. ὁ δὲ διεγερθεὶς καὶ μόλις
d ἑαυτὸν ἀναλαβὼν τί τοῦτ', εἶπεν, Ἡράκλεις; οὐ
σπογγιᾷ τίς μου παρελθὼν τὸ πρόσωπον ἐκκαθα-
ρίσει μεμολυσμένον μαγγανείαις πολλαῖς; ἢ οὐκ
οἴδατε καὶ τὸν καλὸν Ξενοφῶντα ἐν τῷ Συμποσίῳ
ποιοῦντα τὸν Σωκράτην τοιαυτὶ λέγοντα· "νὴ
Δί', ὦ Καλλία, τελέως ἡμᾶς ἑστιᾷς· οὐ γὰρ μόνον
δεῖπνον ἄμεμπτον παρέθηκας, ἀλλὰ καὶ ἀκροάματα
καὶ θεάματα[6] ἥδιστα παρέχεις.—τί οὖν εἰ καὶ μύρον

---

[1] κατὰ τὸν Ἀντιφάνη· στεφάνους ἐνεγκεῖν Casaubon, Meineke:
κατὰ τὸν ἀντιφάνους ἐνεγκεῖν A.
[2] χρηστῶν Casaubon. So χρηστὴν, χριστῷ.
[3] Meineke: διέξοδον A.   [4] αὐτὸς added by Kaibel.
[5] νυστάζοντα added by Schweighäuser after Dalechamps.
[6] θεάματα καὶ ἀκροάματα Xen.

---

[a] Punning on the other sense of στεφανηφόρος, "wreath-
winning," i.e. deserving a wreath.
[b] Kock ii. 123.

at the conclusion of this wreath-laden [a] lecture of mine, in the words of Antiphanes,[b] " to fetch hither two goodly wreaths and a goodly torch lighted with a goodly fire." Thus, indeed, will I make my exit, as in a play, after my speech.

Not many days after that, as if he himself had had a premonition of the silence that was to be his, he died happily, allowing no time for illness, but causing grief to us his companions.[c]

When the slaves passed round perfumes in alabaster bottles and also gold containers, someone noticed that Cynulcus was dozing, and smeared perfume on his face in large quantities. Waking up, but hardly yet returning to consciousness he cried, Great Heracles, what's that? Step up, someone, and wipe over my face with a sponge, dirtied as it is by your superfluous tricks. Or don't you know that even the fine Xenophon in his *Symposium* makes Socrates say something like this [d] : " I swear, Callias, you feast us perfectly ; for not only have you set before us a blameless dinner, but you also provide most pleasant entertainments and spectacles. *Callias* :

---

[c] This graceful tribute to the dead Ulpian, who has been rather roughly treated in this long work, has caused much discussion. See Introd. vol. i. pp. xii-xiii. εὐτυχῶς does not seem in keeping with the violent death of Ulpian the *praefectus praetorio* in A.D. 228 ; consequently the Ulpian of this work, variously called Syrian or Phoenician but never Roman, must have been different, and the date A.D. 228 cannot be used in determining the time when Athenaeus wrote. See W. Dittenberger in *Apophoreton* 1-28, esp. 20-23, F. Hackmann, *De Athen. Naucr. Quaest. Selectae* 23-24, Hirzel, *Der Dialog* ii. 352 note 6. Dittenberger seeks to confine the composition of the *Deipnosophists* within the years 193–197 after Christ.

[d] *Symp.* ii. 204, Athen. 612 a (vol. vi. p. 296).

ἐνέγκαι τις ἡμῖν, ἵνα καὶ εὐωδίᾳ ἑστιώμεθα;[1]—
μηδαμῶς, ἔφη ὁ Σωκράτης· ὥσπερ γάρ τοι ἐσθὴς
e ἄλλη μὲν γυναικεία, ἄλλη δὲ ἀνδρεία,[2] οὕτω καὶ
ὀσμὴ ἄλλη μὲν γυναικί, ἄλλη δὲ ἀνδρὶ πρέπει. καὶ
γὰρ ἀνδρὸς μὲν δή που ἕνεκα ἀνδρῶν οὐδεὶς[3] μύρῳ
χρίεται. αἵ γε μὴν[4] γυναῖκες ἄλλως τε καὶ ἂν[5]
νύμφαι τύχωσιν οὖσαι, ὥσπερ ἡ Νικηράτου τε τούτου καὶ ἡ Κριτοβούλου,[6] μύρου μὲν τί[7] καὶ προσδέονται; αὐταὶ[8] γὰρ τούτου ὄζουσιν. ἐλαίου δὲ
τοῦ ἐν γυμνασίοις ὀσμὴ καὶ παροῦσα ἡδίων[9] ἢ
μύρου γυναιξὶ[10] καὶ ἀποῦσα[11] ποθεινοτέρα. καὶ γὰρ
δὴ μύρῳ μὲν ἀλειψάμενος δοῦλος καὶ ἐλεύθερος
εὐθὺς ἅπας ὅμοιον ὄζει· αἱ δ' ἀπὸ τῶν ἐλευθε-
f ρίων[12] μόχθων ὀσμαὶ ἐπιτηδευμάτων τε πρῶτον
χρηστῶν καὶ χρόνου πολλοῦ δέονται, εἰ μέλλουσιν
ἡδεῖαί τε καὶ ἐλευθέριαι ἔσεσθαι.'' καὶ ὁ θαυμα-
σιώτατος δὲ Χρύσιππος τὴν ὀνομασίαν φησὶ λαβεῖν
τὰ μύρα ἀπὸ τοῦ μετὰ πολλοῦ μόρου καὶ πόνου[13]
ματαίου γίνεσθαι. Λακεδαιμόνιοί τε ἐξελαύνουσι
τῆς Σπάρτης τοὺς τὰ μύρα κατασκευάζοντας ὡς
687 διαφθείροντας τοὔλαιον· καὶ τοὺς τὰ ἔρια δὲ βάπ-
τοντας ὡς ἀφανίζοντας τὴν λευκότητα τῶν ἐρίων.
Σόλων τε ὁ σοφὸς διὰ τῶν νόμων κεκώλυκε τοὺς

---

[1] Xen., A : ἑστιώμεθα Kaibel, Richards, without need.
[2] CE : γυναικεία· ἄλλη δὲ ἀνδρεία κάλλη A, γυναικί, ἄλλη δὲ
ἀνδρὶ καλῇ Xen.
[3] CE : ἔνεκεν οὐδεὶσ A, ἕνεκα ἀνὴρ οὐδεὶς Xen.
[4] ACE, Aristid. ii. 514 : μέντοι Xen.
[5] Xen. : ἂν καὶ ACE.   [6] κριτοβόλου A.
[7] μὲν τί Stephanus : με τι A, μέντοι Xen.
[8] Aristid. : αὗται Xen. codd., ν αυται A (ν seemingly inserted
in the wrong place to correct με τι above it).
[9] Xen. : παρουσία ἀνδρῶν A.
[10] Xen. : γυναιξὶν ἡδίων A.   [11] Xen. : ἀπουσία A.

What, then, if they bring us also some perfume, that
we may feast on fragrance too ? *Socrates* : Not so !
For just as there is one kind of garment for women,
but another for men, so also one kind of smell is
appropriate to a woman, but another for a man. For
the sake of a man, I suppose, no man smears himself
with perfumery. Even in the case of women, especially if they happen to be young brides, like the one
of Niceratus here, or of Critobulus, what need have
they of perfume besides ? For they of themselves
smell sweet.[a] The smell of olive oil in our gymnasia,
when present, is sweeter than perfume on women,
and when absent, is missed more. Slave or freeman,
all smell alike the moment they anoint themselves
with perfume ; but the smells arising from labour
becoming to a freeman require first exertions which
are noble and which take a long time, if they are to be
pleasant and worthy of free men." The most admirable Chrysippus, too, declares that perfumes (*myra*)
took their name from the great toil[b] (*moros*) and fool-
ish labour with which they are obtained. And so the
Lacedaemonians expel from Sparta the manufacturers
of perfumes, on the ground that they spoil the olive
oil ; so, too, those who dye raw wool, because they
destroy the whiteness of the wool. And the wise
Solon in his laws forbade the selling of perfume by

[a] On αὐταὶ τούτου ὄζουσιν Aristid. ii. 514 comments thus :
τοῦτο μὲν οὖν οὕτω δεῖ προσδέξασθαι οἷον αὐταὶ παρὰ ἀνδρὸς
μύρου οὐ προσδέονται, παρ' ἑαυτῶν γὰρ ἔχουσι νυμφαί γε οὖσαι.

[b] For this meaning of μόρος (usually " death," " doom "),
not noticed in L. & S., see Hesych. *s.* μόρου· κόποι, πόνοι,
and *s.* μόρος· πόνος. Of course the etymology given is
untrue. " Chrysippus tam malus grammaticus quam bonus
Stoicus fuit " (Casaubon).

---

[12] Xen.: ἐλευθέρων A. [13] CE: ποτου A.

ἄνδρας μυροπωλεῖν. '' νῦν δὲ τῶν ἀνθρώπων
οὐχ αἱ ὀσμαὶ μόνον, ὥς φησιν Κλέαρχος ἐν γ´ περὶ
Βίων, ἀλλὰ καὶ αἱ χροιαὶ τρυφερὸν ἔχουσαί τι
συνεκθηλύνουσι τοὺς μεταχειριζομένους. ὑμεῖς δὲ
οἴεσθε τὴν ἁβρότητα χωρὶς ἀρετῆς ἔχειν τι τρυ-
φερόν; καίτοι Σαπφώ, γυνὴ μὲν πρὸς ἀλήθειαν
οὖσα καὶ ποιήτρια, ὅμως ᾐδέσθη τὸ καλὸν τῆς
ἁβρότητος ἀφελεῖν λέγουσα ὧδε·

b ἐγὼ δὲ φίλημμ᾽[1] ἁβροσύναν, . . . τοῦτο,[2] καί μοι
τὸ λαμπρὸν ἔρος τὠελίω[3] καὶ τὸ καλὸν λέλογχε·

φανερὸν ποιοῦσα πᾶσιν ὡς ἡ τοῦ ζῆν ἐπιθυμία τὸ
λαμπρὸν καὶ τὸ καλὸν εἶχεν αὐτῇ· ταῦτα δ᾽ ἐστὶν
οἰκεῖα τῆς ἀρετῆς. Παρράσιος δὲ ὁ ζωγράφος,
καίπερ παρὰ μέλος ὑπὲρ τὴν ἑαυτοῦ τέχνην τρυ-
φήσας καὶ τὸ λεγόμενον ἐλευθέριον ἐκ ῥαβδίων ὡς[4]
ἔκ τινων ποτηρίων ἑλκύσας, λόγῳ γοῦν ἀντελάβετο
τῆς ἀρετῆς, ἐπιγραψάμενος τοῖς ἐν Λίνδῳ πᾶσιν
αὐτοῦ ἔργοις·

ἁβροδίαιτος ἀνὴρ ἀρετήν τε σέβων τάδ᾽ ἔγραψεν
Παρράσιος.

ᾧ κομψός τις, ὡς ἐμοὶ δοκεῖ, ὑπεραλγήσας ῥυ-
c παίνοντι τὸ τῆς ἀρετῆς ἁβρὸν καὶ καλόν, ἅτε

---

[1] φίλημμι A.   [2] τοῦτο added from Ox. Pap.
[3] A. S. Hunt: εροσα ελιω A.
[4] ὡς added by Kaibel, who, however, preferred to delete
ἔκ τινων ποτηρίων as a gloss.

---

[a] Athen. 612 a (vol. vi. p. 296), Eust. 1295. 20.
[b] F.H.G. ii. 304, Athen. 543 c-e (vol. v. pp. 460-462), cf.
568 a-d (vol. vi. pp. 66-70).
[c] P.L.G.⁴ iii. 115, Diehl i. 358, Edmonds i. 266, 436, Ox.
Pap. xv. 42.   The moralist Clearchus, for his own purpose,
takes τὸ καλόν=honour, though Sappho is speaking of
178

men.[a] "Nowadays not only the scents that people use," says Clearchus in the third book of his *Lives*,[b] "but also their complexions, have something so luxurious as to make those who use them completely effeminate. But do you imagine that daintiness can comprehend anything luxurious when divorced from virtue? And yet Sappho, truly a woman, if there ever was one, and a poetess besides, nevertheless was ashamed to separate honour from daintiness when she said[c]: 'But I love daintiness, (mark) this, and for me brightness and honour belong to my yearning for the sun'; thus she makes it plain to all that the desire to live contained for her the idea of brightness with honour; for these are natural properties of virtue. Again, the painter Parrhasius, though he indulged in luxury in a way offensive to good taste and beyond his station as an artist, and quaffed, as from wine-cups, his fill of what is called a gentleman's life from his painter's stile,[d] professed at least a regard for virtue when he inscribed over all his works in Lindus this epigram[e]: 'A man who lives in dainty style (*habrodiaitos*) and at the same time honours virtue, hath written these words, even Parrhasius.' Whereupon some wit, who, I imagine, felt great annoyance at him for besmirching the daintiness and honour of virtue, in that he had

physical qualities. For the use of λέλογχε cf. Pind. *Ol.* i. 53 ἀκέρδεια λέλογχεν κακαγόρος, "little gain falls to the lot of slanderers."

[d] See critical note 4. Clearchus in his usual exuberance plays on two meanings of ἑλκύσας "take a pull at," *i.e.* swig or drink, and "derive." ῥαβδίων, the stiles used by an artist in encaustic painting (Plut. *De Fato* 568 A), are extravagantly likened to drinking-cups. His art made him rich, and so raised his social level.

[e] *P.L.G.*[4] ii. 320, Diehl i. 95.

φορτικῶς μετακαλεσαμένῳ εἰς τρυφὴν τὴν δοθεῖσαν[1] ὑπὸ τῆς τύχης χορηγίαν, παρέγραψε τὸ
" ῥαβδοδίαιτος ἀνήρ." ἀλλ᾽ ὅμως διὰ τὸ τὴν
ἀρετὴν φῆσαι τιμᾶν ἀνεκτέον." ταῦτα μὲν ὁ
Κλέαρχος. Σοφοκλῆς δ᾽ ὁ ποιητὴς ἐν Κρίσει[2] τῷ
δράματι τὴν μὲν Ἀφροδίτην Ἡδονήν τινα οὖσαν
δαίμονα μύρῳ τε ἀλειφομένην παράγει καὶ κατ-
οπτριζομένην, τὴν δὲ Ἀθηνᾶν Φρόνησιν οὖσαν καὶ
Νοῦν ἔτι δ᾽ Ἀρετήν, ἐλαίῳ χριομένην[3] καὶ γυμ-
ναζομένην."

d   Τούτοις ἀπαντήσας ὁ Μασσούριος ἔφη· " ὦ
δαιμόνιε ἀνδρῶν, οὐκ οἶδας ὅτι αἱ ἐν τῷ ἐγκεφάλῳ
ἡμῶν αἰσθήσεις ὀδμαῖς ἡδείαις παρηγοροῦνται
προσέτι τε θεραπεύονται, καθὰ καὶ Ἄλεξίς φησιν
ἐν Πονήρᾳ οὕτως[4]·

υγιείας μέρος
μέγιστον ὀσμὰς ἐγκεφάλῳ χρηστὰς ποιεῖν.

καὶ ὁ ἀνδρειότατος δέ, προσέτι δὲ καὶ πολεμικὸς
ποιητὴς Ἀλκαῖος ἔφη·

κὰδ δὲ χευάτω[5] μύρον ἁδὺ καττῶ
στήθεος ἄμμι.

e   καὶ ὁ σοφὸς δὲ Ἀνακρέων λέγει που·

τί μὴν πέτεαι
συρίγγων[6] κοιλώτερα[7]
στήθεα χρισάμενος μύρῳ;

---

[1] Perizonius: τὴν εἰς τρυφὴν δοθεῖσαν A.
[2] Tyrwhitt: κρησὶ A.
[3] Nauck: χρωμένην ACE.   [4] οὗτοσ A.
[5] Bergk: καδδ᾽ ἐχεύσατο A, καδδεχεύατο CE.

180

vulgarly summoned to the gratification of luxury those advantages which luck had brought him, wrote by way of correcting him, ' A man who lives by the painter's *stile*' (*rabdodiaitos*). Nevertheless, since he declared that he honoured virtue, we shall have to tolerate him." So much, then, for what Clearchus says. And the poet Sophocles in the play called *The Judgement*[a] brings on Aphrodite as a goddess of Pleasure, anointing herself with perfume and toying with a mirror, whereas Athena, who is Wisdom and Reason and Virtue besides, anoints herself with olive oil and plays the gymnast.

To these words of Cynulcus Masurius replied : Good Heavens, man, you don't know that the sensations of our brain are soothed by sweet odours and cured besides, even as Alexis says in *Love-lorn Lass*[b] : " A highly important element of health is to put good odours to the brain." And the most brave as well as warlike poet Alcaeus said[c] : " And let one pour sweet perfume over our breasts." Also the wise Anacreon says, I believe[d] : " Why, indeed, are you all of a flutter, anointing with perfume your breast that is hollower than Pan's pipes ? "

[a] *T.G.F.*[2] 209 ; a satyric drama apparently dealing with Paris and the three goddesses.

[b] Kock ii. 368, Athen. 46 a (vol. i. p. 198), Clem. Alex. *Paed.* ii. 8. 68.

[c] *P.L.G.*[4] iii. 162, Diehl i. 429, Edmonds i. 416 ; ending the strophe of which two verses were quoted 674 c-d (p. 110).

[d] *P.L.G.*[4] iii. 257, Diehl i. 451, Edmonds ii. 142. It is of no use to alter the text. Athenaeus has been led by the apt quotation from Alcaeus to introduce a less appropriate one from Anacreon, who is satirizing an old man who ought to know better than to assume the ways of a young lover.

---

[6] σηράγγων Hecker. [7] Bergk : κοιλότερα ACE.

τὰ στήθη παρακελευόμενος μυροῦν, ἐν οἷς ἐστιν ἡ
καρδία, ὡς καὶ ταύτης δηλονότι παρηγορουμένης
τοῖς εὐώδεσι. τοῦτο δ' ἔπρασσον οὐ μόνον τῆς
εὐωδίας ἀπὸ τοῦ στήθους κατὰ φύσιν ἀναφερο-
μένης ἐπὶ τὴν ὄσφρησιν, ἀλλὰ καὶ διὰ τὸ νομί-
f ζειν ἐν τῇ καρδίᾳ τὴν ψυχὴν καθιδρῦσθαι, ὡς Πραξ-
αγόρας καὶ Φυλότιμος οἱ ἰατροὶ παραδεδώκασιν.
καὶ Ὅμηρος δέ φησιν·

στῆθος δὲ πλήξας κραδίην ἠνίπαπε μύθῳ.

καί·

κραδίη δέ οἱ ἔνδον ὑλάκτει.[1]

καί·

Ἕκτορι δ' αὐτῷ θυμὸς ἐνὶ στήθεσσι πάτασσε.

ὃ δὴ καὶ σημεῖον φέρουσι τοῦ τὸ κυριώτερον τῆς
ψυχῆς ἐνταῦθα κεῖσθαι· κατὰ γὰρ τὰς ἐν τοῖς
φόβοις[2] γινομένας ἀγωνίας πάλλεσθαι τὴν καρδίαν
688 ἐπιδηλότατα συμβαίνει. καὶ ὁ Ἀγαμέμνων δέ
φησιν ὁ Ὁμηρικός·

αἰνῶς γὰρ Δαναῶν πέρι δείδια, οὐδέ μοι ἦτορ
ἔμπεδον, ἀλλ' ἀλαλύκτημαι· κραδίη δέ μοι ἔξω
στηθέων ἐκθρώσκει, τρομέει δ' ὑπὸ φαίδιμα γυῖα.

καὶ ὁ Σοφοκλῆς δὲ τὰς ἀπολελυμένας τοῦ φόβου
πεποίηκε λεγούσας·

θυμῷ δ' οὔ τις[3] φαιδρὰ χορεύει
τάρβους θυγάτηρ.

---

[1] ὑλακτεῖ A.　　　　　　[2] Muretus: ψόφοισ A.
[3] δὲ οὔτισ A: δ' οὐκέτι Brunck.

Here he urges the perfuming of the breast, because it contains the heart, obviously because even the heart is comforted by sweet odours. They did this, not merely because fragrance is naturally borne upwards from the breast to the sense of smell, but also because they believed the soul is seated in the heart, as the physicians Praxagoras and Phylotimus [a] have taught And even Homer says [b] : " Then he smote his breast and rebuked his heart, saying." And [c] : " His heart barked within him." Again [d] : " Hector's own heart beat within his breast." All of which, as you know, they adduce as proof that the more authoritative part [e] of the soul resides there ; for in the agitation caused by fear you will find the heart beats most noticeably. The Homeric Agamemon also says [f] : " Dreadfully do I fear for the Danaans, nor is my heart firm within me, but I am tossed to and fro ; my heart leaps forth from my breast, and my doughty limbs tremble." Sophocles, too, makes the women who have been released from their fears say [g] : "No daughter of fear now dances gaily in our breasts."

[a] Wellmann 122-123. Quoted as an authority on food in vol. i. (see Index). In 355 a the name appears as Philotimus, as in Schol. *Il.* x. 10, xi. 424.

[b] *Od.* xx. 17, of Odysseus. See Plato, *Rep.* 441 B.

[c] *Od.* xx. 13.

[d] *Il.* vii. 216.

[e] Also called τὸ ἡγεμονικόν in Stoic terminology ; so Philotimus *ap.* Schol. *Il.* x. 10. See Diog. Laert. vii. 85 (159).

[f] *Il.* x. 93.

[g] *T.G.F.*[2] 297. I follow A. C. Pearson's interpretation, *Fragments of Sophocles* iii. 19 : " an extraordinarily bold figure for ' No heart throbs tumultuously with fear.' " No better explanation could be given than that supplied in the next quotation : " The heart *dances* with fear, but dancing is *gay*" (φαιδρά is neut. plur.).

Ἀναξανδρίδης δὲ τὸν ἀγωνιῶντα παράγει λέγοντα·

b   ὦ πονηρὰ καρδία,
ἐπιχαιρέκακον ὡς εἶ μόνον[1] τοῦ σώματος·
ὀρχῇ[2] γὰρ εὐθὺς ἄν μ᾿[3] ἴδῃς δεδοικότα.

Πλάτων δέ φησι τὸν τῶν ὅλων δημιουργὸν καὶ
τὴν τοῦ πλευμόνος αὐτῇ[4] φύσιν περιθεῖναι,[5] πρῶτον
μὲν μαλακὴν καὶ ἄναιμον, εἶτα σήραγγας ἔχουσαν οἶον σπόγγου κατατετρημένας, ἵν᾿ ἐν τῇ τῶν
δεινῶν προσδοκίᾳ πολλάκις ἀλλομένη τὸν παλμὸν
εἰς ὑπεῖκον καὶ μαλακὸν ποιῆται. ἀλλὰ μὴν
c καὶ τοὺς στεφάνους τοὺς περικειμένους τῷ στήθει
ὑποθυμίδας[6] οἱ ποιηταὶ κεκλήκασιν ἀπὸ τῆς τῶν
ἀνθῶν ἀναθυμιάσεως, οὐκ ἀπὸ τοῦ τὴν ψυχὴν
θυμὸν καλεῖσθαι, ὥς τινες ἀξιοῦσιν.

Τῷ δὲ τοῦ μύρου ὀνόματι πρῶτος Ἀρχίλοχος
κέχρηται λέγων·

οὐκ ἂν μύροισι γραῦς ἐοῦσ᾿ ἠλείφετο.

καὶ ἀλλαχοῦ δ᾿ ἔφη·

         ἐσμυρισμένας κόμας
καὶ στῆθος, ὡς ἂν καὶ γέρων ἠράσσατο.

μύρρα γὰρ ἡ σμύρνα παρ᾿ Αἰολεῦσιν, ἐπειδὴ τὰ
πολλὰ τῶν μύρων διὰ σμύρνης ἐσκευάζετο καὶ
ἥ γε στακτὴ καλουμένη διὰ μόνης ταύτης· ὁ δὲ

---

[1] μόριον Naber.   [2] Canter: ἀρχῇ altered to ἀρχὴ A.

And Anaxandrides brings on the worried man saying [a] : " Oh my poor heart, how true it is that you are the only thing in the body that rejoices in the misery of the rest ; for you dance the moment you see me scared ! " Plato says [b] that the Creator of the universe enveloped the heart with the structure of the lungs, first soft and bloodless, then containing cavities bored throughout it like those of a sponge, in order that when the heart leaps up with apprehension of danger, as it often does, it may throb against something yielding and soft. However, wreaths laid upon the breast are called by the poets *hypothymides* [c] from the exhalation (*anathymiasis*) rising from the flowers, and not because the soul is called *thymos*, as some authorities maintain.

Now the word *myron* (perfume) is used first by Archilochus, when he says [d] : " Being an old woman, she would not be anointing herself with perfumes." In another place, too, he said [e] : " Her locks and breast scented with perfume, so that even an old man would have fallen in love with her." For the gum *smyrna* is called *myrrha* by the Aeolians, since most perfumes (*myra*) were prepared with this gum, and what is called *stakté* [f] (oil of myrrh) is made with

[a] Kock ii. 160.
[b] *Timaeus* 70 c ; Plato's text is here paraphrased, not copied.
[c] Above, 674 c-d (p. 110), Plut. *Qu. Conv.* 647 f.
[d] *P.L.G.*⁴ ii. 392, Diehl i. 219 ; adapted by Pericles in his retort to Elpinice, Plut. *Per.* 28. 4-5.
[e] *P.L.G.*⁴ ii. 391, Diehl i. 219.
[f] *Cf.* vol. ii. p. 379, below, p. 190.

---

[3] μ' added by Kaibel.   [4] τῇ καρδίᾳ C.
[5] C, confirming Kaibel's conjecture : παραθεῖναι AE.
[6] ὑποθυμιάδασ A (so 674 d) C.

d "Ομηρος τὴν μὲν χρῆσιν[1] οἶδε τῶν μύρων, ἔλαια[2] δ' αὐτὰ καλεῖ μετ' ἐπιθέτου·

ῥοδόεντι[3] δ' ἔχριεν ἐλαίῳ.

καὶ ἀλλαχοῦ δὲ λέγει τι τεθυωμένον. καὶ ἡ Ἀφροδίτη δὲ[4] παρ' αὐτῷ τὸν Ἕκτορος νεκρὸν ῥοδόεντι ἔχριεν ἐλαίῳ ἀμβροσίῳ. καὶ τοῦτο μὲν ἐξ ἀνθέων. περὶ δὲ τοῦ ἐκ τῶν ἀρωμάτων σκευαζομένου, ἃ δὴ θυώματα ἐκάλουν, ἐπὶ τῆς Ἥρας λέγει·

ἀμβροσίη μὲν πρῶτον ἀπὸ χροὸς ἱμερόεντος
λύματα πάντα κάθηρεν, ἀλείψατο δὲ χρόα λευκὸν[5]
e ἀμβροσίῳ ἑδανῷ,[6] τό ῥά οἱ τεθυωμένον ἦεν·
τοῦ καὶ κινυμένοιο Διὸς ποτὶ χαλκοβατὲς δῶ
ἔμπης ἐς γαῖάν τε καὶ οὐρανὸν ἵκετ' αὐτμή.

Γίνεται δὲ μύρα κάλλιστα κατὰ τόπους, ὡς Ἀπολλώνιός φησιν ὁ Ἡροφίλειος[7] ἐν τῷ περὶ Μύρων γράφων οὕτως· " ἶρις μὲν ἐν Ἤλιδι χρηστοτάτη καὶ ἐν Κυζίκῳ· ῥόδινον δὲ κράτιστον ἐν Φασήλιδι, καὶ τὸ ἐκ Νέας δὲ πόλεως καὶ Καπύης· κρόκινον δ' ἐν Σόλοις τοῖς Κιλικίοις[8] καὶ ἐν Ῥόδῳ· νάρδινον δὲ τὸ ἐν Τάρσῳ· οἰνάνθη δὲ ἡ ἀρίστη[9]

---

[1] CE: χρίσιν A.   [2] ACE: ἔλαιον Kaibel.
[3] δροσόεντι AE (ῥοδο written above), ῥοδόεντι C (after correction).
[4] CE: τὲ A.   [5] A: λίπ' ἐλαίῳ Hom.
[6] Hom.: εανῷ A, Schol. B Il. xiv. 346 (but with λίπ' ἐλαίῳ).
[7] ἡροφίλιοσ A.   [8] ACE: τῆς Κιλικίας Kaibel.
[9] ἀρίστη CE: om. A.

---

[a] Il. xxiii. 186, Athen. 9 e, 18 e (vol. i. pp. 40, 80) "Ομηρος δὲ τὴν τοῦ μύρου φύσιν εἰδὼς οὐκ εἰσήγαγε μύροις ἀλειφομένους τοὺς ἥρωας πλὴν τὸν Πάριν. Cf. Pliny, H.N. xiii. 1.
[b] Il. xiv. 172 ; of the oil used by Hera.
[c] Herbs and spices burnt as incense.

this exclusively. Homer, indeed, knows the use of perfumes, but he calls them "oils," qualified by some adjective [a] : " She anointed him with rose-scented oil." And elsewhere [b] he tells of something " filled with a sweet smell." In Homer Aphrodite anointed the dead body of Hector " with rose-scented oil, ambrosial." And this, of course, is made out of flowers. But of that prepared from spices, which they used to call *thyomata*,[c] he says, in the description of Hera [d] : " With ambrosia first she cleansed every stain from her lovely body, and anointed her white skin with (oil) ambrosial, soft, which was filled with a sweet smell ; if it were but shaken in the bronze-paved chamber of Zeus, the fragrance of it went even to earth and to heaven."

Certain places produce the best perfumes, as Apollonius, of the school of Herophilus, asserts in his book *On Perfumes*, writing as follows [e] : " The best orris-root is that grown in Elis and in Cyzicus ; of the rose, the best perfume is obtained in Phaselis,[f] also from Naples and Capua ; of the saffron crocus, in the Cilician Soli and Rhodes ; spikenard, in Tarsus ; the best drop-wort [g] is from Cyprus and

---

[d] A good example of a passage quoted from memory (critical notes 5, 6). The trouble began when χρόα λευκὸν " her white body " crept in for λίπ' ἐλαίῳ from *Il.* xiv. 175 χρόα καλὸν ἀλειψαμένη. Then ἀμβροσίῳ ἑανῷ (robe) was suggested by *vs.* 178, ἀμβρόσιον ἑανὸν ἕσατο. The same mistake, ἑανῷ for ἑδανῷ, occurs in all mss. of *h. Ven.* 63. The exact meaning of ἑδανῷ is not known.

[e] From the same source, Pliny, *H.N.* xiii. 1. 2. The word μύρον seems to embrace not only perfumes but oils and salves as well.

[f] Above, 683 b (p. 158).

[g] Theophr. *H.P.* vi. 6. 11, vi. 8. 2 says it is grown for its flowers, but he does not specify the localities.

Κυπρία καὶ Ἀδραμυττηνή[1]· ἀμαράκινον δὲ[2] Κῷον
f καὶ μήλινον. κύπρινον δὲ προκέκριται τὸ ἐν
Αἰγύπτῳ, δευτερεῦον δ᾽ ἐστὶ τὸ Κυπριακὸν καὶ τὸ
ἐν Φοινίκῃ καὶ ταύτης τὸ ἀπὸ Σιδῶνος. τὸ δὲ
παναθηναϊκὸν λεγόμενον ἐν Ἀθήναις· τὸ δὲ μετώπιον καὶ Μενδήσιον κάλλιστα ἐν Αἰγύπτῳ σκευά-
ζεται· σκευάζεται δὲ τὸ μετώπιον ἐξ ἐλαίου τοῦ
ἀπὸ τῶν πικρῶν καρύων. οἱ δὲ χορηγοῦντες,
φησί,[3] καὶ ἡ ὕλη καὶ οἱ τεχνῖται τὸ χρηστότατον
689 ποιοῦσι μύρον, ἀλλ᾽ οὐχ οἱ τόποι. Ἔφεσός γέ τοι
πρότερον, φησί,[4] τοῖς μύροις διέφερεν καὶ μάλιστα
ἐν[5] τῷ μεγαλλείῳ,[6] νῦν δὲ οὔ. ἤκμαζε[7] δὲ καὶ τὰ
ἐν Ἀλεξανδρείᾳ διὰ πλοῦτον καὶ διὰ τὴν Ἀρσινόης
καὶ Βερενίκης σπουδήν. ἐγίνετο δὲ καὶ ἐν Κυρήνῃ[8]
ῥόδινον χρηστότατον καθ᾽ ὃν χρόνον ἔζη Βερενίκη
ἡ μεγάλη.[9] οἰνάνθινον δὲ ἐν Ἀδραμυττίῳ πάλαι
μὲν μέτριον, ὕστερον δὲ πρῶτον διὰ Στρατονίκην
τὴν Εὐμένους.[10] ἡ δὲ Συρία τὸ παλαιὸν χρηστὰ
πάντα παρείχετο, μάλιστα δὲ τὸ τήλινον, νῦν δὲ
οὔ. ἐν δὲ Περγάμῳ πρότερον μὲν ἐξόχως,[11] νῦν
b δὲ οὔ, μυρεψοῦ τινος ἐκπονήσαντος, ἐσκευάσθη

---

[1] A: ἀδραμυτηνὴ CE. [2] δὲ CE: om. A.
[3] φησὶν ἠρόφιλος C. [4] Kaibel: φασὶ A.
[5] ἐν ACE: μὲν Pursan, deleted by Kaibel.
[6] Canter: μεγαλλίωι AE, μεγαλίῳ C.
[7] Canter: ἤκμασε ACE. [8] Canter: κορύνηι A.
[9] A: ἡ Μάγα Schweighäuser. [10] A: εὐμενοῦς C.
[11] Kaibel following Schweighäuser (who preferred ἐξοχῇ):
ἐξόχη A, om. C.

---

[a] This seems to refer to the oil given to victors at the
Panathenaic games, rather than to a special kind of perfume.

Adramyttium ; the best marjoram and quince from Cos. Of henna the Egyptian is judged the best, next to it being the Cyprian and the Phoenician, especially the kind from Sidon. The Panathenaic, as it is called, is made in Athens [a] ; the *metopion* and the Mendesian are made best in Egypt ; the *metopion* is made with the oil obtained from bitter almonds. Apollonius adds, however, that the excellence of the perfume is due in each case to those who furnish the materials, the material itself, and the manufacturers, rather than to the localities. For example Ephesus, he says, in earlier times excelled in perfumes, particularly in the kind called *megalleion*, but does so no longer. Again, those of Alexandria used to be superior because of the city's wealth and the interest taken in them by Arsinoë and Berenice. And in Cyrene, too, the oil of roses was the best in the lifetime of Berenice the Great.[b] Drop-wort perfume in Adramyttium had in old times been mediocre, but later it became of first quality through the influence of Stratonicê, the wife of Eumenes.[c] Syria, in ancient times, supplied all perfumes of excellent quality, especially that from fenugreek,[d] but it is not so to-day. And in Pergamum, in earlier times but not to-day, after a certain perfumer had worked hard at it, there was manufactured in superior fashion

---

[b] Or, reading ἡ Μάγα for ἡ μεγάλη, " Berenice the daughter of Magas," Athen. 550 b-c (vol. v. p. 496 and note *a*). See Callimachus, *Epigr*. lii. (L.C.L. 174 and note *a*).

[c] Eumenes II of Pergamum. In his relations with Stratonicê (of course not to be confused with the mistress of Ptolemy Philadelphus, vol. vi. p. 114) he was the Enoch Arden of antiquity, Livy xlii. 15-16.

[d] See the description of Antiochus Epiphanes, vol. ii. p. 385, iv. p. 489.

τὸ παρ' οὐδενί πω γεγονὸς λιβανώτινον μύρον.[1]
μύρον δὲ χρηστὸν μύρῳ εὐτελεῖ ἐπιχεόμενον ἐπι-
πολῆς μένει· μέλι δὲ χρηστὸν χείρονι ἐπιχεόμενον
εἰς τὸ κάτω βιάζεται· λαμβάνει γὰρ αὐτοῦ καθύπερθεν τὸ ἧττον."

Τοῦ δὲ Αἰγυπτίου μύρου μνημονεύων Ἀχαιὸς
ἐν Ἄθλοις φησιν·

ἰσάργυρόν τ' εἰς χεῖρα[2] Κυπρίου λίθου
δώσουσι κόσμον χριμάτων[3] τ' Αἰγυπτίων.

μήποτε, φησὶν ὁ Δίδυμος, τὴν καλουμένην στακτὴν
c λέγει, διὰ τὴν σμύρναν ἣν εἰς Αἴγυπτον καταγο-
μένην κομίζεσθαι πρὸς τοὺς Ἕλληνας. Ἱκέσιος δ'
ἐν β' περὶ Ὕλης " τῶν μύρων, φησίν, ἃ μέν ἐστιν
χρίματα,[4] ἃ δ' ἀλείμματα. καὶ ῥόδινον μὲν πρὸς
πότον[5] ἐπιτήδειον, ἔτι δὲ μύρσινον, μήλινον· τοῦτο
δ' ἐστὶν καὶ εὐστόμαχον καὶ ληθαργικοῖς χρήσιμον.
τὸ δ' οἰνάνθινον εὐστόμαχον ὂν καὶ τὴν διάνοιαν
ἀπαραπόδιστον φυλάσσει. καὶ τὸ σαμψούχινον[6] δὲ
καὶ ἑρπύλλινον ἐπιτήδεια πρὸς πότον καὶ κρόκινον
d τὸ χωρὶς σμύρνης πολλῆς. καὶ ἡ στακτὴ δὲ ἐπιτήδειος πρὸς πότον, ἔτι δὲ νάρδος. τὸ δὲ τήλινον
καὶ γλυκύ ἐστι καὶ ἁπαλόν. τὸ δὲ λευκόϊνον καὶ
εὐῶδες καὶ σφόδρα πεπτικόν." Θεόφραστος δὲ ἐν
τῷ περὶ Ὀδμῶν συντίθεσθαί φησι μύρα ἀπ' ἀνθέων

[1] ἐκπονήσαντος ἐσκευάσθη τὸ . . . μύρον CE: ἐκπονήσαντοσ τὸ
. . . γεγονὸσ ἐσκευασθη τὸ λ. μ. A.
[2] Heringa (cf. 359 a): εἰσ ἀργυροῦντισ χεῖρα A, ἰσαργύρου
Meineke.
[3] χριμάτων A.   [4] A: χρίσματα C.
[5] Canter: πρὸσ τὸν A.   [6] σαμψύχινον CE.

[a] Discussed by Plut. Qu. Conv. vii. 3.   Cf. Theognis 679
κακοὶ δ' ἀγαθῶν καθύπερθεν.

what had never been made by anyone before, the perfume from frankincense. When good perfume is poured over cheap perfume it remains on the surface ; but good honey poured on inferior honey is forced to the bottom ; for the worse gets the better of it." [a]

Mentioning Egyptian perfumery in *The Games* Achaeus says [b] : "An honour worth its weight in silver they will bestow upon his hand,—Cyprian gems [c] and Egyptian ointments." "Perhaps," says Didymus,[d] "he means what is called *stakté,*[d] because the myrrh imported into Greece is brought down first into Egypt." Now Hicesius in the second book of his work *On Materials* says : "Some perfumes are rubbed on, others are poured on.[e] Rose perfume is appropriate for a symposium, also myrrh and quince ; this last is wholesome and efficacious for patients suffering from lethargic fever. The perfume from drop-wort is wholesome and keeps the brain clear. Those made of marjoram and tufted thyme are appropriate for a symposium, so, too, saffron crocus if not mixed with too much myrrh. But the *stakté* also is appropriate for a symposium, and nard as well. Fenugreek is both sweet and delicate. Perfume from gilliflowers is fragrant and very helpful to digestion." Theophrastus, in his work *On Odours,*[f] says that perfumes compounded from flowers are

[b] *T.G.F.*[2] 747. For Egyptian perfume *cf.* 553 e (vol. v. p. 514).

[c] Probably *smaragdus*, Pliny xxxvii. 5. 17.

[d] Schmidt 305 ; on *stakté* see above, p. 184.

[e] The distinction is not observed in the authors, as regards either the nouns χρῖμα and ἄλειμμα or the verbs χρίομαι and ἀλείφομαι.

[f] vi. 27, Hort (L.C.L.) ii. 350.

μὲν ῥόδινον καὶ λευκόϊνον καὶ σούσινον (καὶ γὰρ
τοῦτο ἐκ τῶν κρίνων), ἔτι δὲ τὸ σισύμβρινον καὶ
ἑρπύλλινον, ἔτι δὲ κύπρινον καὶ κρόκινον[1] βέλτιστον
δ' ἐν Αἰγίνῃ καὶ Κιλικίᾳ. ἀπὸ δὲ φύλλων τὸ μύρ-
ρινον καὶ τὸ οἰνάνθινον· αὕτη δ' ἐν Κύπρῳ φύεται
ὀρεινὴ καὶ πολύοσμος[2]· ἀπὸ δὲ τῆς ἐν τῇ Ἑλλάδι[3]
e οὐ γίνεται διὰ τὸ ἄοσμον. ἀπὸ[4] δὲ ῥιζῶν τό τ'
ἴρινον, καὶ τὸ νάρδινον, καὶ τὸ ἀμαράκινον ἐκ τοῦ
κόστου.''

Ὅτι δὲ διὰ σπουδῆς ἦν τοῖς παλαιοτέροις ἡ τῶν
μύρων χρῆσις[5] δῆλον ἐκ τοῦ καὶ ἐπίστασθαι ποῖόν
τι ἑκάστῳ τῶν μελῶν ἡμῶν ἐστιν ἐπιτήδειον.
Ἀντιφάνης γοῦν ἐν Θορικίοις ἢ Διορύττοντί φησιν·

λοῦται δ' ἀληθῶς;[6] ἀλλὰ τί;
Β. ἐκ χρυσοκολλήτου γε[7] κάλπιδος μύρῳ
Αἰγυπτίῳ μὲν τοὺς πόδας καὶ τὰ σκέλη,
φοινικίνῳ δὲ τὰς γνάθους καὶ τιτθία,
f σισυμβρίνῳ[8] δὲ τὸν ἕτερον βραχίονα,
ἀμαρακίνῳ δὲ τὰς ὀφρῦς καὶ τὴν κόμην,
ἑρπυλλίνῳ δὲ τὸ γόνυ καὶ τὸν αὐχένα. . . .

καὶ Κηφισόδωρος ἐν Τροφωνίῳ·

ἔπειτ' ἀλείφεσθαι πρίω τὸ σῶμά μοι
μύρον ἴρινον[10] καὶ ῥόδινον, ἄγε μοι,[11] Ξανθία[12]·
καὶ τοῖς ποσὶν χωρὶς πρίω[13] μοι βάκκαριν.[14]

---

[1] ἔτι . . . κρόκινον Kaibel (following Dindorf): ἐν δὲ
κύπρωι, καὶ τὸ κρίνον A.
[2] Theophr. (πολύοδμος): πολύγονος ACE.
[3] ἀπὸ . . . ἐν τῇ Ἑλλάδι Theophr.: ἐν δὲ ἑλλάδι A.
[4] Theophr.: διὰ ACE.
[5] CE: χρίσις A.   λοῦτ' αι δου ο αληθωσ A.
192

rose, gilliflower, and *susinon* (for this too is made from flowers of the lily),[a] besides bergamot-mint and tufted thyme, and again henna [b] and saffron crocus; this crocus is best in Aegina and Cilicia. But from the leaves are compounded perfume of myrrh and of drop-wort ; this grows in Cyprus on the hills and is very fragrant ; but from that which grows in Greece no perfume can be made, since the leaf is without scent. From roots, on the other hand, come orris and spikenard and the sweet-marjoram-perfume made from costus-root.[c]

That the use of perfumes was popular in earlier times is shown by the knowledge of what is suitable for each of our members. Antiphanes, for example, says in *The Villagers of Thoricus*, or *Digging Through*[d] : " A. So she's really bathing ? Well, then, what ? B. Yes, she has a box inlaid with gold, and from it she anoints her feet and legs with Egyptian perfume, her cheeks and nipples with palm-oil, one of her arms with bergamot-mint, her eyebrows and hair with sweet marjoram, her knee and neck with tufted thyme. . . ." And Cephisodorus in *Trophonius*[e] : " A. Then you must anoint my body ; buy me some perfume of orris and rose, hurry, Xanthias, and for my feet besides, buy me some asarabacca. B. You loose-

[a] See 513 f (vol. v. p. 310 and note *b*).
[b] See p. 189. *Cf.* French *chypre?*
[c] See Hort ii. 351, 355, 357.
[d] Kock ii. 53, Athen. 553 d (vol. v. p. 514).
[e] Kock i. 800, Athen. 553 a (vol. v. p. 511 and note *f*).

---

7 Musurus: δὲ A (τε 553 d).   8 CE: σισυμβρίωι A.
9 πριῶ A.   10 553 a: μύροντ' ἱρινον A.
11 Kock: ἄγαμαι A.   12 ξανθίου A.
13 πριω χωρίσ A.   14 553 a: βακχαριν A.

B. ὦ λακκόπρωκτε, βάκκαριν[1] τοῖς σοῖς ποσὶν
ἐγὼ πρίωμαι; λαικάσομάρα βάκκαριν;[2]

Ἀναξανδρίδης Πρωτεσιλάῳ·

μύρον τε παρὰ Πέρωνος, οὗπερ ἀπέδοτο
690   ἐχθὲς[3] Μελανώπῳ, πολυτελοῦς Αἰγυπτίου,
ᾧ νῦν ἀλείφει τοὺς πόδας Καλλιστράτου.

μνημονεύει τοῦ μυροπώλου τούτου τοῦ Πέρωνος
καὶ Θεόπομπος ἐν Ἀδμήτῳ καὶ Ἡδυχάρει.
Ἀντιφάνης δ' ἐν Ἀντείᾳ·

παρὰ[4] τῷ μυροπώλῃ γευόμενον κατελίμπανον
αὐτὸν Πέρωνι[5] τῶν μύρων[6]· μέλλει δέ[7] σοι
συνθεὶς[8] φέρειν
τὰ κινναμώμινα[9] ταῦτα καὶ τὰ νάρδινα.

Παρὰ πολλοῖς δὲ τῶν κωμῳδιοποιῶν ὀνομάζεταί
τι μύρον ΒΑΚΚΑΡΙΣ· οὗ μνημονεύει καὶ Ἱππῶναξ διὰ
τούτων·

b   βακκάρι[10] δὲ τὰς ῥῖνας
ἤλειφον· ἐστὶ δ' οἷά[11] περ κρόκος.

Ἀχαιὸς δ' ἐν Αἴθωνι σατυρικῷ·

βακκάρει χρισθέντα καὶ ψυκτηρίοις
πτεροῖς ἀναστήσαντα προσθίαν[12] τρίχα.

Ἴων Ὀμφάλῃ·

                  βακκάρις[13] δὲ καὶ μύρα
καὶ Σαρδιανὸν κόσμον εἰδέναι χροὸς
ἄμεινον ἢ τὸν Πέλοπος ἐν νήσῳ τρόπον.

---

[1] 553 a : βακχαριν A.   [2] βάκκαριν A.
[3] 553 e : χθὲσ A.   [4] Kock : πρὸσ A.
[5] Canter : περὶ A.   [6] τῶν μύρων Kock : μύρων A (sic).

194

oreeched wanton, I am to buy asarabacca for your
feet? I'll go a-wenching with an asarabacca?"
Anaxandrides in *Protesilaus* [a] : " Perfume bought at
Peron's shop, some of which he sold yesterday to
Melanopus, and expensive Egyptian it is too ; with
it Melanopus anoints the feet of Callistratus."
Theopompus also mentions this perfumer, Peron,
in *Admetus* and in *Delighting in Luxury*.[b] And Antiphanes in *Anteia* [c] : " I left him behind at the shop
of Peron the perfumer, tasting the perfumes [d] ; and
after he has agreed on a price he is going to bring
you those made of cinnamon and spikenard."

In many comic poets there is mentioned a perfume
called asarabacca (*baccaris*) ; Hipponax, also, mentions it with these words [e] : " They were smearing
their nostrils with baccaris ; it smells like saffron
crocus." And Achaeus in *Aethon*, a satyric drama [f] :
" Anointed with baccaris, and making his forelock
rise with cooling feathers." Ion in *Omphale* [g] : " To
know about baccaris-ointments and perfumes and
cosmetics of Sardis for the skin is better than knowing the manner of life in Pelops' isle." In these

[a] Kock ii. 151, Athen. 553 d (vol. v. p. 515 and note c).
[b] Kock i. 733, 737.
[c] Kock ii. 24.
[d] For the use of perfumes in wine see 66 c-d (vol. i. p. 288).
[e] *P.L.G.*[4] ii. 476, Diehl i. 273.
[f] *T.G.F.*[2] 749 ; for the title see 270 c note b (vol. iii. p. 214).
[g] *T.G.F.*[2] 736, contrasting Eastern luxury with Spartan
simplicity.

---

[7] δὲ Bergk : τε A.   [8] Kock : συνθείσ σοι A.
        [9] Schweighäuser : κιννάμωμα A.
    [10] CE after correction : βακκάρει ACE.
    [11] Bergk : ἔσθ' οἴη A, ἔστι δ' οἴη CE.
[12] Canter : προσθείαν A.   [13] βάκκαρισ A (*sic*).

ἐν τούτοις Σαρδιανὸν κόσμον εἴρηκε τὸ μύρον, ἐπεὶ
διαβόητοι ἐπὶ ἡδυπαθείᾳ οἱ Λυδοί· καὶ τὸ παρὰ
c Ἀνακρέοντι " Λυδοπαθὴς " ἀκούουσιν ἀντὶ τοῦ
ἡδυπαθής. μνημονεύει τῆς βακκάριδος καὶ Σοφοκλῆς. Μάγνης δ' ἐν Λυδοῖς·

> λούσαντα χρὴ[1] καὶ βακκάριδι κεχριμένον . . .

καὶ μήποτε οὔκ ἐστι μύρον ἡ βάκκαρις. Αἰσχύλος
γὰρ ἐν Ἀμυμώνῃ[2] ἀντιδιαστέλλων φησίν·

> κἄγωγε τὰς σὰς βακκάρεις τε καὶ μύρα.

καὶ Σιμωνίδης·

> κἠλειφόμην μύροισι καὶ θυώμασι
> καὶ βακκάρι.[3]

Ἀριστοφάνης δ' ἐν Θεσμοφοριαζούσαις·

d > ὦ Ζεῦ πολυτίμηθ', οἷον ἐνέπνευσ'[4] ὁ μιαρὸς
> φάσκωλος εὐθὺς λυόμενός[5] μοι τοῦ μύρου
> καὶ βακκάριδος.

ΒΡΕΝΘΕΙΟΥ[6] δὲ μύρου μνημονεύει Φερεκράτης ἐν
Λήροις οὕτως·

> ἔστην δὲ κἀκέλευον, " ἐγχέασθε νῶν
> βρένθειον,[7] ἵνα τοῖς εἰσιοῦσιν ἐγχέῃ."[8]

---

[1] χρὴ λουσάμενον Kock.   Read λουθέντα χρὴ or λούσαντα
χρόα?   [2] ἀμυμόνη A.
[3] CE : βακκάρει A.   [4] Dobree : ἔπνευσ' A.
[5] Dalechamps : λουόμενοσ ACE.   [6] CE : βρενθίου A.
[7] Meineke : ενχεασθαι . . . νων μύρον βρένθιον A.
[8] εἰσιοῦσι ἐγχέῃ A : εἰσιοῦσιν ἐγχέω Meineke.

lines he means by " Sardian cosmetics " the perfume, since the Lydians were notorious for luxurious
living; in fact the word " Lydian-living " in
Anacreon [a] is understood to mean the same as
" luxurious living." Baccaris is mentioned also by
Sophocles,[b] and by Magnes in *The Lydians* [c] : " When
bathed and anointed with baccaris he should . . . "
It may be, indeed, that baccaris is not a perfume, for
Aeschylus in *Amymone* makes some sort of distinction when he says [d] : " As for me, I (loathe) your
smearings of baccaris and your perfumes." And
Simonides [e] : " I began to anoint myself with
perfumes and scents and baccaris." So Aristophanes
in *Thesmophoriazusae* [f] : " O worshipful Zeus, how
that damned clothes-bag, the moment it was untied,
breathed upon me with its perfume and baccaris."

A perfume called *brentheium* is mentioned by
Pherecrates in *Frills*, thus [g] : " I stopped and gave
orders : ' Pour out some brentheium for us two,
that he may have it ready for those who enter.' "

[a] *P.L.G.*⁴ iii. 293, *cf.* Edmonds ii. 204, Schol. Aesch. *Pers.*
41 (on ἀβροδίαιτοι).

[b] *T.G.F.*² 342.

[c] Kock i. 8.

[d] *T.G.F.*² 7, from a satyric drama. It was, in fact, a dry
powder, Hesych. *s.* βάκκαρις· ἔστι δὲ καὶ ξηρὸν διάπασμα τὸ
ἀπὸ τῆς ῥίζης (made from the root).

[e] *P.L.G.*⁴ ii. 455, Diehl i. 254. The iambograph Semonides of Amorgos is meant. Clem. Alex. *Paed.* ii. 64. 3
(p. 196. 54) adds καὶ γάρ τις ἔμπορος παρῆν " for a rich
merchant had arrived "; obviously spoken by an hetaera.

[f] Kock i. 474.

[g] Kock i. 173; the true readings seem to be lost. Hesych.
s. βρενθινά defines these as roots used by women as rouge;
the powder seems to have been sprinkled on the feet after
they were washed on coming in from the street. For βρένθος
used of haughty bearing, putting on airs, see vol. vi. p. 294.

197

ΒΑΣΙΛΕΙΟΥ δὲ μύρου μνημονεύει Κράτης ἐν Γείτο-
σιν λέγων οὕτως·

   γλυκύτατον δ᾽ ὦζε[1] βασιλείου μύρου.

ἡ Σαπφὼ δ᾽ ὁμοῦ μέμνηται τοῦ τε βασιλείου καὶ τοῦ
βρενθείου, λέγουσα οὕτως·

   βρενθείῳ βασιληίῳ.[2]

ΨΑΓΔΗΣ. Ἀριστοφάνης ἐν Δαιταλεῦσιν·

   φέρ᾽ ἴδω, τί σοι δῶ τῶν μύρων; ψάγδαν φιλεῖς;

Εὔπολις δ᾽ ἐν Μαρικᾷ[3]·

   ψάγδαν ἐρυγγάνοντα.

Εὔβουλος δ᾽ ἐν Στεφανοπώλισιν·

   Αἰγυπτίῳ ψάγδανι[4] τρὶς λελουμένη.

Πολέμων δ᾽ ἐν τοῖς πρὸς Ἀδαῖον παρὰ Ἠλείοις
φησὶ μύρον τι ΠΛΑΓΓΟΝΙΟΝ καλεῖσθαι, εὑρεθὲν ὑπό
τινος Πλαγγόνος. ὁμοίως ἱστορεῖ καὶ Σωσίβιος ἐν
Ὁμοιότησιν.

f   Ὡς καὶ τὸ ΜΕΓΑΛΛΕΙΟΝ[5]· ὠνομάσθη γὰρ καὶ τοῦτο
ἀπὸ Μεγάλλου τοῦ Σικελιώτου· οἱ δ᾽ Ἀθηναῖόν
φασιν εἶναι τὸν Μέγαλλον. μνημονεύει δ᾽ αὐτοῦ

---

[1] Porson: δὲ ὦ ζεῦ A.   [2] C Pap.: βρενθείῳ βασιληῖω A.
[3] μάρι καὶ A.   [4] ψαγδανι A.
[5] μεγαλεῖον A, μεγάλλιον CE (C in later hand adds προπαρ-
οξυτόνως, cf. Eust. 974. 2).
198

Royal perfume is mentioned by Crates in *Neighbours*, thus [a] : " He smelt most sweetly of royal perfume." But Sappho mentions the royal and the brentheium together, putting it thus [b] : " You have anointed (your body ?) with royal brentheium."

Psagdes. Aristophanes in *Men of Dinnerville* [c] : " Come, let me see. Which perfume shall I give you ? Do you like psagdas ? " And Eupolis in *Maricas* [d] : " Belching psagdas." Also Eubulus in *Wreath-Sellers* [e] : " Thrice bathed she was with Egyptian psagdan."

Polemon in his *Address to Adaeus* [f] says that there is a perfume used by the people of Elis, called *plangonium*, having been discovered by a woman named Plangôn. The same is recorded by Sosibius also in *Similarities*.[g]

So also the perfume known as *megalleium* [h] ; for that received its name from Megallus, a Sicilian Greek ; but others declare that Megallus was an Athenian. Aristophanes mentions him in *The Tel-*

[a] Kock i. 131. Pliny, *H.N.* xiii. 2. 1 regale unguentum ; alluded to in the story of Demetrius, 577 f (vol. vi. pp. 118-120).

[b] *P.L.G.*[4] iii. 105, Diehl i. 370, Edmonds i. 242, Berlin Papyrus 9722, p. 2, where the reading is very uncertain, but the verb is surely ἐξαλείψαο, translated above.

[c] Kock i. 443, below, 691 c (p. 202).

[d] Kock i. 312. *Maricas* (=κίναιδος Hesych.) was an attack on the demagogue Hyperbolus, *cf.* Aristoph. *Nub.* 551-556. Often quoted by other authors, it is mentioned by Athenaeus only here and below, 691 c.

[e] Kock ii. 199.

[f] Preller 106. Phot. *Bibl.* 532. 15 πλαγγόνιον, ὅπερ εὖρε γυνὴ ᾿Ηλεία καλουμένη Πλαγγών, *cf.* Pollux vi. 104. Πλαγγόν (vol. vi. p. 203), the celebrated hetaera, was a native of Miletus.

[g] *F.H.G.* ii. 630. For Sosibius see *Ox. Pap.* xv. 98.

[h] Athen. 553 b (vol. v. p. 512).

Ἀριστοφάνης ἐν Τελμησσεῦσι[1] καὶ Φερεκράτης ἐν
Πετάλῃ, Στράττις δ᾽ ἐν Μηδείᾳ[2] οὕτως·

  καὶ λέγ᾽ ὅτι φέρεις αὐτῇ μύρον[3]
  τοιοῦτον οἷον οὐ Μέγαλλος πώποτε
  ἥψησεν οὐδὲ Δεινίας[4] ἀγύπτιος[5]
  οὔτ᾽ εἶδεν οὔτ᾽ ἐκτήσατο.

691 τοῦ μεγαλλείου[6] δὲ μύρου μνημονεύει καὶ Ἄμφις
ἐν Ὀδυσσεῖ διὰ τούτων·

  ἐρίοισι τοὺς τοίχους κύκλῳ Μιλησίοις,
  ἔπειτ᾽ ἀλείφειν τῷ μεγαλλείῳ[6] μύρῳ
  καὶ τὴν βασιλικὴν θυμιᾶτε μίνδακα.
  Β. ἀκήκοας σύ, δέσποτ᾽, ἤδη πώποτε
  τὸ θυμίαμα τοῦτο;

Ἀναξανδρίδης Τηρεῖ·

  ἀλλ᾽ οἷα νύμφη βασιλὶς ὠνομασμένη
  μύροις μεγαλλείοις τὸ σῶμ᾽[7] ἀλείφεται.

ΝΑΡΔΙΝΟΥ δὲ μύρου μέμνηται Μένανδρος ἐν
Κεκρυφάλῳ οὕτως·

b ἡδὺ τὸ μύρον, παιδάριον.[8] Β. ἡδύ; πῶς γὰρ οὔ;
  νάρδινον.

Τὸ δὲ χρίσασθαι τῷ τοιούτῳ ἀλείμματι μυρί-
σασθαι εἴρηκεν Ἀλκαῖος ἐν Παλαίστρᾳ[9] διὰ
τούτων·

  μυρίσασα[10] συγκατέκλεισεν[11] ἀνθ᾽ αὑτῆς λάθρα.

---

[1] τελμισσεῦσι A.   [2] Schweighäuser: μήδαι A.
  [3] Erfurdt: λεγοτὶ μυρον φέρεισ αὐτη A.
  [4] δινίασ A.   [5] Kock: αἰγύπτιοσ A.
  [6] μεγαλλίου and μεγαλλίω A.
  [7] Herwerden: μεγαλλίοισι σῶμ᾽ A.
  [8] Dindorf: παιδίον A, παῖ. B. νὴ Δί᾽, ἡδύ Dobree.
  [9] παλαίστραισ A.   [10] Dalechamps: μυρίσασ A.
  [11] A (sic, in a contraction; not ἐγ-).

messians,[a] Pherecrates in *The Broad,*[b] and Strattis in *Medea,* as follows [c] : " And say that you bring her perfume, such perfume as Megallus never yet cooked, and Deinias of Egypt neither saw nor acquired." The megalleium perfume is mentioned by Amphis also in *Odysseus* in these lines [d] : " A. Drape the walls about with Milesian wool, then anoint him with the megalleium perfume, and burn the royal [e] incense. B. Have you ever heard of that kind of incense before now, my master ? " Anaxandrides in *Tereus* [f] : " Like some promised [g] bride of kings, she anoints her body with perfumes of Megallus."

Perfume of *spikenard* is mentioned by Menander in *The Head Dress* thus [h] : " A. This perfume, laddy, is fragrant. B. Fragrant ? Of course it is. It's made of spikenard."

Now the act of anointing with such unguents as these is expressed by the verb *myrizo* (perfume) ; thus Alcaeus in *Palaestra* [i] : " After perfuming her she locked her up with him to take her own place without his knowledge." Nevertheless the noun

---

[a] Kock i. 527. Hesych. *s. μεγάλλειον· μύρον.* Ἀριστοφάνης. "μεταπέμπου νῦν ταῦτα σπουδῇ καὶ μύρον, εὕρημα Μεγάλλου."

[b] Kock i. 186.   [c] Kock i. 720.

[d] Kock ii. 243.   [e] Perhaps = Persian.

[f] Kock ii. 156.

[g] This meaning of ὠνομασμένη (sponsa, desponsata), adopted by Schweighäuser and Meineke, has been questioned, but *cf. Il.* ix. 515, xxiii. 90. For the picture *cf.* Theocr. xv. 23, of the newly-wed Arsinoë, ἀκούω χρῆμα καλόν τι | κοσμεῖν τὰν βασίλισσαν.

[h] Kock iii. 78, Allinson 368.

[i] Kock i. 761 ; a woman foists a substitute on her lover. On this name of a courtesan, Palaestra, see vol. iv. p. 293 note *i*; the plural form of the title (critical note 9) seems to be an error. See Aristoph. *Lys.* 938.

μυρώμασιν μέντοι, οὐ μυρίσμασιν ἔλεγεν[1] Ἀριστοφάνης ἐν Ἐκκλησιαζούσαις·

ἥτις μεμύρισμαι τὴν κεφαλὴν μυρώμασιν.

c Τῆς δὲ λεγομένης σάγδας (μύρον δ' ἐστὶ καὶ
τοῦτο) Ἐπίλυκος ἐν Κωραλίσκῳ·

βάκκαρίς τε καὶ σάγδας ὁμοῦ.

καὶ Ἀριστοφάνης ἐν Δαιταλεῦσιν, καὶ ἐν Μαρικᾷ[2]
Εὔπολις " σάγδαν ἐρυγγάνοντα " λέγων. ὅπερ ὁ
Θυατειρηνὸς Νίκανδρος ἐπὶ τοῦ ἄγαν χλιδῶντος
εἰρῆσθαι ἀκούει, Θεόδωρος δὲ θυμίαμά τί φησιν
αὐτὸ εἶναι.

Παμπόλλου δ' ἐπιπράσκετο Ἀθήνησιν ἡ τοῦ
μύρου κοτύλη, καὶ ὡς μὲν Ἵππαρχός φησιν ἐν
Παννυχίδι, ε´ μνῶν, ὡς δὲ Μένανδρος ἐν Μισο-
d γύνῃ, ι´. Ἀντιφάνης δ' ἐν Φρεαρρίῳ[3] στακτῆς
τοῦ μύρου μνημονεύων φησίν·

στακτὴ δυοῖν μναῖν οὐκ ἀρέσκει μ' οὐδαμῶς.

οὐ μόνον δὲ τὸ τῶν Σαρδιανῶν γένος φιλόμυρον
ἦν, ὡς Ἄλεξίς φησιν ἐν Ἐκπωματοποιῷ·

ἀεὶ φιλόμυρον πᾶν τὸ Σάρδεων γένος,

ἀλλὰ καὶ αὐτοὶ οἱ Ἀθηναῖοι οἱ πάντων τῶν καλ-
λίστων εἰσηγηταὶ τῷ τῶν ἀνθρώπων βίῳ γενόμενοι,

---

[1] Early edd.: ἔλεγον AC.
[2] μαρι καὶ A.
[3] Porson: φρεαρρω A (originally φρεαριω).

---

[a] As if from myrō not myrizō; Eccl. 1117, a maid-servant
congratulates herself on her good luck. Other examples
of μύρωμα are not found in the comedians, though they may

ᾱsed by Aristophanes in *Ecclesiazusae* is *myroma*,[a] not *myrisma* : " For my whole head is perfumed with perfumes (*myromata*)."

What is called *sagda* (this also is a perfume) is mentioned by Epilycus in *Coraliscus*[b] : " Baccaris and sagdas together." So Aristophanes in *Men of Dinnerville* and Eupolis in *Maricas*, when he says : " Belching sagda." This last is understood by Nicander of Thyateira to be said of one who is very luxurious ; Theodorus says it is a kind of incense.

The price of a half-pint of perfume sold at Athens was very high ; according to Hipparchus in *The Vigil*[c] it was five minas ; according to Menander in *Woman Hater*,[d] ten minas. And Antiphanes in *The Villager from Phrearrus*[e] says in mentioning the perfume *stakté* : " I am by no means satisfied with *stakté* that costs only two minas." It was not only " the tribe of Sardians " that was fond of perfumery, as Alexis declares in *The Cup-Maker*,[f] " Ever fond of perfumery is the entire tribe of Sardis," but even the Athenians themselves ; for though they were the people who introduced the noblest practices to the

have been cited and lost here, since the MSS. give the plural ἔλεγον, not ἔλεγεν.

[b] Kock i. 803. For sagda, psagdes, psagdan see above, 690 e (p. 198).

[c] Kock iii. 274. Παννυχίς, like Παλαίστρα, may be a jocose name for an hetaera, as in Lucian, *Dial. Mere.* 9. On the prices here given, ranging from about £10 to £50, see Böckh-Fränkel, *Staatshaushaltung* i. 134.

[d] Kock iii. 97.

[e] Kock ii. 110 ; the deme here mentioned belonged to the tribe Leontis. On στακτή see above, 688 c (p. 185). The dissatisfaction of the woman speaking must have been due to the small quantity ; *cf.* 194 b (vol. ii. p. 378) for a story of its extravagant use.　　　　　　　[f] Kock ii. 320.

παρ᾽ οἷς ἀνυπερβλήτου τιμῆς, ὡς προείρηται, τῶν
μύρων ὑπαρχούσης οὐκ ἀπείχοντο τῆς χρήσεως,[1]
e ὥσπερ οὐδὲ ἡμεῖς νῦν οὕτω πολυτίμων τῶν[2] καλ-
λίστων ὑπαρχόντων ὡς λῆρον εἶναι τὰ ἐν τῷ
Εἰσοικιζομένῳ Ἀλέξιδος ταυτί[3]·

οὐ γὰρ ἐμυρίζετ᾽ ἐξ ἀλαβάστου, πρᾶγμά τι
γινόμενον ἀεί, κρονικόν, ἀλλὰ τέτταρας
περιστερὰς ἀφῆκεν ἀποβεβαμμένας[4]
εἰς οὐχὶ ταὐτόν, μὰ Δία, τὴν αὐτὴν[5] μύρον,
ἰδίᾳ[6] δ᾽ ἑκάστην. πετόμεναι δ᾽ αὗται κύκλῳ
ἔρραινον ἡμῶν θαἰμάτια καὶ[7] στρώματα.
f μή μοι φθονήσητ᾽, ἄνδρες Ἑλλήνων ἄκροι·
ἠλειφόμην ὑόμενος[8] ἰρίνῳ[9] μύρῳ.

Πρὸς θεῶν, φίλοι, ποία ἡδονή, μᾶλλον δ᾽ ὑοσα-
λακωνία[10] θαἰμάτια μολύνεσθαι, ἐξὸν ταῖς χερσίν,
ὥσπερ ἡμεῖς νῦν ποιοῦμεν, ἀρυσαμένους ἀλείφεσθαι
πᾶν τὸ σῶμα καὶ μάλιστα τὴν κεφαλήν. φησὶν γὰρ
ὁ Φιλωνίδης[11] ἐν τῷ περὶ Μύρων καὶ Στεφάνων τὴν
692 ἀφορμὴν τοῦ τὴν κεφαλὴν ἐν τοῖς πότοις λιπαίνειν
ἐντεῦθεν γενέσθαι· τοῖς αὐχμῶσι γὰρ τὰς κεφαλὰς
εἰς τὸ μετέωρον ἕλκεσθαι τὸ λαμβανόμενον· καὶ διὰ
τοῦτο τῶν πυρετῶν διακαιόντων τὰ σώματα τέγ-
γουσι τὴν κεφαλὴν ἐπιβρέγμασιν, ἵνα μὴ πρὸς τὸ
ξηρόν, ταύτῃ δὲ καὶ πολύκενον, ὁρμὴν τὰ παρα-

---

[1] CE: χρίσεως A. [2] Wilamowitz: καὶ A.
[3] ταυτὶ A corrected from ταυτη.
[4] CE (ἀπο om. C): ἀποβεβανμένασ A.
[5] τὰς πάσας Hirschig, τὴν πυγὴν Kock.
[6] CE: ἰδίω A, ἴδιον Kock.
[7] Dindorf: τὰ ACE. [8] Meineke: θυόμενος A.
[9] Canter: ηρινω A. [10] Meineke: ουσαλακωνια A.
[11] Reinesius: μυρωνίδησ ACE.

civilized world, nevertheless when the price of perfumes was exorbitant, as we have just said, they did not abstain from their use any more than we do nowadays, when the best things cost so much that the following lines, spoken in *The New Tenant* of Alexis, seem to describe a mere trifle [a] : " He did not get perfume from an alabaster bottle ; that's something which happens every day, the custom's grown stale ; no, he had four pigeons dipped in perfume, not, I swear, all in the same perfume,[b] but each in her own, and then he let them loose. They, flying all round, sprinkled our cloaks and couch-spreads. ' Grudge it not to me, exalted men of Greece ' [c] ; when I anointed myself it was in a rain of orris-perfume."

The gods are my witness, friends, what delight, or rather what hoggish wallowing it is, to have one's clothes stained, when with our hands we can dip out ointment as we are doing now and anoint the entire body, and especially the head. For Philonides [d] in his work *On Perfumes and Wreaths* says : " The practice of oiling the head in drinking-parties arose from the following cause : when, namely, the head is dry, whatever is taken into the stomach is drawn upward ; for this reason, as the fevers inflame their bodies, men moisten the head with lotions to prevent the partly burned elements from getting a start toward the part that is dry and is moreover

---

[a] Kock ii. 318 ; a comic report of luxurious life in the East, imitating Aristoph. *Acharn.* 65-90.

[b] See critical notes 5 and 6.

[c] Quoted from Euripides' *Telephus*, *T.G.F.*[2] 583 ; parodied in Aristoph. *Acharn.* 497. See Schol.

[d] The mss. give Μυρωνίδης for Φιλωνίδης (above, 675 a) which may be a weak pun suggested by the title of his work.

καιόμενα[1] λαμβάνῃ. τοῦτο δὴ λογισάμενοι καὶ ἐπὶ
τῶν πότων τὴν εἰς τὸ μετέωρον[2] τῶν οἴνων φορὰν
ὑποπτεύσαντες ἐπεσπάσθησαν κεφαλὴν λιπαίνειν,
ὡς ἐλάσσονος τῆς[3] βίας γενησομένης εἰ ταύτην
b προτέγξαιεν. προστιθεὶς δ᾽ ὁ βίος ἀεὶ τοῖς χρειώ-
δεσιν[4] καὶ τῶν εἰς ἀπόλαυσιν καὶ τρυφὴν ἀγόντων
ἐπὶ τὴν τῶν μύρων χρῆσιν ὥρμησεν. χρηστέον οὖν,
ὦ Κύνουλκε Θεόδωρε, μύροις παρὰ πότον τοῖς
ἐλάχιστα καροῦν δυναμένοις, τοῖς στύφουσιν δὲ καὶ
ψύχουσιν ἐπ᾽ ὀλίγον. ζητεῖ δ᾽ ὁ πολυμαθέστατος
Ἀριστοτέλης ἐν τοῖς Φυσικοῖς Προβλήμασι " διὰ
τί οἱ μυριζόμενοι πολιώτεροι; ἢ ὅτι τὸ μύρον διὰ
τὰ ἀρώματα ξηραντικόν ἐστι, διὸ καὶ αὐχμηροὶ οἱ[5]
μυριζόμενοι· ὁ δὲ αὐχμὸς πολιωτέρους ποιεῖ. εἴτε
γὰρ αὔανσις τριχὸς ἡ πολιὰ εἴτ᾽ ἔνδεια[6] θερμοῦ, ἡ
c ξηρότης μαραίνει. διὸ καὶ τὰ πιλία θᾶττον ποιεῖ
πολιούς· ἐκπίνεται γὰρ ἡ οἰκεία τῆς τριχὸς
ὑγρότης."

Ἥδιστον δέ, ἄνδρες φίλοι, ἀναγινώσκων τὴν
ὀγδόην καὶ εἰκοστὴν τῶν Ποσειδωνίου[7] Ἱστοριῶν
περὶ μύρων τι λεγόμενον ἐτήρησα, οὐκ ἀλλότριον[8]
ἡμῶν τοῦ συμποσίου. φησὶ γὰρ ὁ φιλόσοφος· " ἐν
Συρίᾳ ἐν τοῖς βασιλικοῖς συμποσίοις ὅταν τοῖς
εὐωχουμένοις δοθῶσιν[9] οἱ στέφανοι, εἰσίασίν τινες
μύρων[10] Βαβυλωνίων ἔχοντες ἀσκίδια καὶ πόρρωθεν

---

[1] Dalechamps: παρακείμενα ACE.
[2] CE: εἰσ μετέωρον A.   [3] τῆς added by Wilamowitz.
[4] E, χρεώδεσι C: χριώδεσιν A.
[5] αὐχμηροὶ οἱ CE, αὐχμηρότεροι οἱ Clem. Al.: αὐχμηρον
(om. οἱ) A.
[6] CE, Clem.: ἐνδείαι A.   [7] CE: ποσιδωνιου A.
[8] Early edd.: οὐκαλλότριοσ A.
[9] CE: δωθῶσιν A.   [10] CE: μυρω A.

most empty. And so, taking this fact into account, and suspecting that during the drinking-bout the course of the wine is upward to the top, men were induced to oil the head, believing that the violence of the wine would be abated if they moistened the head beforehand. And since human life is constantly adding to the merely useful some of those things which conduce to enjoyment and luxury, it is impelled to the use of perfumes." Therefore, Theodorus-Cynulcus,[a] we must use those perfumes in a drinking-party which have the least stupefying effect, and which are astringent and can cool for a short time. The most learned Aristotle raises the question in his *Problems of Physics*[b] : " Why do those who use perfumes have grey hair sooner? Is it because perfume, through the spices in it, has a drying quality, wherefore the users of perfume become parched? For parching makes people more grey. For whether greyness is a drying up of the hair or a deficiency in heat, certain it is that dryness withers. Hence caps made of felt make men grey more quickly; for the natural moisture of the hair is absorbed by them."

Reading the twenty-eighth book of Poseidonius's *Histories*, I observed a very neat thing said concerning perfumes, which is not out of place in our symposium. For that philosopher says[c] : " In Syria, at the royal symposia when wreaths are distributed among the feasters, certain attendants enter with small pouches of Babylonian perfumes from which,

[a] See 669 e (p. 87 note *e*).
[b] Frag. 235 Rose. Clem. Alex. *Paed.* ii. 8. 69 αἱ ἀφραίνουσαι γυναῖκες βάπτουσαι μὲν τὰς πολιάς, μυρίζουσαι δὲ τὰς τρίχας, πολιώτεραι θᾶττον γίνονται διὰ τὰ ἀρώματα ξηραντικὰ ὄντα.
[c] *F.H.G.* iii. 263, J. 2 A 231.

d ἐκ τούτων περιπορευόμενοι τοὺς μὲν στεφάνους
τῶν κατακειμένων δροσίζουσι τοῖς μύροις, ἄλλο
μηδὲν ἔξωθεν παραραίνοντες." ἐπεὶ δ' ἐνταῦθα τοῦ
λόγου ἐσμέν, "συμβαλοῦμαί τι μέλος ὑμῖν εἰς
ἔρωτα" κατὰ τὸν Κυθήριον ποιητήν, ὅτι Ἰανὸς ὁ
παρ' ἡμῖν θεός, ὃν καὶ πατέρα προσαγορεύομεν,
πρῶτος εὗρεν στέφανον. ἱστορεῖ δὲ τοῦτο Δράκων
ὁ Κερκυραῖος ἐν τῷ περὶ Λίθων γράφων οὕτως·
" Ἰανὸν¹ δὲ λόγος ἔχει διπρόσωπον γεγονέναι, τὸ
μὲν ὀπίσω τὸ δ' ἔμπροσθεν ἔχοντα πρόσωπον. ἀπὸ
τούτου καὶ τὸν Ἰανὸν ποταμὸν καὶ τὸ ὄρος Ἰανὸν
ὀνομάζεσθαι,² κατοικήσαντος αὐτοῦ ἐπὶ τοῦ ὄρους.

e τοῦτον δὲ³ καὶ στέφανον πρῶτον εὑρεῖν καὶ σχεδίας
καὶ πλοῖα καὶ νόμισμα χαλκοῦν πρῶτον χαράξαι.
διὸ καὶ τῶν κατὰ τὴν Ἑλλάδα πολλὰς πόλεις καὶ
τῶν κατὰ τὴν Ἰταλίαν καὶ Σικελίαν ἐπὶ τοῦ νομίσματος ἐγχαράττειν πρόσωπον δικέφαλον καὶ ἐκ
θατέρου μέρους ἢ σχεδίαν ἢ στέφανον ἢ πλοῖον.
τοῦτον δὲ τὴν ἀδελφὴν γήμαντα Καμήσην υἱὸν μὲν
Αἴθηκα, θυγατέρα δὲ Ὀλιστήνην γεννῆσαι. καὶ

f αὐτὸν ὡς μειζόνων ὀρεγόμενον πραγμάτων εἰς
τὴν Ἰταλίαν διαπλεῦσαι καὶ οἰκῆσαι τὸ πλησίον
Ῥώμης ὄρος κείμενον τὸ ἀπ' αὐτοῦ Ἰανοῦκλον
ὀνομαζόμενον."

Τοσαῦτα καὶ περὶ μύρων ἐλέχθη. καὶ μετὰ
ταῦτα πλείστων τῶν μὲν Ἀγαθοῦ Δαίμονος αἰ-
τούντων ποτήριον, τῶν δὲ Διὸς Σωτῆρος, ἄλλων δὲ

---

¹ A : ἴανον C, Suid., ἰάνον codd. Plut.
² Early edd. : ὀνομάζεται A.
³ Kaibel : πρῶτον δὲ A, οὗτος εὗρε πρῶτος CE.

208

as they go round, they shower from a distance the wreaths of the reclining company with perfumes, but sprinkle nothing else upon them." And since we are on this subject, " I will contribute for you a tune in praise of love," as the poet of Cythera phrases it,[a] to this effect, that our Roman god Janus, whom we address as Father, was the first to devise a wreath. This is recorded by Draco of Corcyra in his work *On Stones*, writing as follows [b] : " It is said that Janus is two-faced, having one face behind as well as another in front. From him the Janus River and Hill get their name, because he made his abode on the hill. He was the first, moreover, to devise a wreath, rafts, and boats, and the first to inscribe a bronze coin. Hence many cities of Greece, and many in Italy and Sicily inscribe on their coinage a head with two faces,[c] with a raft or a wreath or a boat on the other side. He married his sister Camêsê and begot a son named Aethex, and a daughter, Olistênê. And being ambitious for larger fortunes, he sailed over the sea to Italy and settled on the hill near Rome which is named after him the Janiculum."

All this was said in connexion with the subject of perfumes. After that discussion ended, most of the guests called for a cup in honour of the Good Daemon, some, in honour of Zeus Saviour, others,

[a] Philoxenus, *P.L.G.*[4] iii. 610, Diehl ii. 133, Edmonds iii. 386. Plato, *Symp.* 185 c ταῦτα . . . περὶ Ἔρωτος συμβάλλομαι, " this is my contribution on Love," Athen. 271 b (vol. iii. p. 218) ; the phrase became proverbial.

[b] *F.H.G.* iv. 402; *cf.* Plut. *Qu. Rom.* 269 A (22), 274 E-F (41), Ovid, *Fasti* i. 229-234. On the coins see Usener in *Strena Helbigiana* 327.

[c] Lit. " a double-headed face." Meineke read κεφαλὴν διπρόσωπον.

ATHENAEUS

Ὑγιείας¹ καὶ ἑτέρων ἑτέρους² ἐπιλεγόντων, τοὺς
τούτων τῶν κράσεων μεμνημένους τῶν ποιητῶν
ἔδοξεν παρατίθεσθαι, ὧν καὶ αὐτῶν μνησθήσομαι.
Ἀντιφάνης μὲν γὰρ ἐν Ἀγροικίσιν³ ἔφη·

Ἁρμόδιος ἐπεκαλεῖτο,⁴ παιὰν ᾔδετο,
μεγάλην Διὸς Σωτῆρος ἄκατον ᾖρέ τις.

Ἄλεξις δ' ἐν Τοκιστῇ ἢ Καταψευδομένῳ·

ἀλλ' ἔγχεον⁵
αὐτῷ Διός γε⁶ τήνδε Σωτῆρος, θεῶν
θνητοῖς ἁπάντων χρησιμωτάτου· πολύ.
Β. ὁ Ζεὺς ὁ σωτήρ, ἂν⁸ ἐγὼ διαρραγῶ,
οὐδέν μ' ὀνήσει. Α. πῖθι⁹ θαρρῶν.

Νικόστρατος Πανδρόσῳ·

κἀγώ, φιλτάτη·
μετανιπτρίδ'¹⁰ αὐτῷ τῆς Ὑγιείας ἔγχεον.
Β. λαβὲ τῆς Ὑγιείας δὴ σύ. Α. φέρε, τύχἀγαθῇ.¹¹
τύχη τὰ θνητῶν πράγμαθ', ἡ πρόνοια¹² δὲ
τυφλόν τι κἀσύντακτόν ἐστιν, ὦ πάτερ.

b ἐν δὲ τῷ αὐτῷ δράματι καὶ τῆς τοῦ Ἀγαθοῦ
Δαίμονος κράσεως μνημονεύει, ἧς καὶ σχεδὸν
πάντες οἱ τῆς ἀρχαίας κωμῳδίας ποιηταί. ἀλλ'
ὅ γε Νικόστρατος οὕτως φησίν·

ἀλλ' ἐγχέασα¹³ θᾶττον Ἀγαθοῦ Δαίμονος
ἀπενεγκάτω μοι τὴν τράπεζαν ἐκποδών.
ἱκανῶς κεχόρτασμαι γάρ. Ἀγαθοῦ Δαίμονος

---

¹ ὑγείας Α.   ² Α: ἑτέρου Kaibel.   ³ Ἀγροίκοις?
⁴ Koppiers: ἐκαλεῖτο Α.   ⁵ ἔγχεον Α.   ⁶ Διὸς ἔτι Cobet.
⁷ Meineke: χρησιμώτατον Α.   ⁸ ἐαν Α.
⁹ Canter: πειθει Α.   ¹⁰ 487 b: μετανιπριαδ' Α.

210

in honour of Hygieia, one naming one divinity, another another; so we decided to adduce in testimony the poets who have mentioned the bowls of wine mixed in honour of these divinities; these poets I will mention by name. Antiphanes, for instance, has said in *Farmer Wives* [a]: "Harmodius was invoked, the paean was sung, everyone raised a mighty bowl of Zeus Saviour." [b] Alexis in *The Usurer* or *Falsifier* [c]: "A. Just pour him out this bowl of Zeus Saviour, by far the most salutary of all gods to mortals. B. That 'Zeus Saviour' won't do me any good if I burst! A. Have no fear; drink!" Nicostratus in *Pandrosus* [d]: "A. And I too, dearest girl; pour him out an after-dinner cup to Hygieia. B. Do you also take some 'Hygieia.' A. Here's to you, good luck! For 'tis luck rules mortals' lives, while providence is a thing blind and inconstant, daddy." In the same play Nicostratus mentions also the mixture to the Good Daemon, a mixture in fact which practically all the poets of the Old Comedy know. [e] But to quote Nicostratus [f]: "Nay, let her pour out quickly the 'Good Daemon' cup and carry the table out of my way. I've had enough of feeding, but I

---

[a] Kock ii. 14. The title as given in A above is probably incorrect; elsewhere it is *The Farmer* or *Farmers* (masc.). For the glee sung in honour of Harmodius and Aristogeiton see below, 695 a-b (pp. 222-224) and 503 e (vol. v. p. 257).

[b] This expression was used as an indeclinable substantive; jokes based on the term are repeated by Aristoph. *Plut.* 1174-1190. For ἄκατος (boat) used of a *phialē* see vol. v. p. 245.

[c] Kock ii. 382.

[d] Kock ii. 224, Athen. 487 b (vol. v. p. 166).

[e] See, for example, vol. v. p. 165.   [f] Kock ii. 225.

---

[11] Dindorf: τυχα αγαθη A.   [12] Porson: πραγματα προνοια A.
[13] ἐνχεασα A.

δέχομαι. λαβοῦσ᾽ ἀπένεγκε ταύτην ἐκποδών.[1]

Ξέναρχος ἐν Διδύμοις·

ὡς ὑπό τι[2] νυστάζειν γε καὐτὸς ἄρχομαι.

c Β. ἡ τἀγαθοῦ γὰρ[3] Δαίμονος συνέσεισε[4] με
ἄκρατος ἐκποθεῖσα φιάλη παντελῶς.
Α. ἡ τοῦ δὲ Σωτῆρος Διὸς τάχιστά γε
ἀπώλεσε ναύτην[5] καὶ κατεπόντωσέν μ᾽,[6] ὁρᾷς.

Ἔριφος Μελιβοίᾳ·

ἐκπεπήδηκας[7] πρὶν Ἀγαθοῦ πρῶτα[8] Δαίμονος
λαβεῖν,
πρὶν Διὸς σωτῆρος.

Θεόφραστος δ᾽ ἐν τῷ περὶ Μέθης " τὸν ἄκρατον,
d φησίν, οἶνον τὸν ἐπὶ τῷ δείπνῳ διδόμενον, ὃν δὴ
λέγουσιν Ἀγαθοῦ[9] Δαίμονος εἶναι πρόποσιν, ὀλίγον
τε προσφέρουσιν, ὥσπερ ἀναμιμνήσκοντες μόνον τῇ
γεύσει τὴν ἰσχὺν αὐτοῦ καὶ τὴν τοῦ θεοῦ[10] δωρεάν,
καὶ μετὰ τὴν πλήρωσιν διδόασιν, ὅπως ἐλάχιστον
ᾖ τὸ πινόμενον· καὶ τρίτον προσκυνήσαντες λαμ-
βάνουσιν ἀπὸ τῆς τραπέζης, ὥσπερ[11] ἱκετείαν τινὰ
ποιούμενοι τοῦ θεοῦ μηθὲν ἀσχημονεῖν μηδ᾽ ἔχειν
ἰσχυρὰν ἐπιθυμίαν τοῦ πότου,[12] καὶ λαμβάνειν ἐξ
αὐτοῦ τὰ καλὰ καὶ χρήσιμα." Φιλόχορος δ᾽ ἐν
δευτέρῳ Ἀτθίδος " καὶ θέσμιον, φησίν, ἐτέθη τότε
e προσφέρεσθαι μετὰ τὰ σιτία πᾶσιν ἀκράτου μὲν
ὅσον[13] γεῦμα καὶ δεῖγμα τῆς δυνάμεως τοῦ ἀγαθοῦ

Meineke: ἐκποδῶν Α.   [2] Porson: ὡσ εὐποτι Α.
[3] γὰρ added by Dindorf.   [4] συνεσισε Α.
[5] Canter: ἀπώλεσεν ἀυτην Α, ἀπώλεσ᾽ ἀνέδην Kock.
[6] Schweighäuser: κατεπόντωσεμ᾽ Α.
[7] Cobet: ἐκπεπιηδεκασ Α.   [8] Dindorf: πρῶτον Α.
[9] ἀγαθοῦ Α: ἀθηναῖοι C.   [10] τοῦ διονύσ ου C.

can accept a ' Good Daemon.' Take up the table,
girl, and get it out of my way." Xenarchus in *The
Twins* [a]: "A. Oh, how I myself am beginning to doze a
little ! B. Yes, that unmixed cup of Good Daemon
I drank up has knocked me out completely. A. And
that cup of Zeus Saviour very quickly wrecked and
sank me, the sailor,[b] as you see." Eriphus in
Meliboea [c]: " You jumped up and left without first
getting a cup of Good Daemon or of Zeus Saviour."

Theophrastus in his work *On Drunkenness* says [d]:
" The unmixed wine which is given upon ending the
dinner and which they call a ' toast in honour of the
Good Daemon ' is taken only in small quantity, just
as a reminder, through a mere taste, of the strength
in the god's generous gift ; and they offer it after
they have been satisfied with food, so that the amount
drunk may be very small ; and after making obeis-
ance three times, they take it from the table,[e] as
though supplicating the god that they may do
nothing indecent or have too strong a desire for the
drinking, and may receive from it all that is noble and
salutary." And Philochorus in the second book of
his *Attic History* says [f]: " In those days the custom
was established that after the food only so much
unmixed wine should be taken by all as should be
a taste and ensample of the good god's power, but

---

[a] Kock ii. 468; the first speaker is yawning uncontrollably.
[b] See critical note 5, and *cf.* the story in vol. i. p. 163.
[c] Kock ii. 430. [d] Wimmer iii. 199.
[e] *i.e.* not passed round among the couches, but drunk by
all the company standing.
[f] *F.H.G.* i. 387 ; *cf.* vol. i. p. 166, vol. v. p. 26.

---

[11] ὥσπερ CE: καὶ ὥσπερ A.
[12] Herwerden: του ποτουτούτου A.
[13] ἀκρατούμενοσ· ὂν A (*cf.* 38 d).

θεοῦ, τὸν δὲ λοιπὸν ἤδη κεκραμένον. δι᾽ ὃ καὶ
τροφοὺς τοῦ Διονύσου τὰς Νύμφας ὀνομασθῆναι.''
ὅτι δὲ δοθείσης τῆς τοῦ Ἀγαθοῦ Δαίμονος κράσεως
ἔθος ἦν βαστάζεσθαι τὰς τραπέζας ἔδειξεν διὰ τῆς
αὐτοῦ ἀσεβείας ὁ Σικελιώτης Διονύσιος. τῷ γὰρ
Ἀσκληπιῷ ἐν ταῖς Συρακούσαις ἀνακειμένης τραπέζης χρυσῆς προπιὼν αὐτῷ ἄκρατον Ἀγαθοῦ
Δαίμονος ἐκέλευσεν βασταχθῆναι τὴν τράπεζαν.
παρὰ δὲ τοῖς Ἐμεσηνοῖς[1] θύοντες τῷ Ἡλίῳ, ὥς
f φησι Φύλαρχος ἐν τῇ ιβ᾽ τῶν Ἱστοριῶν, μέλι
σπένδουσιν, οἶνον οὐ φέροντες τοῖς βωμοῖς, δεῖν[2]
λέγοντες τὸν τὰ ὅλα συνέχοντα καὶ διακρατοῦντα
θεὸν καὶ ἀεὶ περιπολοῦντα[3] τὸν κόσμον ἀλλότριον
εἶναι μέθης.

Ἐμέμνητο δ᾽ οἱ πολλοὶ καὶ τῶν Ἀττικῶν
ἐκείνων σκολίων· ἅπερ καὶ αὐτὰ ἄξιόν ἐστί σοι
ἀπομνημονεῦσαι διά τε τὴν ἀρχαιότητα καὶ ἀφ-
έλειαν τῶν ποιησάντων, καὶ τῶν[4] ἐπαινουμένων ἐπὶ
τῇ ἰδέᾳ ταύτῃ τῆς ποιητικῆς Ἀλκαίου τε καὶ
694 Ἀνακρέοντος, ὡς Ἀριστοφάνης παρίστησιν ἐν
Δαιταλεῦσιν λέγων οὕτως·

ᾆσον δή μοι σκόλιόν τι λαβὼν Ἀλκαίου κἀνα-
κρέοντος.

καὶ Πράξιλλα δ᾽ ἡ[5] Σικυωνία ἐθαυμάζετο ἐπὶ τῇ

---

[1] Wilamowitz: ελλησιν ωσ AC.
[2] CE: δεινα A.   [3] CE: περιπολεύοντα A.
[4] καὶ τῶν deleted by Kaibel.
[5] Casaubon: πράξιλλα δη A, πραξίλλα ἡ CE.

214

after that all other wine must be drunk mixed.
Hence the Nymphs *a* were called nurses of Dionysus."
After the mixture to the Good Daemon had been
given it was customary to have the tables removed,
as is shown in the case of Dionysius of Sicily by
his own sacrilege. For in Syracuse there was a
gold table dedicated to Asclepius ; when Dionysius
had drunk in his honour unmixed wine of the Good
Daemon he ordered the table to be removed.*b* But
among the people of Emesa,*c* when they sacrifice
to the Sun, as Phylarchus declares in the twelfth
book of his *Histories,d* they pour libations of honey,
bringing no wine to the altars ; for they say that the
god who encompasses and controls all things, and
ever traverses the world about, must be hostile to
drunkenness.

The greater part of the guests made mention of
the well-known scolia *e* of Athens ; all of which it is
worth while recalling to your memory because of the
antiquity and simplicity of their composers, especially those who have won high praise for this form
of poetry, Alcaeus and Anacreon, as Aristophanes
shows in *Men of Dinnerville f* : "Take the myrtle
branch and sing me a glee from Alcaeus or Anacreon."
Praxilla of Sicyon, also, was admired for the scolia

a i.e. the fountain-nymphs who supplied the water for the
mixing.
b The sacrilege consisted in appropriating for his own
use a votive offering. Aelian, *V.H.* 1. 20 says the table was
of silver and dedicated to Apollo ; *cf.* Cic. *De Nat. Deor.*
iii. 34. 84.
c In Syria. *d F.H.G.* i. 340, J. 2 A 168.
e On these glees, or convivial songs, see Smyth, *Melic
Poets* xcv-cvii, R. Reitzenstein, *Epigr. u. Skolion* 3-44,
Severyns in *Mél. Bidez* 836.
f Kock i. 449, *cf.* Aristoph. *Nub.* 356, 1365

τῶν σκολίων ποιήσει. σκόλια δὲ καλοῦνται οἱ
κατὰ τὸν τῆς μελοποιίας τρόπον ὅτι[1] σκολιὸς ἦν·
λέγουσιν γὰρ τὰ ἐν ταῖς ἀνειμέναις εἶναι σκολιά·
ἀλλὰ τριῶν γενῶν ὄντων, ὥς φησιν Ἀρτέμων ὁ
Κασσανδρεὺς ἐν δευτέρῳ Βιβλίων[2] Χρήσεως, ἐν οἷς
τὰ περὶ[3] τὰς συνουσίας ἦν ᾀδόμενα· ὧν τὸ μὲν
b πρῶτον ἦν ὃ δὴ πάντας ᾄδειν νόμος ἦν, τὸ δὲ
δεύτερον ὃ δὴ πάντες μὲν ᾖδον, οὐ μὴν ἀλλά γε
κατά τινα περίοδον ἐξ ὑποδοχῆς, τὸ[5] τρίτον δὲ καὶ
τὴν ἐπὶ πᾶσι τάξιν ἔχον, οὗ μετεῖχον οὐκέτι πάντες,
ἀλλ' οἱ συνετοὶ δοκοῦντες εἶναι μόνοι, καὶ καθ'
ὅντινα τόπον ἀεὶ[6] τύχοιεν ὄντες· διόπερ ὡς ἀταξίαν
τινὰ μόνον παρὰ τἆλλα ἔχον τὸ μήθ' ἅμα μήθ'
ἑξῆς γινόμενον, ἀλλ' ὅπῃ ἔτυχον εἶναι[7] σκόλιον
ἐκλήθη. τὸ δὲ τοιοῦτον ᾔδετο ὁπότε τὰ κοινὰ καὶ
πᾶσιν ἀναγκαῖα τέλος λάβοι· ἐνταῦθα[8] γὰρ ἤδη τῶν
σοφῶν ἕκαστος ᾠδήν τινα καλὴν εἰς μέσον ἠξίουν
c προφέρειν.[9] καλὴν δὲ ταύτην ἐνόμιζον τὴν παραί-
νεσίν τέ τινα καὶ γνώμην ἔχειν δοκοῦσαν χρησίμην[10]
εἰς τὸν βίον.

[1] Schweighäuser (cf. Hesych. s. σκόλια): οστισ A.
[2] Joenson: βιβλίωι A.   [3] παρά (?) Kaibel.
[4] ἀλλά γε A: ἀλλὰ CE.   [5] τὸ added by Kaibel.
[6] Casaubon, Ruhnken: καὶ κατατόπον τινα εἰ ACE.
[7] ὅπῃ ἔτυχον μὲν εἶναι C (μὲν marked as incorrect): ὅπου
ἔτυχεν εἶναι A.
[8] Cobet: λάβοιεν· ταῦτα A, λάβοιεν. τηνικαῦτα C.
[9] Coraes: προσφέρειν A, εἰσφέρειν CE.
[10] χρησίμην Kaibel: χρησιμην τε A, καλὴν δὲ ταύτην ἔλεγον,
ὡς παραίνεσιν καὶ γνώμην ἔχουσιν τῷ βίῳ χρησίμην CE.

[a] i.e. involved, intricate.
[b] See Plato, Rep. 398 E, Aristot. Pol. 1342 b 22.
[c] F.H.G. iv. 342, cf. Schol. Plato, Gorg. 451 E, Plut. Qu.
Conv. 615 A-C; on Artemon see 515 e (vol. v. p. 318).
[d] i.e. no longer in regular order round the company (κατὰ

she wrote. Now they are so called not by reason of the manner of their composition, that is, because it was " crooked " (skoliós),[a] though indeed they sometimes speak of tunes composed in the softer varieties of scales [b] as " crooked "; rather, there are three kinds of scolia, as Artemon of Cassandreia says in the second book of his work *On the Use of Books*,[c] comprising all the songs sung in social gatherings. Of these the first kind was that which it was customary for all to sing in chorus; the second was sung by all, to be sure, but in a regular succession, one taking it up after another; and the third kind, which came last of all in order, was that no longer sung by all the company, but by those only who enjoyed the reputation of being specially skilled at it, and in whatever part of the room they happened to be [d]; hence because this method implied a kind of disorder, but only in comparison with the other methods, in that it was carried out neither in chorus nor in the regular order, but in whatever direction they happened to be, it was called the crooked [e] song (scolion). This variety was sung when the songs participated in by all, and obligatory for all, came to their end; from that moment on they required all the trained singers in turn to offer a beautiful song for the common enjoyment. They believed that the beautiful song was the one which seemed to contain advice and counsel useful for the conduct of life.

περίοδον), but in criss-cross fashion at the arbitrary command of the symposiarch, Schol. Aristoph. *Vesp.* 1231 ὅτι οὐκ ἀπὸ τοῦ ἑξῆς (in regular order) ἡ λύρα τοῖς συμπόταις ἐδίδοτο, ἀλλ' ἐναλλάξ, διὰ τὴν σκολιὰν τῆς λύρας περιφοράν, σκόλια ἐλέγετο.

[e] Eustath. *Od.* 1574. 11 (277) assures us that the word does not imply moral obliquity (λόγῳ ψόγου).

Τῶν οὖν δειπνοσοφιστῶν ὁ μέν τις ἔλεγε τῶν
σκολίων τόδε, ὁ δέ τις τόδε· πάντα δ᾽ ἦν τὰ
λεχθέντα ταῦτα·

α΄[1]

Παλλὰς Τριτογένει᾽, ἄνασσ᾽ Ἀθηνᾶ,[2]
ὄρθου τήνδε πόλιν τε καὶ πολίτας,
ἄτερ ἀλγέων[3] καὶ στάσεων
καὶ θανάτων ἀώρων σύ τε καὶ πατήρ.

β΄

Πλούτου μητέρ᾽ Ὀλυμπίαν[4] ἀείδω[5]
Δήμητρα στεφανηφόροις[6] ἐν ὥραις,
σέ τε, παῖ Διός, Φερσεφόνη·
χαίρετον, εὖ δὲ τάνδ᾽ ἀμφέπετον[7] πόλιν.

γ΄

d   ἐν Δήλῳ ποτ᾽ ἔτικτε παῖδα[8] Λατώ,
Φοῖβον χρυσοκόμαν, ἄνακτ᾽ Ἀπόλλω,[9]
ἐλαφηβόλον τ᾽ ἀγροτέραν
Ἄρτεμιν, ἃ γυναικῶν μέγ᾽ ἔχει κράτος.

δ΄

ὦ Πάν, Ἀρκαδίας μέδων[10] κλεεννᾶς,

---

[1] The numbers here prefixed have no ms. authority.
[2] C: ἀθηνα A, Ἀθάνα Bergk.
[3] Hermann: ἀλγέων τε ACE.
[4] Ὀμπνίαν Casaubon.   [5] Early edd.: ειδω A.

218

Well, one of the Deipnosophists would recite this scolion, another that; the following comprise all the scolia which were recited [a] :

1

Pallas, Trito-born, our Lady Athena, guide this our city and her citizens aright, thou and thy Father too, free from pains and factions and death untimely.

2

I sing of Plutus's mother, Olympian [b] Demeter, at the season when wreaths are worn, and thee too, daughter of Zeus, Persephone; hail, ye twain, and guard ye both our city well.

3

In Delos, once upon a time, Leto bore a son, Phoebus of the golden hair, Lord Apollo; ay, and the deer-slaying huntress, Artemis, who holds mighty power over women.

4

O Pan, ruler over glorious Arcadia,[c] dancing

---

[a] *P.L.G.*[4] iii. 643-645, Diehl ii. 182-183, Edmonds iii. 562-564. For comic imitation see Aristoph. *Eccl.* 938-945.

[b] Casaubon's proposal to read 'Ομπνίαν "Bountiful" for 'Ολυμπίαν is tempting, but it involves unwarranted changes to suit the metre.

[c] *Cf.* Pind. frag. 95 (Sandys 564) 'Ω Πάν, 'Αρκαδίας μεδέων . . Ματρὸς μεγάλας ὀπαδέ, said by Schol. Pind. *Pyth.* iii. 139 to come from the Partheneia, Maidens' Songs.

---

6 δημητραστε στεφανηφόροις A.
7 Canter: αμφετον A.
8 CE: τεκνα A, παῖδε Hermann.
9 Ilgen: ἀπόλλων' A, ἀπόλλωνα CE.
10 Hermann: ἰω . . . μεδέων ACE (ἀρκαδίης C).

ὀρχηστὰ Βρομίαις ὀπαδὲ[1] Νύμφαις,
γελάσειας, ὦ[2] Πάν, ἐπ᾽ ἐμαῖς
εὔφροσι[3] ταῖσδ᾽ ἀοιδαῖς[4] κεχαρημένος.

ε΄

ἐνικήσαμεν ὡς ἐβουλόμεσθα,[5]
καὶ νίκην ἔδοσαν θεοὶ φέροντες
παρὰ Πανδρόσου . . . (ὡς φίλην Ἀθηνᾶν).[6]

ς΄

εἶθ᾽ ἐξῆν ὁποῖός τις ἦν ἕκαστος
τὸ στῆθος διελόντ᾽, ἔπειτα τὸν νοῦν
ἐσιδόντα,[7] κλείσαντα πάλιν,
ἄνδρα φίλον νομίζειν ἀδόλῳ φρενί.

ζ΄

ὑγιαίνειν μὲν ἄριστον ἀνδρὶ θνητῷ,
δεύτερον δὲ καλὸν φυὰν[8] γενέσθαι,
τὸ τρίτον δὲ πλουτεῖν ἀδόλως,
καὶ τὸ τέταρτον ἡβᾶν[9] μετὰ τῶν φίλων.

Αἰσθέντος δὲ τούτου καὶ πάντων ἡσθέντων ἐπ᾽
αὐτῷ καὶ μνημονευσάντων ὅτι καὶ ὁ καλὸς Πλάτων
αὐτοῦ μέμνηται ὡς ἄριστα εἰρημένου, ὁ Μυρτί-

---

[1] ὀρχιστὰ βρόμιε ἰὼ πάν C.
[2] Valckenaer: γελασίαισϊω A.
[3] Wilamowitz: εὐφροσύναισ ACE.
[4] Hermann: αοιδαισ αοιδε A, ἀοιδαῖς ἄειδε CE.
[5] Hermann: ἐβουλόμεθα ACE.
[6] Lacuna marked by Kaibel. CE omit παρὰ . . . Ἀθηνᾶν.
[7] Hermann: εἰσιδόντα A, ἰδόντα E, Eust., εἰδόντα C.
[8] ACE: φυὰν καλὸν Schol. Plato, *Gorg.* etc.
[9] Schol. Plato: συνηβᾶν ACE.

220

attendance with the revelling Nymphs, smile joyously on these merry songs of mine.[a]

5

We won as we desired ; ay, the gods have given the victory, bringing it to us from Pandrosus . . . (Pandrosus is mentioned because Athena was her friend).[b]

6

Would that, to see what sort of man each is, we could open his breast and look at his mind, then locking it up once more, regard him surely as our friend.[c]

7

To have health is mortal man's highest boon ; second to that is to be born handsome ; third, to have honest wealth, and fourth, to enjoy youth with our friends.[d]

After the singing of this last to the pleasure of all, who remembered that the noble Plato mentions it [e] as something very well expressed, Myrtilus said that

[a] Cf. Aristoph. Thesm. 978 καὶ Πᾶνα καὶ Νύμφας φίλας ἐπιγελάσαι προθύμως ταῖς ἡμετέραισι χαρέντα χορείαις. With the last verse of the scolion cf. the paean to Asclepius found at Ptolemaïs (Menschieh), Rev. archéol. 1889, 71 χαῖρέ μοι, ὦ Παιάν, ἐπ' ἐμαῖς εὔφροσι ταῖσδ' ἀοιδαῖς.

[b] The words in parenthesis seem to be the remnant of a scholiastic note. Both 4 and 5 refer to the Persian Wars.

[c] Quoted by Eustath. 1574. 16, who says that it is based on a fable of Aesop, wherein Momus blames Prometheus for not placing gates (πύλας) on a man's breast.

[d] This is probably the most frequently quoted of all the scolia ; see Edmonds iii. 565. It was variously ascribed to Simonides or Epicharmus.

[e] Gorgias 451 E.

λος ἔφη Ἀναξανδρίδην αὐτὸ διακεχλευακέναι τὸν
κωμῳδιοποιὸν ἐν Θησαυρῷ λέγοντα οὕτως·

f ὁ τὸ σκόλιον εὑρὼν ἐκεῖνος, ὅστις ἦν,[1]
  τὸ μὲν ὑγιαίνειν πρῶτον ὡς ἄριστον ὂν
  ὠνόμασεν ὀρθῶς· δεύτερον δ' εἶναι καλόν,
  τρίτον δὲ πλουτεῖν, τοῦθ', ὁρᾷς, ἐμαίνετο·
  μετὰ τὴν ὑγίειαν γὰρ τὸ πλουτεῖν διαφέρει
  καλὸς δὲ πεινῶν[2] ἐστιν αἰσχρὸν θηρίον.

695 Ἑξῆς δ' ἐλέχθη καὶ τάδε·

η′

[3] . . . ἐκ γῆς χρὴ κατίδην[4] πλόον,
εἴ τις δύναιτο καὶ παλάμην ἔχοι.
ἐπεὶ δέ κ'[5] ἐν πόντῳ γένηται,
τῷ παρεόντι τρέχειν ἀνάγκη.

θ′

ὁ δὲ καρκίνος ὧδ' ἔφη,
χαλᾷ τὸν[6] ὄφιν λαβών·
" εὐθὺν[7] χρὴ τὸν ἑταῖρον ἔμμεν[8]
καὶ μὴ σκολιὰ φρονεῖν."

ι′

ἐν μύρτου κλαδὶ τὸ ξίφος φορήσω,

[1] Meineke: ἦν ACE. [2] Canter: πίνων ACE.
[3] Supply πόρρωθεν? Stadtmüller ὡραῖον, Wilamowitz τὸν
εὐθύν. [4] A: κατιδεῖν CE.
[5] κ' Dindorf: καὶ ACE. [6] CE: χαλλιτον A.
[7] A: εὔθεα C, εὐθέα E, Eust.
[8] Casaubon: ἐνμὲν A, ἔμεν CE, Eust.

[a] Kock ii. 142.
[b] *P.L.G.*[4] iii. 647-650, Diehl ii. 184-189, Edmonds iii.
564-572.

the comic poet Anaxandrides had poked fun at it in *The Treasure* saying [a] : " That fellow who composed the scolion, whoever he was, that ' health comes first as the highest boon,' described it correctly ; but that ' the second boon is to be handsome, whereas wealth is third,' there, look you, he was crazy ; for after health, wealth holds first place, but a handsome man, if he be hungry, is an ugly beast."

Following this these scolia were recited.[b]

8

The sailor should scan his course from the shore, if so be that he has the power and means ; for once he is on the high seas he must run with whatever comes.[c]

9

Thus spoke the crab as he gripped the snake with his claw : " A comrade should be straight, and not have crooked thoughts." [d]

10 [e]

In a myrtle-branch I will carry my sword, as did

[c] " Look before you leap." Solon *ap.* Herodotus i. 32 σκοπέειν δὲ χρὴ παντὸς χρήματος τὴν τελευτὴν κῇ ἀποβήσεται. Metre and dialect are reminiscent of Alcaeus; it follows in C the remark, ἀρχαῖον σκόλιον κἀκεῖνο.

[d] *Cf.* Aesop. *Fab.* 346 Halm, 291 Chambry.

[e] For this famous scolion, in four strophes (10-13), see Aristoph. *Acharn.* 980 and Schol. (977), Schol. *Vesp.* 1239, Plato, *Gorg.* 451 E. It was, in part at least, attributed to Callistratus, Hesych. *s.* Ἁρμοδίου μέλος. *Cf.* Athen. 503 e (vol. v. p. 257), Edmonds iii. 567 note 3. For the story of the assassination see Herodotus v. 55, vi. 123, Thuc. i. 20, vi. 53, 54, 56, 57, Aristot. *Pol.* 1311 a 34, *Rep. Ath.* 18, 58.

ὥσπερ Ἁρμόδιος καὶ Ἀριστογείτων,
ὅτε τὸν τύραννον κτανέτην[1]
b ἰσονόμους τ' Ἀθήνας ἐποιησάτην.

ια'

φίλταθ' Ἁρμόδι', οὔ τί που[2] τέθνηκας
νήσοις[3] δ' ἐν μακάρων σέ φασιν εἶναι,
ἵνα περ ποδώκης Ἀχιλεύς,[4]
Τυδεΐδην τέ φασι τὸν ἐσθλὸν Διομήδεα.[5]

ιβ'

ἐν μύρτου κλαδὶ τὸ ξίφος φορήσω,
ὥσπερ Ἁρμόδιος καὶ Ἀριστογείτων,
ὅτ' Ἀθηναίης ἐν θυσίαις
ἄνδρα τύραννον Ἵππαρχον ἐκαινέτην.

ιγ'

αἰεὶ σφῶν κλέος ἔσσεται κατ' αἶαν,
φίλταθ' Ἁρμόδιος καὶ Ἀριστογείτων,[6]
ὅτι τὸν τύραννον κτανέτην
ἰσονόμους τ' Ἀθήνας ἐποιησάτην.

ιδ'

c Ἀδμήτου λόγον, ὦ ἑταῖρε, μαθὼν τοὺς ἀγαθοὺς
φίλει,[7]
τῶν δειλῶν δ' ἀπέχου, γνοὺς ὅτι δειλοῖς[8] ὀλίγη
χάρις.

---

[1] ACE: κανέτην Cobet.
[2] Schol. Aristoph.: ἁρμοδίου πω A, ἁρμόδι' οὔ πω CE.
[3] CE: νησσοισ A.   [4] Brunck: ἀχιλλευσ ACE.
[5] διομήδεα in A deleted by Wilamowitz.
[6] Ilgen: ἁρμόδιε καὶ ἀριστόγειτον A.

Harmodius and Aristogeiton, when they slew the
tyrant and made Athens a city of equal rights.

11

Dearest Harmodius, thou art not dead, I ween,
but they say that thou art in the Islands of the Blest,
where swift-footed Achilles lives,[a] and, they say, the
brave son of Tydeus, Diomed.[b]

12

In a myrtle-branch I will carry my sword, as did
Harmodius and Aristogeiton, when at the Feast of
Athena they slew the tyrant Hipparchus.

13

Ever shall your fame live in the earth, dearest
Harmodius and Aristogeiton, for that ye slew the
tyrant, and made Athens a city of equal rights.

14 [c]

Take to heart, my friend, the story of Admetus :
love the brave, but keep aloof from cowards, knowing
that cowards have little favour.

[a] Nothing can be made of the nonsense, in a corrupt
quotation from Plato Comicus, which seems to add ὅ τε
Μίνως " and Minos too "; Kock iii. 728, Demiańczuk,
Suppl. Com. 79.
[b] See critical note 5.
[c] *Cf.* Aristoph. *Vesp.* 1239 and Schol. (1231) ; attributed
to Praxilla, but belonging to the tradition of the proverb,
like No. 20 below. Admetus, driven into exile, took refuge
with Theseus at Athens. The grammarian Pausanias,
quoted by Eustath. 326. 36, refers τοὺς ἀγαθούς to Alcestis,
τῶν δειλῶν to Admetus's father, Pheres. On the " Attic
Scolia " see Wilamowitz, *Aristot. u. Athen.* ii. 322.

[7] Schol. *Vesp.*: τουσ αγαθουσ φιλεισεβου A, τοὺς ἀγαθοὺς
φίλους σέβου CE.   [8] δειλῶν Schol. *Vesp.*, Eust.

ιε´

παῖ Τελαμῶνος, Αἶαν αἰχμητά, λέγουσί σε[1]
ἐς Τροίαν ἄριστον ἐλθεῖν Δαναῶν μετ᾽ Ἀχιλλέα.[2]

ις´

τὸν Τελαμῶνα πρῶτον, Αἴαντα δὲ δεύτερον
ἐς Τροίαν λέγουσιν ἐλθεῖν Δαναῶν μετ᾽ Ἀχιλλέα.[3]

ιζ´

εἴθε λύρα καλά[4] γενοίμαν ἐλεφαντίνα,[5]
καί με καλοὶ παῖδες φέροιεν Διονύσιον ἐς χορόν.

ιη´

εἴθ᾽ ἄπυρον καλὸν γενοίμην[6] μέγα χρυσίον
d   καί με καλὴ γυνὴ φοροίη καθαρὸν θεμένη νόον.

ιθ´

σύν μοι πῖνε, συνήβα, συνέρα, συστεφανηφόρει,[7]
σύν μοι μαινομένῳ μαίνεο,[8] σὺν σώφρονι σω-
    φρόνει.[9]

κ´

ὑπὸ παντὶ λίθῳ σκορπίος, ὦ ἑταῖρ᾽, ὑποδύεται.
φράζευ μή σε βάλῃ· τῷ δ᾽ ἀφανεῖ πᾶς ἕπεται
    δόλος.

---

[1] λέγουσι σ᾽ CE, Eust.: λεγούσησ A.
[2] Eust.: καὶ αχιλλέα ACE.
[3] Edd.: καὶ αχιλλέα A; CE om. No. 16.
[4] καλὴ ACE.   [5] CE: γενοίμην ἐλεφαντίνη A.
[6] γενοίμαν CE: γενοίμην A.
[7] CE: συνστεφανηφόρει A.   [8] CE: μένεο A.
[9] Canter: συν σοφρονήσω σώφρονι A, συσσωφρόνει σώφρονι
CE.

226

15

Son of Telamon, spearman Ajax, they say that
next to Achilles thou wast the bravest of all the
Danaans who went to Troyland.[a]

16

Telamon, they say, was first and Ajax second, after
Achilles, of all the Danaans who went to Troyland.

17

Would that I might become a lovely ivory lyre,
and that lovely lads might take me to join the chorus
of Dionysus.

18

Would that I might become some large new lovely
golden jewel, and that a lovely woman, whose heart
is pure, might wear me.

19

Drink with me, sport with me, love with me, wear
wreaths with me, rage with me when I am raging,
be sober when I am sober.

20

Under every stone, my friend, there lurks a
scorpion. Have a care that he does not sting you;
for any kind of trickery may attend the unseen.[b]

---

[a] Cf. Alcaeus, Edmonds i. 374 Κρονίδα βασίληος γένος Αἶαν,
τὸν ἄριστον πεδ' (=μετὰ) Ἀχιλλέα.

[b] Parodied by Aristoph. Thesm. 528-530, where the Schol.
says it is a proverb attributed to Praxilla. Cf. the fragment
from Soph. Captive Women (T.G.F.[2] 138) ἐν παντὶ γάρ τοι
σκορπίος φρουρεῖ λίθῳ.

κα´

ἁ ὗς τὰν βάλανον τὰν μὲν ἔχει, τὰν δ᾽ ἔραται
λαβεῖν·
θ κἀγὼ παῖδα καλὴν τὴν μὲν ἔχω,[1] τὴν δ᾽ ἔραμαι
λαβεῖν.

κβ´

πόρνη καὶ βαλανεὺς τωὐτὸν ἔχουσ᾽ ἐμπεδέως
ἔθος·
ἐν ταὐτᾷ πυέλῳ τόν τ᾽ ἀγαθὸν τόν τε κακὸν
λόει.

κγ´

ἔγχει καὶ Κήδωνι, διάκονε, μηδ᾽ ἐπιλήθου,
εἰ χρὴ[2] τοῖς ἀγαθοῖς ἀνδράσιν οἰνοχοεῖν.

κδ´

αἰαῖ Λειψύδριον[3] προδωσέταιρον,[4]
οἵους ἄνδρας ἀπώλεσας, μάχεσθαι
ἀγαθούς τε καὶ εὐπατρίδας,
οἳ τότ᾽ ἔδειξαν οἵων πατέρων κύρησαν.[5]

κε´

f ὅστις ἄνδρα φίλον μὴ προδίδωσιν, μεγάλαν[6] ἔχει
τιμὰν ἔν τε βροτοῖς ἔν τε θεοῖσιν[7] κατ᾽ ἐμὸν νόον.

Σκόλιον[8] δέ φασί τινες καὶ τὸ ὑπὸ Ὑβρίου τοῦ
Κρητὸς[9] ποιηθέν. ἔχει δ᾽ οὕτως·

---

[1] Early edd.: ἔχων A.
[2] Porson, confirmed by Pap. Aristot.: εἰ δὴ χρὴ A.
[3] Schol. Aristoph. *Etym. M.*, Suid.: λιψύδριον A, Pap. Aristot.
[4] προδωσεταιροον A.
[5] ἔσαν Aristot., Suid.
[6] Bergk: μεγάλην A.
[7] Early edd.: θεοῖσ A.
[8] CE: σκολιόν A.
[9] CE: κριτοσ A.

228

21

The sow has one acorn, but yearns to take the other ; so I have one fair maid, but yearn to take the other.

22

A harlot and a bath-tender have ever the same habit : both wash the good and the bad in the same trough.

23

Fill up a cup to Cedon, waiter, and forget him not, so long as wine is poured out for brave men.[a]

24

Alas for Leipsydrium, betrayer of comrades, what heroes hast thou slain ! Brave soldiers they, and sons of nobles, who showed on that day what fathers they had.[b]

25

He who betrays not his friend has great honour amongst both men and gods, according to my mind.

Some assert that the poem written by Hybrias of Crete is a scolion. It is as follows [c] : " My great

[a] See Aristot. *Rep. Ath.* 20. Cedon, an Alcmeonid otherwise unknown, led a revolt against Hippias; see Wilamowitz, *Aristot. u. Athen.* i. 38 note 20.

[b] Or, reading ἔσαν for κύρησαν " of what fathers they were." For the defeat of the Alcmeonidae in their revolt against Hippias see Herodotus v. 62, Aristot. *Rep. Ath.* 19, Schol. Aristoph. *Lys.* 665. Leipsydrium was a fort on Mt. Parnes.

[c] *P.L.G.*[4] iii. 651, Diehl ii. 128, Edmonds iii. 572, Eustath. 1574. 7. *Cf.* Archilochus (Athen. vol. i. p. 134) and the song quoted by Sir Walter Scott at the beginning of *Quentin Durward* " La guerre est ma patrie. '

ἔστι μοι πλοῦτος μέγας δόρυ καὶ ξίφος
καὶ τὸ καλὸν λαισήιον, πρόβλημα χρωτός.

696 τούτῳ γὰρ ἀρῶ, τούτῳ θερίζω,
τούτῳ πατέω τὸν ἁδὺν οἶνον ἀπ' ἀμπέλω,[1]
τούτῳ δεσπότας μνοίας κέκλημαι.
τοὶ δὲ μὴ τολμῶντ'[2] ἔχειν δόρυ καὶ ξίφος
καὶ τὸ καλὸν λαισήιον, πρόβλημα[3] χρωτός,
πάντες γόνυ πεπτηῶτες[4] ἐμὸν κυνέοντι, δεσπόταν
καὶ μέγαν βασιλῆα[5] φωνέοντες.

Τούτων λεχθέντων ὁ Δημόκριτος ἔφη· '' ἀλλὰ
μὴν καὶ τὸ ὑπὸ τοῦ πολυμαθεστάτου γραφὲν Ἀριστοτέλους εἰς Ἑρμείαν τὸν Ἀταρνέα[6] οὐ παιάν
ἐστιν, ὡς ὁ τὴν τῆς ἀσεβείας κατὰ τοῦ φιλοσόφου
b γραφὴν ἀπενεγκάμενος Δημόφιλος εἰσέδωκε,[7] παρα-
σκευασθεὶς ὑπ' Εὐρυμέδοντος, ὡς ἀσεβοῦντος καὶ
ᾄδοντος ἐν τοῖς συσσιτίοις ὁσημέραι εἰς τὸν Ἑρμείαν παιᾶνα. ὅτι δὲ παιᾶνος οὐδεμίαν ἔμφασιν
παρέχει τὸ ᾆσμα, ἀλλὰ τῶν σκολίων ἕν τι καὶ αὐτὸ
εἶδός ἐστιν ἐξ αὐτῆς[8] τῆς λέξεως φανερὸν ὑμῖν
ποιήσω·

Ἀρετὰ πολύμοχθε γένει[9] βροτείῳ,
θήραμα κάλλιστον βίῳ,

---

[1] Edd.: ἀμπέλου Eust., ἀμπέλων A (sic) CE.
[2] Hermann: τολμῶντεσ ACE, Eust.
[3] Early edd.: πρόβλημά τε ACE.
[4] Eust.: πεπτηότεσ ACE.   [5] βασιλεα ACE, Eust.
[6] CE: αταρνεαν A.
[7] Gulick: εἰσ αἰδωτε A, εἶπε CE, ἠτιάσατο Lumb.
[8] Casaubon: αρχῆσ A.   [9] CE, Diog. Laert.: ενει A.

wealth is my lance and sword and my goodly shield,
defence for the body. With these I plough, with
these I reap, with these I tread out the sweet wine
from the vine, through these I am hailed as master
of serfs. But all who dare not wield the lance and
sword and goodly shield, defence for the body, cower
and bow at my knee, calling me master and great
king."

After these scolia had been recited, Democritus
spoke : Let me add, too, that the poem addressed by
the most learned Aristotle to Hermeias[a] of Atarneus
is not a paean, as alleged by Demophilus ; he,
suborned by Eurymedon, caused an indictment[b] to
be drawn against the philosopher for impiety, on the
ground that he impiously sang a paean to Hermeias
every day in the common dining-rooms. But that
the song furnishes no evidence of being a paean, but
rather is one kind of scolion in itself, I will make
plain from its own words[c] : " Virtue, attained by
much toil of mortals,[d] fairest prize that life can win,

[a] Or Hermias, Suid. s. Ἑρμίας. A eunuch and originally
a slave, he studied under Plato, becoming an intimate friend
of Aristotle and Xenocrates ; later, when ruler over the
district in Asia Minor near Atarneus and Assos, he was
murdered by the Persians 345–344 B.C. P.-W. viii. 831,
Foucart, Étude sur Didymos, 1907, 130-132.

[b] 323 B.C. Eurymedon was hierophant. On the impiety of
addressing a human being in a paean, originally associated
with praise of Apollo, see Smyth, Melic Poets xxxviii.

[c] Frag. 675, cf. 645 Rose. P.L.G.⁴ ii. 360, Diehl i. 101,
Edmonds iii. 410, Diog. Laert. v. 5-7 ed. Hicks (L.C.L.)
i. 450, Berl. Klass. Texte i. 25-27 (papyrus of Didymus).
Cf. Lucian, Eun. 9, Himerius, Or. vi. 6-7, Wilamowitz,
Aristot. u. Athen. ii. 403-412, Bowra in Class. Qu. 32 (1938),
182-189. The historical source is Hermippus, below, 696 f.

[d] Simonid. 37 (58) ἔστι τις λόγος τὰν Ἀρετὰν ναίειν δυσαμ-
βάτοισ' ἐπὶ πέτραις.

231

σᾶς πέρι,[1] παρθένε, μορφᾶς[2]

c καὶ θανεῖν ζηλωτὸς[3] ἐν Ἑλλάδι[4] πότμος
καὶ πόνους τλῆναι μαλερους ἀκάμαντας[5]·
τοῖον ἐπὶ φρένα βάλλεις
καρπὸν ἰσαθάνατον[6] χρυσοῦ τε κρείσσω
καὶ γονέων μαλακαυγήτοιό θ' ὕπνου.[7]

σεῦ[8] δ' ἕνεχ'[9] οἵ[10] Διὸς Ἡρακλέης[11] Λήδας τε
κοῦροι[12]

πόλλ' ἀνέτλασαν ἔργοις σὰν ἀγρεύοντες[13] δύναμιν.

d σοῖς δὲ πόθοις Ἀχιλεὺς[14] Αἴας τ' Ἀΐδα δόμον[15]
ἦλθον.

σᾶς δ' ἕνεκεν φιλίου μορφᾶς καὶ[16] Ἀταρνέος[17]
ἔντροφος ἠελίου[18] χήρωσεν αὐγάς.

τοιγὰρ ἀοίδιμον ἔργοισ' ἀθάνατόν τέ μιν[19] αὐξήσουσι[20] Μοῦσαι,

Μνημοσύνης θύγατρες,[21] Διὸς ξενίου σέβας
αὔξουσαι φιλίας τε γέρας[22] βεβαίου.[23]

Ἐγὼ μὲν οὐκ οἶδα εἴ τίς τι κατιδεῖν ἐν τούτοις
e δύναται παιανικὸν[24] ἰδίωμα, σαφῶς ὁμολογοῦντος
τοῦ γεγραφότος τετελευτηκέναι τὸν Ἑρμείαν δι'
ὧν εἴρηκεν " σᾶς γὰρ φιλίου μορφᾶς Ἀταρνέος
ἔντροφος ἠελίου χήρωσεν αὐγάς." οὐκ ἔχει δ' οὐδὲ
τὸ παιανικὸν ἐπίρρημα, καθάπερ ὁ εἰς Λύσανδρον

---

[1] βίῳ σᾶς πέρι Pap., Diog.: βιώσασ τε περι A, σᾶς τε πέρι C,
βίῳ σᾶς τε πέρι E.   [2] CE: μορφᾶσ A.
[3] ζηλωτοσ ACE, Pap.: ζαλωτὸς Diog.
[4] ἐν ἑλλάδι Pap., Diog., CE: ἑλλάδι A.
[5] Diog.: ἀκαμάτουσ ACE, ακαμαντος Pap.
[6] Pap.: εἰς ἀθάνατον Diog., τ' ἀθάνατον A.
[7] Diog.: ὕπνουσ A.
[8] ACE: σοῦ Pap., Diog.   [9] CE: ἔνεκεν A.
[10] Wilamowitz: ὁ ACE, οὐκ Brunck, ἐκ Diog.
[11] Diog.: ηρακλησ ACE, Pap.

232

'tis an enviable lot in Greece to die for thy virgin
beauty, and to endure violent, unwearied toils; such
is the fruit thou bestowest on the soul, fruit like that
the Immortals enjoy, better than gold, than noble
ancestors, yea, than soft-eyed sleep. For thy sake
the sons of Zeus, Heracles and those born of Leda,
endured many toils in their quest of power from thee.[a]
In their yearning for thee Achilles and Ajax went
to the dwelling of Hades. For the sake of thy dear
beauty the nurseling of Atarneus, in his turn, hath
made desolate the sun's light. Therefore the Muses,
Memory's daughters, shall exalt [b] him in story, immortal for his deeds, exalting the majesty of Zeus
the god of friendship, and this meed of enduring
friendship."

I know not whether anyone can discern in these
verses anything specially characteristic of the paean;
the writer clearly admits that Hermeias is dead when
he says " for the sake of thy dear beauty the nurseling
of Atarneus hath made desolate the sun's light."
Further, there is no refrain, characteristic of the
paean, as there is in the true paean written in honour

---

[a] See critical note 13.
[b] Or, reading αὐδήσουσι for αὐξήσουσι, which may have
crept in from αὔξουσαι below, " shall cry his name."

[12] ACE, Diog.: κ[ό]ρ[οι] Pap.
[13] σαν αγρευόντεσ A: ἀναγορεύοντες Diog., . . . επουτε . . .
Pap., σὰν ἀνειπόντες " proclaiming thy power" Bowra.
[14] Bergk (Pap.): αχιλλευσ ACE.
[15] Wilamowitz (δόμους Pap.): αἰδαο δόμουσ ACE.
[16] καὶ om. Pap.
[17] Musurus: ατερνεοσ Pap., ἀταρνέως CE, αταρτανεοσ A.
[18] ACE: ἀελίου edd., ἀλίου Wilamowitz.
[19] CE: μην A.   [20] αὐδήσουσι Wilamowitz.
[21] Diog.: θυγατέρεσ A.   [22] Γαρ., Diog.: τεγαρασ A.
[23] Diog.: βεβαίασ A.   [24] CE: παιωνικὸν A.

τὸν Σπαρτιάτην γραφεὶς ὄντως παιάν, ὃν φησι
Δοῦρις ἐν τοῖς Σαμίων ἐπιγραφομένοις "Ωροις
ᾄδεσθαι ἐν Σάμῳ. παιὰν δ' ἐστὶν καὶ ὁ εἰς Κρα-
τερὸν τὸν Μακεδόνα γραφείς, ὃν ἐτεκτήνατο
f Ἀλεξῖνος ὁ διαλεκτικός, φησὶν "Ερμιππος ὁ Καλ-
λιμάχειος[1] ἐν τῷ πρώτῳ περὶ Ἀριστοτέλους.
ᾄδεται δὲ καὶ οὗτος ἐν Δελφοῖς, λυρίζοντός γέ τινος
παιδός. καὶ ὁ εἰς Ἀγήμονα δὲ τὸν Κορίνθιον
Ἀλκυόνης πατέρα, ὃν ᾄδουσιν Κορίνθιοι, ἔχει τὸ
παιανικὸν ἐπίφθεγμα. παρέθετο δ' αὐτὸν Πολέμων
ὁ περιηγητὴς ἐν τῇ πρὸς Ἀράνθιον Ἐπιστολῇ.
καὶ ὁ εἰς Πτολεμαῖον δὲ τὸν πρῶτον Αἰγύπτου
βασιλεύσαντα παιάν ἐστιν, ὃν ᾄδουσιν Ῥόδιοι· ἔχει
697 γὰρ τὸ ἰὴ παιὰν ἐπίφθεγμα, ὡς φησιν Γόργων[2] ἐν
τῷ Περὶ τῶν ἐν Ῥόδῳ θυσιῶν. ἐπ' Ἀντιγόνῳ δὲ
καὶ Δημητρίῳ φησὶν Φιλόχορος Ἀθηναίους ᾄδειν
παιᾶνας τοὺς πεποιημένους ὑπὸ Ἑρμοκλέους[3] τοῦ
Κυζικηνοῦ, ἐφαμίλλων γενομένων τῶν παιᾶνας
ποιησάντων πάντων[4] καὶ τοῦ Ἑρμοκλέους προ-
κριθέντος. ἀλλὰ μὴν καὶ αὐτὸς Ἀριστοτέλης ἐν
τῇ Ἀπολογίᾳ τῆς ἀσεβείας, εἰ μὴ κατέψευσται ὁ
λόγος, φησίν· "οὐ γὰρ ἄν ποτε Ἑρμείᾳ θύειν ὡς
b ἀθανάτῳ προαιρούμενος ὡς θνητῷ μνῆμα κατ-
εσκεύαζον καὶ ἀθανατίζειν τὴν φύσιν βουλόμενος
ἐπιταφίοις ἂν τιμαῖς ἐκόσμησα τὸ σῶμα."[5]

---

[1] καλλιμάχιοσ A.   [2] Casaubon: γεωργοσ A.
[3] Schweighäuser: ἑρμίππου ACE.
[4] πάντων added by Kaibel (πολλῶν Musurus).
[5] σῶμα added by Kaibel: ἐκοσμήσατο A, ἐκόσμουν CE.

---

[a] F.H.G. ii. 485, J. 2 A 146, Plut. Lys. 18.

of the Spartan Lysander, which Duris, in his work entitled *Chronicles of Samos*,[a] says was sung in Samos. A paean, too, is the poem in honour of Craterus of Macedon composed by Alexinus the dialectician, according to Hermippus,[b] the disciple of Callimachus, in the first book of his work *On Aristotle.* This, also, is sung at Delphi to the accompaniment of a lyre played by a boy. Again, the poem sung by the Corinthians in honour of Agêmon of Corinth, Alcyonê's father, has the true paeanic refrain. It is quoted by Polemon the geographer in his *Letter to Aranthius.*[c] So, too, that in honour of the Ptolemy who first became king of Egypt, sung by the people of Rhodes, is a paean. For it has the refrain *ié paián*, according to Gorgon in his work *On the Rhodian Festivals.*[d] To Antigonus and to Demetrius, says Philochorus,[e] the Athenians sang paeans composed by Hermocles [f] of Cyzicus; a contest of all the writers of paeans was held, in which Hermocles was adjudged the best. But returning to Aristotle : he himself says in his *Defence against the Charge of Impiety,* if the speech is not a forgery [g] : " If my purpose had been to sacrifice to Hermeias as a god, I should never have built for him the monument as for a mortal, nor, if I had wished to make him into the nature of a god, should I have honoured his body with funeral rites."

---

[b] *F.H.G.* iii. 46.   [c] Frag. 76, p. 113 Preller.
[d] *F.H.G.* iv. 410. Gorgon (first century B.C. ?) is the authority also for the statement that Pindar's seventh *Olympian* was inscribed in letters of gold in the temple of the Lindian Athena, Schol Pind. *Ol.* vii. 1.
[e] *F.H.G.* i. 408.
[f] See critical note 3 and *P.L.G.*[4] iii. 637.
[g] Frag. 645 Rose.

Τοιαῦτα λέγοντος τοῦ Δημοκρίτου ὁ Κύνουλκος
ἔφη·

τί μ' ἀνέμνασας κείνων κυκλικῶν;[1]

κατὰ τὸν σὸν[2] Φίλωνα, δέον μηδένα[3] τῶν σπουδῆς
ἀξίων λέγειν τι τοῦ γάστρωνος παρόντος Οὐλπιανοῦ. οὗτος γὰρ τὰς καπυρωτέρας ᾠδὰς ἀσπά-
ζεται μᾶλλον τῶν ἐσπουδασμένων· οἷαί εἰσιν αἱ
Λοκρικαὶ καλούμεναι,[4] μοιχικαί τινες τὴν φύσιν
ὑπάρχουσαι, ὡς καὶ ἥδε·

ὦ τί πάσχεις; μὴ προδῷς ἄμμ', ἱκετεύω.
πρὶν μολεῖν καὶ[5] κεῖνον, ἀνστῶ,[6] μὴ κακόν σε[7]
μέγα ποιήσῃ κἀμὲ[8] τήνδε[9] δειλάκραν.
ἁμέρα καὶ δή[10]· τὸ φῶς διὰ τᾶς θυρίδος οὐκ
εἰσορῇς;[11]

τοιούτων γὰρ ᾀσμάτων αὐτοῦ πᾶσα πλήρης ἡ
Φοινίκη, ἐν ᾗ καὶ αὐτὸς περιήει καλαμίζων[12] μετὰ
τῶν τοὺς κολάβρους καλουμένους συντιθέντων.

---

[1] Gulick (κυκλίων Schweighäuser): κυλίκων ACE.
[2] A: σοφόν Dalechamps.   [3] Kaibel: μηδὲν A.
[4] οἷαι (οἶαι) αἱ λοκρικαὶ CE: οἷα εἰσιν οἱ λοκρικαι καλούμενοι A.
[5] μολεῖν Kaibel: καὶ μολιν A, tr. Garrod.
[6] Garrod: ανιστω (sic) A.
[7] σὲ added by Dindorf after ποιήσῃ; tr. Garrod.
[8] Dindorf: ποιήσησ· και με A.   [9] Garrod: την A.
[10] Bergk: καὶ ηδη A.   [11] Meineke: εκορησ A.
[12] A: καλαβίζων Lobeck.

---

[a] The mss. (critical note 1) give κυλίκων "cups," for κυκλικῶν
"commonplace" or "conventional poetry," cf. Callim. Ep.
xxx. 1 (L.C.L. 156) ἐχθαίρω τὸ ποίημα τὸ κυκλικόν. Not
much sense can be made of a reference to cups here, unless

To these remarks of Democritus Cynulcus replied :
" Why hast thou reminded me of those conventional
poems ? " [a] to quote your own Philon,[b] when no one
should mention anything worthy of serious considera-
tion in the presence of our big-bellied Ulpian. For
he likes the more sultry songs more than those of a
serious content ; I mean songs like the Locrian, as
they are called,[c] lascivious [d] in their nature, like the
following [e]: " Oh, what ails you ? Don't betray
us, I implore you. Rise up before my husband re-
turns,[f] lest he do some big injury to you and me
here, miserable woman that I am ! Day is at hand ;
don't you see the light through the window ? "
Indeed, with such songs as these Ulpian's country,
Phoenicia, rings from one end to the other, and in it
he himself used to go about playing on his reed-pipe [g]
in company with the men who compose the pig-songs,

one may take it of the cups or toasts accompanying the
scolia just quoted.
  [b] Since Democritus came from Nicomedia (vol. i. pp. 4,
86), Philon, otherwise unknown, has been thought to be a
poet of that city (in Bithynia).
  [c] Athen. 639 a (vol. vi. p. 448). See Garrod, *Class. Rev.*
37 (1923), 161-162, E. Fraenkel, *Plautinisches* 329, 331 note 2,
Reitzenstein, *Ep. u. Sk.* 139.
  [d] Lit. " pertaining to adulterers."
  [e] *P.L.G.*⁴ iii. 665, Diehl ii. 205, Edmonds iii. 546.
  [f] *Cf.* Herodas i. 42 κεῖνος ἦν ἔλθῃ, where κεῖνος means
" husband." " For tyme it is to ryse and hennes go, Or
ellis I am lost for evere mo ! " *Troilus and Criseyde* 1425-
1426.
  [g] Or, reading καλαβίζων (critical note 12) " dancing the
hootchy-kootchy," see vol. vi. p. 398 note *b*, and for the
dance called κόλαβρος, vol. vi. p. 395 note *g*, *cf.* 164 e, vol. ii.
p. 248. For the reed-pipe, καλάμινος αὐλός, see 182 d (vol. ii.
p. 304). " Their lean and flashy songs grate on their scrannel
pipes of wretched straw," *Lycidas* 123.

εἴρηται γάρ, ὦ καλὲ Οὐλπιανέ, τοὔνομα. καὶ ὅ γε
Σκήψιος Δημήτριος ἐν τῷ δεκάτῳ τοῦ Τρωικοῦ
Διακόσμου φησὶν οὕτως· " Κτησιφῶν ὁ ᾿Αθηναῖος
ποιητὴς τῶν καλουμένων κολάβρων, ὃν καὶ ὁ πρῶ-
d τος μετὰ Φιλέταιρον ἄρξας Περγάμου ῎Ατταλος
δικαστὴν καθεστάκει βασιλικῶν[1] τῶν περὶ τὴν
Αἰολίδα." ὁ δ᾿ αὐτὸς οὗτος συγγραφεὺς κἂν τῷ
ἐννεακαιδεκάτῳ τῆς αὐτῆς πραγματείας Μνησιπτο-
λέμου φησί ποτε τοῦ ἱστοριογράφου τοῦ παρὰ
᾿Αντιόχῳ τῷ προσαγορευθέντι Μεγάλῳ πλεῖστον
ἰσχύσαντος υἱὸν γενέσθαι Σέλευκον τὸν τῶν ἱλαρῶν
ᾀσμάτων ποιητήν. οὗπερ συνεχῶς ᾄδειν εἰώθασιν·

κἀγὼ παιδοφιλήσω· πολύ μοι κάλλιον ἢ γαμεῖν·
e   παῖς μὲν γὰρ παρεὼν κἢν πολέμῳ μᾶλλον
ἐπωφελεῖ."

Καὶ μετὰ ταῦτα ἀποβλέψας εἰς αὐτὸν ἔφη· " ἀλλ᾿
ἐπειδή μοι ὀργίζῃ, ἔρχομαί σοι λέξων τὸν συρβηνέων[2] χορὸν ὅστις ἐστί." καὶ ὁ Οὐλπιανὸς " οἴει
γάρ, ἔφη, κάθαρμα, θυμοῦσθαί με ἐφ᾿ οἷς εἴρηκας
ἢ κἀπ᾿ ὀλίγον[3] σου[4] πεφροντικέναι, ᾿ κύον ἀδδεές';
ἀλλ᾿ ἐπεὶ διδάσκειν μέ τι ἐπαγγέλλῃ,[5] σπονδάς σοι
ποιοῦμαι οὐ τριακοντούτιδας ἀλλ᾿ ἑκατοντούτιδας.
f σὺ δὲ μόνον δίδασκε τίς ὁ συρβηνέων χορός." καὶ
ὅς[6]. " Κλέαρχος, ὦ λῷστε, ἐν δευτέρῳ περὶ Παιδείας
οὑτωσί φησιν· ᾿ λείπεται[7] ὁ συρβηνέων[8] χορός, ὧν

---

[1] βασιλικὸν Meineke.   [2] συρβηναιων A.
[3] Kaibel: ἠ κατολίγον A.   [4] Casaubon: σοι A.
[5] Schweighäuser: ἐπαγγέλησ (sic) A.
[6] καὶ ὅς added by Schweighäuser.
[7] λείπεται Wilamowitz: λείπεται τισ A.   [8] συρβηναιων A.

as they are called. Yes, my fine Ulpian, that is the word. At least Demetrius of Scepsis, in the tenth book of his *Trojan Battle Order*, says [a] : "Ctesiphon of Athens, writer of the so-called pig-songs ; he it was whom Attalus,[b] the first to rule over Pergamum after Philetaerus, established as judge of his realm in Aeolis." And this same historian, in the nineteenth book of the same work,[c] says that Mnesiptolemus, the historian who once wielded large power at the court of Antiochus, called the Great, had a son named Seleucus who composed "joy-songs." The following is one of his which is constantly sung [d] : " I shall be a boy-lover, I like that better than taking a wife ; for a boy can attend me even in battle and help me more."

After this Cynulcus, looking sharply at Ulpian, continued : Well, since you are so angry at me, I am going to tell you what " caterwauling band " means.[e] And Ulpian retorted : What ? Do you think, you outcast, that I am angry at what you have said, or even pay the slightest attention to you, " bold dog " ? [f] But since you profess to teach me something, I will make a truce with you to last not thirty years but a hundred. Do you then just tell me what " the caterwauling band " is. Cynulcus said : My good man, Clearchus in the second book of his work *On Education* has the following [g] : " There remains ' the

[a] Frag. 6 Gaede ; Bevan, *House of Seleucus* i. 200.
[b] *i.e.* Attalus I, since Eumenes came before him, Athen. 445 d (vol. iv. pp. 516-518), *cf.* 577 b (vol. vi. p. 116).
[c] Frag. 13 Gaede. See vol. iv. p. 458 and J. 2 B 890.
[d] Powell 176. For the thought see vol. vi. p. 245.
[e] Above, 669 b (p. 84), 671 c (p. 96).
[f] The words of Hera to Artemis, *Il.* xxi. 481.
[g] *F.H.G.* ii. 313.

ἕκαστος τὸ δοκοῦν ἑαυτῷ κατᾴδει,[1] προσέχων οὐδὲν
τῷ προκαθημένῳ καὶ διδάσκοντι τὸν χορόν· ἀλλ᾽
αὐτὸς πολὺ τούτων ἀτακτότερός ἐστιν ὁ[2] θεατής.
καὶ κατὰ τὸν παρῳδὸν Μάτρωνα·

> οἱ μὲν γὰρ δὴ πάντες ὅσοι πάρος ἦσαν ἄριστοι,
> Εὔβοιός τε καὶ Ἑρμογένης δῖοί τε Φίλιπποι,
> οἱ μὲν δὴ τεθνᾶσι καὶ εἰν Ἀίδαο δόμοισιν.
>
> 698 ἔστι δέ τις Κλεόνικος, ὃν ἀθάνατον λάχε γῆρας,
> οὔτε ποιητάων ἀδαήμων οὔτε θεάτρων,
> ᾧ καὶ τεθνειῶτι λαλεῖν πόρε Φερσεφόνεια[3].᾽

σὺ δὲ καὶ ζῶν, καλὲ Οὐλπιανέ, πάντα μὲν ζητεῖς,
λέγεις δὲ οὐδὲ ἕν.'' καὶ ὅς· '' τίς[4] ἡδέως, ἔφη, ...[5]
τῶν ἐπῶν, ὦ καλέ μου ἑταῖρε, ἕως ἔτι ἐμμένομεν
ταῖς σπονδαῖς.''

Καὶ ὁ Κύνουλκος· '' πολλοί τινες παρῳδιῶν
ποιηταὶ γεγόνασιν, ὦ ἑταῖρε· ἐνδοξότατος δ᾽ ἦν
Εὔβοιος ὁ Πάριος, γενόμενος τοῖς χρόνοις κατὰ
Φίλιππον. οὗτός ἐστιν ὁ καὶ Ἀθηναίοις λοιδορη-
b σάμενος, καὶ σῴζεται αὐτοῦ τῶν Παρῳδιῶν[6]
βιβλία τέσσαρα. μνημονεύει δ᾽ αὐτοῦ Τίμων ἐν

---

[1] Gulick: κατασαιδεῖ A, κατήσαιδεῖ C, καταυλεῖ Kaibel,
κατάσεται Lumb: ἕκαστον . . . δεῖ προσέχοντα CE.
[2] ὁ added by Wilamowitz.
[3] περσεφόνεια CE.
[4] Musurus: καὶ ὅστισ A.
[5] Lacuna marked by Casaubon. Something like the
following may have stood here: καὶ ὅς· ὅστις (so Kaibel)
ἡδέως ἂν ἀκούσαιμι, ἔφη, τίνες εἰσὶν τῶν ἐπῶν παρῳδοί.
[6] παρῳδίων A: παρῳδῶν CE.

[a] Luc. Dial. Mort. 2. 2 ἀκολουθήσων ἀνιῶν καὶ κατᾴδων καὶ
καταγελῶν. Cf. the story of Lucius Anicius in Polybius,
Athen. 615 b-e (vol. vi. pp. 312-314).
[b] Brandt 93, Wachsmuth 148. It is hard to discover in
these verses any relation to the preceding text. Assuming

caterwauling band,' each member of which sings in mockery [a] whatever he pleases, paying no attention to the president and teacher of the band; but even more disorderly by far than they is the spectator in the audience. And to quote the parodist Matron [b]: ' All who were aforetime the bravest,[c] Euboeus and Hermogenes and the godlike Philips,[d] they all are dead and dwell in the halls of Hades.[e] But there is one Cleonicus, to whose lot undying old age has fallen, well acquainted with poets and with audiences,[f] to whom, even when dead, Persephone gave the gift of gabble.' [g] " But you, my fine Ulpian, while still alive ask all questions but answer not a single one. To this he [h] : . . . my noble friend, so long as our truce holds good.

Then Cynulcus : There have been many writers of parodies, my friend; the most famous was Euboeus of Paros, who flourished in the time of Philip. He is the one who specially railed at the Athenians, and four books of his *Parodies* are extant. Euboeus is mentioned by Timon in the first book of his *Satires.*[i]

with Schweighäuser that they belong to the citation from Clearchus, we may suppose that something showing the connexion has been lost.

[c] *Il.* xi. 825.   [d] Cf. *Il.* x. 429.   [e] *Il.* xxii. 52.

[f] *Od.* xvii. 283, Odysseus says of himself, οὐ γάρ τι πληγῶν ἀδαήμων οὐδὲ βολάων. Whoever Cleonicus was, he is here mockingly said to be acquainted with the theatre, back stage and front. For θεατρῶν "audiences" (not θεατῶν as Wilamowitz), cf. Aristoph. *Eq.* 233 τὸ γὰρ θεατρὸν δεξιόν, and often. So Eustath. 1665. 34.

[g] *Od.* x. 494.

[h] We may invent a plausible stop-gap, such as the following : " Because I, he said, should be glad to hear who the parodists of epic poetry are."

[i] Frag. 39 Wachsmuth, Diels, *P.P.G.* iii. 184.

τῷ πρώτῳ τῶν Σίλλων.[1] Πολέμων δ' ἐν τῷ
δωδεκάτῳ τῶν πρὸς[2] Τίμαιον περὶ τῶν τὰς παρῳδίας γεγραφότων ἱστορῶν τάδε γράφει· ' καὶ
τὸν Βοιωτὸν δὲ καὶ τὸν Εὔβοιον τοὺς τὰς παρῳδίας
γράψαντας λογίους ἂν φήσαιμι διὰ τὸ παίζειν
ἀμφιδεξίως καὶ τῶν προγενεστέρων ποιητῶν ὑπερ-
έχειν ἐπιγεγονότας. εὑρετὴν μὲν οὖν τοῦ γένους
Ἱππώνακτα[3] φατέον τὸν ἰαμβοποιόν. λέγει γὰρ
οὗτος ἐν τοῖς ἑξαμέτροις·

c   Μοῦσά μοι Εὐρυμεδοντιάδεω[4] τὴν ποντοχάρυβδιν,[5]
    τὴν ἐγγαστριμάχαιραν,[6] ὃς ἐσθίει οὐ κατὰ
        κόσμον,
    ἔννεφ', ὅπως ψηφῖδι[7] κακὸς[8] κακὸν οἶτον ὄληται[9]
    βουλῇ δημοσίῃ παρὰ θῖν' ἁλὸς ἀτρυγέτοιο.

κέχρηται δὲ καὶ Ἐπίχαρμος ὁ Συρακόσιος ἔν τισι[10]
τῶν δραμάτων ἐπ' ὀλίγον καὶ Κρατῖνος ὁ τῆς
ἀρχαίας κωμῳδίας[11] ποιητὴς ἐν Εὐνείδαις[12] καὶ τῶν
κατ' αὐτὸν Ἡγήμων ὁ Θάσιος, ὃν ἐκάλουν Φακῆν.
λέγει γὰρ οὕτως·

d   ἐς δὲ Θάσον μ' ἐλθόντα μετεωρίζοντες ἔβαλλον
    πολλοῖσι σπελέθοισι,[13] καὶ ὧδέ τις εἶπε παραστάς·
    '' ὦ πάντων ἀνδρῶν βδελυρώτατε, τίς σ' ἀν-
        έπεισε[14]

    [1] σιλλῶν A.   [2] Schweighäuser: περι A.
                [3] ἱππώνακτε A.
    [4] Wilamowitz: ευρυμεδοντιαδεα A, εὐρυμεδοντία δία C.
        [5] ACE: παντοχ. Bergk, Wilamowitz.
        [6] ενγαστρι- A.   [7] ψηφῖσιν Brandt.
    [8] κακὸς added by Cobet.   [9] ACE: ὀλεῖται Cobet.
            [10] CE (see Peppink ii. xix): ἔν τινι A.
    [11] κωνιωδίας A.   [12] εὐνίδαις A.
        [13] Casaubon: σπέλθοισι A, λίθοισι CE.
            [14] CE: τισσαν ἐπι σε A.

242

Polemon, recording the authors of parodies in the twelfth book of his *Address to Timaeus*, writes as follows [a] : " I should say that both Boeotus and Euboeus, the writers of parodies, were men of literary eminence because of the great ingenuity of their wit, and though they came later, they excelled the poets who preceded them. To be sure, the iambograph Hipponax should be set down as the inventor of this type. He says in his *Hexameters* [b] : ' Tell me, Muse, of that maelstrom wide as the sea,[c] that belly-knife,[d] son of Eurymedon who eats indecently,[e] how that he, miserable one, shall in miserable doom perish [f] by stoning at the people's decree by the shore of the unharvested sea.' [g] Parody is employed also by Epicharmus of Syracuse to a small extent in some of his plays ; by Cratinus, the poet of the Old Comedy, in *The Sons of Euneôs* [h] ; and, among his contemporaries, by Hegemon of Thasos, whom they used to call Lentil Porridge. For he says [i] : ' When I returned to Thasos, they pelted me with lumps of filth tossed high, and one standing beside me said, " Foulest man in all the world, who

[a] Preller 76.
[b] *P.L.G.*⁴ ii. 489, Diehl i. 284, Brandt 35.
[c] Or, reading παντοχάρυβδιν (critical note 5) " that all-engulfing maelstrom." Wachsmuth read πολτοχάρυβδιν " porridge-engulfing."
[d] Hesych. *s. ἐγγαστριμάχαιραν· τὴν ἐν τῇ γαστρὶ κατατέμνουσαν.*
[e] *Cf. Od.* xx. 181, viii. 179 for οὐ κατὰ κόσμον.
[f] *Cf. Il.* iii. 417. If the subjunctive ὄληται is correct, the construction borders on indirect discourse, *G.M.T.* 356, 359.
[g] *Il.* i. 316.
[h] Kock i. 32-33.
[i] Brandt 42. See Athen. 406 e (vol. iv. p. 340), Cornford, *Att. Com.* 102 note 4.

καλὴν ἐς¹ κρηπῖδα ποσὶν τοιοῖσδ'² ἀναβῆναι;"
τοῖσι δ' ἐγὼ πᾶσιν μικρὸν μετὰ τοῦτ' ἔπος εἶπον·
" μνῇ μ'³ ἀνέπεισε γέροντα καὶ οὐκ ἐθέλοντ'
   ἀναβῆναι
καὶ σπάνις, ἣ πολλοὺς Θασίων εἰς ὁλκάδα βάλλει

e εὐκούρων⁴ βδελυρῶν, ὀλλύντων τ' ὀλλυμένων τε
ἀνδρῶν, οἳ νῦν κεῖθι⁵ κακῶς κακὰ ῥαψῳδοῦσιν·
οἷς καὶ ἐγὼ σίτοιο μέγα χρῄζων⁶ ἐπίθησα.⁷
αὖθις δ' οὐκ ἐπὶ κέρδος ἀπείσομαι,⁸ εἰς Θασίους
   δέ⁹
μηδένα¹⁰ πημαίνων κλυτὸν ἄργυρον ἐγγυαλίξω,¹¹
μή τίς μοι κατὰ οἶκον Ἀχαιιάδων¹² νεμεσήσῃ,

f πεσσομένης ἀλόχου τὸν ἀχάινον¹³ ἄρτον ἀεικῶς¹⁴
καί ποτέ τις εἴπῃ σμικρὸν¹⁵ τυροῦντ' ἐσιδοῦσα,
' ὦ φίλη, ὡνὴρ μὲν¹⁶ παρ' Ἀθηναίοισιν ἀείσας
πεντήκοντ' ἔλαβε δραχμάς, σὺ δὲ μικρὸν ἐπέψω.'
ταῦτά μοι ὁρμαίνοντι παρίστατο Παλλὰς Ἀθήνη,

---

¹ ἐς added by Brandt here (ἐς καλὴν Musurus): ἐς om.
ACE.
² Casaubon : τοῖσδ' AC, τοῖσιν δ' E.
³ Gulick (μνέα μ' Wilamowitz) : μνῆμ' ACE, λῆμμ' Jacobs.
⁴ ACE : οἰκουρῶν Meineke.
⁵ Casaubon : οἳ καὶ νῦν κιθι A.
⁶ Jacobs, Brandt : οἶσ καὶ εγω μετατοίσιν ταχρηϊζων A.
⁷ Musurus : ἐπόιθησα A, ἔπος ᾖσα Lumb.
⁸ Casaubon : ἀποίσομαι.
                       ⁹ εἰσθασίουσ A.
¹⁰ Brandt : μηθὲν A.   ¹¹ Early edd. : εγγυαλίξων A.
¹² ἀχαιιάδων (sic) A.   ¹³ Casaubon : αχαῖκον A.
¹⁴ Wachsmuth : ἐν οἴκοισ A.
¹⁵ Meineke : εἴπῃσιμικρὸν A.
¹⁶ Wilamowitz : ὡσ φιλιων ωρμην A.

persuaded you to mount our fair platform [a] with such feet as yours ? " To them all I then answered one little word : " 'Twas the lucre that persuaded me, in my old age and unwillingly,[b] to come up here, and my poverty, which drives many Thasians aboard a merchantman, foul men with elegantly trimmed hair, men destroying and destroyed,[c] who to-day chant their vile songs vilely there ; to them even I did yield, for I crave food [d] sorely. Another time I will not rush abroad for gain, but in Thasos, harming no one, I will hand out the glorious silver,[e] so that no Achaean woman may chide me in my house [f] when my wife bakes the Demeter-loaf too meagrely, and one says, seeing the little cheese-cake,[g] " My dear woman, in Athens your husband won fifty drachmas for his singing,[h] yet the cake you have baked is so small ! " As I mused thus, Pallas Athena stood at

[a] Equivalent to βῆμα or θυμέλη. So Brandt : L. & S. s.v. κρηπίς are in error (" half-boot " !). The statement of Aristocles that κρηπῖδες were worn by the hilarodist (vol. vi. p. 346) does not apply here, since Aristocles lived much later. Cf. Zenob. Prov. i. 95 ἀνίπτοις ποσὶν ἀναβαίνων ἐπὶ τὸ στέγος (climbing to the roof with unwashed feet), ἐπὶ τῶν ἀμαθῶς ἐπί τινα ἔργα καὶ πράξεις ἀφικομένων.

[b] Athen. 428 a (vol. iv. p. 438) οἶνος ἄνωγε γέροντα καὶ οὐκ ἐθέλοντα χορεύειν. Cf. 134 c (vol. ii. p. 116).

[c] Il. iv. 451 ἀνδρῶν ὀλλύντων τε καὶ ὀλλυμένων, cf. Il. xi. 83, Plut. Animine an Corp. Aff. 502 A συνέρρωγεν ὀλλύντων καὶ ὀλλυμένων. [d] Cf. Od. xvii. 556-559.

[e] With κλυτὸν ἄργυρον cf. Il. xxiv. 437 κλυτὸν Ἄργος.

[f] Od. ii. 101, Penelope says μή τίς μοι κατὰ δῆμον Ἀχαιιάδων νεμεσήσῃ.

[g] Il. vi. 459 καί ποτέ τις εἴπῃσιν ἰδὼν κατὰ δάκρυ χέουσαν. The ἀχάϊνον should have been a large loaf, baked in honour of Demeter and Korê, Athen. 109 e (vol. ii. p. 16). The poet's wife, unaware of his riches, bakes a paltry cheese-cake instead.

[h] On his success at Athens, 413 B.C., see vol. iv. p. 343.

χρυσῆν ῥάβδον ἔχουσα, καὶ ἤλασεν εἶπέ τε φωνῇ

699 " δεινὰ παθοῦσα, Φακῆ βδελυρά, χώρει 's¹ τὸ
ἀγῶνα."

καὶ τότε δὴ θάρσησα καὶ ἤειδον πολὺ μᾶλλον.'

Πεποίηκε δὲ παρῳδίας καὶ Ἕρμιππος ὁ τῆ[ς]
ἀρχαίας κωμῳδίας ποιητής. τούτων δὲ πρῶτο[ς]
εἰσῆλθεν εἰς τοὺς ἀγῶνας τοὺς θυμελικοὺς Ἡγήμω[ν]
καὶ παρ' Ἀθηναίοις ἐνίκησεν ἄλλαις τε² παρῳδίαι[ς]
καὶ τῇ Γιγαντομαχίᾳ. γέγραφε δὲ καὶ κωμῳδία[ν]
εἰς τὸν ἀρχαῖον τρόπον, ἣν ἐπιγράφουσιν Φιλίννην.
ὁ δὲ Εὔβοιος πολλὰ μὲν εἴρηκεν ἐν τοῖς ποιήμασι[ν]
b χαρίεντα, περὶ μὲν τῆς τῶν βαλανέων⁴ μάχης·

βάλλον δ' ἀλλήλους χαλκήρεσιν ἐγχείησιν.

περὶ δὲ τοῦ λοιδορουμένου κουρέως τῷ κεραμεῖ τῆ[ς]
γυναικὸς χάριν·

μήτε⁵ σὺ τόνδ' ἀγαθός περ ἐὼν ἀποαίρεο, κουρεῦ,
μήτε⁵ σύ, Πηλείδη.

ὅτι δὲ ἦν τις περὶ αὐτοὺς δόξα παρὰ τοῖς Σικελιώταις Ἀλέξανδρος ὁ Αἰτωλὸς ὁ τραγῳδοδι-
δάσκαλος⁶ ποιήσας ἐλεγεῖον τρόπον τοῦτον δηλοῖ·

---

¹ Nauck : χωρεισ A, χώρ' εἰς C, Eust.
² Musurus : ἄλλωστε A.
³ φιλίννην A : Φιλίνην Meineke.
⁴ Dalechamps : βαλανείων ACE.
⁵ Hom., CE : μηδὲ A.   ⁶ τραγωδιδάσκαλος A.

ᵃ Cf. Od. iii. 222 and xix. 33-34 Παλλὰς Ἀθήνη, χρύσεον
λύχνον ἔχουσα.
ᵇ Il. i. 92 καὶ τότε δὴ θάρσησε καὶ ηὔδα μάντις ἀμύμων.

my side, holding her golden wand,[a] and she struck me and spake with her voice : " Shamefully treated as thou art, foul Lentil Porridge, go forth into the contest." And so I took heart,[b] and began to sing more loudly.'

" Parodies were composed also by Hermippus, the poet of the Old Comedy.[c] But the first to enter the contests on the stage was Hegemon, winning victories at Athens with other parodies, but especially with that on *The Battle of the Giants*. He wrote also a comedy in the old style entitled *Philinna*.[d] Then there was Euboeus, who said many witty things in his poems. Thus, on *The Battle of the Bath-Tenders*[e] : 'They hurled at one another their bronze-tipped spears.[f]' And of the barber who quarrelled with the potter over the woman[g] : 'Do not thou, barber, brave though thou art, rob him, nor thou, son of Peleus.' That there was a certain esteem for these writers among the Greeks of Sicily is disclosed by Alexander of Aetolia, the tragic poet, who wrote an elegy in the following manner[h] : 'When the ruth-

[c] *Cf.* the fragment, Athen. 29 e (vol. i. pp. 128-130), Meineke, *Com.* i. 218.

[d] Kock i. 700, *cf.* Athen. 5 b (vol. i. p. 20).

[e] Brandt 52.

[f] *Il.* xviii. 534 ἐγχείησιν " spears " is said jocosely of the barbers' bowls, ἀγγείοισι, which Schweighäuser proposed to read.

[g] Brandt 52 ; *Il.* i. 275, 277, Nestor remonstrates with Agamemnon and Achilles. Hegemon cleverly changes κούρην " maiden " to κουρεῦ " barber." Brandt professes inability to see why the potter is called son of Peleus, " Muddiman's son." This name was often connected with πηλός, mud or clay, Athen. 383 c (vol. iv. p. 232) and 474 d (vol. v. p. 94) ὁ Πηλεὺς δ᾽ ἐστὶν ὄνομα κεραμέως.

[h] Meineke, *An. Alex.* 230, Powell 125, Couat-Loeb, *Alex. Poetry* 111. The text is uncertain at several points.

ATHENAEUS

c ὡς Ἀγαθοκλεῖος[1] λάσιαι φρένες ἤλασαν ἔξω
πατρίδος. ἀρχαίων ἦν ὅδ᾽ ἀνὴρ προγόνων,
εἰδὼς ἐκ νεότητος ἀεὶ ξείνοισιν[2] ὁμιλεῖν
ξεῖνος, Μιμνέρμου δ᾽ εἰς ἔπος ἄκρον ἰὼν
παιδομανεῖ σὺν ἔρωτι ποτὴν[3] ἴσον.[4] ἔγραφε δ᾽
ὤνηρ[5]
εὖ παρ᾽ Ὁμηρείην[6] ἀγλαΐην ἐπέων
πισσύγγους ἢ φῶρας ἀναιδέας[7] ἤ τινα χλούνην,
φλύοντ᾽[8] ἀνθηρῇ σὺν κακοδαιμονίῃ.
τῷ ῥα Συρηκοσίοις καὶ ἔχον[9] χάριν. ὃς[10] δὲ
Βοιωτοῦ[11]
ἔκλυεν, Εὐβοίῳ τέρπεται οὐδ᾽ ὀλίγον.᾽᾽

d Πολλῶν οὖν ἑκάστοτε τοιούτων λεγομένων, ἐπεί
ποτε ἑσπέρα κατελάμβανεν ἡμᾶς, ὁ μέν τις ἔλεγεν
" παῖ, λυχνίον[12]," ὁ δὲ[13] λυχνέα, ὁ δὲ[14] λοφνίαν,[15] οὕτω
καλεῖσθαι φάσκων τὴν ἐκ τοῦ φλοιοῦ λαμπάδα, ὁ
δὲ πανόν, ἄλλος δὲ φανόν, ὁ δὲ λυχνοῦχον, ὁ δὲ
λύχνον, καὶ δίμυξον δὲ λύχνον ἕτερος,[16] ἄλλος δὲ
ἑλάνην, ὁ δέ τις ἑλάνας, τὰς λαμπάδας οὕτω φάσκων καλεῖσθαι παρὰ τὴν ἕλην· οὕτω δ᾽ εἰπεῖν
Νεάνθην ἐν α᾽ τῶν[17] περὶ Ἄτταλον Ἱστοριῶν. καὶ

---

[1] αγαθοκλειοσ A : -κλῆος Jacobs.
[2] Musurus : ξενοισιν A. [3] Headlam : πότην A.
[4] ἴσον A. [5] δ᾽ ὢ ᾽νηρ A.
[6] Musurus : παρομηρέην A.
[7] Weston : πισσυγαση φωρασ αναϊδεασ A.
[8] Powell (Schweighäuser φλύων): φλοιων A.
[9] Hermann : τοια Σ. κ. ἔχων A.
[10] Jacobs : ὡσ A. [11] Casaubon : βοιωτουσ A.
[12] λυχνειον A. [13] Meineke : οἱ δὲ A.
[14] Casaubon : οἱ δὲ A.
[15] ACE : λοφνίδα Kaibel (cf. 701 a).
[16] φιλύλλιος C, see note c.
[17] Early edd.: εατων A.

248

less [a] heart of Agathocles drove them out from their native land. Yet this man sprang from ancient forebears, from youth up he always knew how as stranger to mingle among strangers, and in his mad passion he ascended in equal flight to the height of Mimnermus's verse. Well did the man portray, as he parodied the splendour of Homer's epics, cobblers or shameless thieves or lurcher bubbling over with exuberant mischievousness. Therefore they enjoyed favour in the eyes of the Syracusans. But whosoever listens to Boeotus will take not even small delight in Euboeus.'"

Many subjects of this sort were discussed at all our meetings. When evening overtook us, there would be a call for lamps, one saying "Slave, bring a lychnion," another "lychneus," another "lophnia," [b] asserting that that was the name given to the torch made of bark; others still said "panos" or "phanos" or "lychnuchus" or "lychnos" and another spoke of a lamp with two wicks, [c] another of the "helanê," [d] still another used the plural, *helanai*, asserting that this name for torches was derived from *helê* [e]; this, he said, was on the authority of Neanthes in the first book of his *Histories of Attalus*. [f] And so, one saying

[a] Lit. "hairy," thought to be a sign of brute courage or cunning. On the cruelty of Agathocles see Diod. xix. 6-7.

[b] Or lophnis, below, 701 a.

[e] Philyllius, Kock i. 788 from Pollux vi. 103, below, 700 f (p. 265 note c).

[d] Cf. Hesych. *s.* ἐλένη (*sic*)· λαμπάς, δετή. Lydus, *Ost.* 5 applies the word to St. Elmo's fire. *Cf.* Chapouthier, *Dioscures* 140, below, 701 a.

[e] Hesych. γέλαν (=Ϝέλαν)· αὐγὴ ἡλίου. *Cf.* Pindar, Athen. 601 e (vol. vi. p. 242) δαχθεὶς ἕλᾳ (Bergk's accepted emendation).

[f] *F.H.G.* iii. 4, J. 2 B 895, 2 A 192.

ATHENAEUS

e ἄλλος ὅ τι δή ποτε, ὡς τάραχον γίνεσθαι οὐ τὸν
τυχόντα τῶν ἐπὶ τούτοις πίστεων παρὰ πάντων
λεγομένων. Σιληνὸν μὲν γάρ τις τὸν γλωσσο-
γράφον ἔφασκεν Ἀθηναίους λέγειν τὰς λαμπάδας
φανούς. Τιμαχίδας δὲ ὁ Ῥόδιος δέλετρον τὸν
φανὸν καλεῖσθαι, οἷον, φησίν, οἱ νυκτερευόμενοι
τῶν νέων ἔχουσιν . . .[1] οὓς οὗτοι ἑλάνας καλοῦσιν. Ἀμερίας[2] δὲ γράβιον τὸν φανόν. Σέλευκος
δὲ οὕτως ἐξηγεῖται ταύτην τὴν λέξιν· "γράβιόν
ἐστιν τὸ πρίνινον ἢ δρύϊνον ξύλον ὃ περιεθλασμένον[3]
καὶ κατεσχισμένον ἐξάπτεσθαι καὶ φαίνειν τοῖς
f ὁδοιποροῦσιν. Θεοδωρίδας γοῦν ὁ Συρακόσιος ἐν
Κενταύροις[4] διθυράμβῳ φησίν·

> πίσσα δ᾽ ἀπὸ[5] γραβίων ἔσταζεν,

οἷον ἀπὸ . . . . λαμπάδων.[6] μνημονεύει δὲ γρα-
βίων καὶ Στράττις[7] ἐν Φοινίσσαις.

Ὅτι δὲ λυχνοῦχοι οἱ νῦν καλούμενοι φανοὶ ὠνο-
μάζοντο Ἀριστοφάνης ἐν Αἰολοσίκωνι παρίστησιν·

> καὶ διαστίλβονθ᾽ ὁρῶμεν,
> ὥσπερ ἐν καινῷ[8] λυχνούχῳ,
> πάντα τῆς ἐξωμίδος.

---

[1] Lacuna marked by Wilamowitz.
[2] Casaubon: αμερισ A.   Four lines in A are here destroyed
by chemicals.
[3] Kaibel: ὅπερ (ὃ CE) ἐθλασμένον ACE.
[4] Musurus: ενεκενταυροισ A.   [5] ὑπὸ C, Eust.
[6] There is space for seven letters between ἀπὸ and παδων
in A.
[7] Schweighäuser: μν . . . . . γραβιων κα . . . . . A.
[8] Salmasius: κενω A, Pollux.

---

[a] Schol. Aristoph. Lys. 308 φανὸν πᾶν τὸ φαῖνον ἐκάλουν.
[b] i.e. bait, lure, as in Numenius, another parodist, vol. iii.

250

one thing, another another, no slight confusion arose
in the testimony on these terms, cited from all sources.
Silenus, the compiler of glosses, was adduced by one
as saying that the Athenians called torches *phanoi*.[a]
But Timachidas of Rhodes says that the phanos
is called *deletron*,[b] such, for example, as young men
who roam about at night carry with them . . .
which they call *helanai*. Amerias calls the phanos
a *grabion*. Seleucus interprets this word thus:
" Grabion is the stick of ilex or oak, which when split
and broken all round into splints is set on fire and
gives light to travellers. Theodoridas of Syracuse, for
example, says in *The Centaurs*, a dithyramb [c] : ' And
the pitch oozed from the grabia,' that is from . . .
torches. Strattis, also, mentions grabia in his
Phoenician Women." [d]

As for lychnuchoi, Aristophanes in *Aeolosicon*
proves that what are now called phanoi were given
that name [e] : " And as in a new lantern (lychnuchus)
we can see all of her glistening through her shift."

---

p. 290 ; Hesych. *s.* δέλετρον· φανὸς ὃν οἱ νυκτερεύοντες φαίνουσι.
This use of δέλετρον may have arisen from the practice of
hunting or fishing by night. See the verses from Epicrates
below (p. 255).

[c] Diehl ii. 295. *Cf.* Hesych. *s.* γοβρίαι (*sic*)· φανοί, λαμπτῆρες.

[d] Kock i. 726.

[e] Kock i. 394, Pollux x. 116. The λυχνοῦχος was properly
a lamp-holder or lantern with orifices through which the
light of the lamp inside shone forth. Bekk. *Anec.* 50. 23,
distinguishing the torch (φανός) from the λυχνοῦχος says σκεῦός
τι ἐν κύκλῳ ἔχον κέρατα (panels of horn), ἔνδον δὲ λύχνον
ἡμμένον, διὰ τῶν κεράτων τὸ φῶς πέμποντα. So Arethas, of
the Seven Candlesticks or Seven Churches, λυχνίας (=λυχ-
νούχους) δὲ αὐτὰς ὠνόμασεν, οὐ λύχνους, ὡς τῆς λυχνίας οἰκεῖον
φῶς οὐκ ἐχούσης, ἀλλ᾽ ὄχημα μόνον οὔσης τοῦ λύχνου ὃς ἔχει τὸ
φῶς, Migne, *Patr. Gr.* 106, p. 516.

ἐν δὲ τῷ δευτέρῳ Νιόβῳ προειπὼν λυχνοῦχον

οἴμοι κακόδαιμον (φησίν), ὁ λύχνος[1] ἡμῖν οἴχεται.

εἶτ᾽ ἐπιφέρει·

καὶ πῶς ὑπερβὰς τὸν λυχνοῦχον οἴχεται
κἆλαθέ σε;[2]

ἐν δὲ τοῖς ἑξῆς καὶ λυχνίδιον αὐτὸν καλεῖ διὰ τούτων·

ἀλλ᾽ ὥσπερ λύχνος[3]
ὁμοιότατα καθεῦδ᾽ ἐπὶ[4] τοῦ λυχνιδίου.

Πλάτων δ᾽ ἐν Νυκτὶ Μακρᾷ·

ἕξουσιν οἱ πομπεῖς[5] λυχνούχους δηλαδή.

Φερεκράτης Δουλοδιδασκάλῳ·

ἄνυσόν ποτ᾽ ἐξελθών, σκότος[6] γὰρ γίγνεται,
καὶ τὸν λυχνοῦχον ἔκφερ᾽ ἐνθεὶς τὸν λύχνον.

Ἄλεξις δ᾽ Ἐκκηρυττομένῳ·

ὥστ᾽ ἐξελὼν ἐκ τοῦ λυχνούχου τὸν λύχνον
μικροῦ κατακαύσας ἔλαθ᾽ ἑαυτόν,[8] ὑπὸ μάλης[9]
τῇ γαστρὶ μᾶλλον τοῦ δέοντος προσαγαγών.

Εὐμήδης δ᾽ ἐν Σφαττομένῳ προειπών·

ἡγοῦ μέν· ἢν δὲ . υκνον εἰς τὸ πρόσθ᾽ ἰδὼν
. . . . ατο . ϋμένιδι . . . . s,

ἐπιφέρει·

. . . . λυχνούχῳ[10] . . . κο . . . .

---

[1] Schweighäuser: λυχνουχος A.
[2] Kaibel, following Cobet: καὶ ελαθεσ A.
[3] Pollux: ὁ λύχνοσ A.   [4] Pollux: καθεύδετ᾽ ἐπι A.

In the second *Niobus*, after first mentioning a lantern
(lychnuchos), Aristophanes says [a] : " Alas, wretch
that you are, our lamp is gone ! " He then adds [b] :
" And how could it have stepped over the lantern
and be gone without your knowing it ? " And in the
verses following he calls the lantern *lychnidion*, thus [c]:
" But he was fast asleep, as snug as a lamp fixed in
a lantern." Plato in *The Long Night* [d] : " Of course
the escorts will have lanterns (lychnuchoi)." So
Pherecrates in *Slave-teacher* [e] : " Hurry and come out,
for darkness is coming on, and fetch the lantern
after you put the lamp in it." Alexis in *Banished* [f]:
" So when he took the lamp from the lantern he almost
burnt himself up without noticing as he furtively [g]
put the lamp too close to his stomach." Eumedes
in *Murdered*, after first saying [h] " You lead the way,
but if, looking ahead . . ." continues : " . . . with a

[a] Kock i. 463.   [b] Kock i. 464.
[c] *Ibid.*, Pollux x. 119.
[d] Kock i. 624 ; the title refers to the night in which
Alcmena was visited by both Zeus and Amphitryon.
[e] Kock i. 156.   [f] Kock ii. 332.
[g] Lit. " under the armpit " ; for the general meaning *cf.*
Dem. *Or.* xxix. 12 οὐδ' ὑπὸ μάλης ἡ πρόσκλησις, ἀλλ' ἐν τῇ
ἀγορᾷ " and the summons was not made in secret, but in
the middle of the market-place." *Cf.* 499 e (vol. v. p. 281).
[h] Kock iii. 377. For the present condition of A from
this point on the curious may consult Schöll in *Hermes* iv.
160-173, Kaibel, *Ind. lect. Rost.* for the summer of 1883.

---

[5] πομπῆς Meineke (of course rightly).
[6] Schweighäuser : || ὅτοσ A, κρότος Kaibel.
[7] Schweighäuser : δ' ἐν κηρυττομένωι reported in A, no
longer visible.
[8] Elmsley : ἔλαθεν εαυτον A.
[9] ὑπομαλησ A : ὑπὸ μέθης Herwerden, ὑπὸ μάτης Meineke.
[10] ///υχω A.

Ἐπικράτης δ' ἐν Τριόδοντι ἢ Ῥωποπώλῃ προειπὼν

λαβὲ τριόδοντα καὶ λυχνοῦχον,

ἐπιφέρει·

ἐγὼ δὲ δεξιᾷ γε τόνδ' ἔχω τινά,[1]
σιδηρότευκτον ἐναλίων θηρῶν βέλος,[2]
κερατίνου τε φωσφόρου λύχνου σέλας.

Ἄλεξις Μίδωνι·

700   ὁ πρῶτος εὑρὼν μετὰ λυχνούχου περιπατεῖν
τῆς νυκτὸς ἦν τις κηδεμὼν τῶν δακτύλων.

ἐν δὲ Θεοφορήτῳ ὁ αὐτὸς Ἄλεξις·

οἶμαί γ'[3] ἐπιτιμᾶν τῶν ἀπαντώντων τινὰς
ἡμῖν ὅτι τηνικαῦτα μεθύων περιπατῶ.
ποῖος γάρ ἐστιν φανός, ὦ πρὸς τῶν θεῶν,
τοιοῦτος οἷος ὁ γλυκύτατος ἥλιος;

Ἀναξανδρίδης δὲ ἐν Ὕβρει·

οὔκουν[4] λαβὼν τὸν φανὸν ἅψεις μοι λύχνον;

b ἄλλοι δὲ ἔφασκον φανὸν λέγεσθαι τὴν λαμπάδα, οἱ δὲ τὴν ἔκ τινων ξύλων τετμημένων δέσμην. Μένανδρος Ἀνεψιοῖς·[5]

ὁ φανός ἐστι μεστὸς ὕδατος οὑτοσί·
δεῖ τ'[6] οὐχὶ σείειν, ἀλλ' ἀποσείειν αὐτόθεν.[7]

Νικόστρατος ἐν Πατριώταις·

ὁ κάπηλος γὰρ οὐκ τῶν γειτόνων
ἄν τ' οἶνον ἄν τε φανὸν[8] ἀποδῶταί τινι
ἄν τ' ὄξος, ἀπέπεμψ'[9] ὁ κατάρατος δοὺς ὕδωρ.

---

[1] κτένα "comb" Kock.   [2] Casaubon: μέλοσ A.
[3] γ' Jacobs: γὰρ A (οἶμαι ἐπιτιμᾶν CE).
[4] Casaubon, Porson: ενυβριουκουν A.

254

lantern . . ." Epicrates in *The Trident* or *Huck-ster*, first saying [a] " Take your trident and lantern " continues : " And I in my right hand hold this thing, whatever it is, an iron-forged missile against the beasts of the sea, and the flame of the light-shedding lamp of horn." Alexis in *Midon* [b] : " The first man to invent walking about at night with a lantern (lychnuchos) had a care for his toes." And Alexis again in *God-inspired* [c] : " I fancy that some we meet may blame me for walking about drunk at this hour.[d] But indeed what torch, I ask the blessed gods, is so good as the sweet, sweet sun ? " Anax-andrides in *Violence* [e] : " So take the torch and light the lamp, won't you ? " Others asserted that the lamp is called a phanos, but against this were those who said that the phanos is a bundle of certain split woods. Menander in *The Cousins* [f] : " This torch (phanos) is full of water ; it's not a job of shaking merely,[g] but of shaking it all out and at once." Nicostratus in *Fellow-Countrymen* [h] : " That huckster in our neighbourhood ! If he sells one wine, or a lamp, or vinegar, the scoundrel puts water to it

[a] Kock ii. 285. On the use of the trident in fishing see Plato, *Soph.* 220 D-E; on fishing by night with a lantern, Oppian, *Hal.* iv. 640. See above, 699 e, note b (p. 251).

[b] Kock ii. 351. Among the spurious dialogues attributed to Plato was Μίδων ἢ Ἱπποτρόφος (Horse-Breeder), Diog. Laert. iii. 37 (62). For the sense *cf.* Aristoph. *Eq.* 874 εὐνού-στατόν τε τῇ πόλει καὶ τοῖσι δακτύλοισι.

[c] Kock ii. 325.   [d] While the sun is still shining.

[e] Kock ii. 157.   [f] Kock iii. 20.

[g] To stir the flame.

[h] Kock ii. 225-226, *cf.* Aristoph. *Ran.* 1386.

---

[5] Musurus: ἀνεψιδσ A.   [6] δειτε A.

[7] Bentley: αλλὰ ποδιειν αυτον A.

[8] Early edd.: ἀνστέφανον A.   [9] Musurus: ἀπέπεμψεν A.

c Φιλιππίδης Συμπλεούσαις·

>ὁ φανὸς ἡμῖν οὐκ ἔφαινεν οὐδὲ ἕν.
>Β. ἔπειτα φυσᾶν δυστυχὴς οὐκ ἠδύνω;

Φερεκράτης δὲ ἐν Κραπατάλλοις[1] τὴν νῦν λυχνίαν[2] καλουμένην λυχνεῖον[3] κέκληκεν διὰ τούτων·

>τίς τῶν λυχνείων[4] ἡ 'ργασία; Β. Τυρρηνική.

ποικίλαι γὰρ ἦσαν αἱ παρὰ τοῖς Τυρρηνοῖς ἐργασίαι, φιλοτέχνων ὄντων τῶν Τυρρηνῶν. Ἀντιφάνης[5] δ'[6] Ἱππεῦσι·

>τῶν δ' ἀκοντίων
>συνδοῦντες ὀρθὰ τρία λυχνείῳ[7] χρώμεθα.

Δίφιλος δ' ἐν Ἀγνοίᾳ·

d
>ἅψαντες λύχνον
>λυχνεῖον ἐζητοῦμεν.

Εὐφορίων δ' ἐν Ἱστορικοῖς Ὑπομνήμασιν Διονύσιόν φησι τὸν νεώτερον Σικελίας τύραννον Ταραντίνοις εἰς τὸ πρυτανεῖον ἀναθεῖναι λυχνεῖον[8] δυνάμενον καίειν τοσούτους λύχνους ὅσος ὁ τῶν ἡμερῶν ἐστιν ἀριθμὸς εἰς τὸν ἐνιαυτόν. Ἕρμιππος δὲ ὁ κωμῳδιοποιὸς ἐν Ἰάμβοις τὸ στρατιωτικὸν λυχνεῖον σύνθετον[9] οὕτως ὀνομάζει. ἐν δὲ Φορμοφόροις δράματι·

---

¹ κραπατάλοισ A. ² CE: λυχνειαν A.
³ λυχνειον A: λυχνίον CE. ⁴ λυχνίων A.
⁵ Porson: ἀριστοφάνησ ACE, Eust. 1571. 19.
⁶ τὲ C. ⁷ λυχνίω ACE. ⁸ A: λυχνίον C.
⁹ A: σύνδετον Schweighäuser.

before delivering it." Philippides in *Women in a Boat*[a]: " A. That 'lighter' (phanos) of ours wouldn't light a single thing. B. Well, were you so unlucky that you couldn't blow it into a flame ? "

Pherecrates in *Good-for-Nothings* calls what is now called lychnia (lampstand or lantern) lychneion in these words[b]: " A. What is the workmanship of these lampstands ? B. Etruscan." Indeed manufactures were various among the Etruscans, devoted as they were to the arts. Antiphanes in *The Horsemen*[c]: " We fasten three javelins upright together and use them as a lampstand." And Diphilus in *A Mistake*[d]: " Having lighted a lamp we looked about for a lampstand." Euphorion in *Historical Notes* says[e] that Dionysius the Younger, tyrant of Sicily, dedicated in the town-hall at Tarentum a lampstand capable of holding as many lighted lamps as there are days in the year. The comic poet Hermippus in his *Iambics*[f] calls the military lampstand " compound "; that is his word.[g] In *The*

---

[a] Kock iii. 306. Pollux ix. 30 gives the title Συνεκπλέουσα " sailing out together "; in either case the subject is a woman or women. The pun in φανός and ἔφαινον should be noted; Eustath. 1571. 12 καὶ ὅρα τό, " ὁ φανὸς οὐκ ἔφαινεν," *i.e.* the light did not light.

[b] Kock i. 169. On Etruscan bronzes *cf.* Athen. 28 b-c (vol. i. p. 122).   [c] Kock ii. 54.

[d] Kock ii. 541. Athen. 401 a (vol. iv. p. 314) gives this play to Diphilus or Calliades; P.-W. *s. Kalliades* 1612.

[e] Frag. 24 b, p. 76 Meineke.

[f] Kock i. 248.

[g] The text is uncertain, and reading σύνδετον for σύνθετον (critical note 9) does not help matters. Probably the quotation should stand after the one from Antiphanes above, and we should understand Hermippus to mean that a lampstand " so made " with javelins was " compounded," *i.e.* improvised. *Cf.* below, p. 259 note *h*.

τῇδ' ἐξιόντι δεξιᾷ,[1]
ὦ λυχνίδιον.

e πανὸς δ' ὀνομάζεται τὸ διακεκομμένον ξύλον καὶ
συνδεδεμένον· τούτῳ δ' ἐχρῶντο λαμπάδι. Μένανδρος Ἀνεψιοῖς·

οἶσ'[2] εἰσιὼν
πανόν, λύχνον, λυχνοῦχον, ὅ τι πάρεστι· φῶς
μόνον πολὺ ποίει.[3]

Δίφιλος Στρατιώτῃ·

ἀλλ' ὁ πανὸς ὕδατός ἐστι μεστός.

πρότερος δὲ τούτων Αἰσχύλος ἐν Ἀγαμέμνονι μέ-
μνηται | τοῦ πανοῦ ⟨καὶ Εὐριπίδης[4]⟩ | ἐν Ἴωνι.
ἔλεγ⟨ον δὲ τοῦτον οἱ⟩[5] | πρὸ ἡμῶν κ⟨αὶ ξυλο-
λυχνοῦ⟩|χον, οὗ μνη⟨μονεύει Ἄλεξις⟩ | ἐν Εἰσ-
οικιζ⟨ομένῳ οὕτως⟩

ὁ δὲ ξυλο⟨λυχνοῦχος . . . .
πυρὸς
νὶ
χ
ο
κ⟨. . . . . μνημο-⟩[6]
νε⟨ύει δὲ Θεόπομπος ἐν Εἰρή-
ν⟨ῃ λέγων οὑτωσί· " ἡμᾶς δ' ἀ-⟩
παλ⟨λαχθέντας ἐπ' ἀγαθαῖς⟩

[1] τηδεξιοντι δεξιᾱι A : τῇδ' ἐξιόντι δεῖξον Meineke.
[2] οἶσ' added by Dobree.
[3] Dalechamps : ποιεῖ A.
[4] καὶ Εὐριπίδης added by Meineke.
[5] Kaibel : ἐλει . . . . A. At this point fol. 371ʳ of A has so
much of the second column cut away that only a few letters

258

Porters he says [a]: "As I go out here to the right, O my little lantern (show me the way)." Panos (=phanos) is the name given to wood split into several pieces and bound together; they used it as a torch. Menander in *The Cousins* [b]: "Go in and fetch a torch, a lamp, a lampstand, or whatever you can get; only make a big light." Diphilus in *The Soldier* [c]: "But the torch is full of water." But even before these writers Aeschylus mentions the panos in *Agamemnon*,[d] as does Euripides, also, in *Ion*.[e] Our predecessors called it also "wooden lampstand," mentioned by Alexis in *The New Tenant* thus [f]: "And the wooden lampstand . . . of fire . . .[g]" Theopompus in *The Peace* mentions also the spit-lampholder in these words [h]: "As, for us, by great

[a] Kock i. 243. See critical note 1.
[b] Kock iii. 21, Allinson 318.
[c] Kock ii. 542. *Cf.* above, 700 b.
[d] *Vs.* 284 μέγαν δὲ πανὸν (codd. φανὸν) ἐκ νήσου (Lemnos) τρίτον Ἀθῷον αἶπος Ζηνὸς ἐξεδέξατο.
[e] *Vs.* 195 πανὸν (codd. πτανὸν) πυρίφλεκτον αἴρει τις.
[f] Kock ii. 408.
[g] At this point may be added the compendia in CE and Eustath. 1571. 20 ff., printed separately below, p. 264.
[h] Kock i. 735, from Pollux x. 118, *cf.* vi. 103 τὸ μὲν παρὰ Θεοπόμπῳ τῷ κωμικῷ ὀβελισκολύχνιον, τὸ μὲν σκεῦος ἦν στρατιωτικόν (*i.e.* improvised by soldiers on a campaign, *cf.* above, p. 257 note g), τὸ δὲ ὄνομα ὑπομόχθηρον "rather bad." The speaker is describing his relief at being freed from the inconveniences of life in camp, where torches must be mounted on spits (*cf.* the candle in a bottle), and swords are used as meat-knives.

---

at the left of the column are legible, and correspondingly, a few at the right of fol. 371ᵛ, first column.

[6] Supplied by Kaibel, *cf.* Pollux x. 118, Eust. 1571. 21, CE below, p. 264.

τύχα⟨ις ὀβελισκολυχνίου⟩
καὶ ξ⟨ιφομαχαίρας πικρᾶς⟩
επακ
επισ
ασελ
ωτι
πῶς
μεν
δαίμ
γωδ
ὄισπ
φη
εν
νειμ
απτ
Φιλύ⟨λλιος⟩[1]
π
δι
λα
φ
φ
ι
ξ δ
· · ·
·
·
·

Fol. 371ᵛ first column

[3]ὡς ἐβάδι-
⟨ζον δαῗδας⟩ μετὰ χερσὶν
⟨ἔχοντες.⟩ . . . δὲ τῶν ἄλλων
ἔμενον ἔν

good luck, we are rid of spit-lampholder and bitter
sword-knife" . . . .
. . . .

Philyllius *a* : . . . .
. . . .

" as they went on with torches (*daïdes*) in their
hands " . . . .

a Kock i. 788, below, p. 264, Eustath. 1571. 5 : " Philyllius
calls torches *daïdes*, thus following Homer."

---

[1] Schöll, a certain supplement ; below, p. 264.
[2] Fol. 371ᵛ, last part of first column. Additions by Kaibel.

δέοι κατα
ὅπερ ἔτι
. ρων
ιη
.
.
.
.
.
κάν
ῆι
φησὶ
λεί
οδω
ι εἰσ
ωλι
δ' ενι
λύ
υθέ
υτί
εν
ῆσ
εκ
ου
ψη
χρύ
αφά
ει:
ον
υ
⟨διμύ⟩ζου

two-nose

ει
ὰ
σ
αῖ
. .
. α
. . .

COMPENDIUM IN CE

Ξυλολύχνου δὲ μέμνηται "Αλεξις· καὶ τάχα τούτῳ
ὅμοιόν ἐστι τὸ παρὰ Θεοπόμπῳ ὀβελισκολύχνιον.[1]
Φιλύλλιος δὲ τὰς λαμπάδας δᾷδας καλεῖ. οὐ
παλαιὸν δ' εὕρημα λύχνος· φλογὶ δ' οἱ παλαιοὶ τῆς
τε δᾳδὸς καὶ τῶν ἄλλων ξύλων ἐχρῶντο. " κοιμί-
σαι λύχνον " Φρύνιχος φησί.

Fol. 371ᵛ second column in A

καὶ λύχνον δίμυξον οἴσω[2] καὶ θρυαλλίδ', ἣν δέῃ.[3]
καὶ Πλάτων ἐν Νυκτὶ μακρᾷ·

ἐνταῦθ' ἐπ' αὐτῶν[4] τῶν κροτάφων ἕξει λύχνον
δίμυξον.

μνημονεύει τοῦ διμύξου λύχνου καὶ Μεταγένης ἐν
701 Φιλοθύτῃ καὶ Φιλωνίδης ἐν Κοθόρνοις. Κλεί-

---

[1] ὀβελισκόλυχνον CE. Eust. 1571. 21 τάχα, φασίν, ὅμοιός
ἐστι τῷ παρὰ Θ. ὀβελισκολύχνῳ. See G. and H. 358.
[2] With the syllable σω the second column of fol. 371ᵛ
becomes entirely legible. The words preceding added by
Porson.
[3] Early edd. : ην δε νι A.
[4] Kock : ἄκρων A, ἐντεῦθεν ἐπ' ἄκρων Meineke.

---

[a] Yet the word λύχνος occurs Od. xix. 34, quoted at 698 f
note a (p. 246), possibly meaning torch-holder; Batrachom.

264

Compendium in CE

A " wooden lamp " is mentioned by Alexis ; it may be that the " spit-lamp " in Theopompus is similar to it. Philyllius calls torches *daïdes*. The lamp is not an ancient invention [a] ; for light the ancients used torches of pine and other woods. " To put a lamp to sleep " is a phrase used by Phrynichus.[b]

" I will fetch a two-nose lamp and wicks, if need be." [c] Plato, also, in *The Long Night* [d] : " There, on his very temples, he'll have a two-nose lamp." This kind of lamp is mentioned also by Metagenes in *Fond of Sacrifices* [e] and by Philonides in *The Buskins*.[f]

180, and in Alcaeus, Athen. 430 d (vol. iv. p. 450) τί τὰ λύχν' ὀμμένομεν; Very early Minoan lamps in Walters, *B.M. Cat. Gr. and Rom. Lamps*, p. 24, Broneer, *Corinth* iv. 11.

[b] Kock i. 377, from Pollux vii. 178 : ἔπειτ' ἐπειδὰν τὸν λύχνον κατακοιμίσῃ " then, when he has put the lamp to sleep."

[c] Probably from Philyllius, above, p. 260, Kock i. 788 ; *cf.* Pollux vi. 103. See also p. 249.

[d] Kock i. 624, *cf.* above, 699 f, p. 252.

[e] Kock i. 708, Pollux vi. 103 δίμυξον ἢ τριμυξον, ὡς ἐμοὶ δοκεῖ, *cf.* x. 115.

[f] Kock i. 255, Pollux x. 115 ὥσπερ οἱ δίμυξοι τῶν λύχνων.

ταρχος δ' ἐν ταῖς Γλώσσαις λοφνίδα[1] φησὶ καλεῖν
Ῥοδίους τὴν ἐκ τοῦ φλοιοῦ τῆς ἀμπέλου λαμπάδα.
Ὅμηρος δὲ τὰς λαμπάδας δετὰς ὀνομάζει·

καιόμεναί τε δεταί, τάς τε τρεῖ ἐσσύμενός περ.

ἐλάνη δὲ ἡ λαμπὰς καλεῖται, ὡς Ἀμερίας φησίν,
Νίκανδρος δ' ὁ Κολοφώνιος ἐλάνην τὴν τῶν κα-
λάμων δέσμην. λύχνα δὲ οὐδετέρως εἴρηκεν
b Ἡρόδοτος ἐν δευτέρᾳ Ἱστοριῶν. λυχνοκαυτίαν δέ,
ἣν οἱ πολλοὶ λέγουσιν λυχναψίαν, Κηφισόδωρος
ἐν Ὑῖ.[2]

Καὶ ὁ Κύνουλκος αἰεί ποτε τῷ Οὐλπιανῷ ἀντι-
κορυσσόμενος ἔφη· " ἐμοὶ δέ, παῖ δωρόδειπνε,
ἀσσαρίου κανδήλας πρίω, ἵνα κἀγὼ κατὰ τὸν καλὸν
Ἀγάθωνα ἀναφωνήσω τάδε τὰ τοῦ ἡδίστου Ἀρι-
στοφάνους·

ἐκφέρετε πεύκας κατ' Ἀγάθωνα φωσφόρους."

καὶ ταῦτ' εἰπὼν

οὐρὰν ὑπίλας[3] ὑπὸ λεοντόπουν βάσιν,

ὑπεξῆλθεν τοῦ συμποσίου ὑπηλὸς κάρτα γενόμενος.
Τῶν δὲ πολλῶν τὸ ἰὴ παιών[4] ἐπιφθεγγομένων ὁ
c Ποντιανὸς ἔφη· " τὸ ἰὴ παιών,[4] ἄνδρες φίλοι,

---

[1] Musurus: λοφίδα A.   [2] Schweighäuser: υἱεῖ A.
[3] Valckenaer: ὑπήλασ' A.   [4] ἰη παιών A.

---

[a] Above, 699 d, p. 248 ; Hesych. s. λοφνίδια· λαμπάδια.
[b] Il. xi. 554, xvii. 663, of a lion driven off by hunters.
δεταί means " bound together," of splints or faggots soaked
in pitch or oil.
[c] Above, 699 d, p. 249 and note d.
[d] Frag. 89 Schneider, p. 120.
[e] ii. 62, of the Festival of Lamps, Λυχνοκαΐη, in the city
of Sais, on which see How and Wells's note. τὰ λύχν(α) is

Cleitarchus in his *Glossary* says the Rhodians call the torch made from the bark of the vine, a *lophnis*.[a] And Homer has a word *detai* for torches [b] : " And blazing torches, from which he shrinks, though he is eager to attack." The torch is also called *helanê*,[c] as Amerias asserts, and Nicander of Colophon calls the bundle of reeds *helanê*.[d] The plural of *lychnos* (lamp) is neuter, *lychna*, in Herodotus, second book of his *Histories*.[e] What most people speak of as *lychnapsia* (lamp-lighting) is called *lychnokautia* by Cephisodorus in *The Pig*.[f]

Thereupon Cynulcus, who was always butting against Ulpian, said : Boy, waiter ! Buy me a penny-worth [g] of candles, for I want to declaim these words which sweetest Aristophanes quotes from the beautiful Agathon [h] : " Bring ye out, as Agathon said, the light-bearing sticks of pine." And after quoting " wrapping his tail beneath his lion-foot legs," [i] he sneaked out of the party, for he had become very sleepy.

Since most of the company were now beginning to utter the refrain, *ié paión*,[j] Pontianus said : As to

Porson's emendation for the unmetrical τὸν λύχνον in Alcaeus, quoted above, p. 264 note *a*.

[f] Kock i. 802. I follow the punctuation and interpretation of Sophocles, *Lexicon s.* λυχναψία as against Kock (see also Eust. 1571. 22, whom Kock accuses of misunderstanding Athenaeus). With λυχναψία, found also in *Amherst Pap.* ii. 70, 10 and *I. G. Rom.* iv. 117, *cf.* περὶ λύχνων ἁφάς Herod. vii. 215. λυχνοκαυτία occurs only here.

[g] He uses the old form, *assarius*, of Lat. *as*, as also the Lat. *candela*, torch.   [h] *T.G.F.*[2] 766, Kock i. 544.

[i] Wittily adapted from Eur. *Oedipus*, *T.G.F.*[2] 532, of the Sphinx, οὐρὰν ὑπίλασ' ὑπὸ λεοντόπουν βάσιν καθίζετο, "wrapping her tail . . . she sat down," Aelian, *N.A.* xii. 7.

[j] Above, 696 f, p. 234.

μαθεῖν βούλομαι εἴτε παροιμία ἐστὶν εἴτε ἐφύμνιον
εἴτε τι ἄλλο." πρὸς ὃν ὁ Δημόκριτος ἔφη·
" Κλέαρχος ὁ Σολεὺς οὐδενὸς ὢν δεύτερος τῶν τοῦ
σοφοῦ Ἀριστοτέλους μαθητῶν ἐν τῷ προτέρῳ περὶ
Παροιμιῶν ' τὴν Λητώ,' φησίν, ' ἐκ Χαλκίδος τῆς
Εὐβοίας ἀνακομίζουσαν εἰς Δελφοὺς Ἀπόλλωνα καὶ
Ἄρτεμιν γενέσθαι περὶ[1] τὸ τοῦ κληθέντος Πύθωνος
σπήλαιον. καὶ φερομένου τοῦ Πύθωνος ἐπ' αὐτοὺς
d ἡ Λητὼ τῶν παίδων τὸν ἕτερον ἐν ταῖς ἀγκάλαις
ἔχουσα, προσβᾶσα[2] τῷ λίθῳ τῷ νῦν ἔτι κειμένῳ
ὑπὸ τῷ ποδὶ τῆς χαλκῆς εἰργασμένης Λητοῦς, ὃ
τῆς τότε πράξεως μίμημα γενόμενον[3] ἀνάκειται
παρὰ[4] τὴν πλάτανον ἐν Δελφοῖς, εἶπεν " ἵε παῖ."
(τυχεῖν δὲ τόξα μετὰ χεῖρας ἔχοντα τὸν Ἀπόλλωνα.) τοῦτο δ' ἐστὶν ὡς ἂν εἴποι τις " ἄφιε παῖ "
καὶ " βάλε παῖ." διόπερ ἀπὸ τούτου λεχθῆναί φασιν
τὸ ἵε παῖ καὶ ἵε παιών.' ἔνιοι δὲ παρεγκλίνοντές
τε τὴν λέξιν καὶ ψιλοῦντες[5] ἐπὶ τοῖς[6] δεινοῖς ἀλε-
e ξητήριόν τινα παροιμίαν λέγουσιν ' ἰὴ παιών ' καὶ
οὐχὶ ' ἵε παῖ.' πολλοὶ δὲ καὶ ἐπὶ τοῖς τέλος ἔχουσιν
ἐπιφθεγγόμενοι οἱ μὲν ἐν παροιμίᾳ φασὶν οὕτως
τοῦτο δὴ τὸ λεγόμενον ' ἰὴ παιών,' διὰ δὲ τὸ λίαν
ἡμῖν εἶναι σύνηθες λανθάνον ὂν ἐν παροιμίᾳ· οἱ δὲ
τὸ τοιοῦτο λέγοντες οὐχ ὡς παροιμίαν. τὸ δὲ ὑφ'
Ἡρακλείδου τοῦ Ποντικοῦ λεχθὲν φανερῶς πέ-
πλασται, ἐπὶ σπονδαῖς τοῦτο πρῶτον εἰς τρὶς εἰπεῖν

---

[1] CE: παρα A.　　　　　　[2] AC: προβάσα E.
[3] ὃς . . . γενόμενος CE.　　[4] περὶ C.
[5] ψιλοῦντες added by Kaibel, cf. Schol. Il. xv. 365.
[6] At this point A, fol. 372ʳ, second column, is badly
damaged by acids.

that *iê paión*, my friends, I should like to know
whether it is a proverb, refrain to a hymn, or something else.   In answer to him Democritus said :
Clearchus of Soli, who was second to none among the
disciples of wise Aristotle, tells us in the first of his
two books *On Proverbs* [a] that " Leto, bringing Apollo
and Artemis up to Delphi from Chalcis in Euboea,
arrived near the cave of the beast called Python.
When the Python rushed upon them, Leto, still
holding one of the children in her arms, mounted the
stone still lying at the foot of the Leto wrought in
bronze—a representation of the deed done at that
time which is set up beside the plane tree in Delphi
—and cried, ' At him, my son ! ' (It happened that
Apollo had a bow in his hand.) This cry, ' *hie pai* '
is as much as to say, ' Hurl, son,' or ' Shoot, son.'
From this, they therefore say, came the expression
hie pai or *hie paión*." But some authorities, altering
the word by pronouncing it with the smooth breathing, say that it is a kind of proverb uttered to ward
off danger, and is *iê paión*, not *hie pai*.[b] Many use
it as an ejaculation when a job is finished ; some of
these say that this saying, *iê paión*, is proverbial, but
because of its familiarity we forget that it is proverbial ; but others who use it deny that it is a
proverb.[c] But the assertion of Heracleides of Pontus [d]
is plain fiction, namely, that " at libations the god

[a] *F.H.G.* ii. 318. *Cf.* the fine chorus on this theme Eur.
I.T. 1234-1282.

[b] This was the doctrine of the school of Crates, as against
Aristarchus. On *Il.* xv. 365, ἦιε Φοῖβε, the Schol. says
Ἀρίσταρχος δασύνει (writes with the rough breathing), ἀπὸ τῆς
ἔσεως (shooting) τῶν βελῶν οἱ δὲ περὶ τὸν Κράτητα ψιλῶς (with
smooth breathing) ἀπὸ τῆς ἰάσεως (from his healing power).

[c] With παροιμία as used here *cf.* " slogan."   [d] Voss 51.

τὸν θεὸν οὕτως ' ἰὴ παιάν, ἰὴ παιάν, ἰὴ παιάν.'[1]
ἐκ ταύτης γὰρ τῆς πίστεως τὸ τρίμετρον καλού-
f μενον ἀνατίθησι τῷ θεῷ, φάσκων τοῦ θεοῦ διὰ[2]
τοῦθ' ἑκάτερον εἶναι τῶν μέτρων, ὅτι μακρῶν μὲν
τῶν πρώτων δύο συλλαβῶν λεγομένων ' ἰὴ παιάν '
ἡρῷον γίνεται, βραχέως[3] δὲ λεχθεισῶν ἰαμβεῖον[4]·
διὰ δὲ τοῦτο δῆλον ὅτι καὶ τὸν χωλίαμβον[5] ἀνα-
θετέον αὐτῷ. βραχειῶν γὰρ γινομένων εἰ[6] δύο τὰς
ἁπασῶν τελευταίας συλλαβὰς εἰς μακρὰν ποιήσει
τις, ὁ Ἱππώνακτος ἴαμβος ἔσται."

Μετὰ ταῦτ' ἤδη μελλόντων καὶ ἡμῶν ἀνίστασθαι
ἐπεισῆλθον παῖδες φέροντες ὁ μέν τις θυμιατήριον,
ὁ δὲ . . . .[7]
τοῦ συμποσίου . . . . . . δε | ⟨λιβ⟩α⟨ν⟩ωτοῦ
⟨θυμίασ⟩ιν ποι|⟨ήσας⟩ — — — δὴ . . . |
— — — — — ηιθυταυ | — — — — — τὰ τὸν |
— — — — αν. τήν . . . . . . ενορ . . . .
οι | . . . . . . ὸ . . . . καὶ τόδε ε | . . . . ς .
τοῦ θ⟨υμι⟩ατηρίου | . . . . . καὶ ἐ . τοῦ
⟨λι⟩βανωτοῦ, | τοῖς θεοῖς πᾶσι καὶ πάσαις | εὐξά-
μενος, ἐπισπείσας[8] | τοῦ οἴνου καὶ δοὺς κατὰ | τὸ
νόμιμον τὸ[9] ἐπιχώριον τὸ | λοιπὸν τοῦ ἀκράτου
τῷ | διδόντι ἐκπιεῖν παιδὶ | τὸν εἰς τὴν Ὑγίειαν
702 παι|ᾶνα ᾄσας τὸν ποιηθέν|τα ὑπὸ Ἀρίφρονος
τοῦ Σι|κυωνίου τόνδε·

---

[1] Kaibel following Casaubon: ἰὴ παιὰν ἰὴ παιών A, ἰὴ παιάν
ἰέ παιών CE.
[2] διὰ added by Kaibel.
[3] CE: βραχέων A.   [4] CE: ἰαμβίον A.
[5] Kaibel: ἴαμβον ACE.

270

was the first to utter the refrain three times, ' iê
paián, iê paián, iê paián.' " In this belief he ascribes
to the god the trimeter, as it is called, alleging that
" to the god belong both types of trimeter, for the
reason that if the first two syllables are pronounced
long, *iē pāiān* becomes a heroic measure,[a] but if pronounced short, it is an iambic measure ; but on this
showing it is clear that the limping iambus [b] must
also be ascribed to Apollo. For if (the first syllable
in each measure being considered short) one prolongs
the last two syllables of all, the verse will belong to
the type represented by Hipponax."

Thereupon, as we were now on the point of arising
to depart, slaves entered in succession, one bearing
a censer, another (cups for a libation) . . . (Then
Larensis, our host), having performed the rite of
purification with frankincense . . . prayed to all
the gods and goddesses ; he then made libation of
wine, and after giving, according to the custom of
the place, the remainder of the unmixed wine to
the slave who had served it to drink up, he sang the
following paean to Hygieia composed by Ariphron of

---

[a] Two spondees, forming a " measure " of the heroic
verse, or hexameter, which he regards as a trimeter.
[b] The trimeter scazon, choliambus, or Hipponactean,
$\cup-\cup-\ |\ \cup-\cup-\ |\ \cup--\cup.$

---

[6] εἰ deleted here by Wilamowitz following Casaubon,
reading εἰ μακρὰς for εἰς μακρὰν.

[7] Here the last three lines of fol. 372r, second column, have
vanished. What follows, in col. 1 of 372v, is to me illegible.
The supplements are due to Schöll.

[8] Kaibel: ἐπισπάσασ A.

[9] τὸ added by Kaibel. CE have here: ὅτι ἔθος ἦν ἀναστᾶσι
τοῦ δείπνου καὶ σπείσασι τὸ λοιπὸν τοῦ ἀκράτου τῷ διδόντι παιδὶ
ἐκπιεῖν διδόναι.

Ὑγίεια, πρεσβίστα μακάρων, μετὰ σοῦ ναίοιμι τὸ
   λειπόμενον βιοτᾶς, σὺ δέ μοι πρόφρων σύνοικος
   εἴης·
εἰ γάρ[1] τις ἢ πλούτου χάρις ἢ τεκέων
ἢ[2] τᾶς ἰσοδαίμονος[3] ἀνθρώποις βασιληίδος ἀρχᾶς[4]
   ἢ πόθων,

b οὓς κρυφίοισ᾽ Ἀφροδίτας ἄρκυσιν[5] θηρεύομεν,
ἢ εἴ τις ἄλλα θεόθεν ἀνθρώποισι τέρψις ἢ πόνων
   ἀμπνοὰ[6] πέφανται,
μετὰ σεῖο, μάκαιρ᾽ Ὑγίεια,[7]
τέθαλε πάντα καὶ λάμπει Χαρίτων ὀάροις[8]
σέθεν δὲ χωρὶς οὔτις εὐδαίμων ἔφυ.[9]

καὶ ἀσπα|σάμενος ἡμᾶς φιλοφρό⟨νως⟩[10] . . . ἀπο-
μάττοντας . . . |[11] . . . . οἴδασιν ο⟨ἱ πα⟩λαιοί.[10]
Σώπατρος γὰρ ὁ ⟨φλυακο⟩γράφος[12] ἐν τῷ ἐπιγραφομένῳ δράματι Φακῆ λέγει οὕτως·

   κρεανομοῦμαι καὶ τὸν ἐκ Τυρρηνίας[13]
   οἶνον σὺν ὀκτὼ λαμβάνειν ἐπίσταμαι.

Ταῦτα, φίλτατε Τιμόκρατες, κατὰ τὸν Πλάτωνα
c οὐ Σωκράτους νέου καὶ καλοῦ παίγνια, ἀλλὰ τῶν

---

[1] CE: ἢ γὰρ A.
[2] ἢ added from Sext. Emp.
[3] CE: εἰσοδαίμονος A.
[4] τ᾽ ἀρχᾶς CE: ἀρχὰς A.
[5] ἄρκυσιν CE: ἄρκουσι A, ἄρκυσι Inscr. Epid., ἔρκεσι Cod. Ottob.
[6] CE: ἀνπνοὰ A.
[7] CE: ὑγεια A.

272

Sicyon [a] : " Hygieia, most revered of the blessed
gods, with thee may I dwell for the rest of my life,
and be thou the gracious inmate of my house. For
if there is any delight in wealth or in offspring, or
in royal dominion which makes men equal to gods,
or in those desires which we seek to capture by
Aphrodite's hidden nets, or if any other joy or sur-
cease from toil hath been revealed to men by the
gods, it is with thy help, blessed Hygieia, that they
all flourish and shine in the Graces' discourse.
Without thee, no man is happy." He then em-
braced us fondly . . . wiping the hands . . . known
to the ancients. Sopater, the writer of farces, says
in the play entitled *Lentil Soup* [b] : " I can carve
meat for myself, and I know how to take Tuscan
wines with any party of eight."

These remarks, my very dear Timocrates, are not,
to quote Plato,[c] the light jests of a young and noble
Socrates, but the serious thoughts of the wiseacres

[a] *P.L.G.*⁴ iii. 595-597, Diehl ii. 130, Edmonds iii. 400,
Kaibel, *Epigr. Graeca* 1027, pp. 433-435 (= *I.G.* iii. 171,
p. 66), Bowra, *Class. Qu.* 32 (1938), 182. Lucian, *Pro Laps.
inter Salut.* 6, quoting the beginning, describes the poem
as τὸ γνωριμώτατον ἐκεῖνο. It seems to have remained a
favourite for many centuries, for Ariphron lived *ca.* 400 B.C. ;
Max. Tyr. 7. 1, p. 75 Hobein. See also Sext. Empir. 11. 49,
p. 386 Mutschmann, quoting similar phrases from Licym-
nius; Plut. *Virt. Mor.* 450 A, *Frat. Amor.* 479 A. See also
P. Maas, *Epid. Hymnen* 148, 160.

[b] Kaibel 196. On the number at table see p. 95.

[c] *Epist.* ii. 314 c τὰ δὲ νῦν λεγόμενα Σωκράτους ἐστὶν καλοῦ
καὶ νέου γεγονότος.

⁸ ὄαροις Cod. Ottob. confirming Crusius: ὄαροι or ὄαρει A
(so Schöll), ὄαρ C, ὄαρι γρ. ὄαρ E.

⁹ ἔφυ added from Sext. Emp.: om. ACE.

¹⁰ So Schöll.   ¹¹ Three lines are here lost in A.

¹² Casaubon.   ¹³ Musurus: τυρρηνέασ A.

ATHENAEUS

δειπνοσοφιστῶν σπουδάσματα. κατὰ γὰρ τὸν
Χαλκοῦν Διονύσιον·

τί κάλλιον ἀρχομένοισιν[1]
ἢ καταπαυομένοισ᾽ ἢ τὸ ποθεινότατον;

ΑΘΗΝΑΙΟΤ ΝΑΤΚΡΑΤΙΤΟΤ ΔΕΙΠΝΟϹΟΦΙϹΤΩΝ : ΙΕ :

[1] Casaubon (yet see Schroeder on Pind. frag. 89): ἀρχομένοιο
ACE.

at dinner. As the Bronze Dionysius says [a] : " What nobler theme for you and me is there, either at the beginning or at the close, than that which we desire the most ? " [b]

[a] *P.L.G.*[4] ii. 264, Diehl i. 75, imitating Pindar frag. 89, *P.L.G.*[5] i. 419, Sandys (L.C.L.) 564. On his name see above, 669 d (p. 86).

[b] This seems like a lame and impotent conclusion, and indeed we could wish for a more lucid verse. Throughout the work Timocrates has expressed desire to hear all he could of the parties at which Athenaeus was present.

GREEK INDEX

The numbers refer to volume and page of this edition

GREEK INDEX

279

GREEK INDEX

GREEK INDEX

281

βασιλικοὶ (συμποτικοὶ ?)
νόμοι 1 14, cf. 322 ;
βολβοί 1 278
βασυνίας 6 482
βατάνη 2 124 ; βατάνιον
1 122, 2 268
βάτια = συκάμινα 1 224
βατιάκιον 5 52, 126
βατίς 1 448, 2 104, 170, 3
212, 284-286, 322-326,
340, 374, 402, 468, 486,
4 112, 116, 240
βάτος 1 224, 3 284-286
βάτραχος (fish) 2 104, 3
284-286, 326, 450, 482,
486, 4 326
βαυκαλίς 5 54
βελόνη = ἀβλεννής, ῥαφίς
1 370, 390, 3 434, 450,
452, 4 110, 326
βεμβράδες 3 288-292, 302,
350, 370
βέρβερι 1 400
βέφυρα = γέφυρα 6 350
βήρηξ 2 38. See βάραξ
βῆσσαι 5 52
βιβλία ἄμπελος 1 136 ;
βίβλινος οἶνος 1 134,
136
βιβλιακοὶ χαρακῖται 1 98
βιβλιολάθας 2 136
βῖκος 5 54
βίος ἀληλεμένος 6 464
βιστάκια 6 508

βίττακος = ψίττακος 1 284
βλάχνον = πτέρις 1 268
βλέννος 3 292
βλέπειν 6 70, 71 note e
βλεψίας = κεφαλῖνος 3 376
βλῆμα 2 36
βλίτον 1 288
βλωμιαῖοι ἄρτοι 2 36
βόα = σάλπη 3 446
βόαξ, βῶξ 3 286, 288, 306,
374, 406, 446, 460, 480,
4 110
βοὴν ἀγαθός 2 328, 334
βολβῖναι 1 278
βολβιτίνη 3 430
βολβός 1 20, 238, 262,
266, 276-280, 2 102, 104,
112, 4 324
βολβοφακῆ 2 220
βολίζη 3 200
βολίς 1 454
βομβυλιός 3 178, 5 54-56
βοσκάδες 4 290
βότις 3 286, 452
βότρυς 1 206, 7 2-6 ;
βοτρυοσταγῆ ἔρνη 1
128
βούγλωσσος 2 122, 3 294,
372, 432, 468, 484, 486,
4 112
βουκεφάλια 2 448
βουκολιασμός 6 334
βουκολισμός 6 330, 334
βουνιάς 1 16, 4 172

βοῦς (fish) 3 284, 446 (?),
  4 112
βουτυροφάγοι 2 182
βράβυλα 1 216-218
βραττίμη 2 36
βρένθειον μύρον 7 196
βρένθις 1 300
βρέχειν (ἐπὶ τοῦ πίνειν) 1
  100
Βριγινδαρίδες. See Βρυγινδαρίδες
βρίγκος 3 448, 450, 4 326
βρίζαι 4 526
βρίζειν = καθεύδειν 4 20
βρομιάδες 5 56
βροτοκέρτης = κουρεύς 1
  424
Βρυγινδαρίδες 6 524
βρυσοί 1 390, 391 note e
βρύτεα = στέμφυλα 1 246
βρῦτον, βρῦτος 4 526
βρώματα 1 154, 204, 6 462
βύβλος (στεφανωτρίς) 7
  120
βυκανηταί, βυκανισταί 6
  314
βυσαύχην 1 276
βύστακες 2 152
βωλητινὸς ἄρτος 2 30
βῶξ. See βόαξ
Βώρμος 6 338

γάδος 3 418
γαθεῖν = χαίρειν 1 424

γάλα 1 188, 250, 2 174
γαλαθηνοί 4 292-294
γαλακτοτρόφος 2 172
γαλακτουργοί 6 276
γαλεάγρα 6 318
γαλέη, γαλῆ, γαλεός 1 448,
  2 104, 122, 3 22, 282,
  286, 314-324, 400, 418,
  448, 480, 4 112, 240,
  326
γαλλαρίας, γαλλερίας 3
  402, 418
γαμοποιία 2 340
γάρον, γάρος, ὀξύγαρον 1
  24, 292, 2 62, 4 160
γαρότας = βοῦς 1 424
γαστήρ (meat) 6 354
γάστραι (turnips or cab-
  bages) 4 170
γάστρις (nut-cake) 6 498
γαστρολογία 1 444, 2 236
γαστρονομία 1 18, 244, 2
  24
γελαρίης 3 418
γελοιασταί 3 108, cf. γε-
  λοιάζειν 1 172
γελώνιος πλακοῦς 6 493
  note d
γελωτοποιοί 6 304
γενεᾶτις τρίγλη 3 460, 462
γενειοσυλλεκτάδαι 2 214
γενναῖος 7 4 and note d
γεράνειον 1 268
γέρανος, Γεράνα 5 280

GREEK INDEX

GREEK INDEX

ἔγχυτοι 2 280, 6 476-478, 496

ἐδέατροι 2 148, 276, 278

ἐδέσματα 2 86, 88, 6 462

ἐθελονταί 6 350

εἶ (the letter E) 5 58

εἴδατα 2 374

εἰκοσήρης 2 420; εἰκόσορος 2 436

εἰλαπίναι, εἰλαπιναισταί 3 64, 4 140-142; Ζεὺς Εἰλαπιναστής 2 290

εἰλέατροι 2 276

εἰλεός (vine) 1 136

εἵλωτες 3 192, 220

ἑκατερίδες (dance) 6 398

ἐκβολάς (μήτρα) 1 434

ἐκκλησιαστὴς οἰκόσιτος 3 116

ἐκκύλιστοι (wreaths) 7 132 and note 4

ἐκπίνειν = προπίνειν 5 224

ἐκτομίς 1 434

ἔλα, ἔλη 6 242, 7 248, 249 note e

ἐλᾶαι 1 242-246, 2 128

ἔλαιον 1 132, 290-292. See μύρα

ἔλαιον, ἔλαιος (bird) 1 282

ἐλάνη 7 248, 250, 266

ἔλαφος (cake) 6 490

ἐλεάται 3 220

ἐλεδώνη 3 216, 430

ἐλεοδύται 2 284, 286

ἐλεός 2 276, 284, 286

ἐλέπολις 2 432, 472

ἐλευθέριον (ὕδωρ) 7 178

ἐλεφάντινοι αὐλοί 2 306

ἐλεφάντινον τάριχος 2 46, 48

ἐλεφαντόπους κλίνη 1 208

ἐλέφας (cup) 5 66-68; (elephant) 6 270

ἐλέωτρις 3 400

ἔλη. See ἔλα

ἑλικτοὶ στέφανοι 7 138

ἐλίχρυσος 7 144

ἐλλοί (fishes) 3 246

ἔλλοπες ἰχθύες 3 384

Ἑλλώτια, Ἑλλωτίς 7 128

ἔλοψ 2 122, 3 268, 282, 320, 346, 384, 4 100

ἔλυμοι αὐλοί 2 302, 6 436

ἔμβαμμα 4 168

ἐμβασικοίτας 5 68

ἐμβολάδες. See ἐπεμβολάδες

ἔμβρωμα 1 48

ἐμμέλεια 1 88, 6 394, 402, 406

ἐμπέπτας 6 484

ἐμπυριβῆται τρίποδες 1 164

ἐνδόσιμον 6 6, cf. 5 344

ἐν ἕλει Ἀφροδίτη 6 94

ἔνηφι 1 430, 7 4

ἐνιαυτός (cup) 5 48

ἐν καλάμοις Ἀφροδίτη 6 94

θυρσίων (tursio) 3 394 ; in
the form Θύρσος 3 482
θυρσόλογχος 2 406, 408
θυώματα 7 186

ἰάκχα, ἰακχαῖος στέφανος
7 128
ἴακχος = χοῖρος 1 424
ἰάλεμος 6 334
ἰαμβική (dance) 6 394
ἰαμβισταί 2 344
ἴαμβοι = αὐτοκάβδαλοι 6
352
ἰαμβύκαι 6 432, 446
ἰάς 7 156
ἴγδις 6 396
ἴδιος (?), ὄρχησις 6 396
ἴε παῖ 7 268
ἱερὰ ἄμπελος 1 132
ἱέραξ (fish) 3 468-480, 4
110
ἱεροκῆρυξ 2 182
ἱερόν 3 144
ἱεροποιός 2 182
ἱερὸς ἰχθύς 3 268-276, 4 70
ἱεροστολισταί 2 398
ἰὴ παιάν, παιών 7 234, 266
ἰθύφαλλοι 2 94, 6 352
ἴκταρ (fish) 3 480
ἱλαρῳδοί 6 340-342
ἰλλάς 1 282
ἱμαῖος 6 330, 334
ἱμαλίς 2 12, 6 330
ἱμερτὸν ὕδωρ 1 178

ἱμονιά 2 272
ἰξοφάγος 1 282
ἴον 7 148, 156
'Ιουλιανός (cake) 6 496
ἰουλίς, ἴουλος (fish) 3 276,
368, 472
ἴουλος, οὖλος 6 330, 334,
336
'Ιουλώ (Demeter) 6 332
ἰοχέαιρα (asp) 1 426
ἰπνίτης ἄρτος 2 14, 42, 134
ἰπνολέβης 1 422
ἱππίδια, ἵπποι (fish) 3 366,
374
ἵπποι (? πῖποι) 4 170 note 4
ἱππόπορνος 6 52
ἵππος (in slang) 5 404,
405 note f, 6 52, 53
note d
ἵππουροι 3 364-366, 434,
448-450
ἴρινον μύρον 1 198, 2 126,
384, 7 186
ἶρις 7 150-152, 186
ἰσθμιακόν, ἴσθμιος
(wreath) 7 126
ἴσθμιον (cup) 5 84 ; (of a
well and a sword) 7 126
ἰσίκια 4 204
ἰσχαδοπῶλαι 2 86
ἰσχάς (fig) 1 132, 238, 322,
328, 330, 436, 6 522-
528 ; (olive) 1 244
ἰσχάς = ἄγκυρα 1 428

294

GREEK INDEX

ἴτρια 1 252, 2 82, 6 468, 490, 500
Ἰφικρατίς 5 78
ἴφυα 1 272
ἰχθύα 1 26
Ἰχθυόεσσα 1 132
ἰχθυοπῶλαι 3 10-22
ἰχθυοπώλαινα 6 296
ἰχθυοτροφεῖον 2 440
Ἰωνιάδες 7 148
Ἰωνικολόγος 6 342, cf. 7 64
ἰωνίσκος 3 476
ἴωπες 3 348, 480, 482

καδίσκος 5 88
Καδμεῖα γράμματα 1 353 note g
κάδος 5 84-88, 6 148
καθάρυλλοι 2 20
κακκάβαι, κακκαβίδες 2 268, 4 262
κακκάβιον 2 270
κάκκαβος 1 312, 2 170, 172, 270
κακόσιτος 3 114, 118
κάκτος 1 306, 308
καλαβίζω, καλαμίζω 6 398 note b, 7 236 note 12, 237 note g
καλαθίσκος (dance) 6 398
καλαμαύλης 2 300
καλάμινος αὐλός 2 304
καλάμου στεφάνωμα 7 108

καλασίρεις 5 370
καλλαβίδες (dance) 6 398, 492
καλλαρίας, γαλαρίας, χελλαρίης 3 418
καλλίνικος 6 330
καλλίουλος 6 332
καλλιστρούθια σῦκα 1 326
κάλλιχθυς 3 268, 322, 476
καλλιώνυμος 3 268, 4 110
καλοφόροι 2 152
καλπίον 5 98
Καλύκη 6 336
κάλχαι 7 152
καμασῆνες 4 16
καμινίτης ἄρτος 2 42
κάμμαροι 1 456, 3 278, 286, 374
κάμματα, καμματίδες 2 140, 142
κάναθρον 2 132, 136
Κανδαύλας (Hermes) 5 323 note j
κάνδαυλος, κάνδυλος 1 38, 2 110, 180, 5 322-326, 6 478, 7 58
κανδῆλαι 7 266
κανθαρίς 3 468
κάνθαρος 5 88-94
κανυσῖνος (coat) 1 420
καπάνα = ἀπήνη 4 394; καπανικὰ δεῖπνα 4 394
καπνίας οἶνος 1 138, 2 106
καπνιστὰ κρέα 2 198

GREEK INDEX

GREEK INDEX

299

GREEK INDEX

303

GREEK INDEX

λυχναψία **7** 266
λυχνεῖον **7** 256
λυχνεύς (marble) **2** 430;
(lamp) **7** 248
λυχνία **7** 251 note *e*, 256
λυχνίδιον **7** 252
λυχνίον **7** 70, 248
λυχνοκαυτία **7** 266
λύχνος **7** 248, 264, 266
λυχνοῦχος **7** 248-252
λώτινοι αὐλοί **2** 304
λωτός **1** 316, **2** 304, **6** 518-
520, **7** 126-128

μαγαδίζειν **6** 426
μάγαδις **2** 304, 306, **6** 422-
442
μαγγανεία **1** 40
μαγείραινα **6** 296
μαγειρικὰ σκεύη **2** 244,
250, 266
μαγειρίσκος **3** 312
μάγειρος **2** 274-286, **3** 294,
302-316, **7** 30-50
Μαγίδες (in Delos) **2** 284
μαγίς (in Cyprus) **7** 52
μαγῳδός **6** 342, 346
μάδρυα **1** 218
μᾶζαι **1** 238, 244, 262, **2**
36-42, 74, 104, 138, 172,
180, 216, 228, **7** 52
μαζίον **1** 258
μαζονόμοι **2** 180; μαζο-
νόμια **2** 404, 416

μαζός (fish) **3** 446
μαζῶνες **2** 180
μαθαλίδες **5** 166
μαινίδιον **3** 388, 456
μαινίς **1** 16, 274, **3** 24, 98,
278, 322, 326, 404, 462,
478, **4** 36, 122, 124
μαίσων **7** 32-34
μαιῶται (fish) **3** 400
μακτιστρίαι, μακτριστίαι
6 394
μακτρισμός (ἀπόκινος) **6**
394, 396
μακωνίδες **2** 20-22
μαλάκια **3** 420, 430, 432,
454, **4** 116
μαλακοκόλαξ **3** 160
μαλάχη **1** 254, 266
μαλόδρυα **1** 218
Μάνερως **6** 338
μάνης **5** 166-168, **7** 72, 76,
78, *cf.* 79 note *b*
μανία **5** 24-26, *cf.* **6** 120,
121 note *h*, 122
Μαντινικὴ ὅπλισις **2** 202
μάντις = κράμβη **4** 176
μάξεινος **3** 418, **4** 8
μάραγδος **1** 404
μάραθον **1** 244, 308, **2** 104
μαργαρίτης **1** 398-404
μαρυπτόν **6** 496
μάσπετον **1** 434
μάσταξ **7** 52
μαστίχη **7** 52

GREEK INDEX

μαστός (cup) 5 166
ματερία 2 30
ματτύα, ματτύη, ματτύης 2 142-146, 7 50-60
Μεγάλαρτος 2 12
μεγαλλεῖον 5 512, 7 188, 198
Μεγαλόμαζος 2 12
μέγαρον 2 376
μέθυ 4 144
μεθύειν 1 174
μέθυσος 1 6 and note c, cf. μεθύσης 7 172
Μειλίχιος Διόνυσος 1 338
μείουροι στίχοι 6 414
μελαινίδες = κόγχοι 1 370
Μελαινὶς Ἀφροδίτη 6 172
μελάνδρυαι, μελάνδρυες 2 62
μελάνουρος 2 120, 3 216, 386, 406, 434, 440, 464, 4 108, 540
μελανόφαια σῦκα 1 336
μελεαγρίδες 7 12-16
μέλη (cups) 5 162, 163 note h
μεληδὸν ὠπτημένα 2 198
μελίκηρα 1 380
μελικηρίδες 6 500
μελιλώτινος στέφανος 1 316, 7 130, 172
μελίνη 2 14
μελίπηκτα 1 38, 40, 2 82, 184, 282, 450, 6 504

μελιτοῦττα μᾶζα 2 38
μελίττιος οἰνίσκος (?) 1 126
μελιτώματα 6 490
μεμβράδες 3 84, 98, 278, 292, 416, 478, 4 118, 326
μεμβραδοπώλης 2 86
μένανδρος (παρθένος) 1 422
μενεκράτης (στύλος) 1 424
μενέσται (πενέσται) 3 188
μεσάγκυλα δόρατα 5 44
μέση κωμῳδία 3 314, 4 26
μεσόκοποι αὐλοί 2 302
μεσόλευκος 2 474, 5 430, 6 352
μεσόμφαλοι φιάλαι 5 242, 244
μεσπίλη 1 218, 220, cf. 6 512, 513 note c
μεσπιλώδης 1 332
μεταδόρπια 6 456
μετάκερας 1 180, 2 72, 74
μετάνιπτρον 5 164-166
μετώπιον 7 189
μήκων (in the pinna) 1 376, 378, 394; (plant) 2 30, 104
μηκώνια 1 378
μῆλα 1 120, 218, 256, 264, 346-356
μήλινον μύρον 1 198
μηλοφόροι 5 312-314
μήτρα 1 6, 414-416, 430-436

GREEK INDEX

μηχανή (in drama) 3 4
μικροσιτία (Pythagoreans) 2 234
μικροτράπεζοι (Greeks) 2 100
μιλιάριον 1 422
μιμαίκυλα 1 220, 222
μίσυ 1 268
μίτλος 1 368
μιτροχίτωνες 5 358
μνοία 3 186, 7 230
μνῶται 3 200
μογγάς (dance) 6 394
μόθακες 3 220, 6 331 note e
μόθων (dance) 6 330
μολόχη 1 254
μολπή 1 60, 66
μόναυλος 2 290, 296-300, 312; μοναύλιον 2 300
μονοκάλαμος σῦριγξ 2 312
μονομάχος 2 202
μονοσιτεῖν 1 190, 204
μονοφαγεῖν 1 34, 36
μονοχίτων 6 180
Μοντιανόν (?) 6 496
μόρα 1 188, 222-226
μόρμυλος, μόρμυρος 2 122, 3 408
μόρος = πόνος 7 176
μόρσιμος τύχη 1 424
μορφασμός (dance) 6 396
μόστηνα (?) 1 226
μόσχοι (πέτηλοι) 4 202

μουκηροβαγός 1 230
μούκηρος (μύκηρος) 1 228, 230
μουστάκια (cakes) 6 496
μοχλὸς φόβου = φύλαξ 1 428
μυελὸς λευκός = ἐγκέφαλος 1 286
μύες 1 366-398, 2 48, 60, 104, 3 266, 322, 366, 374, 386, 486, 4 110 (?)
μνηφόνος = σκίλλα 4 182
μυίσκαι 1 388
μύκηροι, μούκηροι 1 228, 230
μύκητες 1 262-266
μυκτηριστής 2 348
μυλαικὰ σῦκα 1 336
μύλλοι (cakes) 6 492
μύλλοι (fish) 2 52, 3 448, 484, 4 326
μῦμα 7 30, 50
μυξῖνος 3 376, 4 112
μύξος 3 376
μύρα 1 198, 2 126, 210, 228, 288, 384, 7 176, 184-208
μύραινα 1 16, 2 104, 122, 3 352, 380, 402, 404, 484
μυρίνης οἶνος 1 140
μυρίσαι 2 282, 7 200
μυρίσματα, μυρώματα 7 202
μύρμαι 3 408, 442

306

μυροποιοί 6 276, *cf.* 7 186
μῦρος 3 404
μύρρα 7 184
μυρρίναι 1 324
μυρσίνης στέφανος 7 116
μυρτίδες 1 230
μυρώματα 7 202
μυστήριον (double meaning) 1 424
μυστίλη 2 82
μυστριοπώλης 2 86
μύστρον 2 82-86, 94
μῶκος 1 156, 2 326, *cf.*
   καταμώκησις 1 240

νάβλας 2 294, 296
ναβλιστής 2 306
νᾶνος (ἄρτος) 6 488
νᾶπυ 1 122, 256, 304, 2
   112. 272, 4 158-162
νάρδινον μύρον 1 198, 384,
   7 186, 200
νάρκη, νάρκα 2 4, 104, 3
   84, 284, 326, 362, 400,
   410,450,486, 4 112,326
ναρκίον 2 170
νάρκισσος 7 144, 148-150
ναστός 2 24, 6 492
Ναυκρατίτης στέφανος 7
   96, 118-122
ναυμάχος 2 204
ναυτίλος 3 428
νεασπάτωτον 6 350
νεβροῦ κῶλα (αὐλοί) 2 306

νεήλατα 6 483
νέκταρ 1 140, 168, 188
νεκταροσταγής 1 126, 132
νεοδαμώδεις 3 220
Νεστορίς, Νέστορος δέπας
   5 168-198
νεῦρα 1 22, 23 note *a*
νευρομῆτραι 4 306 note 3
νευροσπαστεῖσθαι 4 266
νεφροί = ὄρχεις 4 238
νεφρομῆτραι 4 306
νηρίτης 1 384, 396
νηριτοτρόφοι νῆσοι 1 370
νησιώτης οἶνος 1 142
νῆστις 1 202, 432, 448, 2
   170,172, 3 380,382, 398
νῆτται 4 288-290
νηττίον 1 284
νιβατισμός (dance) 6 394
Νικολᾶοι φοίνικες 6 522
νικύλεα (?) σῦκα 1 330
νιπτήρ 2 492
νίτρον 2 268
νόμιον (pastoral) 6 336
νόμοι βασιλικοί (?) 1 14;
   πολιτικοί 1 8
νοσσὰς ὄρνις 2 282
νόστος 6 330
νύμφη (niche) 2 390
νώγαλα 1 128, 204-206, 6
   356 note *a*
νωγαλεύματα 1 204, 372
νωγαλίζειν 1 124, 206
νωτιδανὸς γαλεός 3 318

GREEK INDEX

ξανθίας (θύννος) 4 114
ξανθόχρωτες 3 464, 486
ξενίαι, ξενικαὶ τράπεζαι 2 154, 156
ξενικὸς θᾶκος 2 156
ξενύδριον 2 108
ξει ὦνες 2 376
ξηροβατικός 1 426
ξηροπυρίτας ἄρτος 2 34
ξηροτήγανον 3 30
ξηροτροφικός 1 426
ξηροφαγία 2 30
ξιφίας 3 354, 412, 4 100
ξιφισμός (dance) 6 398
ξιφομάχαιρα 7 260
ξυλίνη κύων 1 306
ξυλοθήκη 2 440
ξυλολύχνος 7 264
ξυλολυχνοῦχος 6 258
ξύλου παράληψις 6 398
ξυλοφόροι 2 152

ὀβελίας ἄρτος 2 22
ὀβελιαφόροι 2 22
ὀβελισκολύχνιον 7 259
note h, 260, 264
ὄζαινα 3 480
οἰκέται 3 200
οἰκετιεύς 2 238
οἶκος 1 206, 208
οἰκόσιτος 3 114-116
οἶναι = ἄμπελοι 1 152
οἰνάνθη, οἰνάνθινον 7 186, 188

οἰνάς 4 282, 284
οἰνίσκος 1 26, 128
οἰνιστηρία 5 204 and
note a
οἰνολογεῖν 1 176
οἰνοηθηταί 6 276
οἰνομανής 5 26
οἰνοποτεῖν 5 4
οἰνόπται 4 424
οἶνος 1 12, 42, 70, 112-
150, 198, 206, 228, 250,
2 106, 126, 168, 260
οἰνοῦττα μᾶζα 2 38
οἰόνους 1 152-154
οἰτόν 1 270
ὀλβιογάστωρ 4 246, 248
ὀλιγοδρανεῖν 1 100
ὀλιγόσιτος 3 114-118
ὄλισβος 5 502, 7 122
ὄλλιξ (?) 5 204, 205 note c
ὄλμος 5 200
ὀλόκυρος 7 148
ὀλόλευκος 2 52, 410
ὀλονθοφόρος συκῆ 1 336
ὀλόπυρος 4 340
ὀλοφυρμός 6 334
ὄλπη 5 206
ὄλυραι 2 14
Ὁμαιμῆς 1 424
Ὁμηρισταί 6 340
ὁμομηλίδες 6 514
Ὁμόνοια 5 248
Ὀμπνία 7 218 note 4
ὀμφακίας οἶνος 1 114, 116

308

GREEK INDEX

ὀρτυγομήτρα 4 276

ὄρτυξ 4 272-278

ὀρύα = χορδή 1 406, 4 158

ὄρυζα 2 198; ὀρυζίτης
πλακοῦς 6 496

ὀρυκτοὶ ἰχθύες 4 4-6

ὀρφακίνης 3 414

ὀρφίσκος 3 370

ὀρφός, ὀρφώς 1 22, 3 282,
322, 340, 362, 370, 414,
450, 472, 476, 482, 4
14, 32, 42, 60, 108, 326

ὄρχεις 4 238

ὄρχησις 1 62, 66-70, 88-
96, 2 38, 6 386-408

ὅς (for ὅ not Homeric)
5 194

ὀσμύλιον 3 456, 480

ὀσμύλος 3 430

ὀστακός = ἀστακός 1 450

ὀσταφίς = ἀσταφίς 1 450

ὄστρακα. See ὄστρεα

ὀστρακίδες 1 248, 2 82,
6 498, 509 note ƒ

ὀστρακίτης (cake) 6 498

ὀστρακόδερμα 3 428, 4 96,
100

ὄστρεα, ὄστρεια, ὄστρακα
1 30, 58, 374, 378, 2
4, 8, 3 38, 208, 4 10,
102

ὀτόστυλλον (?) 1 308

οὖ (the letter O) 5 56-58

οὖθαρ 4 306, 7 20

οὖλοι 6 332

οὔπιγγοι 6 334

οὐρανόπολις (Rome) 1 88

οὐρανοσκόπος 4 110

οὐρία 4 290

οὖς Ἀφροδίτης 1 378

ὀφθαλμοί = οἰνόπται 4 424

ὀφρυανασπασίδης 2 236

ὀψάριον 2 108, 4 240-244

ὀψαρτυσία 1 20, 112, 252,
2 34, 246, 282

ὀψοδαίδαλος 1 434, 452,
2 16

ὀψομανής 5 26

ὄψον 1 24, 3 242, 245 note
e, 246 note a, 6 128,
7 50

ὀψοποιία, ὀψοποιοί 1 18, 5
496, 6 276

ὀψόπωλις 1 24

ὀψοφάγος 1 22, 90, 432, 3
246, 4 66-68, 5 26

ὀψωνάτωρ, ὀψώνης 2 276

ὀψωνία 2 48

παγκαρπία 5 88, 6 500,
cf. 2 82

πάγουρος 1 450, 3 432

πάγχορτοι σῖτοι 1 430

παιάν 7 230-234

παίδεια = παιδικὰ ᾄσματα
6 238

παιδιά 1 60, 64

παιδικά 6 46

310

GREEK INDEX

παιδικοὶ αὐλοί **2** 302, 304, 6 424
παίειν (in cookery) **4** 452, 6 464
παισά (cakes) **6** 492
παλαιομάγαδις **2** 305 note 5, **6** 426
παλίουρος **6** 510
πᾶνα = panem **2** 22
Παναθηναϊκόν **5** 204; μύρον **7** 188
πανδαισία **4** 338
πάνδημος Ἀφροδίτη **6** 76
πανδουριστής **2** 306
πάνδουρος **2** 298, 310
πανός, πανία, πάνια **2** 22
πανός = φανός **7** 248, 258
πανόσμεον **7** 164
πανσπερμία **6** 500
παντόμιμος **1** 88
παραβίη **4** 526
Παράβυστος **3** 156
παραγκωνιστής **3** 160
παραγοράζειν **2** 276
παραδεδειπνημένος **4** 414
παραδειπνίδες **2** 32
παραινετήρ **1** 60
παραμασύντης **2** 114
παρασάγγης **2** 66
παράσιτος **2** 286, **3** 54-114
παρασταθέντες (Crete) **5** 40
παραστάται = ὄρχεις **4** 290
παραυλίζεσθαι **2** 360

παραφέρειν **4** 220
παραχορηγεῖν **2** 140, 142
παρετυμολογῶν **1** 154
παρευδιασταί **4** 10
παρθένιοι (ἀποστολικοί) **6** 406; (αὐλοί) **2** 302, **6** 424
παριαμβίδες **2** 308
παροιμία **7** 268, 269 note c. See Proverbs
παροίνιος (dance) **6** 396
πάροινος **4** 516, **6** 146
παροψίς **1** 260, 262, **4** 162-168
παροψωνεῖν **2** 276
παρῳδία, παρῳδοί **1** 20, **7** 240-248
πάσασθαι = ἀπογεύσασθαι **1** 104
πατάνιον **2** 270
παταξάτω τις (slang) **4** 520
πατρόπολις **1** 432
Παυλινιανόν (cake) **6** 496
πέξις **1** 268
Πελειάδες, Πλειάδες **5** 178-192
πελειάς = περιστερά **4** 284, 288
πελίκαι **5** 204-206
πελίχνη **2** 22, **5** 206
πέλλα, πελλίς **5** 206-208
πελλητήρ **5** 208
πέλτης = κορακίνος **2** 64

311

GREEK INDEX

GREEK INDEX

πρόαρον 5 204
προγεύστης 2 276, 280
πρόδρομα σῦκα 1 332
πρόδρομος οἶνος 1 132
πρόκνιδες 6 528
Προμάλαγγες 3 152
πρόμοι = ἄρχοντες 1 424
προπίνειν 5 224
προπόλιον 6 352
πρόπολος 3 200
πρόπομα 1 252, 254, 260, 280, 288
προπόσεις 1 60, 4 458-462
προσκεφάλαιον 1 120, 208, 5 314
προσκήνιον 6 312
προσοδιακοὶ τρόποι 6 406
προσπελάται 3 220
προτένθης 2 278, 280
πρότροπος οἶνος 1 132, 198
Προυσιάς 5 50, 212-214
προχοΐδες 5 212
προχύτης 5 212
πρυτανικαὶ ἐσθῆτες 2 182
πρωτερικὴ συκῆ 1 334
πρωτογεύστης 2 278
πτισάνη 1 198, 202, 248, 2 104, 182, 220, 4 566
πτωματίδες (?) 5 156
πυάνιον 6 500
πύανον 4 338
Πυθαγορισμός 2 232
πυλεών 7 128, 146

πυός 1 448, 2 104
πυραλλίς 4 284
πυραμοῦς 1 252, 2 34, 6 494
πυρῆνες = κῶνοι 1 248
πυρίεφθα 7 30
πυρνὸς ἄρτος 2 36, 172
πυροῦντες 4 120
πυρρίχη (dance) 6 392, 396, 400, 402, 406
πύτινος 3 474
πωλύπος. See πολύπους

ῥαβδοδίαιτος 5 460, 7 178
ῥαβδοῦχοι 6 312
ῥαβδοφόροι 6 418
ῥάδια 2 292; ῥαδιεστέρα 4 422
ῥαππαύλης 2 300
ῥαφανίς 1 242, 246, 248, 308
ῥάφανος 1 150, 246, 284, 2 50, 56, 112
ῥαφίς 3 366, 370, 400, 434, 476, 4 110. See βελόνη
ῥάφυς 4 172
ῥέοντα 5 214
ῥήγεα καλά 1 210
ῥίζα = κολοκάσιον 1 314, 316
ῥίνη 2 104, 120, 3 22, 284, 318, 400, 432-436, 448, 4 112, 116, 326

GREEK INDEX

σελῆναι = φθόεις 5 176
σεληνίτιδες γυναῖκες 1 250
σέλινον 1 266, 7 168, 169
  note a
σέμελος 1 276
σεμίδαλις 1 120, 2 12, 26,
  40, 88 116, 280
σεμνοπαράσιτον ἔθνος 3 68
σερίς 1 308
σεσερῖνος 3 370
σέσιλοι 1 274
σεῦτλα (τευτλία) 4 180,
  5 254, 6 348
σηπία 1 132, 242, 246,
  2 8, 104, 118, 3 216,
  314, 356, 420, 422, 430,
  450-456, 466, 468, 482,
  4 36, 112, 116, 326, 330
σηπιδάριον 1 372; σηπίδιον
  1 448, 3 348, 358, 398,
  456, 4 124, 178
σησαμίδες 6 398, 492, cf.
  2 282
σησαμίτης ἄρτος 2 34
Σήσαμοι 2 284
σητάνια μῆλα 1 348
σία 1 266, 320
σιαγών 1 404, 406
σιαλίς 4 276
σίδη 6 516
σιδηρῖτις 7 148
σικελίζειν 1 96
σίκιννις,   σικιννιστής
  (dance) 1 88, 6 394, 400

σικιννοτύρβη 6 330
σικύα 1 256, 298, 4 188 ;
  Σικύας 3 156
σικυός, σίκυς 1 256, 296,
  298, 318, 320
σικυωνία 1 256
σιλόδουροι (soldurii, Caes.
  B.G. iii. 22. 1) 3 122
σίλουρος 2 54, 108, 3 38,
  288, 400
Σιμαλὶς Δημήτηρ 2 12
  note 1
σιμὴ χείρ 6 398
σιμόν 6 316
σῖμος (fish) 3 400
σιμῳδοί 6 340-342
σίναπυ,   σίνηπυ 1 291
  note b, 298, 2 112, 4
  158-160
σίνδρων 3 200
σινόδους 3 448
σίσαρον 2 60
σίταρχος 2 178
σιτευτοὶ δέλφακες, μόσχοι
  7 20, 22 ; ὄρνιθες 7 20 ;
  χῆνες 4 234, 7 22
σιτόκουρος 3 114-118
σίττυβος 2 270
Σιτώ 2 12
σκαλίας (? σκόλιον) 1
  308
σκάλλιον (cup) 5 222
σκαμωνίας ὀπός 1 122
σκάρος 3 98, 366, 370,

317

GREEK INDEX

319

τράγος (fish) 3 476, 4 8, 112

τραγῳδίας εὕρεσις 1 172, cf. 3 2

τράκτα = καπύρια 2 32

τράπεζα 1 212, 214, 2 154, 156, 3 32, 6 460, 462, 470, 7 170

τραπεζοκόμος, τραπεζοποιός 2 274, 284, 286

τραπεζορήτωρ 1 98

τραχηλισμός 1 64

τράχηλοι 1 376, 378, 4 390

τράχουρος 3 440, 466

τρεχέδειπνος 1 14, 3 90

τρεψίχρως 3 428

τρήρωνες πελειάδες 5 182

τριακοντήρης 2 420

τριγκοί 3 288, 446

τρίγλα, τρίγλη, τριγλίς 1 22, 26, 28, 372, 2 118, 3 98, 216, 248, 276, 292, 314, 326, 348, 368, 406, 436-468, 482, 486, 4 36, 62, 110, 122, 124, 326, 540

Τριγλανθίνη Ἑκάτη 3 462

τριγλῖτις 3 278, 290

τριγόλας 3 460

τρίγωνον, τρίγωνος 2 44, 296, 306, 310, 6 432, 7 64

τρίδουλος 6 208

τριήρης (cup) 5 216, 236,

238; (house) 1 162-164

τρίμετρον 7 268-270

τρῖμμα 1 138

τριπορνεία, τρίπορνος 6 156, 208

τρίπους 1 164, 166, 212, 214; τριπόδιον 1 312

τρίπους (musical instrument) 6 438-442

τρίφορος 1 334

τρίφυλλον 7 168

τριχάς 1 282

τριχίας, τριχίδες, τριχίδια 3 350, 358, 450, 476-482, 4 118, 326

τρίχορδος 2 308

τροχοπέδη 1 426

τρυγέρανος 6 182

τρυγίας οἶνος 1 136

τρυγῳδία 1 172, cf. 2 48

τρυγών 3 284, 390, 464, 486, 4 38, 326

τρυμαλιή 6 344

τρύφη 3 206, 7 60

τρωγάλια 6 460

τρωξαλλίς 2 50

τῦκα = σῦκα 6 350

τυκτά (Persian) 2 166

τυλάς 1 282

τύμπανα 6 346

τυροκόσκινον (cake) 6 498

τυρός, τυρίδιον 1 284, 2 18, 30, 274, 7 28-30

GREEK INDEX

τυροῦται δέμας 1 434
τύφλη (fish) 3 400

ὕαινα, ὑαινίς, ὕες 3 372,
468, 470, 486
ὑάκινθος 7 138, 160
ὑγιάτης Διόνυσος 1 156
ὑγίεια (μᾶζα) 2 38 ; (bowl)
7 208-210
ὑγροτροφικός 1 426
ὕδνα 1 266-270
ὑδνόφυλλον 1 270
ὕδραυλις 2 290-294
ὑδροθήκη 2 440
ὑδρόμελι 1 266
ὑδροπόται 1 190-192
ὕδωρ 1 176-202, 2 66, 70-
78 ; πρὸς ὕδωρ εἰπεῖν 1
190
ὕες. See ὕαινα
ὕκης 3 276, 322, 348, 366,
438, 470-476
ὑμέναιος 6 334
ὕπαρχος = σατράπης 5
394
Ὑπερειὰς ἄμπελος 1 136
ὑπερμαζᾶν 7 52
ὑπερτέλειοι αὐλοί 2 302, 6
424
ὑπερῷον 1 250
ὑπηνέμιον ᾠόν 1 250
ὑπήτρια 4 308
ὑπόγαστρα ταρίχια 2 42
ὑπογάστριον, ὑπογαστρί-

διον 2 34, 52, 172, 3
356, 4 308
ὑπογλωττίς 7 124, 132
ὑποδώριος ἁρμονία 6 366-
368
ὑπόθεσις (plot) 6 346
ὑποθυμίδες 7 110, 130, 184
ὑποκρητηρίδιον 2 450
ὑπολαμπάς 5 424 and
note c
ὑποπάρθενος ἁλμάς 2 110
ὑποπόδιον βασιλικόν 5 3 4
ὑποπύθμενες 5 190
ὑπόρχημα 1 90, 2 344, 6
388, 400, 406 ; ὑπορχη-
ματικὸς τρόπος 1 66
ὑποστήματα 2 392
ὑπόσφαγμα σηπίης 3 456
ὑπότρητοι αὐλοί 2 302
ὑποτυρίδες (ὀποτυρίδες ?) 6
498
ὑπόχυτος οἶνος 1 138
ὑπώπιον 1 420
ὗς (swine), see σῦς ; 6 135
note c
ὗς (fish) 3 468-470, 478, cf.
377 note c ; = καπρίσκος
4 110 (ὗς to be read for
μῦς)
Ὑστήρια 1 412
ὑστιακόν 5 238
ὕσ(σ)ωπος 2 212, 3 470

Φαβωνιακόν (cake) 6 496

322

GREEK INDEX

φάγημα 1 392
Φαγήσια, Φαγησιπόσια 3 238
φάγρος 3 212, 322, 348, 350, 400, 416, 448, 450, 470-474, 482, 4 110, 116, 326
φαινίνδα 1 64
φαινόλης 1 418, 420
φαιὸς ἄρτος 2 36
φακῆ, φακός 1 20, 132, 292, 2 104, 210-228; Φακῆ 1 20, 2 220 (read 'Ἰθάκη ?), 4 340, 7 242; φάκινον βρῶμα 2 220; φάκινος ἄρτος 2 222
φάλαιναι 4 14
φαλαρίδες 3 462, 4 290
φαλλοφόροι 4 516, 6 350
Φανερά = Delos 4 566
φανός 7 248, 250, 256, cf. 2 298, 299 note 4
φαρμακίτης οἶνος 1 132
φάσηλοι 1 242
φασιανικοί, φασιανοί 4 246-252, 7 8-10
φασκάδες 4 290
φάσκωλος 7 196
φάσματα 1 84
φάσσαι 4 280-288
φατνώματα 2 388, 440
φαύλια μῆλα 1 348-354
φαυλίαι ἐλᾶαι 1 244, 292
φάψ 4 282

Φεβρουάριος μήν 1 422
φεραῖος (fish) 3 378
φήρ = θήρ 6 322
φθοῖς (cake) 5 176, 6 496
φθοίς (phiale) 5 246
φιάλη 3 42, 5 238-246
φιβάλεω σῦκα 1 324, 326, 332
φιδίτιον, φιδίτης 2 134, 140-152, 288, 322
φιλάδελφον 7 154
φιληλιάς 6 334, 335 note j
φίλιχθυς 1 26, 446
φιλόβοτρυς 3 244
φίλοινος 1 148, 4 462
φιλόμηλος 3 244
Φιλοξένειοι 1 22
φιλοπλάκουντος 6 474
φιλοπότης 4 462
φιλόσυκος 3 244
φιλοτάριχος 2 78
φιλοτησία 5 246
φιλοτράπεζος 2 32
φιλύρα, φιλύρινος 1 218, 5 502, 7 138
φιττάκια 6 508
φλογίδες 7 16-18
φλύακες 6 350; φλυακογράφος 1 368
Φοινίκη 1 120 (read Κύπρος ?)
φοινίκινος οἶνος 1 128, 250
φοίνικος ἐγκέφαλος 1 306, 310, 312

323

GREEK INDEX

φοῖνιξ 1 120, 128, 206, 306, 310, 312, 6 516-522

φοῖνιξ (musical instrument) 2 306, 6 432, 438

φοξῖνος 4 326

φοξός 5 128

φορμύνιος συκῆ 1 326

φούλλικλος 1 64

φουμῶσος τυρός 2 30

φουρνάκιος ἄρτος 2 30

φρατρικὰ δεῖπνα 2 320

φρέαρ ἀργυροῦν 2 368, 5 10

φρεατιαῖον ὕδωρ 2 74

φρύγιον (scent) 6 378, 379 note h

φρυκτοί (fish) 3 24, 358

φύκης, φυκίς 2 4, 104, 3 98, 264, 326, 368, 434, 440, 448, 450, 4 108, 326

φυλετικὰ δεῖπνα 2 320

φυλλάς 2 114, 140

φυλλίς 2 60

φυλλοτρῶγες (Greeks) 2 100

φῦσα (fish) 3 400

φύσιγγες 1 298

φυσίκιλλος 2 134

φύσκη 1 248, 2 104

φύστη, φυστή 2 36, 104, 128, 172, 180

φωκίδες (pears) 6 514

φωλάδες 1 378, 390

φῶτιγξ, φωτίγγιον 2 296-304

χάλκαι (flower) 7 164

Χαλκεῖα 5 251 note g

χαλκεύς (fish) 3 478

χαλκίδες (fish) 3 442, 444, 452, 468, 476-480, 484, 4 110

χαλκίδες = θεράπαιναι 3 200

Χαλκιδικὰ ποτήρια 5 248

χαλκιδικαί (fish) 3 478

χαλκός 3 42-54

χαμαικέρασος 1 220

χαμαίπιτυς 7 148

χαμαιτύπαι 3 172

χάνναι, χάννοι (fish) 3 366, 418, 434, 474, 4 108

χαρακῖται βιβλιακοί 1 98

χάραξ (fish) 4 110

χαρίσιος πλακοῦς 6 488, 7 80

Χαριτοβλέφαρος (Demetrius) 6 200, cf. 7 170

χαριτογλωσσεῖν 2 244, 250

χεδροπά 1 242

χειή 5 112

χεὶρ καταπρηνής, σιμή (dance) 6 398; κατὰ χειρὸς ὕδωρ 4 348-352, 356-360, 7 170

χειρόμακτρον 4 356-360

325

GREEK INDEX

ENGLISH INDEX

The numbers refer to volume and page of this edition

ENGLISH INDEX

Aeschines of Athens, orator and political opponent of Demosthenes 2 325 note *f*, 3 7, 91, 4 39, 211, 5 221 note *e*, 247 note *h*, 451 note *b*, 6 47, 91, 7 5 note *h*

Aeschreas, character in Dioxippus' *Miser* 5 83

Aeschrion of Samos, writer of iambic verse 3 331, 4 23 (Diehl i. 288)

Aeschylides, writer on agriculture (third century B.C. ?) 6 513

Aeschylus of Alexandria 6 231

Aeschylus, tragic poet 1 459, 6 383. *Agam.* (284) (296) 7 259, (916) 6 97. *Pers.* (?) 1 370 note 2. *Prom.* (297) 2 251, (816) 4 73. Lost plays : Ἀθάμας 1 165, 3 419-421. Ἀμυμώνη 7 197. Γλαῦκος Πόντιος 1 375. Δαναίδες 6 233. Ἠδωνοί 5 123. Ἡλιάδες 4 423, 5 73, 185 (?). Ἰξίων 2 305. Κάβειροι 4 193, 443. Κρῆσσαι 1 225. Λυκοῦργος 4 527. Μυρμιδόνες 5 201, 6 239, 249. Ὀστεολόγοι 1 75, 5 45, 7 75. Παλαμήδης 1 51. Περραιβίδες 1 371 (?), 5 105, 329. Προμηθεὺς Λυόμενος 7 113. Πρωτεύς 1 293, 4 283. Σφίγξ 7 113. Φιλοκτήτης 4 283. Φινεύς 4 411. Φορκίδες 4 321. Φρύγες 1 225. Titles unknown : 1 370 note 2, 371, 427, 3 361, 4 143, 201, 437 and note *f*, 5 185, 385, 6 413. Costumes of 1 93-95 ; dedicated his works to Time 4 75 ; drunk when writing 1 97, 4 443 ; used Sicilian words 4 321

Aeson, father of Jason 6 93

Aesop 2 493, 5 200 note *a*, 7 221 and note *c*

Aethex, son of Janus 7 209

Aethiopia, south of Egypt and Libya 1 297, 2 21, 411 ; slaves from 2 177 ; birds 4 250 ; in Homer 4 147 ; in Mimnermus 5 73

Aethiops of Corinth,

333

ENGLISH INDEX

343

ENGLISH INDEX

Antiphanes, poet of the Middle Comedy 1 462, 6 3. Ἀγροῖκος 3 365, 407, 4 123-125, 277, 293, 521, 6 65, 7 211. Αἴολος 4 513, 5 511. Ἀκέστρια 3 365, 4 323, 6 159. Ἀκοντιζομένη 4 499. Ἀλείπτρια (see Alexis) 2 71. Ἁλιευομένη 4 37, 6 159. Ἄλκηστις 2 69, 5 513. Ἀνταῖος 5 469. Ἄντεια (see Alexis) 2 87-89, 7 195. Ἀργυρίου Ἀφανισμός 4 355. Ἀρκάς 4 513, 6 159. Ἁρπαζομένη 4 319. Ἀρχεστράτη 3 449 and note 4. Ἄρχων 2 153. Ἀσκληπιός 5 155. Αὐλητής 6 329. Αὐλητρίς 4 57. Αὑτοῦ Ἐρῶν 4 567, 7 133. Ἀφροδίσιον 4 535-537. Ἀφροδίτης Γοναί 5 167-169, 7 71-73. Βάκχαι 4 501. Βοιωτίς (?) 1 361, 4 165-167, 5 95, 6 515. Βομβυλιός 2 83, 235. Βούσιρις 1 207. Βουταλίων, see Ἀγροῖκος. Γάμοι 1 407, 2 231, 271. Γανυμήδης 4 581. Γάστρων, see

Κνοιθιδεύς. Γόργυθος 4 43. Δευκαλίων 2 53, 6 493. Δηλία 4 189 and note 7. Δίδυμοι 2 89, 3 71, 4 223, 417. Διορύττων, see Θορίκιοι. Διπλάσιοι 5 257. Δραπεταγωγός 2 235. Δυσέρωτες 1 433-435. Δύσπρατος 3 179-181, 7 47. Δωδώνη 5 375. Εὐθίδικος 2 269, 3 453. Ζακύνθιος 5 513. Θαμύρας 3 347. Θορίκιοι ἢ Διορύττων 5 515, 7 193. Ἰατρός 2 295. Ἱππεῖς 5 255, 7 257 and note 5. Καινεύς 4 463. Κᾶρες 2 115. Καρίνη 5 255. Κηπουρός 6 159. Κιθαριστής 7 149. Κιθαρῳδός 4 53. Κλεοφάνης 1 425, 6 55. Κνοιθιδεὺς ἢ Γάστρων 3 291-293, 4 533. Κορινθία 1 411. Κουρίς 2 59, 3 363. Κύκλωψ 3 327, 4 323. Κώρυκος 2 233, 4 159, 353. Λαμπάς 5 165 (bis). Λάμπων 3 381, 4 417. Λεπτινίσκος 6 465. Λευκάδιος (?) 1 297. Λεωνίδης 4 413. Λημνίαι 3 37, 163. Λυδός 4 517.

349

ENGLISH INDEX

95 ; Thessalian 6 177 ;
second cup to 1 159 ;
shrine 2 429, 439 ;
swine to 1 411-413 ;
tree of 1 363 ; temple
6 135 ; verses to 6
193 ; wine called
Aphrodite's milk 4 513;
Aphrodite Leaena 3
139 ; Lamia 3 139 ;
Phila 3 145, 151 ;
Pythionicê 6 209 ; por-
trayed by Apelles 6
187 ; by Praxiteles 6
159. Ἀναδυομένη 6 187,
Ἀργυννίς 6 253, Ἑταίρα
6 23, 87, Ζεφυρῖτις 3
431, Καλλίπυγος 5 519,
Μελαινίς 6 173, Πάνδη-
μος 6 77, 411, 7 37,
Ποντία 6 75, Πόρνη 6
93, Τρυμαλῖτις 6 345
note e. See Cypris
Aphrodite's delight (lily)
7 161
Aphrodite's ear (shell
fish) 1 379
Aphthonetus, cook 4 217
Aphyae 3 279, 459, 6
161
Apia, Apidanê, early
name of Peloponnesus
6 229, 513
Apician pastry 6 497

Apicius, Roman prodigal
2 265, 510, 3 321 (?)
Apicius, two culinary ex-
perts of this name 1 viii,
29, 31, 2 264 note b, 3
321 (?), 5 459
Apidanê, see Apia
Apion of Alexandria,
grammarian 1 73, 462,
3 321, 5 243, 6 469, 7
143
Apollas, writer on cities
of Peloponnesus 1 277,
462, 4 171
Apollo, god of knowledge
and prophecy 1 425,
427, 3 331 ; son of
Leto 4 187 ; musical 6
413 ; amours 3 273 ;
at Acharnae 3 57, 61 ;
at Amyclae 2 133, 139,
3 45 ; crow associated
with 4 129 ; Delian
mission to 3 57 ; grove
in Lycia 4 15 ; in
Homer 1 97, 5 7, 29
note e, cf. 2 119 ; in
song 7 219 ; lyre sacred
to 4 79, cf. 3 373, 6
385, 413 ; oracle at
Delphi 2 491, 3 53,
145, 6 267 ; ordained
wreath 7 103 ; paean to
2 137 ; Phalaris spared

ENGLISH INDEX

ten when drunk 4 443.
Αἰολοσίκων 1 411, 2
29, 3 243, 4 185, 7 251.
Ἀμφιάραος 2 221. Ἀνά-
γυρος 2 111, 3 349, 4
245, 6 515. Βαβυλώνιοι
1 375, 5 117, 203.
Γεωργοί 1 325, 2 23, 5
7, 6 515. Γῆρας 2 17,
111, 3 291. Γηρυτάδης
1 411, 429, 2 29, 221, 3
177, 383, 443, 4 153,
163, 5 155, 501, 503, 6
195, 515. Δαίδαλος 3
421, 453 note *f*, 4 165,
169, 195. Δαιταλῆς 1
19, 2 55-57, 89, 269,
311, 315, 3 341, 4 169,
223 note *f*, 311, 5 153,
379, 6 489, 7 77-79, 199,
203, 215. Δαναΐδες 1
249, 2 37, 3 457, 4 311,
415, 6 485. Δηλία 4
189, 191. Δράματα ἢ
Νίοβος 3 351, 5 211, 7
253. Ἥρωες 4 353.
Θεσμοφοριάζουσαι 1 127,
449, 2 49, 3 457, 6 335,
7 197. Κένταυρος 6 395.
Κώκαλος 2 211, 5 117.
Λημνίαι 3 341, 357, 399,
4 161. Νεφέλαι (earlier
edition) 5 123. Νῆσοι
(title not mentioned) 1

245. Νίοβος see Δρά-
ματα. Ὁλκάδες 1 391,
2 23, 53, 3 483. Πελαρ-
γοί 3 111, 4 169, 253.
Πόλεις (?) 1 373, 2
139. Προαγών 1 345,
411, 4 221, 413, 415,
5 119, 121. Σκευαί (?)
6 389, 391. Σκηνὰς
Καταλαμβάνουσαι 2 269,
3 289. Ταγηνισταί 1
415, 2 21, 277, 3 211,
283, 4 199, 357, 395,
415, 7 125. Τελμησσῆς
1 215, 3 387, 389, 7 201.
Τριφάλης 5 367. Φοί-
νισσαι 1 273, 385, 387,
2 203. Ὧραι 4 187, 7
7. From extant plays:
Acharn. (vs. 85) 2 101,
(459) 5 121, (524) 6 79,
(606) 3 413, (616) 4
357, (786) 4 199, (872)
2 29, (875) 4 255 and
291, (889) 3 341, (1092)
6 491. *Birds* (67) 4
249, (101) 4 299, (249)
4 255, (269) 4 299,
(304) 4 257, (566) 3
463, (695) 1 251, (707)
4 255, (761) 4 255,
(884) 4 301 and 303,
(1377) 5 503. *Clouds*
(103) 2 355, (109) 4 249

(122) 5 59, (339) 1 283,
(362) 2 477, (455) 1 407,
(559) 3 341, (665) 4 197,
(961) 4 223, (983) 4 67,
(1196) 2 279. *Eccle-*
siazusae (707) 1 335,
(843) 2 17, (1117) 7 203.
Frogs (134) 1 287, (294)
6 61, (1304) 6 435.
Knights (83) 2 67, (92)
5 43, (124) 5 5, (160) 1
405, (198) 5 5, (237) 5
249, (300) 1 405, (356)
1 407, (361) 3 399,
(599) 5 145, (631) 4 161,
163, (662) 3 479, (864)
3 341, 343, (1094) 5
51, (1178) 1 407, (1289)
4 523. *Lysistrata* (203)
5 249, (549) 1 387,
(1110) 2 208 note *a.*
Peace (27) 2 285, (122)
2 23, (143) 5 163, (540)
4 421, (563) 2 57, (788)
4 279, (804) 4 57, (916)
5 153. *Plutus* (179) 6
195, (254) 2 208 note *a,*
(720) 1 293, (812) 3 33,
(1005) 2 275, (1128)
4 169. *Thesmophoria-*
zusae (458) 7 143.
Wasps (330) 4 243,
(493) 3 417, (510) 3 341,
(511) 4 293, (855) 4 421,

(884) 1 387, (1127) 3
483, (1208) 2 335, (1214)
2 337, (1216) 6 463.
Titles unknown : 1 95,
133, 211, 221, 231, 293,
2 287, 3 397, 4 513,
523, 5 153, 249, 6 527,
7 267

Aristophanes of Byzan-
tium 1 21 note *a,* 93,
333, 357, 369, 463, 2
305, 343, 3 29, 87, 185,
289, 4 27, 199, 239, 251,
351, 359, 5 153 note *h,*
157, 227, 6 63, 147, 163,
335, 7 33, 51, 57

Aristophanes of Thebes,
historian 1 181, 463

Aristophon, Athenian
orator 6 117

Aristophon, painter 5 414
note *b*

Aristophon, poet of the
Middle Comedy 1 275,
463, 3 71, 73, 359, 5
85, 325 note *c,* 509, 6
25, 43

Aristotle 1 27, 399, 463,
2 323, 325, 335, 469, 4
25, 97-105, 305, 6 9-11,
61, 179, 7 107. Ἀπο-
λογία 7 235. Ἐρωτικά
6 47 (?), 7 109. Εὐ-
γένεια 6 7. Ζῴων

366

ENGLISH INDEX

Callias, Athenian orator
4 51

Callias of Athens, author
of Γραμματικὴ Θεωρία
(Τραγῳδία) 3 241, 4 531,
555-557

Callias, second of the
name, father of Hip-
ponicus Ammon (*ca.*
500 B.C.) 5 427

Callias, third of the name,
son of Hipponicus, rich
Athenian 1 99, 464, 2
267, 315, 353, 481, 483,
489,497,3285,5277,425

Callias, son of Lysima-
chus, poet of the Old
Comedy 1 97, 247,
465, 2 141, 303, 3 283,
285, 375, 4 63, 5 165,
367, 6 117, 7 75. See
Diocles

Callias of Mytilene, grammarian 1 369, 465

Callias of Syracuse, his-
torian 5 453

Callicles of Calymna, ship-
wright mentioned by
Menander 5 95

Callicrates, admiral of
Philadelphus 3 431

Callicrates, father of the
demagogue Callistratus
2 257

Callicrates, parasite of
Alexandria 3 133

Callicrates, poet of the
New Comedy 6 159

Callicrates of Sparta,
toreutic artist 5 41

Callimachus, archon at
Athens 2 483

Callimachus of Cyrene 1
19, 105, 245, 255, 303,
305, 315, 413, 465, 2
161, 467, 3 97, 137, 275,
429, 471, 481, 4 7, 27,
257, 259, 269, 285, 291,
351, 507, 5 111 (read
Ἰκίου for οἰκείου), 215,
6 155, 475, 7 81, 83,
87, 235

Callimedon, Athenian
orator, called Crayfish
1 431, 433, 447, 3 91,
4 37-45, 151, 6 311

Callinus 5 369

Calliopê 4 379 and note *b*

Calliphanes, noted for
learning 1 17

Callippides, tragic actor
5 419

Callippus 5 285, 529

Callippus (?) 7 80 note 2,
81 note *b*

Callisthenes, Athenian
orator 4 37, 49

Callisthenes, historian 4

391

the fire in winter 1 237;
for sleeping 1 75, 123,
209 ; Sicilian 1 209
Council of Five Hundred
2 275 note *a*, 487, 3 27,
104 note *a*, 4 543 note *b*
Courtesans 1 111, 2 7,
215, 6 3, 17, 21, 65-69 ;
camp followers 6 95 ;
courage of 6 93, 199 ;
fees 6 77, 151, 185, 217 ;
generosity 6 203-205,
cf. 83-85, 89, 115, 121 ;
imported by Aspasia 6
79 ; learning 6 147, 171 ;
lure of 6 23 ; names of
6 121, 147, 161, 167 ;
none in Ceos 6 289 ;
patriotism 6 97 ; sanc-
tioned by Solon 6 77 ;
with Alcibiades and
Themistocles 6 103,
111 ; witty sayings 6
121-159
Courts 2 361, 6 191, 197
Crabs 1 367, 393, 403, 449,
451, 455, 457 ; from
Parium 1 397
Cranaus, glutton 4 387
Craneia, nymph 1 337
Cranes 2 107, 4 281
Crane-truffle 1 269
Crannon, city in Thessaly
1 183

Crassian cake 6 495
Crassus 3 137, 227
Craterus, Macedonian
officer 5 439, 531, 6
251, 7 235
Crates of Athens, poet of
the Old Comedy 1 207,
221, 2 47, 49, 57, 3 117,
203, 4 173, 276 note 6,
295, 395, 443, 5 119,
6 335, 7 199
Crates of Mallos, Per-
gamene scholar 2 35,
477, 493, 515, 3 55, 59,
4 45, 161, 5 183, 205,
221, 6 159, 457, 7 3,
269 note *b*
Crates of Thebes, Cynic
philosopher and poet
2 219, 515, 4 413, 591,
6 189. See Diels *P.P.G.*
iii. 219, Diehl i. 106
Crates, toreutic artist 5
41
Crathis river 3 213, 5
341 and note *c*
Cratinus, sacrificed him-
self for Athens (seventh
century B.C.) 6 247, 249
Cratinus, poet of the Old
Comedy 1 171 (Powell
4), 466, 3 207, 5 201
and note *e*, 7 243.
Ἀρχίλοχοι 1 373, 399, 2

(ὄρνιξ), 285, 545, 5 41,
59 (σάν for σίγμα), 153
note *f*, 157 (λεπαστά),
6 349, 7 61 ; mode in
music 6 365 ; Muse 6
325 ; Sicily 2 447

Doricha, mistress of
Sappho's brother 6 213

Dorieus, epigrammatist 4
371

Dorion, writer on fishes,
and flute-player 2 51,
3 269, 279, 291, 319,
333, 349, 365, 369, 371,
377, 379 note *b*, 391-
393, 403-409, 415-419,
435, 441, 449, 451, 475-
481, 487, 4 31-35, 471

Doris, wife of Dionysius
the Elder 5 449

Dorotheus, historian 3
245

Dorotheus of Ascalon or
Sidon 3 485, 4 357, 5
133-135, 221, 7 31, 51

Dorpia, personification in
Philyllius 2 278

Dorus, a handsome boy 6
45

Dorylaeum, in Phrygia
1 187

Dosiadas, historian of
Crete 2 153-155, 3 187,
cf. 6 243 note *f*

Dotis, nymph 3 329

Dotium 3 181, 498

Dove 1 111, 2 93, 107,
113, 145, 147, 173, 4
281-289, 5 179. See
Pigeon, Pleiades

Dowry 2 103, 6 5, 15, 21

Draco, Athenian law-
giver 5 283, 6 75

Draco, character in Di-
philus 3 309

Draco of Corcyra, writer
on petrology (first cen-
tury ?) 7 209

Dracontiades, in Matron
2 123 ; pigeons 4 289

Draughts (πεττεία) 1 73,
75, 83

Dreams, of lovers 6 105

Dress, comeliness and
dignity of 1 91, 93.
See Clothing

Dressing, sour 1 297, *cf.* 2
43, 45, 63

Drimacus, leader of
Chian slaves 3 193-
197

Drinking 1 37-61, 99, 101,
157-163, 193, 199, 2 61,
71, 81, 89, 191, 371, 3
171, 4 147, 399, 415-529,
5 147. See Cups,
Symposia

Drinking-horns 2 189,

419

4 293, 505, 5 237, 7 5.
Κέρκωπες 4 391, 6 65.
Κλεψύδρα 6 65. Κύ-
βευταί 5 81. Λάκωνες
ἢ Λήδα 2 7, 3 487-489,
4 223, 5 7. Μήδεια 3
347. Μυλωθρίς 5 203.
Μυσοί 4 391. Νάννιον
(see Philip) 6 73.
Ναυσικάα 3 383. Νεοτ-
τίς 5 59. Ὀδυσσεὺς ἢ
Πανόπται 5 117. Οἰδί-
πους 3 75. Οἰνόμαος ἢ
Πέλοψ 7 133. Ὀλβία
6 455 (see H.S.C.P. 50,
1939, p. 10). Ὀρθάννης
1 453, 2 9, 11, 29, 3 31,
4 421. Πάμφιλος 5 91.
Παννυχίς 6 71. Πορνο-
βοσκός 2 11, 4 185.
Προκρίς 4 413, 5 513.
Προσουσία ἢ Κύκνος 3
349. Σεμέλη ἢ Διόνυσος
1 157, 5 7. Στεφανο-
πώλιδες 4 237, 6 15, 7
137, 139, 199. Σφιγ-
γοκαρίων 1 345, 4 537-
541, 5 511. Τιτᾶνες 3
31. Τίτθαι 1 453, 3
399, 7 171. Φοῖνιξ 4
297. Χάριτες 5 337.
Χρύσιλλα 6 23. Ψάλ-
τρια 5 7. Titles un-
known : 1 33, 101, 111,

113, 123, 127, 151, 187,
189, 207-209, 215, 227,
285, 289, 2 33-35
Eucleia, hetaera 6 147
Eucleides, Athenian ar-
chon (403-402 B.C.) 3
483 (?), 6 117
Eucleides, parasite 3 89,
129
Eucleides of Athens,
owned a large library
1 11
Eucrates, grammarian (?)
2 23
Eucrates, nicknamed Κό-
ρυδος, parasite 3 83-89,
105
Eudemus, defender of
Aristotle 6 60 note c
Eudemus. See Euthy-
demus
Eudicus, clown (fourth
century B.C.) 1 87
Eudoxus of Cnidus 3 245,
295, 4 275, 5 296 note
b, 469 note f
Euegorus, priest in Eu-
bulus 5 117 and note
3
Euergetes. See Ptolemy
Euhemerus 7 33
Euius (Dionysus) 4 145
Euius of Chalcis, flute-
player 5 437

3 381, **4** 55, 209, 217-219, 307, **5** 253-255

Euphronius, poet and grammarian **5** 207, 503 note g

Euphrosynê, hetaera **6** 147

Eupolis, comic poet **1** 469. Αἶγες **1** 407, 455, **3** 291, 349, **4** 221, 353, 433. Ἀστράτευτοι **4** 297-299. Αὐτόλυκος **1** 385, **2** 481, **4** 169. Βάπται **1** 207, 231, **2** 311, **4** 177, **7** 69, 75. Δῆμοι **1** 455, **2** 71, **3** 421, **4** 193, 349. Εἵλωτες **2** 133, **4** 313, **6** 447. Κόλακες **1** 99, 431, **2** 489, **3** 65, 285, 477, 479, **4** 311, **5** 277, 417, **6** 399, 493. Μαρικᾶς **7** 199, 203. Πόλεις **4** 277, 425. Προσπάλτιοι **3** 465. Ταξίαρχοι **1** 229, **2** 275. Φίλοι **3** 199. Χρυσοῦν Γένος **4** 199, 339, 349, **7** 23, 31. Titles unknown : **1** 9, 77, 243, 247, 297, **5** 247, **6** 361

Euripides, against athletes **4** 373 - 375; as wine-pourer **4** 423 ; epigram by **1** 267 ; epigram by **1** 267 ; epi-

nicion for Alcibiades **1** 13 ; killed by dogs **6** 225 ; mocked by Laïs **6** 141 ; library **1** 11 ; and Sophocles **6** 259, 525 ; throw of dice so named **3** 113 ; woman-lover and -hater **6** 15, 253. *Aeolus* **2** 225, **6** 57, 141. *Andromache* **1** 15. *Andromeda* **5** 109, 429, **6** 33. *Antigone* **5** 363 and note *e*. *Antiope* **4** 409, **7** 125. *Augê* **6** 235. *Autolycus* **4** 373-375. *Bacchae* **1** 169, 173-175, **2** 323, **4** 59, 143, **5** 467. *Cretan Women* **1** 417, **5** 261, **6** 455. *Cyclops* **1** 103, 159, **6** 511, **7** 31. *Danaê* **1** 175, **2** 225. *Eurystheus* **5** 225. *Heracles* **4** 353, **6** 281, 337. *Hippolytus* **2** 69, **5** 395, **6** 75, 235, 455. *Ion* **7** 259. *Iphigenia in Aulis* **6** 41, 73. *Medea* **2** 213, **3** 241, **4** 143, 557, **6** 119, 141, 157. *Melanippê* **5** 359, 475, **6** 305, 307. *Oedipus* **7** 267. *Oeneus* **7** 69. *Orestes* **4** 205. *Peiri-*

ENGLISH INDEX

ENGLISH INDEX

451

ENGLISH INDEX

481

ENGLISH INDEX

79 ; temple on Helicon 6 391 ; worship 5 483 ; in the poets : Alcman 6 239, Anacreon 5 19, Antiphanes 1 11, Archilochus 6 383, Bacchylides 5 235, Hedylus 2 301, Hesiod 2 343, Ibycus 6 51, Matron 2 117, cf. 6 85, Philoxenus 4 47, 6 225, Phoenix 4 129, Phrynichus 1 193, Pindar 2 369, Pratinas 6 369, Stesichorus 2 343, Stratonicus 4 87, cf. 2 343, Timotheus 2 69 ; in pun of Telesphorus 6 319 ; bird-cage of 1 99 ; Socrates possessed by 2 495

Museum at Alexandria 1 99, 2 421, cf. 351 (Athens), 3 81, 7 129

Mushrooms 1 263-269

Music, accompanied dancing 1 69, 71, 91 ; concerted 6 329 ; effect on the soul 6 375-389 ; innovations in 1 81, 6 325, 355, 361, 409, 411, 447 ; terms used in 5 345, 6 7, 79, 7 45, 217 ; varied 2 345

Musical instruments 1 3, 2 291-317, 6 419-449, 7 63, 65 note a. See also Flute, Lyre

Mussels 1 367-379, 389-391, 395-401, 2 49, 61, 105

Mustacea, pastry 6 497

Mustard 1 123, 257, 291 note b, 299, 305, 2 113, 125, 273, 4 161-163

Mycerinus, Egyptian king 4 485

Myconos, island in the Cyclades 1 33, 4 68 note 5

Mygdonians, in Ephippus 4 71

Myiscae 1 389

Mylasa, in Caria 4 79, cf. 31

Mylloi, cakes of sesame and honey 6 493

Myma, stew 7 31, 51

Myndus, seaport in Ionia, wine of 1 143, 145, 249

Mynnacus, shoe-maker 4 89

Mynniscus of Chalcis, tragic actor 4 61-63

Myra, seaport in Lycia, best rue from 1 257

Myraena, Lamprey, personification 3 353

501

ENGLISH INDEX

an arrogant person **2**
467

Pythodelus, prodigal
mentioned by Axio-
nicus **2** 255

Pythodorus, Athenian
archon **3** 57

Pythodorus, of the deme
Aexone **5** 521

Pythodorus of Sicyon, his
son a favourite of Ono-
marchus **6** 261

Python, slain by Apollo
5 436 note *a*, **7** 269

Python of Byzantium,
orator **5** 499, 545, **6** 210
note *b*

Python of Catana, author
of *Agên* (?) **1** 223, **6** 163,
210 note *b*, 211

Python, lover of Nico **6**
145

Pythonicus, Athenian
profligate **2** 499

Quail **1** 285, **4** 273-279,
7 11

Quince **1** 257, 349-351, **6**
239, **7** 189 ; perfume **1**
199

Quintilii, wrote on agri-
culture **6** 509 and note *g*

Quintus Oppius **2** 463

Quirian pastry **6** 497

Quirinal, in Rome **4** 139
note *g*

Radishes **1** 241, 247, 249,
309, 319, 321

Raisins **1** 121, 297, **2** 113,
273, **6** 129, **7** 51

Ram (κριός), variety of
chick-pea **1** 239, 241 ;
of conch **1** 375

Rape, rape-turnip (βου-
νιάς) **1** 17, **4** 173

Ray (βατίς) **1** 449, **2** 105,
171, **3** 285-287

Razor-fish (σωλῆνες) **1**
367, 373, 377, 379, 385,
389, 399, **2** 61

Reapers' songs **6** 333,
339

Reclining at meals (κατα-
κλίνεσθαι) **1** 79 (*cf.* 51
and note *d*, **6** 275),
103, 207, 209, **2** 133,
147-151, 163, 175, 183,
195, 213, 227, 323, 337,
353, **5** 433, 465

Red Sea **2** 311, **3** 447, **7**
115

Reed (κάλαμος), cakes
strung on **2** 143 ;
Cyprian **1** 273 ; flute
2 301 ; (δόναξ) razor-
fish **1** 389

Refrigeration **2** 73, 77, 81

530

ENGLISH INDEX

fish 3 485 ; fish-eating oxen 4 67 ; hanging as a sport 2 207 ; Iphicrates in 2 103, 5 403 ; musical instrument called *phoenix* 6 439, cf. 2 307 ; *oiton* 1 269-271 ; parade 2 381; relations with Athens 5 501, with Philip 3 121, 4 535, 5 139 note *f*, 401, 6 15 ; ribbon-seller (in Eupolis) 3 465-467 ; silver-mines 3 223 ; Spartacus from 3 225 ; Strymon river 3 347 ; tattooing 5 365 ; Themistocles' mother from 6 111, also Timotheus' 6 115 ; Thracians in Ephesus 6 199 ; thyme 7 151

Thraso, in Terence 6 169 note *c* ; parasite 3 135

Thrasybulus, son of the tyrant Xenocrates of Agrigentum 5 43, 127

Thrasydaeus of Thessaly 3 123

Thrasyleon, in a riddle 4 533

Thrasyllus, son of Pythodorus, went insane 5 521 and note 1 (for the story, cf. Horace, *Ep.* 2. 2. 128)

Thrasyllus of Athens, friend of Alcibiades 5 415

Thrasymachus of Chalcedon, sophist 4 383, 563 ; in Plato 5 267, 268 note *a*, 289 and note *c*, cf. 3 238 note *b*

Thrasymedes, son of Nestor, in Homer 7 39

Thria, in Attica 3 151, 509

Thriambus, epithet of Dionysus 1 131

Thrinacria, name of Sicily in the *Odyssey* 1 57

Thrush 1 111, 281-283, 2 95, 107, 147, 6 481 ; fish so-called 3 369-371

Thryallis (Wick), hetaera so named 6 147

Thucydides, son of Melesias, opponent of Pericles 5 273 ; his son Stephanus 3 55

Thucydides, son of Olorus, historian. (i. 6) 5 303 note *a*, (i. 20) 6 37 note *c*, (i. 70) 1 101, (i. 132) 5 422 note *c*, (i. 138) 5 421, (iii. 82) 3 149 note *d*, (iv. 96) 2

Timaea, wife of King Agis 5 417, 6 103

Timaeus, in Plato's dialogue 4 227, *cf.* 5 271 note *d*

Timaeus of Cyzicus, tried to gain sole rule 5 287 and note *c*, *cf.* 271 note *d*

Timaeus of Tauromenium, historian (nicknamed Epitimaeus 3 223). (i.) 2 199, 5 329, (iii.) 3 223, (vii.) 5 449, 6 97, (ix.) 2 243-245, 3 189, *cf.* 223, (xiii.) 3 471, 6 177, (xxii.) 3 127-129, (xxviii.) 5 81. Other fragments : 1 151, 163-165, 2 345, 433, 4 53, 479, 5 335 (*bis*), 339-341, 351-355, 359, 6 249. *Reply to* 1 353, 2 13 (Polemon), 3 223 (Istrus)

Timagoras, Athenian at the court of Artaxerxes 1 211, 3 133, *cf.* 145

Timandra, Corinthian hetaera, mother of Laïs 5 419, 6 103 note *f*

Timanthes, painter, rival of Parrhasius 5 462 note *a*

Timarchus, commentator on Eratosthenes 5 243

Timasion, in the army of Cyrus the Younger 2 191

Timocharidas, poet 6 343 note *h*

Timocles, poet of the Middle Comedy (also of tragedy ? 4 344 note *a*). Αἰγύπτιοι 3 345. Δακτύλιος 3 323, 4 241. Δῆλος 4 49. Δημοσάτυροι 2 253. Διονυσιάζουσαι 3 5-7. Διόνυσος 4 345. Δρακόντιον 3 69-71. Ἐπιστολαί 3 83, 93. Ἐπιχαιρέκακος 3 83-85. Ἥρωες 3 9, 4 569. Ἰκάριοι Σάτυροι 4 41 (*cf.* 2 59), 51, 345-347. Καύνιοι 3 83. Κένταυρος ἢ Δεξαμενός 3 83. Κονίσαλος 4 453. Λήθη 4 345. Μαραθώνιοι 6 83. Νέαιρα 6 65, 189. Ὀρεσταυτοκλείδης 6 67. Πολυπράγμων 4 41. Πορφύρα 3 433 (see Xenarchus). Πύκτης 3 111. Σαπφώ 4 39. Φιλοδικαστής 3 103. Ψευδολῃσταί 2

ENGLISH INDEX

THE LOEB CLASSICAL LIBRARY

VOLUMES ALREADY PUBLISHED

LATIN AUTHORS

AMMIANUS MARCELLINUS. J. C. Rolfe. 3 Vols.

APULEIUS: THE GOLDEN ASS (METAMORPHOSES). W. Adlington (1566). Revised by S. Gaselee.

ST. AUGUSTINE: CITY OF GOD. 7 Vols. Vol. I. G. E. McCracken. Vol. II. W. M. Green. Vol. III. D. Wiesen. Vol. IV. P. Levine. Vol. V. E. M. Sanford and W. M. Green. Vol. VI. W. C. Greene.

ST. AUGUSTINE, CONFESSIONS OF. W. Watts (1631). 2 Vols.

ST. AUGUSTINE: SELECT LETTERS. J. H. Baxter.

AUSONIUS. H. G. Evelyn White. 2 Vols.

BEDE. J. E. King. 2 Vols.

BOETHIUS; TRACTS AND DE CONSOLATIONE PHILOSOPHIAE. Rev. H. F. Stewart and E. K. Rand.

CAESAR: ALEXANDRIAN, AFRICAN AND SPANISH WARS. A. G. Way.

CAESAR: CIVIL WARS. A. G. Peskett.

CAESAR: GALLIC WAR. H. J. Edwards.

CATO AND VARRO: DE RE RUSTICA. H. B. Ash and W. D. Hooper.

CATULLUS. F. W. Cornish; TIBULLUS. J. B. Postgate; and PERVIGILIUM VENERIS. J. W. Mackail.

CELSUS: DE MEDICINA. W. G. Spencer. 3 Vols.

CICERO: BRUTUS AND ORATOR. G. L. Hendrickson and H. M. Hubbell.

CICERO: DE FINIBUS. H. Rackham.

CICERO: DE INVENTIONE, etc. H. M. Hubbell.

CICERO: DE NATURA DEORUM AND ACADEMICA. H. Rackham.

CICERO: DE OFFICIIS. Walter Miller.

CICERO: DE ORATORE, etc. 2 Vols. Vol. I: DE ORATORE, Books I and II. E. W. Sutton and H. Rackham. Vol. II: DE ORATORE, Book III; De FATO; PARADOXA STOICORUM; DE PARTITIONE ORATORIA. H. Rackham.

CICERO: DE REPUBLICA, DE LEGIBUS, SOMNIUM SCIPIONIS. Clinton W. Keyes.

1

THE LOEB CLASSICAL LIBRARY

CICERO: DE SENECTUTE, DE AMICITIA, DE DIVINATIONE. W. A. Falconer.

CICERO: IN CATILINAM, PRO MURENA, PRO SULLA, PRO FLACCO. Louis E. Lord.

CICERO: LETTERS TO ATTICUS. E. O. Winstedt. 3 Vols.

CICERO: LETTERS TO HIS FRIENDS. W. Glynn Williams. 4 Vols.

CICERO: PHILIPPICS. W. C. A. Ker.

CICERO: PRO ARCHIA, POST REDITUM, DE DOMO, DE HARUSPICUM RESPONSIS, PRO PLANCIO. N. H. Watts.

CICERO: PRO CAECINA, PRO LEGE MANILIA, PRO CLUENTIO, PRO RABIRIO. H. Grose Hodge.

CICERO: PRO CAELIO, DE PROVINCIIS CONSULARIBUS, PRO BALBO. R. Gardner.

CICERO: PRO MILONE, IN PISONEM, PRO SCAURO, PRO FONTEIO, PRO RABIRIO POSTUMO, PRO MARCELLO, PRO LIGARIO, PRO REGE DEIOTARO. N. H. Watts.

CICERO: PRO QUINCTIO, PRO ROSCIO AMERINO, PRO ROSCIO COMOEDO, CONTRA RULLUM. J. H. Freese.

CICERO: PRO SESTIO, IN VATINIUM. R. Gardner.

[CICERO]: RHETORICA AD HERENNIUM. H. Caplan.

CICERO: TUSCULAN DISPUTATIONS. J. E. King.

CICERO: VERRINE ORATIONS. L. H. G. Greenwood. 2 Vols.

CLAUDIAN. M. Platnauer. 2 Vols.

COLUMELLA: DE RE RUSTICA, DE ARBORIBUS. H. B. Ash, E. S. Forster, E. Heffner. 3 Vols.

CURTIUS, Q.: HISTORY OF ALEXANDER. J. C. Rolfe. 2 Vols.

FLORUS. E. S. Forster; and CORNELIUS NEPOS. J. C. Rolfe.

FRONTINUS: STRATAGEMS AND AQUEDUCTS. C. E. Bennett and M. B. McElwain.

FRONTO: CORRESPONDENCE. C. R. Haines. 2 Vols.

GELLIUS. J. C. Rolfe. 3 Vols.

HORACE: ODES AND EPODES. C. E. Bennett.

HORACE: SATIRES, EPISTLES, ARS POETICA. H. R. Fairclough.

JEROME: SELECT LETTERS. F. A. Wright.

JUVENAL AND PERSIUS. G. G. Ramsay.

LIVY. B. O. Foster, F. G. Moore, Evan T. Sage, A. C. Schlesinger and R. M. Geer (General Index). 14 Vols.

LUCAN. J. D. Duff.

LUCRETIUS. W. H. D. Rouse.

MARTIAL. W. C. A. Ker. 2 Vols.

MINOR LATIN POETS: from PUBLILIUS SYRUS to RUTILIUS NAMATIANUS, including GRATTIUS, CALPURNIUS SICULUS, NEMESIANUS, AVIANUS, with " Aetna," " Phoenix " and other poems. J. Wight Duff and Arnold M. Duff.

OVID: THE ART OF LOVE AND OTHER POEMS. J. H. Mozley.
OVID: FASTI. Sir James G. Frazer.
Ovid: HEROIDES AND AMORES. Grant Showerman.
OVID: METAMORPHOSES. F. J. Miller. 2 Vols.
OVID: TRISTIA AND EX PONTO. A. L. Wheeler.
PETRONIUS. M. Heseltine; SENECA: APOCOLOCYNTOSIS.
W. H. D. Rouse.
PHAEDRUS AND BABRIUS (Greek). B. E. Perry.
PLAUTUS. Paul Nixon. 5 Vols.
PLINY: LETTERS, PANEGYRICUS. B. Radice. 2 Vols.
PLINY: NATURAL HISTORY. 10 Vols. Vols. I-V and IX.
H. Rackham. Vols. VI-VIII. W. H. S. Jones. Vol. X.
D. E. Eichholz.
PROPERTIUS. H. E. Butler.
PRUDENTIUS. H. J. Thomson. 2 Vols.
QUINTILIAN. H. E. Butler. 4 Vols.
REMAINS OF OLD LATIN. E. H. Warmington. 4 Vols.
Vol. I (Ennius and Caecilius). Vol. II (Livius, Naevius,
Pacuvius, Accius). Vol. III (Lucilius, Laws of the XII
Tables). Vol. IV (Archaic Inscriptions).
SALLUST. J. C. Rolfe.
SCRIPTORES HISTORIAE AUGUSTAAE. D. Magie. 3 Vols.
SENECA: APOCOLOCYNTOSIS. Cf. PETRONIUS.
SENECA: EPISTULAE MORALES. R. M. Gummere. 3 Vols.
SENECA: MORAL ESSAYS. J. W. Basore. 3 Vols.
SENECA: NATURALES QUAESTIONES. T. H. Corcoran. 2 Vols.
SENECA: TRAGEDIES. F. J. Miller. 2 Vols.
SIDONIUS: POEMS AND LETTERS. W. B. Anderson. 2 Vols.
SILIUS ITALICUS. J. D. Duff. 2 Vols.
STATIUS. J. H. Mozley. 2 Vols.
SUETONIUS. J. C. Rolfe. 2 Vols.
TACITUS: AGRICOLA AND GERMANIA. Maurice Hutton: DIA-
LOGUS. Sir Wm. Peterson.
TACITUS: HISTORIES AND ANNALS. C. H. Moore and J.
Jackson. 4 Vols.
TERENCE. John Sargeaunt. 2 Vols.
TERTULLIAN: APOLOGIA AND DE SPECTACULIS. T. R. Glover;
MINUCIUS FELIX. G. H. Rendall.
VALERIUS FLACCUS. J. H. Mozley.
VARRO: DE LINGUA LATINA. R. G. Kent. 2 Vols.
VELLEIUS PATERCULUS AND RES GESTAE DIVI AUGUSTI.
F. W. Shipley.
VIRGIL. H. R. Fairclough. 2 Vols.
VITRUVIUS: DE ARCHITECTURA. F. Granger. 2 Vols.

THE LOEB CLASSICAL LIBRARY

GREEK AUTHORS

ACHILLES TATIUS. S. Gaselee.

AELIAN : ON THE NATURE OF ANIMALS. A. F. Scholfield. 3 Vols.

AENEAS TACTICUS, ASCLEPIODOTUS AND ONASANDER. The Illinois Greek Club.

AESCHINES. C. D. Adams.

AESCHYLUS. H. Weir Smyth. 2 Vols.

ALCIPHRON, AELIAN AND PHILOSTRATUS : LETTERS. A. R. Benner and F. H. Fobes.

APOLLODORUS. Sir James G. Frazer. 2 Vols.

APOLLONIUS RHODIUS. R. C. Seaton.

THE APOSTOLIC FATHERS. Kirsopp Lake. 2 Vols.

APPIAN'S ROMAN HISTORY. Horace White. 4 Vols.

ARATUS. *Cf.* CALLIMACHUS.

ARISTOPHANES. Benjamin Bickley Rogers. 3 Vols. Verse trans.

ARISTOTLE : ART OF RHETORIC. J. H. Freese.

ARISTOTLE : ATHENIAN CONSTITUTION, EUDEMIAN ETHICS, VIRTUES AND VICES. H. Rackham.

ARISTOTLE : THE CATEGORIES. ON INTERPRETATION. H. P. Cooke ; PRIOR ANALYTICS. H. Tredennick.

ARISTOTLE : GENERATION OF ANIMALS. A. L. Peck.

ARISTOTLE : HISTORIA ANIMALIUM. A. L. Peck. 3 Vols. Vols. I and II.

ARISTOTLE : METAPHYSICS. H. Tredennick. 2 Vols.

ARISTOTLE : METEOROLOGICA. H. D. P. Lee.

ARISTOTLE : MINOR WORKS. W. S. Hett. " On Colours," " On Things Heard," " Physiognomics," " On Plants," " On Marvellous Things Heard," " Mechanical Problems," " On Invisible Lines," " Situations and Names of Winds," " On Melissus, Xenophanes, and Gorgias."

ARISTOTLE : NICOMACHEAN ETHICS. H. Rackham.

ARISTOTLE : OECONOMICA AND MAGNA MORALIA. G. C. Armstrong. (With METAPHYSICS, Vol II.)

ARISTOTLE : ON THE HEAVENS. W. K. C. Guthrie.

ARISTOTLE : ON THE SOUL, PARVA NATURALIA, ON BREATH. W. S. Hett.

ARISTOTLE : PARTS OF ANIMALS. A. L. Peck ; MOVEMENT AND PROGRESSION OF ANIMALS. E. S. Forster.

ARISTOTLE : PHYSICS. Rev. P. Wicksteed and F. M. Cornford. 2 Vols.

ARISTOTLE: POETICS; LONGINUS ON THE SUBLIME. W. Hamilton Fyfe; DEMETRIUS ON STYLE. W. Rhys Roberts.

ARISTOTLE: POLITICS. H. Rackham.

ARISTOTLE: POSTERIOR ANALYTICS. H. Tredennick; TOPICS. E. S. Forster.

ARISTOTLE: PROBLEMS. W. S. Hett. 2 Vols.

ARISTOTLE: RHETORICA AD ALEXANDRUM. H. Rackham. (With PROBLEMS, Vol. II.)

ARISTOTLE: SOPHISTICAL REFUTATIONS. COMING-TO-BE AND PASSING-AWAY. E. S. Forster; ON THE COSMOS. D. J. Furley.

ARRIAN: HISTORY OF ALEXANDER AND INDICA. Rev. E. Iliffe Robson. 2 Vols.

ATHENAEUS: DEIPNOSOPHISTAE. C. B. Gulick. 7 Vols.

BABRIUS AND PHAEDRUS (Latin). B. E. Perry.

ST. BASIL: LETTERS. R. J. Deferrari. 4 Vols.

CALLIMACHUS: FRAGMENTS. C. A. Trypanis.

CALLIMACHUS: HYMNS AND EPIGRAMS, AND LYCOPHRON. A. W. Mair; ARATUS. G. R. Mair.

CLEMENT OF ALEXANDRIA. Rev. G. W. Butterworth.

COLLUTHUS. *Cf.* OPPIAN.

DAPHNIS AND CHLOE. *Cf.* LONGUS.

DEMOSTHENES I: OLYNTHIACS, PHILIPPICS AND MINOR ORATIONS: I-XVII AND XX. J. H. Vince.

DEMOSTHENES II: DE CORONA AND DE FALSA LEGATIONE. C. A. Vince and J. H. Vince.

DEMOSTHENES III: MEIDIAS, ANDROTION, ARISTOCRATES, TIMOCRATES, ARISTOGEITON. J. H. Vince.

DEMOSTHENES IV-VI: PRIVATE ORATIONS AND IN NEAERAM. A. T. Murray.

DEMOSTHENES VII: FUNERAL SPEECH, EROTIC ESSAY, EXORDIA AND LETTERS. N. W. and N. J. DeWitt.

DIO CASSIUS: ROMAN HISTORY. E. Cary. 9 Vols.

DIO CHRYSOSTOM. 5 Vols. Vols I and II. J. W. Cohoon. Vol. III. J. W. Cohoon and H. Lamar Crosby. Vols. IV and V. H. Lamar Crosby.

DIODORUS SICULUS. 12 Vols. Vols. I-VI. C. H. Oldfather. Vol. VII. C. L. Sherman. Vol. VIII. C. B. Welles. Vols. IX and X. Russel M. Geer. Vols. XI and XII. F. R. Walton. General Index. Russel M. Geer.

DIOGENES LAERTIUS. R. D. Hicks. 2 Vols.

DIONYSIUS OF HALICARNASSUS: ROMAN ANTIQUITIES. Spelman's translation revised by E. Cary. 7 Vols.

EPICTETUS. W. A. Oldfather. 2 Vols.

THE LOEB CLASSICAL LIBRARY

EURIPIDES. A. S. Way. 4 Vols. Verse trans.

EUSEBIUS: ECCLESIASTICAL HISTORY. Kirsopp Lake and J. E. L. Oulton. 2 Vols.

GALEN: ON THE NATURAL FACULTIES. A. J. Brock.

THE GREEK ANTHOLOGY. W. R. Paton. 5 Vols.

THE GREEK BUCOLIC POETS (THEOCRITUS, BION, MOSCHUS). J. M. Edmonds.

GREEK ELEGY AND IAMBUS WITH THE ANACREONTEA. J. M. Edmonds. 2 Vols.

GREEK MATHEMATICAL WORKS. Ivor Thomas. 2 Vols.

HERODES. *Cf.* THEOPHRASTUS: CHARACTERS.

HERODIAN: C. R. Whittaker. 2 Vols.

HERODOTUS. A. D. Godley. 4 Vols.

HESIOD AND THE HOMERIC HYMNS. H. G. Evelyn White.

HIPPOCRATES AND THE FRAGMENTS OF HERACLEITUS. W. H. S. Jones and E. T. Withington. 4 Vols.

HOMER: ILIAD. A. T. Murray. 2 Vols.

HOMER: ODYSSEY. A. T. Murray. 2 Vols.

ISAEUS. E. S. Forster.

ISOCRATES. George Norlin and LaRue Van Hook. 3 Vols.

[ST. JOHN DAMASCENE]: BARLAAM AND IOASAPH. Rev. G. R. Woodward, Harold Mattingly and D. M. Lang.

JOSEPHUS. 9 Vols. Vols. I-IV. H. St. J. Thackeray. Vol. V. H. St. J. Thackeray and Ralph Marcus. Vols. VI and VII. Ralph Marcus. Vol. VIII. Ralph Marcus and Allen Wikgren. Vol. IX. L. H. Feldman.

JULIAN. Wilmer Cave Wright. 3 Vols.

LIBANIUS: SELECTED WORKS. A. F. Norman. 3 Vols. Vol. I.

LONGUS: DAPHNIS AND CHLOE. Thornley's translation revised by J. M. Edmonds; and PARTHENIUS. S. Gaselee.

LUCIAN. 8 Vols. Vols I-V. A. M. Harmon. Vol. VI. K. Kilburn. Vols. VII and VIII. M. D. Macleod.

LYCOPHRON. *Cf.* CALLIMACHUS.

LYRA GRAECA. J. M. Edmonds. 3 Vols.

LYSIAS. W. R. M. Lamb.

MANETHO. W. G. Waddell; PTOLEMY: TETRABIBLOS. F. E. Robbins.

MARCUS AURELIUS. C. R. Haines.

MENANDER. F. G. Allinson.

MINOR ATTIC ORATORS. 2 Vols. K. J. Maidment and J. O. Burtt.

NONNOS: DIONYSIACA. W. H. D. Rouse. 3 Vols.

OPPIAN, COLLUTHUS, TRYPHIODORUS. A. W. Mair.

PAPYRI. NON-LITERARY SELECTIONS. A. S. Hunt and C. C.

Edgar. 2 Vols. LITERARY SELECTIONS (Poetry). D. L. Page.

PARTHENIUS. *Cf.* LONGUS.

PAUSANIAS: DESCRIPTION OF GREECE. W. H. S. Jones. 4 Vols. and Companion Vol. arranged by R. E. Wycherley.

PHILO. 10 Vols. Vols. I-V. F. H. Colson and Rev. G. H. Whitaker. Vols. VI-X. F. H. Colson. General Index. Rev. J. W. Earp.

Two Supplementary Vols. Translation only from an Armenian Text. Ralph Marcus.

PHILOSTRATUS: THE LIFE OF APOLLONIUS OF TYANA. F. C. Conybeare. 2 Vols.

PHILOSTRATUS: IMAGINES; CALLISTRATUS: DESCRIPTIONS. A. Fairbanks.

PHILOSTRATUS AND EUNAPIUS: LIVES OF THE SOPHISTS. Wilmer Cave Wright.

PINDAR. Sir J. E. Sandys.

PLATO: CHARMIDES, ALCIBIADES, HIPPARCHUS, THE LOVERS, THEAGES, MINOS AND EPINOMIS. W. R. M. Lamb.

PLATO: CRATYLUS, PARMENIDES, GREATER HIPPIAS, LESSER HIPPIAS. H. N. Fowler.

PLATO: EUTHYPHRO, APOLOGY, CRITO, PHAEDO, PHAEDRUS. H. N. Fowler.

PLATO: LACHES, PROTAGORAS, MENO, EUTHYDEMUS. W. R. M. Lamb.

PLATO: LAWS. Rev. R. G. Bury. 2 Vols.

PLATO: LYSIS, SYMPOSIUM, GORGIAS. W. R. M. Lamb.

PLATO: REPUBLIC. Paul Shorey. 2 Vols.

PLATO: STATESMAN. PHILEBUS. H. N. Fowler; ION. W. R. M. Lamb.

PLATO: THEAETETUS AND SOPHIST. H. N. Fowler.

PLATO: TIMAEUS, CRITIAS, CLITOPHO, MENEXENUS, EPISTULAE. Rev. R. G. Bury.

PLOTINUS. A. H. Armstrong. 6 Vols. Vols. I-III.

PLUTARCH: MORALIA. 16 Vols. Vols. I-V. F. C. Babbitt. Vol. VI. W. C. Helmbold. Vol. VII. P. H. De Lacy and B. Einarson. Vol. VIII. P. A. Clement, H. B. Hoffleit. Vol. IX. E. L. Minar, Jr., F. H. Sandbach, W. C. Helmbold. Vol. X. H. N. Fowler. Vol. XI. L. Pearson, F. H. Sandbach. Vol. XII. H. Cherniss, W. C. Helmbold. Vol. XIV. P. H. De Lacy and B. Einarson. Vol. XV. F. H. Sandbach.

PLUTARCH: THE PARALLEL LIVES. B. Perrin. 11 Vols.

POLYBIUS. W. R. PATON. 6 Vols.

THE LOEB CLASSICAL LIBRARY

Procopius : History of the Wars. H. B. Dewing. 7 Vols.
Ptolemy : Tetrabiblos. *Cf.* Manetho.
Quintus Smyrnaeus. A. S. Way. Verse trans.
Sextus Empiricus. Rev. R. G. Bury. 4 Vols.
Sophocles. F. Storr. 2 Vols. Verse trans.
Strabo : Geography. Horace L. Jones. 8 Vols.
Theophrastus : Characters. J. M. Edmonds ; Herodes, etc. A. D. Knox.
Theophrastus : Enquiry into Plants. Sir Arthur Hort. 2 Vols.
Thucydides. C. F. Smith. 4 Vols.
Tryphiodorus. *Cf.* Oppian.
Xenophon : Anabasis. C. L. Brownson.
Xenophon : Cyropaedia. Walter Miller. 2 Vols.
Xenophon : Hellenica. C. L. Brownson.
Xenophon : Memorabilia and Oeconomicus. E. C. Marchant. Symposium and Apology. O. J. Todd.
Xenophon : Scripta Minora. E. C. Marchant and G. W. Bowersock.

VOLUMES IN PREPARATION

GREEK AUTHORS

Aristides : Orations. C. A. Behr.
Musaeus : Hero and Leander. T. Gelzer and C. H. Whitman.
Theophrastus : De Causis Plantarum. G. K. K. Link and B. Einarson.

LATIN AUTHORS

Asconius : Commentaries on Cicero's Orations. G. W. Bowersock.
Benedict : The Rule. P. Meyvaert.
Justin-Trogus. R. Moss.
Manilius. G. P. Goold.

DESCRIPTIVE PROSPECTUS ON APPLICATION

CAMBRIDGE, MASS.	LONDON
HARVARD UNIV. PRESS	WILLIAM HEINEMANN LTD